Making Men into Fathers

Fatherhood is on the political agenda in many countries, often cast in terms of crisis. One side of the policy debate focuses on fathers as deadbeat dads who do not provide financial support and care for their children. The other revolves around making men into active and engaged fathers. However, these policies are often at odds with the employers' reluctance to accommodate work schedules to fathers' needs. In *Making Men into Fathers*, prominent scholars in gender studies and the critical studies of men consider how varied institutional settings and policy logics around cash and care contour the possibilities and constraints for new models of fatherhood, determining the choices open to men. From different historical and societal perspectives, the authors provide new insights into the studies of men as gendered subjects, including the role of transnational and global issues of fatherhood, and the emergence of men's movements, contesting and reimaging fatherhood.

BARBARA HOBSON is a Professor of Sociology and holds a chair in Sociology and Gender Studies at Stockholm University. She is also director of the Advanced Research School in Comparative Gender Studies, a program for international research exchange and advanced doctoral studies. Her most recent book publications include an edited collection, *Gender and Citizenship in Transition* (2000) and a co-edited collection, *Contested Concepts. Gender and Social Politics* (2001).

Making Men into Fathers

Men, Masculinities and the Social Politics of Fatherhood

Edited by

Barbara Hobson

CAMBRIDGE UNIVERSITY PRESS

PUBLISHED BY THE PRESS SYNDICATE OF THE UNIVERSITY OF CAMBRIDGE
The Pitt Building, Trumpington Street, Cambridge, United Kingdom

CAMBRIDGE UNIVERSITY PRESS
The Edinburgh Building, Cambridge CB2 2RU, UK
40 West 20th Street, New York, NY 10011-4211, USA
477 Williamstown Road, Port Melbourne, VIC 3207, Australia
Ruiz de Alarcón 13, 28014 Madrid, Spain
Dock House, The Waterfront, Cape Town 8001, South Africa

http://www.cambridge.org

First published 2002

Printed in the United Kingdom at the University Press, Cambridge

Typeface Plantin 10/12 pt.   *System* LaTeX 2$_\varepsilon$ [TB]

A catalogue record for this book is available from the British Library.

Library of Congress Cataloguing in Publication Data
Making Men into Fathers: Men, Masculinities, and the Social Politics of
Fatherhood / edited by Barbara Hobson.
     p.   cm.
Includes bibliographical references and index.
ISBN 0 521 80927 4 (hardback) – ISBN 0 521 00612 0 (paperback)
1. Fatherhood.   2. Fathers – Government policy.   3. Men – Government
policy.   4. Masculinity.   5. Men's movement.   I. Hobson, Barbara Meil.
HQ756.M33   2001
306.874′2 – dc21   2001035699

ISBN 0 521 80927 4 hardback
ISBN 0 521 00612 0 paperback

Contents

Figures

Tables

Preface

There is a chapter missing from this book, a chapter about the making of *Making Men into Fathers*. It would begin in 1995 in Stockholm in a conference room on the twenty-fifth floor overlooking the harbor. The chapter would try (most likely in vain) to recapture those first three days of intense conversations between the authors of this book, several of whom are central figures in the international debates on gender and welfare states, and two of whom are among the leading figures in the critical studies of men.

Over the next four years the authors of this book met many times, sometimes in the heart of the dark Swedish winter. Our conversations continued; our friendships developed. Our dialogues cut across borders, both geographic and disciplinary. We challenged and energized each other, particularly the junior scholars, Anna Gavanas, Helena Bergman, and Livia Oláh, who brought new perspectives and ideas to our discussions. The original title of the project, Fathers and the State, was discarded since it did not capture the dynamic and complex processes we were writing about. Nor did it encompass the multidimensional views of the authors or of the book, which were being continuously reconfigured and recast in our discussions, through our heuristic triangles. Trudie Knijn presented her rotating and overlapping triangles (the institutional and domestic); David Morgan his inspirational third father triangle. Ann Orloff kept up the provocative questions about men's interests. My scholarship has been enriched by the making of this book. In addition I developed a deep sense of what collaboration meant in terms of the framing of a book, its theories and core concepts. I feel privileged to have been able to bring together this excellent group of scholars and to learn so much from them.

By providing generous program grants designed to develop new research areas, the Riksbankens Jubeleumsfond made possible this kind of creative and exciting endeavor. I acknowledge the important role played by the director, Dan Brandström. The many books and theses that have resulted from this research program are indebted to his strong support for comparative gender studies (CGS). His deep commitment to interdisciplinary and international research in the social sciences has been crucial for the emergence of new research agendas. I would also like to thank Kerstin Stigmark at the Riksbankens Jubeleumsfond for her administrative support.

The extraordinary team of doctoral students in the CGS research program has constituted an invaluable resource for testing ideas, for perceptive and critical readings of the manuscripts, and for locating obscure references. In this context, I would like to express my gratitude to Michelle Ariga, Sanja Magdelenic, Livia Oláh and Maria Tornqvist as well as two guest researchers, Roisín Flood and Katrin Kriz. Finally, I wish to express a special additional thanks to Michelle Ariga, who is both my doctoral student and administrator for our journal. Without her boundless energy and amazing editorial and computer skills, we would not have been on time for our production schedule.

I am grateful also to Ann Orloff for her comments on drafts of the Introduction and to David Morgan for his theoretical insights, which appear in the Introduction and Epilogue. Finally I would like to thank Jacob Von Post and Reijo Rüster for allowing us to use their photographs.

I dedicate this book to Joe De Pierre, who is a real new father – as opposed to the virtual ones that appear in policy discourse. He made me realize how much bonding and caring for one's own children increases one's capacity for emotional contact and empathy with others.

Barbara Hobson

Introduction

Barbara Hobson and David Morgan

The very title of this book, *Making Men into Fathers*, suggests the weak bonds between men and fatherhood. Men father but do not necessarily assume the responsibilities of fatherhood. This is more true in recent decades; fewer men enter fatherhood and more leave it, according to studies on both sides of the Atlantic (Jensen 1998a; Oláh, Bernhardt and Goldscheider in this volume). The growing number of solo mother families also is an outcome that reflects the decoupling of fathers from fatherhood. But this is only part of the story. There are visible actors seeking to forge the links between manhood and fatherhood, as seen in the strident men's movements affirming men's rights to father and their responsibilities to fatherhood. The Million Man march in the United States in 1995 was perhaps the most dramatic statement of a grass roots mobilization of African American men connecting manhood and fatherhood. The message leaders articulated was that poor black men were not allowed to play their normal roles as family leaders and breadwinners because they were excluded from educational and labor market opportunities (Messner 1997). Not to be ignored in this discussion is the emergence of men's groups claiming father's rights for custody of children after divorce.

The making of men into fathers is also obvious in media representations of men's involvement with fathering. A host of films in the 1990s are narratives of fathers who become reconciled to their sons, such as *Liar Liar* (the absent father) or *The Full Monty* (the failed provider). There is a positive and confident imaging of solo fathers in films, which mirrors changing perceptions around the ability of fathers to be primary caregivers, in effect undermining the naturalized relationship of mother and child. Nevertheless, it is through policy discourse, new laws and practices that the most conscious and purposeful attempts have been made to connect men to fatherhood – fathers both inside and outside of marriage.

Policy makers have turned their gaze on men as fathers, most often expressed as a "crisis of fatherhood." In some respects this is old wine in new bottles. Throughout the twentieth century, there have been

1

laments and jeremiads about the decline of the family and marriage, and anxieties about divorce and single-parent families. These accounts most often blamed mothers for "family breakdowns," but fathers were also culpable as Jane Lewis's study in this volume illustrates.

In the current discourse, the crisis in fatherhood is woven into the warp of the crisis in welfare states. We find a tendency in nearly all Western welfare states to reduce, or even withdraw, support for solo mothers. One rationale for these policies is a sense that the state is picking up the tab for never-married fathers and divorced fathers, by supporting solo mothers. This perception has led to the coining of new epithets, such as "deadbeat dads" as well as the increased policing of them by state bureaucracies (see Lewis; Municio-Larsson and Pujol Algans; Orloff and Monson in this volume).

There is also a new content to the debates on fatherhood in our era, which is not only the result of high divorce rates and single-parent families, but also reflects the fractal-like complexity in family forms, with competing claims of mothers, biological fathers and social/household fathers.[1] Divorced fathers who are seeking custody often are at odds with repartnered fathers claiming rights over children who are not their biological children. These conflicting claims involve both cash and care.

In policy discourse, the question of who pays for the kids is now paired with who cares for the kids. This is also visible in the reconfigurations of family law that reflect a greater recognition of fathers' rights to shared custody. Joint custody is feasible in most legal systems in Western welfare states, and it is a norm in the Scandinavian countries. Sweden has the highest levels, where 91 percent of divorced couples agree to joint custody. Not only the principles of law in many countries – the acknowledgement of fathers' claims in custody cases and the rights of children to be cared for by two parents – but also the legal terminology in divorce mirror a change in the assumptions about fatherhood. For example, in legal discourse, "residential parent" has replaced the term of guardian; parental responsibility is a phrase that often appears in formal texts on custody cases (Berns 2000).

Despite these shifts in discourses, and even changes in court practices, with more men now being awarded shared custody, fathers' responsibilities as defined in law and policy are still largely directed toward cash, not care. Consider the increased surveillance and interventions against fathers who do not assume financial responsibility for children. These include attachment of wages and, in rare instances, US judges in some localities sentence fathers to prison who fail to make support payments.

There is no law or policy as of yet that penalizes non-residential fathers who fail to maintain contact with their children.

The social politics of fatherhood: cash and care

This book is about the social politics of fatherhood looking across time and space. We ask why and in what context fatherhood came on the agenda in different countries. Our comparative perspectives allow us to unpack the rhetorical layers in the crisis in fatherhood as well as to track the importance of policy legacies, political constellations and mobilized constituencies. We also turn our lens toward global processes that contribute to the sense of crisis, but appear amorphous in their consequences. The point of departure in this book is that what is perceived as a crisis in fatherhood involves competing and conflicting social politics that revolve around the dimensions of cash and care, the obligations and rights of fatherhood. Our purpose is to situate these politics in the broader context of policy regimes, ideological and cultural frames of family and gender, and structural changes in post-industrial globalizing economies.

To say that fatherhood and motherhood are socially constructed is commonplace in the social sciences. But what is interesting about the social politics of fatherhood are both the convergences in policy and practices as well as the diverse interpretations of these changes and policy responses. As for convergences, we can see that, over the last decade in Western Europe and the United States, the two-earner family is becoming the norm. More mothers are labor-force participants, rather than housewives, in most European and North American countries, and, in the Netherlands, one of our cases, the turn around has been dramatic over the last ten years. Nevertheless, time budget studies show that, while men's involvement in unpaid carework has increased slightly in some countries, it is a drop in the bucket in relation to the loss in women's full-time carework. This shift in valences of greater women's employment with little or no change in the division of unpaid work is characterized in public discourse as a care deficit (Hochschild 1995) which affects not only childcare, but the care of the elderly and disabled.

Two of our cases, Sweden and the Netherlands, have adopted proactive policies for increasing a father's caregiving. Sweden has introduced the most direct policy formula in the mandated month of parental leave, known as the daddy month. Although the policy is gender neutral, it requires that each parent take at least one month's leave or lose the full benefit for that month, it was aimed at fathers (see Bergman and Hobson in this volume). The Dutch government has spearheaded a policy to create options for couples seeking a more equal division of family and work by instituting flexible work and parental sharing schemes in the Netherlands (see Knijn and Selten in this volume).

With the European Union Directive on parental leave in 1996, all European fathers now have the right to fourteen weeks of parental leave. The 1993 US care leave law gives parents (and others) who work for large employers (with 50 or more employees) unpaid leave. The European Directive does not mandate a level of payment either and several countries, including three of our cases, Britain, Spain and the Netherlands, do not have a national policy with a paid benefit.[2] Obviously these formal rights do not necessarily lead to a change in father practices. With the exception of the Scandinavian countries, the number of men who take any leave remains minuscule; most fathers are unable to shoulder the loss of income or feel entitled to make claims upon their employers, particularly in an era of market competitiveness and job insecurity.

Another set of convergences can be seen in the rising number of divorces and single-parent families alluded to previously. Among our cases, the United States represents the most dramatic case in which 40 percent of children do not live with their biological fathers; by age eighteen, almost half will have lived apart from their fathers for some part of their lives (Gillis 2000). However, studies show that divorce does not always result in absent or marginalized fathers. In a survey of non-resident fathers in Britain (Bradshaw et al. 1999) found that only 3 percent of the fathers had no contact with their children after separating from or divorcing the mother; 45 percent had contact at least once a week (Bradshaw et al. 1999: 81). Smart and Neale in their study in Britain, *Family Fragments?* (1999), maintain that, after divorce, fathers can have strong bonds and frequent contact with their children. Although nearly one half of children have no personal contact with non-residential fathers in the United States (Stephens 1996), non-residential fathers with joint legal custody tend to have more frequent contact (Seltzer 1998). The Swedish data show that there are fewer and fewer fathers who lose contact with children after divorce, and there has been a rise in joint residential custody (see Bergman and Hobson in this volume).

What we find in our five cases are parallel discourses on fatherhood concerning divorced and never-married men's failure to meet economic responsibilities as well as the importance for fathers to stay involved with children. But there are diverse interpretations of the causes and different measures and policy options being considered. In US and British policy discourse, terms such as "delinquent fathers" (in the United States) and "problem fathers" (in Britain) reflect the emphasis on the moral framing of the absent and marginalized father. These interpretative frames carry coercive measures to combat fatherlessness that appear backward-looking, such as mandated paternity in which women who do not name the father risk losing state benefits, currently a policy in the United States and Britain. Policy proposals in the United States put forward by conservative groups include restricting divorce, though this does not appear to be a very feasible option given the widespread acceptance of no-fault divorce. However, not all policy interventions to revitalize fatherhood in an era of high divorce have been retrogressive. We are not surprised that our cases suggest the following pattern: when the discourse in absent fatherhood is framed in more structural terms, such as precarious employment and unemployment in a post-industrial economy, it tends to produce policies with positive incentives rather than penalties, and a greater emphasis on care rather than the economic obligations of fatherhood.

Masculinity politics

The social politics of fatherhood cannot be divorced from masculinity politics. Men's authority in the family and male breadwinning are at the core of masculinity politics. This is particularly true of the new religious men's movements, such as the Promise Keepers in the United States, which affirm traditional gender roles and men's decision-making in families. Though not concerned with men's role in the family *per se*, mythopoetic men's groups, inspired by Robert Bly and the cult of homosociality, also seek to reinvigorate essentialist notions of manliness and return to gender distinctiveness. Some scholars in men's studies argue that these movements are driven by fear of feminization and a changing gender order (Kimmel 1996; Muesse 1996; Messner 1997).[3] Anna Gavanas' study (in this volume) presents a complex picture of contesting claims and competing masculinities, a mosaic of politics within masculinity politics. For example, African American men's radicalized masculinity politics is primarily understood in terms of the lack of economic and political power, rather than as a response to women's achievements. Gavanas maintains that organizations representing poor and minority men within fatherhood politics do not pit themselves against women or feminists, but against white male privilege. Other scholars challenging the thesis of a unitary crisis of masculinity, such as Griffen (1990) and Connell (1995, 1998), argue that men are not necessarily on the defensive, and that the changes in gender relations can produce different responses. In our cases, we find examples of men's collectivities advocating a more encompassing egalitarian family model (Bergman and Hobson; Knijn and Selten in this volume) in which men carve out a space for their fathering.

The crisis in fatherhood and male breadwinning

Discussions of the crisis in fatherhood are often linked to the demise of the male breadwinner role. Scholars writing about men and masculinities emphasize that it is important to take along a long-distance lens when making these connections. The father as the family provider emerged as a norm in the wake of the industrial revolution as fathers were removed from the practical work of the household (Gillis 1997; Griswold 1992). Nevertheless, the single-male breadwinner norm was not possible for most working-class men, many of whom never married. And working-class men who did marry enlisted their children and wives to contribute to the family economy. The single-male breadwinner family among white families across classes existed for only a short period, peaking in the 1950s, with high rates of marriage and full-time housewives in Western Europe and North America, while for non-white families it has seldom been an operative – much less feasible – goal. By the 1980s and 1990s, the statistics told another story: rises in women's labor-force participation accompanied by high rates of unemployment and underemployment for men undermined the possibilities for sustaining a male breadwinner family. The shift from industrial to service sector jobs has meant that working-class men most committed to a single-earner family model have had the least likely chances of obtaining it. In the United States, structural changes have had the greatest impact on African American men, where class interacts with racial stratification (Majors and Gordon 1994; Wilson 1996). Faludi (1999), turning her attention to men and masculinities in her book, *Stiffed*, characterizes the collapse of men's economic authority, from shipyard closures to the downsizing and consolidations of corporations, as the most visible layer in the masculinity crisis. It is important to keep in mind that, although structural economic changes in the United States and across the developed world have had most impact on unskilled workers, who are disproportionately people of color, they are not limited to this group (Esping-Andersen 1999).

Fatherhood: a global crisis?

Alongside the growing numbers of men who lack resources to be breadwinners for their families, there is a group of men who are cut off from fatherhood because they are wedded to a work culture that does not allow them the time for emotional involvement. Bob Connell (1998) has coined the phrase, "trans-national business masculinity," to characterize men in the highest income brackets (the top 20 percent), whose upward mobility is contingent on their geographical mobility and wholehearted commitment to financial success. According to the findings of Oláh, Bernhardt and Goldscheider (in this volume), the United States appears to be the country in the forefront of this trend, where there is a significant proportion of upper-middle-class educated men who have opted not to father.

Although work cultures in different societal contexts can be more or less sensitive to parenting, the tendency is toward greater time pressures on working parents in a globalizing economy (see Hearn in this volume). Low fertility rates, expressed in women's birth strikes and more couples deciding to be childless, are the most visible signs. But there are more subtle effects within the daily practices of parenting, what Arlie Hochschild (1996) refers to as the "emotionally downsized family," that involves both men and women in the corporate workplace who feel more at home at work than at home.

Globalizing processes penetrate families in direct and indirect ways. As Jeff Hearn argues in his essay, globalization is not a distant phenomenon but is experienced locally. Individual fathers lose jobs as a result of the restructuring of work, and employment and unemployment policies are governed by transnational organizations, both corporations and governmental. Models of welfare move across the Atlantic and within Europe, carrying with them models of fatherhood that reconstitute the relationships within the state, market and family. The most obvious set of relationships can be seen in the extent to which the state actively supports fathers to provide for their children and care for them. European Union debates and Directives seeking to limit working hours are connected to discourses on fatherhood. But the countervailing tendencies, the growth of unlimited hours contracts, and performance-related and/or commission-based systems, undermine these initiatives.

Fatherhood and welfare policy regimes

The social politics of fatherhood naturally takes us into the theoretical terrain of states and supra-states, welfare regimes and social policy. In shifting our focus toward men as subjects in social policy, we also embrace a body of theory on gender and welfare states. The basic critique of feminist research to the models of welfare policy regimes was that they were "gender blind," that dominant theories ignored women's experiences as mothers, wives, workers and citizens. This meant leaving out the dimensions of care, sexuality and reproduction, which shaped the contours of women's social and political rights. But missing in this dialogue on welfare states and policy regimes has been an analysis of gender that considered how men were embedded in policy. Nor does the comparative welfare regime literature investigate men's gendered positions in social policy; men are seen as members of particular classes, status groups or as citizens (Orloff and Monson in this volume).

In fact, gendering the welfare state has produced a wide literature on models of motherhood and care (Leira 1992; Knijn and Kremer 1997; Lewis 1998). Because men were center stage in mainstream comparative research – as the average worker or citizen with or without social rights – feminist researchers did not see men, masculinities and fatherhood as part of the gendering project. Rather, men in mainstream welfare state research were viewed as gender-neutral citizens who happened to be men. When men were treated as subjects, they were working-class men mobilizing power resources (Korpi 1989) or men as heads of households who should be protected against the vagaries of the market. Gendering of welfare states entails incorporating the experiences of men – not only as earners, but also as fathers, and as heterosexual or homosexual partners.

Men as fathers and their fatherhood have been implied in, but not integrated into, the theorizing on gender logics in welfare states. In the studies of solo mothers and social policy, the research has addressed the degree to which the state compensated women for their caring roles in terms of services, care allowances and income support after divorce (Hobson 1994; Hobson and Takahashi 1997; Lewis 1997b; Winkler 2001). The right to form an independent household without the risk of poverty was bound together with a range of policies that allowed women to be decoupled from dependence on a husband's wage or being forced to marry or enter into familial relationships, the process Ruth Lister (2000) referred to as defamilization. In their recent study, O'Connor et al. (1999) include men in their analysis of the social right to form autonomous households.

Lewis (1992) in conceptualizing the gender regime typology, based on strong, moderate and weak breadwinner ideologies, focuses on variations in policy formulas around the division of unpaid and paid work. This division reflects different policy logics around women's access to the labor market: their ability to combine paid work and carework either through state supports or the market. Variations in gender regimes also mirror the extent to which benefits are organized around a single-earner family and male breadwinners are privileged through tax subsidies for dependent wives. If we turn the lens toward men as fathers and the construction of fatherhood, we find the meaning and content of what a strong, moderate and weak breadwinner society is may have to be reconceived, since men as fathers are embedded in family law and social policy, with different economic responsibilities for their fatherhood. This entails paying attention to divorced and never-married fathers and their financial obligations to support wives and children. It also involves considering what the rights of fathers are to custody and decision-making over a child's welfare in non-marital families.

Theoretical framework of the book

The idea that men are made into fathers recognizes the extent to which fatherhood is bound up with institutions, embedded in law and shaped by policy. Though the case studies in this book challenge dominant welfare regime typologies, they nevertheless build upon them, beginning with the assumption that the social politics of fatherhood is connected to state and market institutions. As the discussion above reveals, this model assumed that the family was a unit with degendered subjects, a way of organizing welfare or structuring the eligibility of benefits. How to analyze the competing claims of mothers, fathers and children together with the role of states and markets in shaping them requires other models reflecting these complex interrelations. As a basis for conceptualizing our various cases, we imagined these relationships as three interfacing triangles as seen in Figure 1: the welfare regime institutional triangle, the domestic/relational triangle of wife, husband and parent/child, and the fatherhood triangle. Suppose we begin with the familiar institutional welfare state triangle of state, market and family. It is important to keep in mind that this is a heuristic device, which provided the building blocks for policy regime typologies: the extent to which states governed the market enabled workers to be less dependent upon market forces, illustrated in the connecting state/market sides of the triangle. Turning to the family at

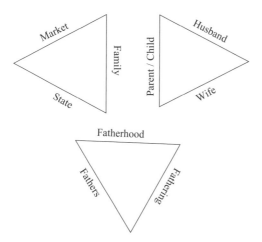

Figure 1 Institutional, domestic and fatherhood triangles.

the base of the triangle (see Figure 1), policy regimes reflect differences in the degree to which the state provides benefits and services or relies on the family as a form of welfare (the state/family sides) and the extent to which the market is the source of benefits and services for families, the family/market sides (Esping-Andersen 1990; O'Connor et al. 1999; Taylor-Gooby 1996).

By incorporating the domestic triangle into the analysis,[4] we are tracking feminist insights on the dynamic interplay between states and markets and the power relations within the family that result from economic dependency on a male breadwinner. Among the countries analyzed in this book, we can see variations in social policy incentives and disincentives for perpetuating a male breadwinner norm, for example in high marriage subsidies (tax advantages given to men who are the sole earners in families) in Germany and the Netherlands; disincentives in Sweden with family members being taxed as individuals; and tax penalties for dual-earner couples in the US and Britain. Everyday practices of parenting reflect the interfacing of the relational and institutional triangles. For instance, couples who espouse egalitarian family norms before children are born come up against a host of constraints when faced with the actual decisions around caretaking responsibilities, for example whether the parental leave is to be shared or not. This involves not only income loss, as men are the higher earners in most families, but rigid policy formulas, and, for fathers, the prejudice of male co-workers and bosses toward men who want to exercise their rights as fathers.

We have included the additional triangle of fatherhood, fathering and fathers in order to capture the complex interplay between institutions and practices. Since these different categories are often conflated, which obscures the distinctions between the construction of fatherhood through laws, policies and discourses, and the practices of fathers, we define them in greater detail below.

Fathers

In the case of the term "Father" we are concerned with processes by which this term becomes attached to a particular individual. We reveal the distinction between the biological and the social father and analyze the ways in which societies privilege the biological fathers.

Fatherhood

If fathers are seen in relational terms to mothers and children and as elements of social structure, fatherhood can be seen as the cultural coding of men as fathers. Here, we are dealing with the rights, duties, responsibilities and statuses that are attached to fathers, as well as the discursive terrain around good and bad fathers. The tension between "cash" and "care," one of the threads in this book, is analyzed in terms of tensions within fatherhood discourses.

Fathering

If the words "father" and "fatherhood" are well established in the English language and readily translatable into other languages, the same cannot be said for the third term, "fathering." The parallel terms are, clearly, "mothering" (as opposed to "motherhood") or, possibly, "parenting." In formal terms, the distinction might seem to signify one between being and doing, between a status or identity and a set of practices. However, we want to suggest that fathering practices do not always require the actual co-presence of a child as when, for example, a father puts in a request for paternal leave.

The links between the fatherhood triangle and the institutional triangle are fairly obvious. Men are configured as fathers through civil laws around marriage, divorce and custody. They are also contoured as fathers in welfare state policies directed at workers and parents, through the governance of the market in policies that de-commodify workers, which is revealed in the division of work time and family time. The relations within individual families shape fathering and the practices of fathers, as seen in the division of care and decision-making within the household. Perhaps the most complex sets of relationships in the fatherhood triangle are those surrounding divorce, where not only mother and child and new partners come into play, but also the state has a crucial role to play in the organization of care and cash regarding the divorced or non-marital father: what are his rights of access to, and custody of, his children? What are his economic obligations? Which fathers are recognized as having rights and obligations, the biological or social/household caretaking father?

Regime typologies and fatherhood models

Institutions are crucial in shaping the rights and obligations of fathers in divorce, and one might expect a fit between the welfare regimes and models of fatherhood. Suppose we consider our basic dimensions of cash and care in relation to divorce and separated fatherhood within the framework of the conventional welfare policy regime typology (Esping-Andersen 1990). As the welfare regime typology is fairly well known, we summarize briefly the three regime types: the Social Democratic type is characterized by decommodifying and universalistic programs; the Corporatist type relies on social insurance schemes, which have generous transfer payments, but where social rights are related to class and status; and the Liberal type is distinguished by its means-tested assistance and the strong role of the market in providing welfare. We are interested in different paradigmatic cases of these regimes. For the Liberal type, the US and Britain provide the cases applied. For the Social Democratic type, Sweden is the case most often cited; the Netherlands has been included in the Esping-Andersen model of Social Democratic regimes, but more recently placed in the Corporatist Conservative group, in which Germany represents the typical case. In this book we also consider Spain; analysts have debated whether distinctive "familiastic" policy approaches characterize Southern European countries and they have suggested that they be treated as a separate category: Latin Rim Countries (Liebfried 1993; Ferrara 1996; Esping-Andersen 1999). Others have placed Spain in the Corporatist fold (Guillén and Matsaganis 2000).

There are different dimensions that one might consider in constructing a father regime typology. Suppose we take the principle employed for motherhood, women's right to form an independent household, that is, not to be economically dependent on husbands or partners. In the case of fatherhood, we would have to broaden the formulation to include the right to form a family, as men are rarely economically dependent on women. But, in effect, this dimension would mirror Esping-Andersen's (1990) model employing the dimensions of the stratifying effects of welfare regimes and the decommodifying social policies that weaken a man's dependence on the market, though including additional policies for parenting. We might consider also the key issue in chapter 1 of this book, a father's capacity to repartner. This formulation captures a man's economic obligations to his biological children, but not his rights to care.

For the purposes of this comparative analysis, we have constructed a very simple model of fatherhood using our five cases, along two general dimensions: rights to custody and care and obligations (economic responsibilities for child support and alimony).[5] Following Lewis' (1992) model for male breadwinner typologies, we use three levels for each dimension (strong, moderate and weak).

As Table 1 shows, we do not find a neat fit between the welfare regime typology and the fatherhood typology drawn from our cases. Not surprisingly, the welfare regime typology does not speak to fathers' rights since the family is not analyzed in terms of competing interests. However, one might have expected more correspondence between policy regime types and the degree of obligations. Given the assumptions in the typology, it would seem likely that Liberal welfare states would support strong obligations, since the family is a mainstay of welfare. This is true in Britain

Table 1. *Policy regimes and fatherhood regimes*

Policy regime type	Countries	Fatherhood obligations	Fatherhood rights
Social Democratic	Sweden	W	S
Liberal	UK	S	M
	US	M	M
Conservative Corporatist			
	Germany	M	M
	Netherlands	W	W
(Latin Rim)	Spain	W	W

M = moderate; S = strong; W = weak.

but not as true in the United States (Table 1). Whereas in Britain the family plays a more central role in social policy, market reliance is stronger in the US, where both women and men are supposed to support themselves through market work (O'Connor et al. 1999).

We assume that Conservative Corporatist welfare states should have moderate obligations as a result of two tendencies, state support for families and children, as can be seen in the advanced income maintenance scheme (see Ostner in this volume), in conjunction with a strong male breadwinner model. With its highly institutionalized support of families and individualized benefits, we should expect countries within the Social Democratic regime to have weak obligations. What we find is that the Netherlands and Sweden both have weak obligations, but not for the same reasons. In the former, the state has generously supported solo-mother families, though this has changed in the 1990s (Knijn and Kramer 1997). Solo mothers have been forced into the labor market, and have higher poverty rates. However, there are no initiatives to increase the economic responsibilities of fathers. In Sweden, the dual-earner family model has assumed that women will be earners in their own right, and those with a weak economy have supplementary housing and social assistance benefits, as do all low-income families (Hobson and Takahashi 1997); solo-mother poverty rates are low. In Spain, with its norms around family responsibility for welfare, the policies surrounding the economic obligations of fathers are weak, despite the attempts to tighten the laws in recent years. The lack of state support presupposes that the mother's parents and extended family will provide support for divorced mothers (Municio-Larsson and Pujol Algans in this volume). If we include Hungary, which appears in the comparative demographic essay on fatherhood and fathering (see Oláh, Bernhardt and Goldscheider in this volume), we might expect a pattern similar to Sweden, a society with a dual-earner model and substantial provisioning for families. But Hungary has been, and continues to be, a country within which fathers have strong economic obligations and weak rights for custody (Goode 1993; Kamarás 1986). Strong male breadwinner norms do not wholly explain the treatment of divorced fathers in social policy along the dimensions of cash and care. Our two cases with weak father obligations, the Netherlands and Sweden, have been placed at opposite ends of the gender regime typology of strong and weak male breadwinner regimes (Lewis 1992). One might assume alternatively that strong male breadwinner regimes, with their traditional family forms, would place more restrictions on men's rights to joint custody among divorced and never-married fathers. This is true for two of our cases, the Netherlands and Spain, but not Germany or Britain.

How do we account for these variations in fatherhood regimes? As the chapters in this book reveal, there are multifarious social, political, economic and cultural sources for them. Institutions play a crucial role, both national and supranational. Through laws and policies, all states indirectly or directly shape the different borders of fatherhood, fathering and father identities, and this varies over time as well as across societies. These include legal parameters that define who the father is and on what basis (the biological or the social/household father). Policy frameworks shape the kinds of choices men make as fathers and foster certain kinds of identities and interests. Public discourse creates hegemonic ideologies around fatherhood, which can be enabling or constraining for fathers. A growing emphasis on fatherhood and care has provided men with discursive resources to make claims upon their employers. These same ideologies, when they are at odds with cultural and ethnic practices of fathering, can lead to conflict in families and divorce.

We find different incentives and disincentives for fatherhood in terms of time and money. In the past, men without economic resources delayed fatherhood or did not form families. In Sweden, the institution of Stockholm marriage, in which men and women published their banns but never married (Matovic 1984), was a way for men to cohabit, have children, but not bear the formal responsibilities of fatherhood. With the emergence of modern welfare states in the early twentieth century, a range of social and labor market policies, social insurance schemes, unemployment benefits and child allowances supported fatherhood. Tax benefits did, and continue to, offer incentives for single-earner male breadwinner fathers. In the current day, social policy also affects men's ability to repartner and form new families (Oláh, Bernhardt and Goldscheider in this volume).

Variations in family law also play a crucial role in shaping the negotiations in marriage and divorce. These include the conditions for divorce and the division of property after divorce, which affects men's power inside and outside marriage as well as the calculation of economic costs in divorce. All states privilege heterosexual marriage and fatherhood (Collier 1995) though many states allow non-marital fathers the same rights as married fathers; few allow homosexual men to adopt children. Even in countries where homosexual partnership is recognized in law, such as Sweden, fatherhood and the adoption of children by homosexual couples is highly contested.

Political constellations comprised of social actors, men's movements, the mobilization of the religious right, and both grassroots feminism and femocrats in government, are forces shaping the patterns of fatherhood, fathering and the claim-making of men as fathers. Men's agency has been a crucial component in the configurations of fatherhood. Men have organized as workers, claiming their role as breadwinners when demanding higher wages and attacking the deskilling of their jobs in terms of their manhood. However, they have not until very recently represented themselves as fathers. Alongside the more visible fathers' rights movements, individual men have made claims upon courts, their employers and within their families to be recognized as father–carers. The well-known case of the German father who was unsuccessful in challenging his country's maternal leave policy in the European Court of Justice in 1985, paved the way for a gender-neutral EU Directive a decade later.[6]

By employing a framework that analytically distinguishes fathers, fatherhood and fathering, we are able to highlight similarities and differences in policies and discourses around fatherhood as well as the diverse practices of fathering over time.

These distinctions provide a means of characterizing historical change. As several of the chapters in this volume underscore, a major influence on the current concern with fathers has been the weakening of the single (male) breadwinner model. Once again we emphasize that in ideology, and to a lesser extent in practice, it occupied a relatively short period of historical time, although it was often presented as something eternal and firmly rooted in the natural order of things. Within this natural order, the husband of the mother was assumed to be the father of the children and the discourses of fatherhood and the practices of fathering were closely bound together through breadwinning responsibilities. Although these notions of fatherhood belong to a distinct historical epoch, the assumptions surrounding the male breadwinner model are by no means dead and, directly or indirectly, may still be influential (Warin et al. 1999).

What is persistent in the ideologies and daily practices linking father-hood and male breadwinning is more difficult to uncover in gender-neutral formulations of family policy. For example, conservative ideologies supporting a traditional gendered role division in the family often sit comfortably with neo-liberal ideologies that take for granted an adult-worker model composed of individuals who do not depend upon support from the state (see Gavanas; Lewis; Orloff and Monson in this volume; Larner 2000). In societies with a hegemonic dual-earner model, the rights and duties of fatherhood have been replaced with the rights and duties of parenthood. But, like the fitting of Chinese boxes one inside the other, there appear to be many caches to store the ideological contents of male breadwinning. These can be seen in the outcomes of the daily decisions over time and money (Takahashi forthcoming), the gender segregation of jobs (Nermo 2000) and the stiffer penalties accorded to men who take advantage of their rights to care (Sundström 1994); all assume that men are the main breadwinners.

The authors in this volume highlight the contradictions in fatherhood ideologies and father practices. Our cases reveal different adaptations to the weakening of the male breadwinner norm, the one-and-a-half bread-winner family (Holland), the three-quarter breadwinner family (Sweden) and the never-married solo mother (in the US) (see Oláh, Bernhardt and Goldscheider; and Orloff and Monson in this volume).

It is important to keep in mind that variations in this uneven process in the weakening of the male breadwinner norm exist both across time and space as well as among different groups of men and their understandings of masculinities. And these are linked to their perceptions of the division of authority in the family and their roles as providers. One can find radical dissonance between hegemonic ideologies supporting the egalitarian family and dual-earner breadwinner model, and the assumptions, norms and religious values of Christian fundamentalist and Muslim fathers. For example, in Sweden, Iranian Muslim men often blame the high rates of divorce in their families on women's participation in paid work and their contact with secular ideas (Darvishpour forthcoming). These men are no longer the only providers, and often they are the more vulnerable provider, since they are more likely to be unemployed than Swedish men. This means that in daily practice they may take on more father-ing tasks, though not necessarily adhering to the ideologies of egalitarian fatherhood within the larger society.

The distinctions between fathers, fatherhood and fathering may be of some help in beginning to sort out the different strands in current debates and anxieties about fathers in modern society. More than this, this exploration of these differences may be helpful in understanding some of the contradictions and conflicts within some of these debates. While these three terms are linked, it has already been intimated that they do not necessarily fit neatly together under all circumstances and to begin to disentangle some of the different strands of meaning is also to begin to identify some possible sources of tension.

For one illustration, we return to the debates concerning "absent" fathers. It has been suggested that such concerns have tended to focus upon issues of fatherhood, on the more legalistic understandings of the duties and responsibilities of fathers, often expressed in cash terms. Several of the empirical accounts discussed in this current volume show the growth and emergence of various pro-fathers groups developing partly in response to these public claims about the responsibilities attached to fatherhood. In so far as these counter-claims are expressed in terms of rights (visiting, access, decision-making in terms of education or, more generally, claims for equal treatment), they may also be seen as reinforcing the idea of fatherhood, even where there may be some disagreement about some specific aspects. However, these claims might also use the rhetoric of fathering in order to underline them. Thus the American Coalition for Fathers and Children highlights the slogan "Children Need Both Parents." In these contexts, fatherhood rights become the opportunities to practice fathering.

In another area at this level of public debate, there are increasing claims for and developments within the areas of parental leave and more flexible working practices. Again, the key points of reference may be fathering practices and the desire to have these recognized as valid claims upon the time and the resources of others, whether these others be the state or employers. Yet, in so far as these concerns are expressed in the form of rights or demands for legislative change or alternative working practices, they may also be seen as part of a process where the boundaries of fatherhood are being shifted.

We can also see some of the tensions between fathers, fathering and fatherhood at the more immediate or micro-level of everyday family practices. The stable nuclear family model is less dominant than it once was, and there has been increasing focus upon arrangements which are variously described as "step," "reconstituted," or "bi-nuclear" (Moxnes 1993) families; terms that more accurately reflect the range of family forms. Divorce and separation are increasingly the major causes of these growing complexities. Thus it is increasingly likely that a child will have the experience of one or more than one household in the course of growing up, and the resulting links between different households will vary according to the wishes and expectations of the various parties involved. Here the recognition of biological and social/household fathers comes into play. We know that different legal frameworks give preference to biological fathers in assigning rights to care and decision-making, but it is unclear how much this affects daily practices of social/household fathers who reside with children.

This leads into another discussion concerning men's interests (Orloff and Monson 1997) connected to fatherhood and fathering. By unpacking the assumed relationships between fathers, fatherhood and fathering, the chapters in this volume call into question the notion of men's interests. First, on the level of the constructions of fatherhood, the chapters addressing the situation of poor and minority men reveal that not all men derive benefit from the scripted cultural ideals of masculinities that connect men's economic power to their authority in the family. Secondly, we imagine competing interests of men as fathers: among social and biological fathers around fathers' rights and obligations. There are diverse politics among fathers supporting a more traditional family and those advocating more egalitarian forms of fathering. Gay fathers are often pitted against heterosexual fathers in custody battles and struggles for the rights to adopt children. As Bob Connell (1995) astutely recognizes, not only are there multiple masculinities, but hierarchies of masculinities.

Men are often embedded in social policy in contradictory ways, a point underscored in Jeff Hearn's analysis of the research on fatherhood from the perspective of the critical studies of men. This is obvious if we consider the different treatment of men as fathers (by race, ethnicity and class) or by marital status (divorced men versus married men) or sexual orientation (gay men versus heterosexual men) (Hearn and Gavanas in this volume). That studies of men and masculinities use the plural form underscores the point that men have multiple identities and interests. By situating our analysis of men's power within the two triangles of the state, market and family and the husband, wife and parent/child, we recognize that men as fathers have different positions in their workplaces, in their families, and in their access to making claims on the state.

Summary of the book

Making Men into Fathers is a unique collection in that it brings comparative perspectives to the study of the social politics of fatherhood. The book consists of six case studies: England, Germany, the Netherlands, Spain, Sweden and the United States. These are societies in which fatherhood has been a central issue on the public agenda. Our six cases represent a cross-section of policy regime types. Moreover, in choosing these cases, we sought to reflect the range of male breadwinner societies in Lewis's typology of strong, moderate and weak male breadwinner models.

The case studies are foregrounded by the opening statistical chapter on who fathers, which looks at men as biological and household fathers. Oláh, Bernhardt and Goldscheider analyze men's patterns of partnership, remarriage and coresidence using cases representing three geographic culture areas: Northern Europe, Central/Eastern Europe and Western Europe/North America. They consider how the costs of fathering, analyzed in terms of children and repartnership, are shaped by different institutional frameworks in Sweden, Hungary and the United States.

Several of the case studies use a long-distance lens from which to view the changing discourses and policy around the logics of gender in welfare states, and the changing emphasis from cash to care in different welfare states. Three of the chapters take us back to the early decades of the twentieth century. Orloff and Monson examine how men as fathers are addressed in US policy from the first decades of the twentieth century and the foundations of welfare policy to the position of men as fathers in more recent US social policy. They argue that men have been situated not as fathers *per se*, or even as citizen workers, but as employees with ties to particular employers, rather than direct ties to the state through their role as fathers. Hobson and Bergman trace the coding of fatherhood in policy and law, beginning with the 1917 law establishing paternity and financial obligations, to the recent laws and policy that seek to enforce fathers' caring responsibilities through compulsory joint custody. They claim that the Swedish welfare state has had one of the most regulatory and highly interventionist policies toward men as fathers. Sweden also represents the case in which the shift from cash (obligations) to care (rights) has been most dramatic. Lewis follows the problem of fathers over time in British policy beginning at the turn of the century. Historically, the British case exemplifies the strong male breadwinner model, and the policy shift in the 1980s and 1990s mirrors earlier concerns about stable families and the authority of fathers. She argues that the main concern of past policy makers has been to perpetuate family relationships beyond divorce. Moreover, recent initiatives, such as the *unpaid* parental leave, do not respond to the profound changes in family structure and the gendered "care gap" that family policies have so far failed to address.

Although fatherhood is being reshaped and recast in many societies, several of our cases reveal fluid and shifting fields of action and reaction. Knijn and Selten in their study of the Netherlands maintain that there has been a dramatic shift in the discourse on fatherhood in the Netherlands. They document a growing emphasis on fathers' roles as carers within a society that remains one of the paradigms of the strong male breadwinner model. New policies and incentives are woven together with the policy legacies of the past, and patterns of power and dependency in families.

Perhaps this is most obvious is the case of the two Germanys after unification. Ilona Ostner argues that unification has made visible different models of fatherhood in the two Germanys, which have produced different sets of expectations about fathers' rights and obligations as carers and breadwinners. Yet the associations of fatherhood with the Nazi past has made it difficult to bring issues of contemporary fatherhood on the political agenda. The search for a new role for fathers in unified Germany must come to terms with these legacies as well as confront the shifting patterns of paid and unpaid work in highly competitive labor markets.

A common thread in all five case studies is the shifting parameters of family law and the resurgence of men as actors both resisting policy change and advocating alternative policies in cases of divorce and custody. In the chapter on Spain, a revised family law framed in accordance with EU guidelines confronts traditional ideologies and practices. Municio-Larsson and Pujol Algans, in their narratives of divorce cases in Spain, point out the difficulty of implementing the law that is deeply resented by men who in the past did not accept any responsibility for former wives and children of former marriages. Of course, these laws are difficult to implement everywhere.

In Spain and in other countries, divorced men have organized to oppose new laws to increase men's share of the costs of children as well as to gain more rights in custody cases. More recently, men have organized to reassert fathering in masculinist terms. Anna Gavanas, in her chapter on the Fatherhood Responsibility Movement in the United States, offers an in-depth analysis of the broad constituencies and complex sets of organizations, actors and claims in a movement that seeks to reaffirm the importance of men as fathers. Her groups range from the Promise Keepers with a fundamentalist base to the Fragile Families initiative organized by urban policy makers of African American men. Through her rich sources of interviews she analyzes the commonalties among groups united around the family and the child with varying constituencies by race, class, religion and urban/rural differences; she also locates the lines of controversy around issues of marriage, the state and feminism.

Two final chapters locate our case studies in a terrain of Theorizing Men, Masculinities and Fatherhood. Jeff Hearn provides a multilayered analysis of the historical relations of men to the state, which encompasses both links between men and welfare and the role of transnational and global perspectives in the construction of men as fathers. David Morgan's Epilogue grapples with the many theoretical challenges that emerge from this book, including the question of whether one can speak about hegemonic masculinities and fathering. This is complicated, even if we consider them as moral identities, in light of the changing patterns of care and breadwinning in many families and the plurality in masculinities and fatherhoods.

Making Men into Fathers emerged from a four-year dialogue between scholars involved in the critical studies of men and feminist researchers on the welfare state. We met across countries, disciplines and methodologies, making and remaking ourselves as scholars of states, societies and the family, as theorists on men and masculinities, and feminism. Our gendered lens was constantly being readjusted and refocused. A wide-angle frame helped us to discern the varied discursive arenas, policies and practices in what has been compressed into a single image, the crisis in fatherhood. The perspective we gained from our historical analysis allowed us to track the continuities and ruptures in an era where traditional ideas of fatherhood are being recast and reconfigured.

Part 1

Who fathers?

1 Coresidential paternal roles in industrialized countries: Sweden, Hungary and the United States

Livia Sz. Oláh, Eva M. Bernhardt and Frances K. Goldscheider

There have been dramatic changes in family patterns throughout the industrialized world during the last third of the twentieth century. Male–female relationships have become less committed, at least as indicated by the rapid rise in divorce and in cohabitation, which in most countries also involves less commitment than marriage. The couple relationship has become a much less central and stable element in adults' lives, both for men and for women.

These patterns are frequently noted. Less frequently noted, however, is a clear concomitant: that parenthood has become a much less central and stable element in men's lives, not only compared with the past, but particularly as compared with its role in the lives of women. In all of the countries undergoing these changes, the connections between men and children have become complex. Men are increasingly unlikely to live with their own biological children, struggling (some more and some much less successfully) to maintain rewarding and supportive relationships with them, yet increasingly likely to live with other children, the children of their current partner, with whom it is not clear at all what sorts of relationships should be established or maintained. In David Morgan's terms (see Morgan in this volume), the core meaning of "fatherhood" is challenged when men are confused about how to "father" either their absent biological children or the children (of their partner) with whom they do live. It is often not totally clear in either case whether they should be considered "fathers" at all. Their partner's children normally have a biological father, and their biological children's mother often has a new partner who is living with them.

Although there has been much more change in the relationships between men and children than in those between women and children, the focus of most theorizing about recent changes in the family has been on women, their increased independence, their increased aspirations and their presumed reduced dependence on men. If one way to view the gender revolution is that it is reducing the separation between the work sphere of men and the home sphere of women, then the focus of most re- search and theories has been on the ways that women have become more nearly equal with men in the sphere of work, with almost no attention to the implications of this complexity in men's parental roles for men's equality or inequality in the sphere of the family.

In addition to the increase in men's parental role complexity, many industrialized countries have experienced a considerable increase in the support states provide for families. Like separation and repartnering, this change also raises different issues for men than for women, since the traditional element of the father's role in the family division of labor is financial support. State support for families with children is generally seen as pro-family, although not always (Popenoe 1988, 1991). A con- sideration of families in gendered perspective, however, suggests that the type and extent of state support for families might have very different implications for the family roles of men than for those of women.

Research on the effects of family policy has shown that public poli- cies differentially reinforce family types. Some primarily provide support that reinforces gender relations based on "separate spheres" for men and women, with payments made to men that substitute for women's wages. This system allows women to stay home but provides little or no afford- able day-care if they wish to continue working, and also provides little job security when they want to return to work. Other systems of family support tend to reinforce gender equality, since payments are made to custodial parents; employed parents have access to substantial parental leave with job guarantees; and subsidized day-care is available to both employed and student parents (Sundström 1991). These two systems are also distinguished as "male breadwinner" and "worker–carer" mod- els (Leira 1992; Lewis 1992; Hobson 1994).

There is another dimension on which family support policies differ, and that is whether they serve as a complement to men's financial roles or as substitutes for them (Cox and Jakubson 1995). The latter has been the case in the United States, where the major programs that provide sup- port to children both have been strongly means-tested and have normally required that no man be present in the household. Although these policies have changed, most agree that the changes are not perceived either by the administrators at the local level or by applicants (Moffitt et al. 1998).

Both of these new trends, then, the growth in state support and the decrease in relationship stability, mean something quite different for men than for women. State support can either reinforce men's traditional roles or encourage egalitarian ones (such as the Swedish "daddy month," a month of parental leave that is only available to men), or it can drive them from the family altogether. The growth in complex paternal roles, with biological children that are often absent and stepchildren who are often present, also has effects with an important economic component. While there is no legal obligation for men to support these stepchildren unless there is formal adoption (Moffitt et al. 1998), most men realize that this is unrealistic, and that the children will be claimants on their income, at least while they remain together in the household.

There is actually little evidence one way or the other on whether men treat their partner's children as "their own." Most of these children have a living biological father who may dilute the strength of the paternal relationship. Further, men in these relationships can be much less confident that the relationship will last, since cohabiting relationships tend to be short-lived and second marriages have even higher rates of dissolution than first marriages when stepchildren are present (White and Booth 1985). Although they must live together and interact on a daily, even hourly basis, the relationships between the children and their mother's partner are only very weakly institutionalized as *parental* relationships. If the couple is married, the woman's husband becomes the children's "stepfather," but in the case of cohabitation there is not even a name for the relationship between the children and their mother's new partner.

In Sweden, men who cohabit with a woman with children are sometimes referred to as "social," "pretend" or "plastic" fathers. None of these terms, however, is well established or generally accepted. In this chapter we will use the term "household father" and call such children "household children." We have struggled with this concept, first using the term "informal father," thereby emphasizing the lack of a legal tie binding such men and children. We have chosen, however, to use a more positive term, one that emphasizes the actual structure of their relationship, which is based on coresidence. Although most biological fathers also live with their children, we will call those who do "biological fathers" to maintain the distinction between them and the growing numbers of men who no longer live with their biological children, whom we will call "absent fathers," and those who have become fathers by joining children in their households (household fathers).

The proportion of men who are living as household fathers is not small. In the three countries which we will be studying, the proportion of men in their late 20s or early 30s who are living with at least some household children among those living with children at all is 5 percent in Hungary, 10 percent in Sweden, and 14 percent in the United States. Hence, it has become increasingly important to know what sorts of men undertake the task of being household fathers, and how they differ from men in relationships which involve only biological children. How does the different obligation to support affect the processes linking income and parenthood? Does the provision of substantial state support for families mean that men make different calculations when they consider a union involving household fatherhood instead of or in addition to biological fatherhood than otherwise similar men might make in countries where such support is weak? Do societal gender-role attitudes influence men in their decision-making about becoming household fathers? We will address these issues by examining the extent to which men with more resources are more likely to be in more committed relationships, and whether this difference is greater for marital relationships than for cohabiting ones and greater in countries with less than more state support, controlling for other factors likely to influence men's family roles.

In this chapter, we begin a cross-national investigation of the relationships between men and children, focusing on cases that vary systematically in the extent of state support to families and on the extent of social support for separate spheres for men and women. We examine Northern Europe (Finland, Norway and Sweden), focusing on Sweden; Central/ Eastern Europe (the former East Germany, Hungary and Poland), focusing on Hungary; and Western Europe/North America (France, the former West Germany, Canada and the United States), taking the United States as our focus in this category.

Background

In order to study factors affecting the types of coresidential paternal roles men hold in these three countries, we need to consider factors at the level of the state and at the level of the individual. At the state level are factors that affect all men in a given country, which in our case are the state-level differences in support for families and in gender-role attitudes. At the individual level are factors that differ among men, since an important question is *which* men become household fathers. Below we discuss both sorts of factors.

Country-level factors: state family support and gender role equality

Our primary, multivariate analysis focuses on three countries, Sweden, Hungary and the United States. These countries differ in a number of ways. They have different histories, very different sizes and different geographic locations. Nevertheless, they represent an opportunity for systematic comparative analysis, based on their differences and similarities.

The recent histories of social policy for Sweden, the smallest country of these three in terms of population (8 million), and of the United States, which is more than 30 times as large (270 million) are described elsewhere in this volume (Hobson and Bergman for Sweden; Orloff and Monson for the United States). Below we provide a short description of Hungary's recent history.

Hungary is a small country in central Europe, with a population of about 10 million. As part of the Austro-Hungarian Empire prior to 1918, and even up to the mid-1940s, Hungarian socioeconomic development was not much different from that of Western Europe, with central roles for the Church (especially the Catholic Church) and for the patriarchal family, in which men worked outside the home but few married women did.

After World War II, Hungary, together with the other states in the region, became part of the Soviet sphere of influence, which had major implications for the economy, politics and public policies. The rebuilding of the half-destroyed country required the work of both men and women in the early post-war years. The demand for female employment remained high due to massive industrial development and the ruling socialist ideology's commitment to full employment and "gender equality." The state–socialist concept of gender equality was, however, limited to women's and men's equal labor force participation. Also, the low level of wages increased the need for full-time working dual-earner couples.

There was no effort to require equal sharing of unpaid work (e.g. household work, childrearing and care for the sick and elderly), however, or to provide equal access to decision-making positions either in the economy or in the other spheres of public life. "Family-friendly" social policies and an extended network of social services (especially public child care) facilitated the combination of parenthood and employment for women, hardly addressing men at all. Thus, despite increases in equality in the extent of employment, pre-war gender relations were maintained within the family and the society during the forty years of socialism to a far greater extent than was the case in Sweden or the United States.

The power of using the three countries for contrast lies in two dimensions that distinguish them clearly. The first is the difference in the level and structure of state support for families, which can affect the ability of parents to combine working and family life by easing their economic and time costs, or, in the extreme, to remain with their children and still receive support. The second is the difference in the level of social support for actually combining work and family life in terms of the preferred gender-role attitudes in each of these three countries. Most research on gender issues has focused primarily on differences in attitudes.

This three-country contrast allows us to weigh the importance of this dimension against that of the structural dimension of state support.

State support for families

A major difference between the United States, Sweden and Hungary is in the level of public support provided to children and the terms under which it is provided (summarized in Table 2) (Adamik 1991; Sundström 1991; Sundström and Stafford 1992; Sainsbury 1996). Both Sweden and Hungary had particularly generous policies at the time the data used in this study were collected, although each country has experienced some decline in support in the mid-1990s. Direct state support to families is almost non-existent in the United States.

Sweden In Sweden, the cost of childrearing is reduced through four major policy programs. First, parents can be absent from work with cash benefits for many months (usually more than a year). Secondly, there is a universal system of child allowances, which provided about 12 percent of net income for a family with an average industrial worker's wage in 1985 (Wennemo 1994). Thirdly, there is a means-tested housing allowance. Fourthly, the highly subsidized public child-care system greatly facilitates the combination of gainful employment and parenthood, and thus further decreases the costs of children. Whether the parents are married or cohabiting is not a factor in determining eligibility for benefits. Single parents[1] are also not discriminated against, either positively

Table 2. *Public support provided to families with children in the United States, Sweden and Hungary*

Policy program	USA	Sweden	Hungary
Maternity/parental leave	not statutory until 1993	statutory (paid)	statutory (paid)
Child/family allowance	none	statutory (universal)	statutory
Housing-related benefit	none	housing allowance (means-tested)	"baby bonus" (for young couples buying a dwelling)
Subsidized public child care	none	yes	yes
Special program for single parents	AFDC (means-tested)	none	none
Tax allowance for children	yes	none	none

or negatively, except for a small supplement to the child allowance they received prior to 1996. The Swedish tax system, however, does not allow any tax deduction related to childrearing.

The parental leave program

Before 1974, only mothers were entitled to leave, which provided a maximum of six months and a 65 percent income replacement. After 1974, parents became free to divide the leave between themselves, with a replacement level of 90 percent of previous earnings, a job-guarantee, and pension entitlement. The benefit is taxable. The period of paid leave was extended several times, reaching fifteen months by the end of the 1980s, though the last three months only provided a flat-rate benefit. Non-employed parents are also eligible for a flat-rate benefit for the same period as the leave for employed parents. The system is highly flexible. The benefit can be used on a full-time or a part-time basis up to the child's eighth birthday (Sundström 1996). For children born in 1995 or later, one month of income-related leave is reserved for the father and one for the mother. (For more detail, see Hobson and Bergman in this volume.)

Child allowance

A child allowance was introduced as a universal benefit in 1947. It was paid to the mother for each child in the family (and included only children, unlike in other countries that provided benefits only for higher-order children). In 1982, an additional benefit (in Swedish: "flerbarnstillägg") was introduced for third and additional children, and its amount increased according to the number of children (Lavin 1987). This higher allowance was abolished for children born after 1995, but reintroduced for third and additional children after January 1, 1998.

Housing allowance

In the mid-1930s, a housing allowance was introduced as a means-tested benefit in Sweden. It was paid to families with at least three children. In 1947, families with two children also became eligible for it and after 1958, even families with only one child. The old system was replaced by a new program in 1968. Further reforms took place in the late 1980s and in the early 1990s, but the benefit has remained means-tested over time (SOU 1995: 133).

Subsidized public child care

The Swedish public day-care system began in the 1960s but expanded greatly after the mid-1970s. It is provided by municipalities and financed mainly by government subsidies, together with parents' fees which are normally based on their income. Public child care is available only for parents of pre-school children who study or are gainfully employed for at least twenty hours per week (Gustafsson and Stafford 1994). In the early 1990s, about 60 percent of children below the age of seven received care in the public day-care system (Statistics Sweden [SCB] 1995).

Hungary Hungary until recently had a very similar package of policies that reduced the cost of children: a parental leave program, family allowances, housing-related benefits and a public day-care system. The family allowance, which averaged about 17 percent of the net income per child (Krausz 1992), was paid as a universal benefit to all families with children. Although there was no housing allowance in Hungary, from the 1970s to the 1990s the state provided a significant one-time benefit for young married couples with children who wanted to build or buy a dwelling. The individual-based tax system, as in Sweden, did not provide any tax allowance for dependent children in Hungary. (This has changed in 2000 to a relatively low tax-deduction for working parents based on the number of children in the family.) However, marital status did matter for some benefits[2] in Hungary and single parents receive more public support than average two-earner families, in contrast to Sweden.

The parental leave program

Until the mid-1960s, mothers could take only a short paid leave after birth in spite of the socialist full-employment policy that required both women's and men's full-time labor market participation. In 1967, women became entitled to a leave with job security, in addition to a fully paid five-month long maternity leave after the birth, and a flat payment ("GYES") of about 40 percent of an average female wage until the child was 2.5 years old. In 1969, the leave was extended to the child's third birthday. Men were not eligible for child-care leave until 1982, but even then they could take leave only when the child was at least one year old.

In 1985, the period of fully paid maternity leave was extended to six months, and leave during the following six-month period was earnings-related (75 percent of the previous wage, or 65 percent in case of shorter previous employment), called child-care pay ("GYED"). Those not eligible for GYED, for example students, could still receive GYES, since both programs were available until the mid-1990s. At the beginning, only mothers could use GYED. In 1986, it was extended by half a year and fathers became entitled to leave for children 12–18 months of age. Starting in 1987, GYED could be used until the child's second birthday (Adamik 1991). In 1996, GYED was abolished and GYES became a means-tested benefit. Unpaid parental leave was still available for parents who were not eligible for cash benefits according to the means-test. In 1999 the means-test for GYES was abolished. Since 2000 working parents are, again, eligible for GYED with a benefit level of 70 percent of the previous wage.

Family allowance

A family allowance was introduced in Hungary in 1938, one of the first countries in Europe to do so (Gordon 1988). During the socialist period, it was restricted to employment in the state-sector (although after the mid-1950s it also covered members of agricultural co-operatives). After 1990, the employment requirement was abolished. While at first only large families received the benefit, one-child families became eligible in 1983. The amount of the allowance has varied according to family type, i.e. single parents and those with disabled children have received higher benefits (Krausz 1992; Jarvis and Micklewright 1992). In 1996, the family allowance was converted to a means-tested program, but became again a universal benefit in 1999.

Housing-related benefit

During socialism there was a constant shortage of housing in Hungary, especially in urban areas, with rental housing only available through the municipalities. In the late 1960s, it became possible to buy a house or apartment. From the 1970s, young couples who took a loan from the bank to build or buy a dwelling received part of the loan as a one-time benefit they did not have to pay back if they had children or "promised" to have one child within three years or two children within six years after taking the loan, a kind of "baby bonus." Only couples below the age of 35 were eligible to make such a "promise." If they did not have the promised children in the period given in the contract, they had to pay the "baby bonus" back as a part of the original loan. The benefit was abolished at the end of 1994.

Subsidized public child care

Hungarian child-care institutions were run by municipalities and by big companies, and were mainly financed by state subsidies. Parents' fees were quite low and based on their income (Adamik 1991). In the transition period, many day-nurseries have closed and others were privatized; the rest are run by the reorganized municipalities with significantly higher financial contribution from the parents than in the past.

United States There is much less state support for families with children in the United States than in either Sweden or Hungary. While private employers not uncommonly have offered maternity benefits, there was no national legislation on parental leave until 1993, and, even then, only unpaid leave was provided.[3] There is almost no subsidized day-care (Panayotova and Brayfield 1997), which makes the cost to working families very high. The major program of support for children (AFDC) is strongly means-tested and the benefit level is low in most states. AFDC is a federal–state program, that provides cash benefits to single-parent families. Other benefits, such as food stamps, Medicaid, day-care and housing are normally tied to receipt of AFDC. A work requirement was adopted for single mothers in the program in 1972, but it was not strictly enforced. During the 1980s, eligibility conditions became more restrictive and eligibility to the related in-kind benefits was reduced (Sainsbury 1996).

The American tax system, however, does provide a tax allowance for families with dependent children, unlike in Sweden and Hungary. It is much less generous than the direct support provided by these two countries. In 1985 it averaged around 4 percent of net income for families with an average industrial worker's wage (Wennemo 1994).

Also in contrast to the Swedish and Hungarian systems, the United States provides no national program of medical insurance, often a considerable expense to families with children. The only program that provides subsidized medical care to children (Medicaid) is strongly means-tested. Like AFDC, Medicaid, in addition to stringent means-testing, was also restricted to single-parent families until the last few years, so that families could expect their benefits to go to zero if a male entered the family, particularly if the couple married (Moffitt et al. 1998). Even under the new rules that lifted the restriction to single-parent families, the stringent means-testing implies that all but extremely low-earning prospective partners can expect the benefits to be withdrawn upon their entry into the household. In terms of state support for families with children, then, the United States stands out, by providing almost none, either in terms of financial support, which eases the burden of parents (and particularly men) to "provide" or in terms of family leave, which makes it more feasible to plan adult lives that include both family and paid work (particularly for women). These differences in the structure of state support for families with children can have a substantial influence on demographic behavior patterns and on patterns of coresidence.

Gender-role attitudes

When it comes to gender relations, there are major differences between these countries in levels of social support for egalitarian gender relationships. Women's participation in higher education and in the labor force has reached high levels in each of the three countries (despite some differences in the use of part-time employment).[4] Nevertheless, no real transformation of gender relations has occurred in Hungary or in other state–socialist countries. In these countries, respondents typically express strong support for men's primacy in the public sphere of work and politics, and the centrality of the family in women's lives (Szalai 1991), with the result that employed mothers carry a double burden of paid work and domestic chores.

Americans are more egalitarian in their attitudes toward women's involvement in non-traditional roles (e.g. employment and politics) than Hungarians (Panayotova and Brayfield 1997). Support for mothers to hold paid employment increased dramatically in the United States (Thornton 1989). There has been much less change in actual behavior in terms of domestic tasks, which resulted in the development of a double burden in the United States, as in Hungary (sometimes called the "second shift"), for employed women (Hochschild 1989). Men in the United States have increased the time they spend caring for families (Goldscheider and Waite 1991), with the result that, while fathers spent less time on domestic tasks than single men in the 1960s, this has now reversed (Gershuny and Robinson 1988).

Swedes have been more successful in moving traditional gender relations in the home to greater equality (Baxter and Kane 1995). A portion of the family leave benefit is only available to fathers. Gender equality has been on the active policy agenda at least since the mid-1960s, and from early on the idea of a transformation of gender roles included the notion that at the same time as women got more involved in non-family activities men should take their share of domestic responsibilities (Bernhardt 1992; Hobson and Bergman in this volume).

In terms of attitudes toward gender-role equality, then, our second country-level dimension, it is Hungary that differs the most, in contrast to the situation on the dimension of state support for families, where the United States is the most distinctive. While we take the two dimensions together, the picture seems to be that in the United States women feel a strong commitment to combine work and family but have great difficulties doing so because of the lack of supportive programs. In addition, the costs of parenthood are very high for men. In Hungary, in contrast, state support for families serves primarily to ease the financial burdens of the population (since as we will see, most live in families with children), and to allow exhausted women to reclaim their domestic roles to the extent possible, which reinforces men's traditional position in the family. Only in Sweden are attitudes and policies congruent, providing support for both fathers and mothers to work and to care.

Individual-level factors: theories of family formation

We expect that there will be individual factors, in addition to the structure of state support and expected gender roles, that will influence the types of families men (and women) form. We draw primarily on general theories of union formation (cohabitation versus marriage) and fertility for our choice of explanatory variables. Demographic studies on connections between men and children have been largely indirect; they examine how having already had children affects the likelihood that a *woman* enters a new union. These studies have also focused almost entirely on marriage and on the United States (Koo et al. 1984; Chiswick and Lehrer 1990; but see Ermisch and Wright 1991 on Great Britain). They have typically found that the presence and sometimes the number of children reduce women's likelihood of marrying. Bennett, Bloom and Miller (1995) also find that children depress the likelihood of union formation, but the negative effect is less for cohabitation than for marriage, which suggests that children reduce the extent of men's commitment to the relationship.

There is much less evidence on how children affect men's likelihood of union formation. Bernhardt (2000) found that men who had children were more likely to enter a second union than men who reported no children in their first union. However, few of these children lived with their fathers. Smith, Zick and Duncan (1991) looked at widowers, where presumably most of the children lived with their fathers, and showed that dependent children also reduce middle-aged (<60) men's likelihood of remarriage after widowhood, although the reduction is much less than is the case for women with children.

However, there is no research on how the presence of the children of a potential partner would influence a person's likelihood of forming a union with that partner. Based on the research that takes the parent as the unit of analysis, we expect that the effect of children would be negative, if only for financial reasons. This is particularly likely to be the case in societies that provide little state support for the expenses of children. Societal gender-role attitudes can further strengthen the negative effect of partners' children, at least for countries with more traditional gender relations. To predict entering a union with children, we will treat such unions as non-normative, and in that sense inferior unions, and derive our expectations from the body of theory developed to study racial inter-marriages, which are also non-normative unions.

Theories predicting entry to marriage and parenthood lead us to expect that those with more resources are both more desirable as marriage partners and more ready themselves to take on these adult roles. However, this effect should be weaker for cohabitation than for marriage, since the planning horizon for cohabitation is less. With regard to the effect of pre-existing children, intermarriage theory predicts that those considering entering unions that are less desirable normally "trade" some other characteristic. For example, a white man considering marrying a black woman can do so with a lower occupational status than he would need to attract an otherwise comparable white partner (Monahan 1976; Schoen and Wooldredge 1989).

This logic with regard to children is reinforced by taking the point of view of the individual, him/herself. Since people are likely to prefer to invest more resources into biological and adopted children, many of those with more resources might avoid entering situations where the potential for investment in household children is high. These effects should be stronger in a society that provides little financial support for children, such as the United States, than in Sweden or Hungary, where support for children is extensive, both via entitlement programs (family allowances, national health care, and free education at all levels) and means-tested poverty prevention programs. There is some evidence of such an income pattern in the United States, where the incomes of men in stepfamilies and cohabiting families are substantially lower than the incomes of men in other families (Sweet and Bumpass 1989), particularly if children are present (Duncan and Hoffman 1985). Hence, our major hypothesis for this analysis is: higher socioeconomic status should increase the likelihood of being in a union, but lower status is needed to be in a union with a partner with coresident children than to be in a union with a partner without children. The effect should be greater for marriage than for cohabitation, and greater in the United States than in Sweden or Hungary.

As for the effect of gender-role attitudes, men with more traditional gender-role attitudes are probably more likely to be in a union. Although they should also be more likely to want children, men with traditional gender-role attitudes might be more reluctant to be in a union with a partner with coresident children, given the non-traditional nature of such relationships.

It is also important to control for other factors likely to influence various dimensions of the union formation process, particularly those likely to have an effect on the parental behavior of those entering such unions. The major types of measures which we consider as controls are indicators of a man's life-course progress (age), background (family structure and number of siblings) and whether he is an absent father.

Data, concepts and methods

Our analysis proceeds in two steps, based on two sets of data and two analytic methods. We will begin with an overview of the family statuses of men and women in ten countries in Europe and North America. We will then narrow our focus to men in three countries, Sweden, Hungary and the United States. At both steps, our goal is to maximize the similarities in the ways we construct our measures in order to reveal similarities and differences in the processes underlying different family statuses, and, in particular, how men attain different types of parenthood.

Data

In our overview analysis of the family roles of men and women in industrialized countries, we use data from a set of countries in Europe and North America. These are drawn from the "Fertility and Family Surveys in Countries in the ECE Region" project, which is being carried out by the Population Activities Unit of the United Nations Economic Commission for Europe. This project has involved the development of core and module questionnaires and the co-ordination of efforts among the twenty industrialized countries that undertook surveys on family and fertility between 1989 and 1996, all of which have been or are in the process of being converted to standard recode files and archived in Geneva.

Our more focused analysis of men and of the factors linked with being in different paternal roles uses data from three separate nationally representative surveys of Sweden, Hungary and the United States. (For details on these surveys see Sweet et al. 1988; Granström 1997; Kamarás 1999.)

Concepts

Our central concepts focus on types of family status. We distinguish throughout between families that include partners, those that include children, and those that include both. In our multi-country analysis, we use these concepts in their simplest form. In our three-country analysis, we distinguish partnerships by whether they are marital or cohabiting and children by whether the coresidential children are a man's "household" or "biological" children. We use measures of education and gender-role attitudes to predict who holds which family statuses in each country. We also control age, childhood family structure (parental marital status and number of siblings) and absent fatherhood. We have attempted to construct these measures to maximize their similarity among all countries, both for our multi-country and three-country analyses. With the exception of gender-role attitudes, where we had to use the only available information from each survey, our measures are almost fully identical in their construction. They are described in Table 3.

Methods

Our descriptive analysis focuses on differences between the family statuses of men and women. We focus on life course, country and gender differences in living in partnerships and parenthood. Our goal is to establish gender differences in these major axes of family structure before beginning the process of unraveling the factors underlying these differences with our multivariate analysis. Our multivariate analysis uses multinomial logistic regression with a dependent variable based on combinations of men's parental and partnership statuses.[5]

Results

First, we show men in the United States, Sweden and Hungary in a broader context. We compare them both with women and with men in the other countries in their "region," and focus on the ages of young and middle adulthood. In this portion of the analysis, we do not distinguish partnerships by whether they are marital or cohabiting, or parents by whether the children are biological or not.

Multi-country analysis

Data for women aged 20–24, 30–34 and 40–44 in the period around 1990 are shown for 10 countries (Table 4) and for men aged 25–29, 30–34 and 40–44 for as many of the same countries as the data allowed (Table 5). In all of these countries, these data show a basic life-course pattern: the young are most likely to be living with neither partner nor children, or with a partner only. Men enter unions and become parents at later ages than women, and are much less likely than women in every country to be single parents. Regional differences, however, are substantial, and there are differences in the extent to which our target countries typify their region.

Table 3. *Definitions of independent variables*

Variables	Sweden, 1992–3
Age	age at survey (28, 33, 43). Reference category = age 28
Education	
low (reference)	elementary school (6–8 years) and at most 2 years of vocational school
medium	upper-secondary-school diploma and possibly some vocational
high	university studies (with or without degree)
Family structure in childhood	(composition of family during the greater part of childhood (<16 years)
non-bio parents	stepfather/stepmother or single parent
intact (reference)	biological or adoptive parents (incl. widowed)
Siblings	number of full or half brothers and sisters
Gender-role attitudes	respondent's image of ideal family situation with children under age 7
	1 = Both parents work and share the responsibility for home and children equally
	2 = Man works full-time, woman works part-time and bears the primary responsibility for home and children
	3 = Only the man has a job while the woman bears the primary responsibility for home and children
Absent father	has biological or adopted children who live with their mother

	Hungary, 1992–3
Age	age at survey. Age 2 = 31–35; Age 3 = 40–44; Age 1 = 26–30 (ref.)
Education	
low (reference)	up to elementary (4–8 years) and vocational school (+3 years)
medium	up to upper-secondary-school diploma and some vocational (4 years)
high	university studies (with or without degree)
Family structure in childhood	composition of family during most of childhood (<15 years)
non-bio parents	stepfather/stepmother or single parent
intact (reference)	biological parents (incl. widowed)
Siblings	number of full or half brothers and sisters
Gender-role attitudes	four questions combined to create a scale; recoded E = egalitarian, I = intermediate, T = traditional *agreement or disagreement with the following:

Table 3. (*cont.*)

Variables	Hungary, 1992–3
	– marriage as an institution has lost its importance nowadays
	– if a single woman wants to have children without living together with a man, she should be allowed to do what she likes
	– I do not mind any sacrifices in order to have a good relationship with my spouse/partner, even if it jeopardizes my other goals
	– I do whatever it takes in order to promote my career
Absent father	has biological or adopted children who live with mother

	United States, 1988–9
Age	age at survey. Age 2 = 31–35; Age 3 = 40–44; Age 1 = 26–30 (ref.)
Education	
low (reference)	high school or lower
medium	some college, vocational school, or associate's degree
high	bachelor's degree or higher
Family structure in childhood	
non-bio parents	ever lived with stepparent for four months or more, or parents separated/divorced or never lived with biological father
intact (reference)	lived with two biological parents through childhood or death of parent
Siblings	number of full brothers and sisters
Gender-role attitudes	
	five questions combined to create scale from 5 to 31; recoded 1 = egalitarian (5–13), 2 = intermediate (14–22), 3 = traditional (23–31)
	*approval or disapproval of the following:
	– mothers who work full-time when their youngest child is under age 5
	– mothers who work part-time when their youngest child is under age 5
	– children under 3 being cared for all day in a day-care center
	*agreement or disagreement with the following:
	– man earns the main living and woman takes care of the home and family
	– pre-school children suffer if their mother is employed
Absent father	Has minor children living elsewhere

Table 4. *Percentage of women living in different family types in selected European and North American countries, 1988/1992*

	Age Group at Interview											
	20–24				30–34				40–44			
Country	both	partner	child	neither	both	partner	child	neither	both	partner	child	neither
Finland	16[a]	38[a]	4[a]	43[a]	69	15	6	10	69	11	11	10
Norway[b]	27	31	5	37	76	7	9	9	78	9	9	5
Sweden[b]	21	36	5	38	71	9	12	9	66	12	13	8
former East Germany	35	13	6	46	78	3	13	7	76[c]	5[c]	12[c]	7[c]
Hungary	37	17	4	42	80	4	10	6	79[d]	3[d]	14[d]	4[d]
Poland	37	14	3	46	82	5	5	8	79	5	12	4
France	14	24	4	58	66	11	12	12	74	5	14	7
former West Germany	13	18	2	67	64	13	8	16	66[c]	11[c]	9[c]	14[c]
Canada	13	22	7	57	64	15	9	12	70	11	9	10
USA	23	19	12	46	64	9	15	12	52	24	13	11

Source: NSFH and FFS

Note: both = living with partner and child(ren); partner = living with partner, no child(ren); child = living with child(ren), no partner; neither = living without partner and child(ren). [a]22–24 years of age; [b]exact ages 23, 33 and 43; [c]age group 35–39; [d]40–41 years of age.

Central and Eastern European women are the most likely to have both a partner and children at all ages, although the differences are most marked in their early twenties, while they are the least likely to live with a partner only. Women in Western Europe/North America are the most likely to postpone family formation, and to live alone (i.e. without partner and children) even in their early thirties. Having a partner but no children is most common among young Nordic women compared to women in other regions.

Hungarian women closely resemble the patterns shown by Polish women and those from the former East Germany. Swedish women more closely resemble other Nordic women than women in other regions but are somewhat more likely to be single parents than are Norwegian or Finnish women. The US women, however, do not fit closely with women in other countries (whether West European or Canadian) in several ways. They are more likely than others to be single parents, particularly at young ages. The oldest US women (aged 40–44 in 1988) are also much less likely to live in partnerships with children. That group of women had their children very young, and US children leave home earlier than those in most of these countries (Cherlin 1997).

When we turn our attention to men (Table 5), we see that the regional differences are quite similar to those for women, with the highest proportions living with both a partner and children in Central and Eastern Europe and the lowest proportion in Western Europe/North America. Swedish men are more typical of their region than Swedish women, falling between the levels of Finnish and Norwegian men at each age. Hungarian men enter unions and parenthood somewhat less rapidly than the other two Central and Eastern European countries and, like men in the former East Germany, have fewer children than Polish men. US men closely resemble Western European and Canadian men at age 40–44, in being more likely to live without children among those in partnerships than men in Northern or Central/Eastern Europe, but this seems to represent a different process for US men. At young ages, they move rapidly into parenthood (close to the Northern European pattern) but, by their early 40s, they are the most likely to live with a partner but with no children. Hence, while the pattern for the other countries in the Western European/North American grouping seems to reflect late childbearing, the US pattern seems more likely to be the result of the much higher level of partnership dissolution in the United States than in other countries. Most of these men are too young to have children who have left home; hence, it is more likely that they have left their children, to live in many cases with a childless woman.

To summarize the differences between the regions and between men and women, we present Figure 2, which shows the percentage of men and

Table 5. *Percentage of men living in different family types in selected European and North American countries, 1988/1992*

	Age Group at Interview											
	25–29				30–34				40–44			
Country	both	partner	child	neither	both	partner	child	neither	both	partner	child	neither
Finland[a]	28	32	0	40	65	10	2	24	61	19	3	17
Norway[b]	47	25	1	27	–	–	–	–	78	8	3	11
Sweden[c]	37	26	1	36	61	12	2	25	70	10	4	17
former East Germany	54	12	2	32	75	8	1	16	75[d]	7[d]	3[d]	16[d]
Hungary	45	16	0	39	71	6	1	22	74	9	3	15
Poland	56	9	0	35	72	5	0	23	86	4	1	9
France	30	24	0	45	64	12	1	23	75	7	2	16
former West Germany	28	21	0	51	52	18	3	27	63[d]	15[d]	2[d]	20[d]
Canada	31	27	1	41	54	19	1	26	73	10	3	14
USA	36	23	1	40	59	17	1	23	62	21	2	15

Source: NSFH and FFS

Note: both = living with partner and child(ren); partner = living with partner, no child(ren); child = living with child(ren), no partner; neither = living without partner and child(ren).

[a] age groups 25–29, 35–39 and 45–49; [b] exact ages 28 and 43; [c] exact ages 28, 33 and 43; [d] age group 35–39.

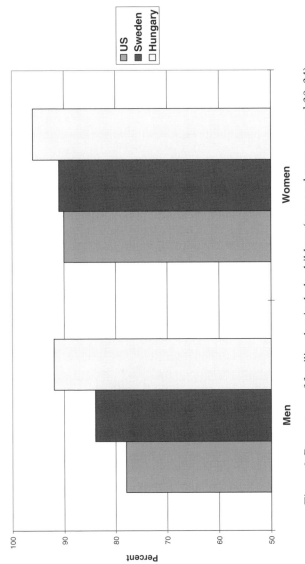

Figure 2 Percentage of families that include children (men and women, aged 30–34).

women in families who have children living with them. We only present differences for those aged 30–34, to avoid the differences in life-course timing we saw in the more detailed analysis. Regional differences are most pronounced among men: Hungarian men living in families are the most likely to live with children and US men are the least, more commonly living with partners only. The pattern of differences is the same for women, but considerably muted. Differences between men and women are thus greatest for the United States and least for Hungary, a pattern also found in a related analysis that excluded North American countries (Jensen 1998b). This leads us to our central question: what is going on in these three countries to have such a strong effect on men's coresidence with children? To address this question, we turn to our detailed analysis of three countries.

Three-country analysis

For this analysis, we combine the three types of parental statuses (no children, some "household" children and only biological children), and the three partnership statuses (no partner, a cohabiting partner and a spouse). Because many of the nine possible combinations of statuses are rare (in one or more countries), we have collapsed them into a set of six by combining three pairs of possibilities. First, we combine the two groups with children who live outside a partnership, creating a category of "single parent," since almost no single parents in any of these three countries live with children who are not their biological children. Secondly, we combined those who are not living with children and have no partner with those with a cohabiting partner, since they have no legal commitments, creating a category of "no spouse, no (coresident) children." Finally, we combined those in cohabiting unions with only biological children with those where some or all of the children are not their own, creating the category "cohabiting, some children." This was done primarily because both categories were too small to analyze separately in the United States and Hungary. This is not the case in Sweden, since many raise joint biological children in a cohabiting union, at least for a while.[6] Hence, we have six categories to analyze: married with biological children only, married with no children, married with at least some household children, cohabiting with children, living with children but no partner, and unmarried without children. The first group is the reference category for the regression.

Men in these three countries differ sharply in family status (Table 6). We summarize the key differences in Figure 3, which examines men aged 30–34 (as we did in Figure 2), but distinguishes types of parental relationships for men who live in a family based on some committed tie, either parental or marital (i.e. those not in the "no spouse, no children

Table 6. *Men's family status by age in Sweden, Hungary and the United States*

Family/household status	Total	Age[a]		
		26–30	31–35	36–50
Sweden				
Married, no children	5.0	6.0	4.5	4.3
Married, household children	2.8	1.2	3.7	3.9
Cohabiting, children	13.3	17.2	18.3	6.3
Single parent	2.0	0.8	2.1	3.3
No spouse, no children	37.7	56.2	32.3	22.2
Married, only bio children	39.1	18.6	39.1	60.0
Total	100.0	100.0	100.0	100.0
N	1661	646	381	634
Hungary				
Married, no children	6.1	10.8	3.5	5.2
Married, household children	3.4	2.0	2.5	4.5
Cohabiting, children	2.8	3.4	2.5	2.6
Single parent	1.0	–	0.8	1.5
No spouse, no children	24.0	36.4	24.7	17.7
Married, only bio children	62.7	47.4	66.0	68.5
Total	100.0	100.0	100.0	100.0
N	1442	352	356	734
USA				
Married, no children	18.4	18.2	11.8	21.5
Married, household children	5.2	4.6	6.4	4.9
Cohabiting, children	2.4	4.1	3.2	1.3
Single parent	1.6	1.2	1.4	1.8
No spouse, no children	24.4	38.5	24.6	18.1
Married, only bio children	48.1	33.4	52.6	52.4
Total	100.0	100.0	100.0	100.0
N	2925	791	748	1386

[a]For Sweden, exact ages are 28, 33 and 43; for Hungary, the oldest age group is 36–44.

category). Men in Hungary and Sweden are much more likely to live with children than are men in the United States, as we saw earlier, but these two countries differ in the proportions of coresident children who are biological or household. On this dimension, Hungary is distinctive, with a much smaller proportion of household children than in Sweden; men in the United States more closely resemble those in Sweden. Swedish men are distinctive in their somewhat higher proportions who are single parents (although in no case is this level very high). Hence, it is important to see what factors affect men's occupancy of these statuses among these three countries.

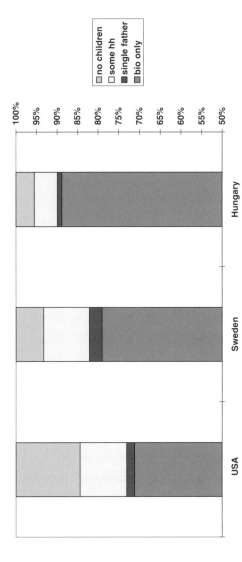

Figure 3 Men's parental status in committed families in the United States, Sweden and Hungary, 1988–1992 (age 30–34).

Table 7. *Determinants of men's family status in Sweden, Hungary and the United States (married, only biological children = reference category)*

	Married no kids	Married other kids	Cohabiting some kids	Single parents	No spouse no kids
Sweden					
Age 2	−1.03**	0.08	−0.68**	0.20	−1.41**
Age 3	−1.58**	−0.34	−2.29**	−0.10	−2.48**
Education:					
medium level	0.04	0.10	−0.42*	−0.25	−0.02
high level	0.44	−0.55	−0.82**	−0.48	−0.17
Not two bio parents	−0.02	−0.21	0.47″	0.79	0.30
Sibsize	0.06	0.03	−0.06	−0.08	−0.06
Traditional gender-role attitudes	0.11	−0.11	−0.15	−0.62*	−0.19*
Absent father	1.33**	2.29**	1.75**	2.90**	2.57**
Hungary					
Age 2	−1.59**	−0.14	−0.59	na	−0.81**
Age 3	−0.59*	0.39	−0.85″	na	−1.76**
Education:					
medium level	−0.62*	−0.06	−0.15	−0.71	−0.33″
high level	0.19	0.38	−1.58	−0.57	−0.33
Not two bio parents	−0.33	0.68	0.21	0.40	0.12
Sibsize	−0.31**	0.03	0.18*	0.25*	−0.09″
Traditional gender-role attitudes	−0.03	−0.29	−0.67*	0.22	−0.06
Absent father	0.29	3.17**	3.95**	2.59**	4.00**
USA					
Age 2	−0.99**	−0.22	−0.70**	0.46	−0.76**
Age 3	−0.61**	−0.38	−1.67**	0.95*	−1.00**
Education:					
medium level	0.30″	−0.12	−0.69*	0.28	0.12
high level	0.76**	−0.79**	−1.40**	−0.40	0.49**
Not two bio parents	−0.21	0.45*	0.85**	0.13	0.34*
Sibsize	−0.12**	−0.05	0.02	−0.08	−0.06**
Traditional gender-role attitudes	−0.20″	−0.15	−0.51*	0.08	−0.14
Absent father	1.17**	1.76**	2.10**	1.13**	1.72**

$**p < 0.01$; $*0.01 < p < 0.05$; $″0.05 < p < 0.10$.

The main results of the multivariate analysis are presented in detail in Table 7, and show the effects of a man's age, education, indicators of parental family characteristics, measures of traditional attitudes, and whether he is an absent father on whether he lives in various types of family situations. We present first the results for Sweden, then those for

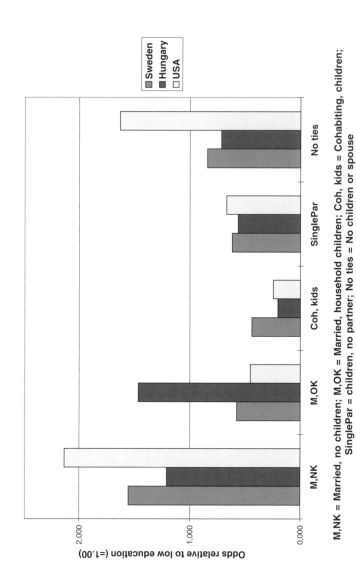

Figure 4 Effect of high education on men's family status.

M,NK = Married, no children; M,OK = Married, household children; Coh, kids = Cohabiting, children; SinglePar = children, no partner; No ties = No children or spouse

Hungary, and last those for the United States. Each of the coefficients shows a contrast with the state of being "married and living with biological children only." The first two columns present the contrasts with men in other married statuses, either with no coresident children or with at least some children who are not their biological offspring. The contrast between being married with children and cohabiting with children is presented in col. 3 (which are primarily biological children in Sweden, but "household" children in the United States and Hungary); col. 4 presents the same contrast for the few men who live with children but no partner, and col. 5 shows differences between those who are not in a legally committed family relationship either through marriage or parenthood and those in the reference category of married, living with biological children only. Since this table is complex, however, we show key results graphically, and transform the logit coefficients into odds relative to 1.00 (the reference category).

The results indicate that men in the United States, Sweden and Hungary find themselves in different types of families for many of the same reasons. There are broad similarities in the effects of a man's age, education, parental family structure, gender-role attitudes and absent father status, although there are a few interesting and potentially important differences.

Life course

The life-course pattern shows that, in each country, the youngest men are unmarried and childless (with large negative coefficients). Young men are also likely to be cohabiting in households with children (at least in the United States and Sweden). The oldest men tend to be married with children, whether biological or not, with the exception of those who have in some sense passed through that stage, and are single parents.

Education

The results for education again show some broad similarities, but with considerably greater differences, which marks the United States as particularly exceptional. We will focus primarily on the results that contrast those with "high" and "low" educations (Figure 4). In each country, men with high educations are less likely to be unmarried men living with children – whether as single parents or as members of a cohabiting couple – than to be married men with biological children (holding constant differences among them by age, attitudes and parental background).

Nevertheless, the presence and type of children is linked with differences among the married categories. In both the United States and

Sweden, men with high educations are less likely to be married and living with household children than to be in one of the other married categories (although the difference is smaller and not significant in Sweden), which suggests that women with children are not able to negotiate as successfully for higher status men than are women who have not yet had children. Interestingly, this pattern does not appear in Hungary, although there are too few stepfathers in Hungary for this result to be meaningful.

The United States is exceptional in two respects, each of which means that more educated men avoid all but the least demanding of family commitments. US men with high educations are less likely to live with any children when they are married than men in the other two countries, not just household children (the US is the only case in which there is a significant difference between married men with and without children). In fact, highly educated men avoid forming committed families at all. The United States is the only country in which men with high educations are likely to be unmarried with no children – the "no ties" category; in the United States, high education increases the odds of being in this family category.

Absent father

In each of these three countries, men who have non-coresidential children are likely to be in any family category other than the reference category of "married, with biological children." The effects are generally strongest in Hungary and weakest in the United States, which suggests that men who are absent fathers are most likely to go on to marry and have more biological children in their new relationship in the United States and least likely to do so in Hungary (Table 7). The reverse pattern can be observed for men's likelihood of being in a relationship that includes household children. Although, in all three countries, men who are absent fathers are substantially more likely to be household fathers than biological fathers, this is less the case in the United States and more the case in Hungary, with Sweden intermediate.

A particularly interesting result is that men who have children living elsewhere are very likely to be single parents, themselves. This is the case in all three countries. Evidently, men who have custody of children often do not take all of their children, sharing them, residentially, with their former partners. This is most dramatic in Sweden. Men with non-coresident children are 18 times as likely to be single parents as to have gone on to form a new biological family in Sweden, compared with the United States, where the odds are only three times as high (calculations not shown). Although it is likely that men in Sweden live with the older children, or with the boys, this is nevertheless a striking example of the impact of the Swedish system of support for working parents, together with its strong encouragement to men to take family responsibilities. Most men in the United States, and likely in Hungary as well, would consider active parenthood totally inconsistent with their central career role.

Among the other findings, a few deserve comment, although most are not our focus here. Family background has several interesting effects. Men who grew up with more siblings are more likely to live with children, themselves, with the strongest effects in Hungary and the weakest in Sweden. Hungarian men from larger families are more likely to be single parents, and to cohabit with children than to be "normal" married biological parents. They are also significantly less likely to be childless, if they are married, or outside a committed family relationship altogether (which is also the case for men with more siblings in the United States). Although this result reinforces the not always intuitive interpretation that those who grow up in more family-centered homes are more interested in carrying on the tradition, it also suggests that this pattern is most common in countries with more traditional gender-role attitudes.

Those who did not experience a stable, two-parent family in childhood are also generally more likely to be found in less conventional family forms (Figure 5), particularly as stepfathers (in the United States and Hungary, although the result is only significant for the United States) and as cohabiting fathers (in the United States and Sweden). In Sweden, such men are also particularly likely to be single parents, and, in each country, they have a tendency to avoid family ties altogether. The strongest effects of this factor appear for men in the United States. This result is consistent with other research that shows that the effects of coming from a non-traditional family, nearly always very powerful in the United States (McLanahan and Sandefur 1994), are rarely as powerful elsewhere (Evans et al. 1995; Jonsson and Gähler 1997). This suggests that the problems faced by such children can be mitigated by supportive policies.

Interestingly, we found almost no effects of holding traditional gender-role attitudes on men's family statuses in any of these countries. The least traditional men are more likely to be cohabiting fathers in the United States and Hungary but not Sweden (Table 7, col. 3), whereas, in Sweden, egalitarian attitudes are linked with being a single father. This latter result seems almost obvious – presumably most of these men feel that they are being "both father and mother" successfully – except that it is not the case in either the United States or Hungary.

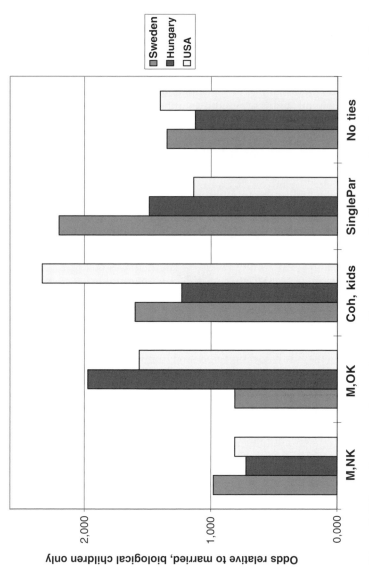

Figure 5 Effect of not growing up in a stable, two-parent family on men's family status in Sweden, Hungary and the United States.

Discussion

These three industrialized countries, each with high levels of female labor force participation, differ substantially in the ways men are included in families. Hungary is at one extreme, with its men more likely to live in families with children than the men in the other two countries, and those children are the most likely to be biological children. Swedish men are also much more likely to live with children than men in the United States, suggesting that strong state support for families is linked with men's greater involvement in the lives of children. In Sweden, fathers' involvement in their children's lives is strongly promoted by the state also after the divorce, considering the high level of joint custody found there. In 1992, 82 percent of divorced parents in Sweden maintained joint custody (Statistics Sweden 1993), compared with 16 percent in the United States at about the same time (NCHS 1995).[7]

The high proportions of household fathers in both Sweden and the United States, as compared to Hungary, suggest that there is a link between egalitarian gender roles and instability in relationships in these countries, which is reflected in the high rates of repartnering and increased complexity in the family lives of men. Yet, this is not a strong link, since, despite gender-role attitudes that are considerably more egalitarian than those in the United States, Sweden has much lower rates of marital dissolution (around 12 divorces per 1,000 married women, compared to 20 for the United States).

Within each country, men who are household parents are quite different from men living with biological children in terms of age, education and childhood family characteristics. These differences vary according to whether the relationship is a marital or cohabiting one. Further, the similarities and the differences in social policy and in societal gender-role attitudes among these three countries help us to begin to understand the role of the state, in its direct provision of support for families, as well as the influence of community gender roles, on men's residential connections with children.

We find these three countries quite similar in some respects. In each country, men who are older, from non-traditional families, and have more siblings are more likely to be in some sort of a coresidential, committed family relationship than other men are, although, in the United States, low education also predicts committed family membership. In each country, young men can only attain families by entering cohabiting relationships with women who already have children; this status, like that of "no spouse, no kids," is also predicted by low socioeconomic status and having come from non-intact families. This evidence that cohabitation is a less desirable state which men with more resources avoid is the case not only in the

United States and in Hungary, but also in Sweden, despite the presumed greater acceptability of cohabitation in Sweden. These results are consistent with several recent studies that show that cohabitation in Sweden is not as similar to marriage as many Swedish social scientists had believed. Hoem and Hoem (1992) have shown that cohabiting unions have considerably higher dissolution risks than marital unions. Further, a recent analysis (Duvander 1999) of the transition from cohabitation to marriage shows a clear pattern of higher socioeconomic status increasing the likelihood of marriage. This positive selection into marriage is also apparent in Björnberg (2001), who shows, for example, that cohabiting parents have a more precarious attachment to the labor force.

In Sweden, unlike in the United States or in Hungary, however, men with less traditional gender-roles are not drawn particularly to cohabitation. In Sweden, holding more egalitarian gender-role attitudes is only strongly predictive of being a single parent, an extremely rare status (if considerably more common in Sweden than in the United States or Hungary). To the extent that traditionalism in gender roles is linked with traditionalism in general, in Sweden cohabitation is also "traditional," unlike in Hungary or the United States. (This result may also reflect the fact that the children in cohabitational unions in Sweden are more likely to be biological children than household children.)

There are more significant differences between stepfathers and married biological fathers in the United States than in Hungary or Sweden. Stepfathers do not differ significantly from married biological fathers in any respect in Hungary or Sweden. In the United States, men who are poorly educated and from other than two-parent biological families are significantly more likely to be stepfathers than married biological fathers. The role of resources has less influence on whether men undertake to become household fathers instead of biological fathers in Sweden and Hungary than in the United States. In the United States, men with high education avoid household fatherhood more strongly than in Sweden and Hungary; only those who have experienced family break-up in their own childhoods are more likely to undertake the task of raising another man's children. It is possible that the greater support for families across the board in Sweden and Hungary than in the United States has contributed to the overall lower selectivity of biological fatherhood.

The role of men's socioeconomic status appears more complex, however, when we consider the anomalous effects of education in the United States compared with Hungary and Sweden. In these two countries, the classic pattern of men's "good provider" roles appears intact, with the more educated more able to establish long-term, committed relationships with a partner, and to have children in these unions. In the United

States, in contrast, the most educated appear to avoid fatherhood, either outside of marriage or within marriage.

It is plausible that by providing support for families, both Sweden and Hungary have made it more possible for men to remain in them, and to maintain their traditional roles as providers. In the United States, in contrast, the private costs of families have escalated to such an extent that men, who disproportionately bear these costs (despite increased help from women), have been turning away from family relationships. This is particularly the case among those who have the most resources to provide to families and hence the most to lose.

This result parallels one that has often troubled feminists when they have considered the effect of state support on *women's* roles. Where there are policies that allow part-time work, or parental leave, women take advantage of them disproportionately, which costs them in terms of career advancement both relative to men in their own country and also relative to women in countries with few such benefits. In the United States, it is likely that at least high-status women have made more rapid professional progress than in Sweden or Hungary. State support may slow progress toward gender equality, since it also reinforces men in their traditional "provider" roles. Also, as seen in Sweden, state support can promote men's greater involvement in children's lives and thus strengthen their roles as fathers (both as married biological fathers and as household fathers), which benefits families. In the long run, this can stimulate the development toward more egalitarian relationships between men and women, and thus promote gender equality.

Part 2

Men in social policy and the logics of cash
and care

2 Citizens, workers or fathers? Men in the history of US social policy

Ann Shola Orloff and Renee A. Monson

How are fathers treated in US social policy? One might well be stumped by such a question. Recent American social policy debates have swirled around single mothers on welfare and the need to get them into the workforce; only secondarily has attention alighted on the fathers of their children and the need to get them to pay child support. Debates about retirement provision, far weightier than welfare in terms of expenditures and population covered, have been principally about financing; the family status of the workers who collect these benefits is politically beside the point. Indeed, the most salient fact about the treatment of fathers in US social policy is the virtual absence of programs targeting them *as fathers*. The US welfare state is cross-nationally unusual in the extent to which coverage is limited to elderly, retired workers (both men and women) and very poor single parents, mainly women. The majority of the working-aged population – men, women, fathers, mothers and their children – is simply left outside the umbrella of state social protection, forced to rely on private sources of cash and care: markets and families. But this gap in provision, which is arguably the most consequential feature of the US social policy regime for men who are fathers, has received far less attention from policy makers or policy analysts than welfare or social security. Thus, a presumed "crisis of fatherhood" is linked by some analysts to targeted cash assistance ("welfare") programs, but not to the overall shape of the US policy regime; to the extent it is framed as a problem of the entire society, it is construed as largely cultural (e.g. Blankenhorn 1995).

In this chapter, we offer an exploratory analysis of men in the US social policy regime, in comparative perspective. Our aim is to sketch out how we can go about understanding the gendered position of men, especially as fathers, as shaped by social policy, and the ways in which this varies across countries and over time. Analysts such as R. W. Connell (1995) argue that the state is central to the constitution of gender, and we see our analysis as contributing to understanding this process. But we should note that we will examine only one set of state policies important for the constitution of gender – the system of social provision, including programs of social insurance and assistance, in the context of the overall welfare regime (including the absence of public provision as well as private benefits). Family law has been a key site for examining the regulation of gender and sexuality, including fatherhood (see, e.g. Fineman 1995, and discussions around gay/lesbian families and partnerships in the wake of the passage of the Defense of Marriage Act in 1996); however, for reasons of space, we will examine this arena only insofar as it has become involved in the state's social welfare functions – paternity establishment and child support enforcement, which have been linked intimately with welfare reform. Indeed, one might argue that the focus on large-scale social provision offers a new angle of vision on how masculinities and fatherhood are constructed for parts of the population that for the most part escape the regulatory apparatus of the courts.

Gendered policy regime analysis, as developed by Orloff in earlier work, is well suited to illuminating the political construction of men's gendered positions, including as breadwinners, fathers and husbands (Orloff 1993a; O'Connor et al. 1999). In the United States, welfare regime analysis historically underlines the strong emphasis on markets and families rather than on states as sources of cash and care, along with the underdevelopment of social rights and state efforts to guarantee employment. Without citizenship-based benefits or publicly supported employment, citizens depend on employment or families for income and many benefits. This produces distinctive gendered consequences: men have been forced to depend on employment for income and on family members, usually women, for care, with little help from the state in terms of income or services. Women have depended on families – their husbands – for the bulk of their income, sometimes supplemented by employment; single mothers were either forced to work or, sometimes, could turn to the state to substitute partially for husbands' income; this has been changing as married women contribute an increasing amount of income to families through their own employment, and employment is supposed to replace the state in the case of single mothers. Employed women have had to depend on kin or private services for care. Thus, while most Americans have had to depend directly or indirectly on the market for income and families for care, women have historically had more reliance on the state than have men – indeed, part of the very definition of proper masculinity, and good fatherhood, in the United States has been economic self-support. Comparatively speaking, American men must depend more on employment to sustain households, and receive far less support from the state than do men in other advanced capitalist countries. And US men's political and social identities are thus forged outside the welfare state; in terms of gaining capacities to head households – to be fathers – their status as employees of particular corporations, which are often the source of important benefits as well as income, is more significant than their status as worker–citizens.

Historically, economic conditions (especially relatively high wages) and the legal toleration of discrimination in favor of white male breadwinners meant that many men were able to provide for their families relatively well. After the development of some key social insurance programs in the 1930s, the US system of social provision, though less-developed than European welfare states, nonetheless provided a sufficient "backup" for most men so that they could continue to head households if out of work temporarily or when retired. But in the 1970s and 1980s anti-discrimination legislation broke the hold of white men on "good jobs" while economic conditions, unfettered by institutionalized labor regulations, shifted in ways unfavorable to many blue-collar men. Men in disadvantaged positions in the labor market – disproportionately men of color and unskilled men – are often left unable to sustain households. In short, male breadwinning and fatherhood have been less protected politically in the US than elsewhere, and the capacity to father is based on labor market status. Moreover – as Oláh, Bernhardt and Goldscheider (in this volume) show – the state provides few positive incentives to induce men to take up fatherhood.

In the following section, we review the contributions of scholars investigating gender and welfare states, including their suggestions about analytic frameworks. What are the relevant dimensions of social policy regimes as they affect gender relations, or the "gender regime of the welfare state," and men as *men – in their gendered social positions*, not in their guise of "universal citizens or workers"?

Research on gender and welfare states: implications for men as fathers

Among comparative analysts, the US welfare state – if the American system of social provision is indeed seen as deserving of the term – is seen as a laggard, permitting levels of poverty, inequality and hardship, such as lack of medical insurance, that are unacceptable in other parts of the developed world. Particularly high levels of poverty among sole-parent families give the laggard image a racial and gendered character. At most, working-class and poor men, too, might be understood as disadvantaged by the underdevelopment of the citizen's wage and the holes in the US safety net. Recently, analysts have begun to incorporate private as well as public sources of employment, income and services into the analyses of systems of social provision (Esping-Andersen 1999). Social policy *regimes* vary in terms of the relative contributions of states, markets and families to welfare and the character of state social provision. The United States is a liberal regime, which features a strong role for markets and relatively limited state provision; citizens must secure their living from the market – there is little decommodification, to use Esping-Andersen's term. However, the comparative welfare regime literature does not investigate men's *gendered* situations – to the extent men are seen as targets of social policy, it is as members of particular classes or status groups, or as citizens. Thus, it is not clear how men's gender positions, including their situations as breadwinners or fathers, are affected by the cross-nationally specific features of the US system of social provision, such as the strong reliance on markets.

Among gender-sensitive scholars and feminists in the United States, the American welfare state is seen in gendered terms, though the substance of those terms differs. Some analysts see the US welfare state as "patriarchal," or, at the least, unfavorable to women's interests, because of the high rates of poverty among women-maintained households, the gender gap in poverty rates, the lack of a citizenship entitlement to paid leave or social assistance. Feminists have also shown that the welfare state differentiates by gender: commodification is limited to men, who – if healthy and able-bodied – are expected to be gainfully employed. But until the very recent past, women have not been subject to commodification, or the "work ethic"; rather, they are subject to requirements related to sexual morality and domestic capabilities – what Abromovitz (1988) calls the "family ethic" (see also Mink 1995; Goodwin 1997). In another important strand of the gender-sensitive literature, that which identifies a "two-tier" gendered welfare state in the US, men serve as a foil for demonstrating women's inequality, as when analysts ask if women's benefits and programs are as good as men's, or if men's and women's prescribed roles are the same (see, e.g. Pearce 1986; Nelson 1990). In this view, the two tiers of social policy reflect and recreate gender stratification: one tier, "welfare," is targeted on the problems of families, serves mainly women and is stingy and intrusive, and another, "social security," is targeted on the problems resulting from labor markets (e.g. retirement), serves (retired) wage-earning men, and offers more generous benefits and honorable treatment (the fact that the wives of these men and other women are the majority of social security beneficiaries is less often remarked upon). The "top" tier seems to be held as an ideal; the implicit criticism of the system is that women and/or people suffering from family "failures" are not treated as well as are men or those confronting labor market problems. But in none of these strands of research are men's gendered positions in this system the focus of investigation, nor have researchers done systematic comparative analyses of men in gendered social policy regimes. Of course, feminists are increasingly engaged in comparative work, and we now know quite a lot about cross-national and historical variation in policies affecting women as solo mothers, widows, wives, citizens and workers (O'Connor 1996; Orloff 1996; Haney 1998; O'Connor et al. 1999: ch. 1; among other things, it is clear that not all systems can be characterized as "two-tier" like the US [Sainsbury 1996]). Yet the task of investigating cross-national policy variation in the treatment of men – as gendered citizens, workers, fathers – is only beginning.

Jane Lewis's (1992, 1997a) concept of "male breadwinner" regimes, with countries manifesting strong, modified or weak (tending to a dual-earner model) versions, is suggestive for comparative investigations of the impact of welfare states on men, given that men's principal gender role in the West has been "breadwinner." Lewis's exercise was particularly concerned with gendered assumptions about family forms: that families were and should be on the breadwinner–caregiver model. In her formulation, men are privileged in access to jobs, enjoy advantages in tax treatment and welfare programs and are paid family wages. What varies in this framework are the extent to which women were excluded from paid work, and the generosity of benefits given to male breadwinners: the gender division of labor. Lewis was less concerned with outcomes, but concedes that as one looks at a greater range of male breadwinner regimes, differences among countries in outcomes become clear, even if assumptions about the desirability of male breadwinner–female housewife families is the same.

But what of men? While it seems that there is little systematic cross-national variation in men's take-up of domestic and caring work, research by Kathleen Gerson (1993), Bob Connell (1995) and some others – each based on research in a single country – indicates that there is variation among men in access to jobs sustaining a breadwinner position, as well as in the time devoted to fathering. In Gerson's (1993) study of family roles among a group of American men of different class and racial backgrounds, she found many men who were unwilling or unable to sustain breadwinning roles. But, while a small minority of the non-breadwinner men she interviewed for her study turned to an egalitarian division of paid and unpaid labor with their partners, the majority of these men turned to an "autonomous" role bereft of most family ties, leaving the work of caregiving relegated to the mothers of their children. It seems quite possible that if we explicitly examined different men's situations, rather than assuming they are everywhere "unencumbered workers," we might find historical and cross-national variation, in addition to being better able to specify the character of differences within countries. We noted above

Esping-Andersen's (1990, 1999) attention to significant differences in the institutional architecture and character of social rights in different regime types. We should be able to combine the insights of gender regime analysis and mainstream regime analysis, for example to examine differences in how breadwinners' positions are secured, even if the logic of male breadwinning and the gender division of labor are similar. In short, we need a multidimensional approach to social policy regimes and gender relations which accounts for variation in outcomes not only in gender differentiation, but also in inequality, autonomy/dependency and the institutional arrangements sustaining employment, income and caregiving, and supporting households, for both men and women (O'Connor et al. 1999; see also O'Connor 1993; Orloff 1993a). Please note that this concept is complementary to the notion of "fatherhood regimes," but not the same; indeed, we are making the case for considering how policy regimes either undergird or detract from fathers' capacities to father and states' attempts to enforce fatherhood obligations.

Following Lewis (1992), most attention has focused on the gender division of labor and the concomitant gender *differentiation* in political identities and interests, and the ways this has contributed to *inequality* between men and women – components of *stratification*. We see distinctly different patterns of women's paid and unpaid work, with associated differences in gender ideologies, particularly ideals of motherhood. While countries do differ in terms of the patterns of labor force participation among women and associated policy supports, there is little systematic information about how social provision affects patterns of men's paid and unpaid work. Indeed, it would seem that there is not much cross-national variation in men's positions in the division of paid work and unpaid caregiving work – everywhere, they are paid workers. But are men in fact everywhere breadwinners, that is, workers able to support caregiving wives? Do men receive special recognition as fathers or as husbands? And what form does this take? Some regimes offer men the opportunity to take parental leave, that is, to participate in caregiving; others give married men or fathers cash benefits to supplement their wages to compensate for the financial burden of supporting a family. In the US, access to parental leave is gender-neutral, but the leave is unpaid. Some countries have developed active labor market policies to ensure employment – and sometimes this is aimed explicitly at men, to bolster their capacities to be breadwinners; elsewhere this can be gender-neutral. Other countries – and it appears that the United States falls into this category – offer little or no special help of any kind to fathers. Clearly, these are different ways of approaching men as fathers, and of institutionalizing cultural assumptions and ideals of fatherhood. The "two-tier" concept is about stratification in that it calls attention to the ways in which states differentially value family roles for women and worker roles for men. Notable in the US case is the extent to which the state does not ameliorate market-generated inequalities among workers; men of different classes thus have quite different levels of resources, significant when they want to form households.

Some of these cross-national differences might be traced to different cultural assumptions and ideologies about fatherhood (e.g. should men be caregivers as well as wage earners, or leave caregiving to women). Yet others reflect differences in countries' institutional arrangements, or *state–market–family relations*, in producing income and welfare; the relative emphasis on states, markets or families is critical. The characteristics of social programs also have gender effects; the eligibility requirements and character of different benefit or service programs determine how they function to reinforce or subvert dominant market or gender relations. Scholars have been especially interested in the extent to which social provision is organized in terms of *citizenship rights*, particularly *social rights*. An important social right *vis-à-vis* the market is *de-commodification*, which protects individuals from total dependence on the labor market for survival. For Esping-Andersen (1990), decommodification is at the core of the state's emancipatory potential, but he is thinking of the situation of workers (implicitly male) *vis-à-vis* the market, not about men in terms of their position in gender relations. Yet benefits that offer a "back-up" to family wages do affect men's capacities to be breadwinners (and were understood in this way). But not all social groups have equal access to the jobs that allow personal independence and access to decommodifying benefits. *Access to paid work* and to the *services that facilitate employment* for caregivers are critical gender dimensions of welfare regime variability given the importance historically of women's exclusion from employment, and linkage of citizenship rights to employment. But this is also of significance for men, for markets may not reliably produce employment for men (any more than for women). To the extent that employment is the basis for access to citizenship rights and household formation, countries' variable commitment to full employment or active labor market policies is significant for both men and women.

Social rights to benefits are also significant *vis-à-vis* gender (and generational) relations within families. In earlier work, Orloff (1993a) focused on the ways in which welfare benefits, provision of services and employment regulations affect the *capacity to form and maintain an autonomous household*, a dimension which indicates an individual's ability to survive and support their children without being forced to marry or enter into other family relationships. This is of clear relevance for women, whose autonomy has been compromised by familial dependencies (not those that are the result of a need to be cared for because of age or disability, but those resulting from economic dependence). But this dimension should be generalized to ask how different sorts of supports for households – including those of men – affect the balance of power between men and women within marriages and families, and men's as well as women's capacities to support families.

Different groups gain access to capacities for household formation and maintenance in different ways depending on the institutional mix of states, markets and families in the provision of care and cash, and whether or not states offer any social right to a job, or to the resources needed to sustain a household. In all Western states, the vast majority of men gain the capacity to head households through their market work; since their inception, most income maintenance programs served as "back-ups" to the family wage system, allowing men to continue to support their families when they lose their wage-earning capacities temporarily (unemployment, temporary illness or disability) or permanently (retirement, disability). Until recently, however, women did not have equal access to such programs, principally because they were not in full-time employment, although in some cases because program rules discriminated against women explicitly. Even now, most men retain a significant amount of freedom of choice relative to family and household formation given their advantaged labor market positions, with the welfare state acting as a back-up, even as some of the family supporting components of income maintenance programs have been cut back in some places. State policies have differed in how – and if at all – the capacity to form and maintain households is supported for men and for women – or for some groups of men and women. For example, some states have supported men's breadwinning and women's stay-at-home motherhood for a favored "race"/ethnicity or class whose reproductive capacities are valued, while denying such supports to others. (Moreover, the capacity to form an autonomous household implies more than individual independence – it also gets at whether women and men are allowed to have as well as to support families, thus reflecting the character of regulations of sexuality, custody, reproduction, marriage, divorce and household composition. We might call this *access to family*, or the "right to a family.")

But, while we see cross-national variation in levels of women's economic dependence (Hobson 1994), it would seem that most men are independent and autonomous (with respect to decisional autonomy; of course, they, like everyone else, at times depend on the care of others). But are there significant cross-national variations in terms of *how* their economic independence – and associated personal autonomy and capacity to head households – is secured? Do states variably support or mandate men's support of dependents? Many (though not all) feminist analysts have interpreted enhanced child support collection as (*de facto*) enforcing men's breadwinner role and states do differ in the extent to which they ask men as individuals to pay for their offspring as opposed to getting children's support from general revenues. Pension and unemployment compensation programs also vary in terms of whether or not dependents' allowances are added to basic payments (O'Connor et al. 1999); family allowances vary in level and in terms of whether mothers or fathers are beneficiaries (Wennemo 1994). And, of course, it is important to consider the extent to which racial, ethnic, class or other differences affect support to men – historical studies show that these differences have affected states' support to men for fathering children as well as to women for caring for their own children (e.g. see essays in Bock and Thane 1991 and Koven and Michel 1993).

In the remainder of this chapter, we explore how men have been treated over time in US social policy, with special attention to their roles as fathers. We are interested in the institutional sources of support for fathers – states, markets, families, as well as how men as fathers have been positioned *vis-à-vis* households' needs for cash and care. Institutionally, the market has predominated in sustaining men as fathers, with the partial exception of the New Deal era, when state provision assumed an unusually strong role (relative to earlier and later periods). To the extent that state social policies address men as fathers – which is quite limited – they are expected to contribute cash rather than care; but, for the most part, the "privacy" of family life in the liberal regime means that men and women are left free – from state interference or support – to construct their households as they will, but only as they can afford.

Men as fathers in the development of US social policy

The United States is seen by most analysts as a liberal policy regime, where liberalism in social policy is taken to imply a preference for private rather than state provision, and a reluctance to interfere politically with the functioning of the market – market capitalism constrains the role of the state *vis-à-vis* economy and society. The United States has consistently been characterized by a restricted role for the state in the provision of income and services, relative to markets and employers, as compared with the systems of social provision in other developed countries. This feature of American institutions of social provision has had important gender consequences, which we attempt to sketch out below. The predominant understanding has been that men's positions as heads of household were to be secured by private employment, where men would earn family wages. Social provision has been understood only as a back-up for men's family wages in times of temporary or permanent unemployment. The American welfare state, unlike some of its European counterparts, is seen not to have a role to play – equalizing income, offering health protection or retraining, mediating wage bargains – in the everyday life of working-aged men and their families. Thus, it has been the market and employers rather than the state which have appeared to be the primary guarantors of men's breadwinning positions. And, in fact, this vision has some empirical validity, as long as we remember that markets cannot actually function without certain political guarantees, and that "private" familial arrangements are needed to ensure necessary caregiving and reproduction. Moreover, while direct public provision of income and services may be politically off limits, the US state has in the last three or four decades developed considerable regulatory capacities, which have been significant in securing more equal access to employment for women of all races and people of color, for example. But, while there have been efforts to open existing employment to formerly discriminated populations, there is still little effort to secure employment for all who want to work or to bolster the income of the poorest. This has left many men (as well as women), disproportionately people of color, without the means to support families.

It is important to keep in mind that liberalism is not a coherent doctrine with obvious social policy implications. A commitment to precluding substantial public provision of services and income and limiting the extent of income redistribution does set limits on policy-making. Still, there have been recurring debates among adherents of liberalism over the extent to which state intervention is necessary to undergird responsible individual initiatives, mitigate against market and family "failures" and ensure a "level playing field" by guaranteeing certain rules of the game and social minima; these pit "classical" or "neo"-liberals against "social" or "new" liberals (Orloff 1993b: ch. 5; O'Connor et al. 1999: ch. 2). In American usage, "liberalism" usually refers to "social liberals" – those who are willing to use the state, at least to some degree, to guarantee social minima and regulate markets. Liberalism has also been associated with a range of different gender ideologies, from support for the traditional gender division of labor and the male breadwinner family to gender egalitarianism. Support for men's or women's "independence" has not always entailed the willingness to use the state – a recurrent theme in US policy history is the notion that full citizens need not rely on public help of any kind; rather, they should secure their means of support from the market. Thus, neo-liberalism – for example, in the US Republican Party – reflects ambivalence about how to support men's breadwinning positions and "traditional" families, and whether fully to apply liberal principles to women or to encourage their dependence in the context of family "unity." In the changed context of women having won political rights, and much higher proportions of women working for pay, support for applying liberal principles to women as well as to men is more common than in the past (e.g. among *"laissez-faire* feminists" [Klatch 1990]) – but this can mean simply asking women, like men, to enter the competitive struggle in the market, without any state "interference" (or assistance). Social liberalism, too, has been associated with different views about gender relations. In its initial phases, social liberalism, as in the case of the New Deal in the United States, contributed to new public supports for breadwinner families and for women's unpaid caregiving, sometimes even if they were without husbands. Today, this is a matter for debate, but many favor using public means to ensure women's independence, to bolster men's wage-earning capacities, or to help low-wage parents.

Gender difference in early US social policy and politics

The origins of modern welfare provision are to be found in the late nineteenth and early twentieth centuries, when, across most countries in the industrializing West, there emerged new forms of social protection for citizens against a range of different problems of income interruption and economic dependency – old-age pensions or insurance, unemployment compensation, benefits for single parents and the like. These replaced (sometimes only partially at first) the old systems of poor relief which had stood as the sole protection against utter destitution, but at the price of citizenship rights.

A new generation of historical scholarship has revealed the gendered origins of modern welfare, complementing earlier accounts which focused almost exclusively on the dynamics of political economy, class and state. During this formative era, alliances of overwhelmingly male working-class movements and male intellectual, political and reform elites advocated programs that would give public benefits to male breadwinners that they might continue to support their families financially even when they lost their jobs or wage-earning capacities. But, in addition, in what has been called a "maternalist" strand of welfare politics (Koven and Michel 1993), women and some men reformers in the first half of the twentieth century proposed state support to women in their roles as mothers as well as protective labor legislation for women workers and infant and maternal health programs. Some reformers also fought for the "endowment of motherhood" for all mothers, which would confer political recognition on the work of mothering as well as provide an independent income, and would also free women from economic dependence on husbands. This general approach did not succeed, at least partly because of men's opposition (Lake 1992; Pedersen 1993). Thus, both welfare politics and the actual early systems of modern social provision were deeply gendered. The initial programs of social provision established across the West were designed to fit and reinforce the dominant form of the gender division of labor, with men as breadwinners and women as primary caretakers and domestic workers (and sometimes as secondary wage earners). In no case were these programs intended to provide *alternatives* to the market for men or to marriage for women (although that was to some extent their unintended consequence, particularly as programs expanded in the post-World War II years).

The risks associated with family break-up, along with limited protection against work accidents, were among the first to be protected against through modern social provision by the American states. This was quite different from the pattern of policy initiations in Europe, where protections against work accidents were accompanied by new provision for those forced to retire due to old age; thus, labor market problems were the initial breakthroughs in modern social provision (Skocpol 1992; Orloff 1993b). Following a campaign by a number of women's voluntary groups, and despite the resistance of most of the forces of organized private charity, almost all states had enacted mothers' pension programs by the 1920s (Skocpol 1992). Mothers' pensions offered cash assistance to a relatively limited clientele of widowed, and in some cases divorced, deserted or never-married, mothers with children at home. These programs were a back-up for the "failures" of the family wage system for women who lacked a breadwinner, allowing some women and their children to survive without husbands, but in relatively deprived circumstances.

Women professionals, social reformers and trade unionists also succeeded in having established several federal administrative agencies specializing in the concerns of women and children, in securing federal funding to states to establish infant and maternal health programs available to all women, and in passing protective labor legislation (e.g. hours laws, minimum wage statutes and safety legislation) directed at women workers. Although many reformers preferred protection for both men and women, judicial obstacles to a universal approach pushed for a strategy of protecting women workers as mothers, with the hope that this would eventually pave the way for protection for men. But other social forces, including employers, most politicians and the national leadership of the American Federation of Labor (AFL), were committed to the ideas of voluntarism, which held that men should and could earn their living as individuals freely contracting with employers (Orloff 1993b: ch. 4). Unfettered labor markets were the province of full citizens – that is to say, men. Only because women were "different" could they be protected (and even this protection was contested by those who wanted unalloyed *laissez-faire*).

While programs and laws aimed at women as mothers and workers were succeeding, protections aimed at male workers were less successful than analogous programs in Europe and the Antipodes. Protection against the failures of the labor market for (predominantly male) wage earners was relatively limited in this early phase of modern American social protection, with the sole exception of state-level workmen's compensation legislation, passed in almost all states, which required employers to insure their workers against industrial accidents and sometimes established state regulatory boards. By the 1920s, a handful of states had enacted old-age pension laws, but these were extremely limited – more elderly people got assistance through poor relief and veterans' pensions than they did from these early laws. However, as in other industrializing and urbanizing countries (see Hobson and Bergman in this volume), American states passed new laws in this period which stiffened regulation aimed at fathers who failed to provide for their children, applied especially to those whose families applied for relief (Willrich 2000) (an antecedent to the welfare reform–child support enforcement link seen in more recent times). Breadwinning did not get much help from the state, but states would enforce it.

Social protection was understood as only for the vulnerable – not men, who were to be self-reliant. While Progressive-Era reformers entertained notions of public support to individual initiatives, by the business-dominated 1920s, it was reliance on the market alone that was celebrated. Some private companies did establish very limited programs for their employees ("welfare capitalism"). The market was expected to provide for (male) workers, who were in turn expected to provide for their wives. It was only with the economic collapse of the Great Depression that faith in market solutions to welfare problems was shaken, ushering in Roosevelt's New Deal.

The New Deal and a welfare state for (male?) workers

The Social Security Act, the "charter legislation" for the current American version of the welfare state, was passed in 1935, in the midst of the Depression with President Franklin Roosevelt's New Deal. In contrast to the Progressive Era, women's groups were relatively quiescent, and, despite participation of a number of women social scientists and officials in the Committee on Economic Security, headed by Labor Secretary (and first woman Cabinet member) Frances Perkins, which drafted the Social Security Act, women's issues did not emerge on the political agenda. Rather, concern focused on the plight of unemployed and forcibly retired wage earners, understood as male breadwinners (Hobson 1993). Labor standards legislation was extended to men for the first time in the United States with passage of the Fair Labor Standards Act in 1938. A number of other initiatives – both public benefits and public employment – addressed the concerns of male wage earners. Had they all survived the 1930s, the United States might have had a welfare state that guaranteed the position of male wage earners in both working age and retirement. In the Australian case described by Castles (1994), a "wage earners' welfare state" accomplished this through protectionist economic policy and direct wage regulation, supplemented by pensions. Social-democratic initiatives in this period laid the groundwork for active labor market policies (Weir 1992), again supplemented by social provision for the aged or others deemed unemployable. But, in the US case, public provision for working-aged men, taking the form of innovative public employment schemes like the Works Progress Administration, were not continued past the economic crisis (Amenta 1998). Instead, only provision for the unemployed and those considered unemployable – the elderly, single mothers (mostly but not only white) – continued past the war, while working men were again to rely on the market.

There was strong backing from Roosevelt, Democratic politicians, the organized elderly (of both sexes) and unions for some sort of social protection for the aged. Popular groups preferred some sort of non-contributory pension. However, policy elites in charge of drafting legislation, pushed by Roosevelt himself, established in the Social Security Act actuarially strict contributory social insurance programs against the risks of income loss due to retirement and unemployment for wage earners – almost all, though not exclusively, men (Orloff 1993b: ch. 9). Fiscal concerns were central in determining elite preferences for a contributory program; these then worked toward a system under which men as wage earners would be advantaged *vis-à-vis* those without labor market experience. Congress included provisions that ensured these would also be principally white men by excluding certain occupational groups dominated by people of color and women of all races (Lieberman 1998). Retired workers would claim benefits by working for a minimum number of years in a covered occupation and making contributions through a payroll tax evenly split between employers and employees (in contrast to most countries, there is no government contribution). Gendered labor market arrangements in the United States, as elsewhere, made it likely that men would be most able to claim retired-worker benefits in such a system. However, while social insurance was based on assumptions that men would be the majority of wage earners, in fact, anyone, male or female, could be a wage earner and establish entitlement to retired-worker benefits. In contrast, at around the same time, Britain established a similar contributory system, but with one key difference – women could opt for paying reduced taxes and give up their right to independent benefits – the "married woman's option," now phased out, on the assumption that they would get spousal benefits based on their husbands' contributions.

Within only a few years, the old-age insurance program was fundamentally altered by the addition of dependents' and survivors' benefits in the 1939 Amendments to the Social Security Act. Interestingly, this policy shift stemmed in part from a different aspect of liberal ideology and practice – not wanting to build up substantial cash reserves under state control. (Similar political actors undermined the expansion of non-contributory old-age pensions, also given federal funding in the Social Security Act.) Thus, extra benefits were coupled with a change to pay-as-you-go financing, resulting in financial bonuses to the early cohorts of social security recipients. The policy makers drafting these amendments were driven by the logic of the male breadwinner: they wanted women out of the labor force, and assumed that male breadwinners would be able to support their spouses and, after their deaths, survivors (minor children, widowed spouses) (Kessler-Harris 1995). Survivors' and dependents' benefits were made available for all widows and spouses of covered wage earners.

But support to families was to be limited to those without a male breadwinner (and only some of these). The Social Security Act also gave federal funding to the mothers' pensions programs, which were renamed Aid to Dependent Children (ADC). It may be worth noting that ADC was made explicitly gender-neutral – fathers or any other caretaker of children could claim them, which sets these benefits for sole parents apart from those available in other countries (e.g. Canada and Australia), where they went to women only; however, almost all US claimants have been women. Until 1961, the only two-parent families eligible for what was now known as Aid to Families with Dependent Children (AFDC) were those in which one parent was incapacitated. Again, the assumption was that a healthy man should be able to support himself and his dependents, and should not need state assistance except in cases of temporary unemployment. While access to caregiving support was gender-neutral, it was also decidedly residual, reserved only to the poorest mothers without husbands to support them – for the most part, caregiving and the support of families was a private matter and not the government's business. Many people of color were excluded from coverage by leaving administration to states; where women of color were a significant part of the labor force – most of the South – they could be denied assistance as "employable mothers" (Lieberman 1998).

Unemployment insurance, financed through employer contributions, was also legislated on the national level in the 1935 Social Security Act. In addition, the New Deal featured innovative programs of public works and public employment, but these did not survive the 1930s (Amenta 1998). With mobilization for war, unemployment dried up, but concerns about employment resurfaced after World War II. Full-employment initiatives were proposed in the 1940s, but these were defeated by a newly energized conservative coalition, as unions found their political capacities undermined, and only a watered-down Employment Act was passed (Lichtenstein 1989; Weir 1992). Moreover, with federal proposals for health insurance and other benefits stymied by a more conservative political climate, newly organized workers turned to collective bargaining to gain benefits from employers (Stevens 1988). Workers in auto, steel and other mass-production industries gained coverage equal to or superior to those nationally guaranteed to workers in Europe – but, of course, not all workers or citizens had access to these benefits. Other public policies also contributed to men's capacities to head households and get by on a single wage, but these were outside the "welfare state," as defined in political discourse. Obviously, the economic expansion and relatively high wages of the time were critical. But, in addition, veterans' benefits, expanded widely with the G.I. Bill, which gave support to home ownership and education (Skocpol 1996), and general support to suburbanization and inexpensive housing helped to undergird the baby boom and "traditional" – meaning breadwinner/caregiver – families (Hayden 1984). Thus, many US male breadwinners understood their positions as sustained by *private* arrangements, *not* by the welfare state.

Work and payroll taxes were significant in establishing men's identities as worker–citizens, but, on the public side, veteran status was also key in gaining access to state benefits, and private employment was an important source of welfare. Fatherhood received scant public recognition in the US welfare state. Again, there are significant contrasts to other countries, where men's position as breadwinners received more substantial state support – thus, men had citizen identities as workers and as fathers. States were the source not only of old-age insurance, but also of health insurance for workers' families. Family allowances were established in the 1940s across the West. In some places (e.g. the other [majority] English-speaking countries), these went to mothers, but, in many European countries, family allowances took the form of wage supplements to fathers

(Wennemo 1994). In the Antipodes, the states directly regulated wages, and ensured that male workers got a breadwinner's wage (Castles 1994; but, in Australia as well as in the United States, the World War II cohort received substantial public benefits outside the welfare state).

Thus, programs of social provision in the United States, as initiated in the 1930s and institutionalized in the two following decades, were designed to fit and reinforce the gender division of labor as manifested in male breadwinner–female carer families, and the income security system was marked by a work/family dualism. As this structure of modern social provision was institutionalized at a time when the work and family patterns of men and women were far more distinctive than they are today, work-related programs have tended to serve men, while almost all of the clients of family-related programs have been women. These policies further institutionalized the gender division of labor, and underlined distinctive gender identities: worker in the case of men, wife or mother in the case of women. Differentiation by gender and by social function (work and caregiving/domestic work) was the explicit aim of social policy. Inequality in the benefits available to men and women was its concomitant, whether the explicit aim of policy or not. Women – at least "good" ones – were exempted from the compulsion to participate in the labor market (as well as from the opportunity to do so!) because of their caregiving work. But, for men, there was no alternative to employment except under strict conditions of eligibility – in the short-term, unemployment insurance, or, when permanently retired, old-age insurance (or, pensions). The only route to honorable coverage for men was through wage-earning, for women, through marriage to a wage earner. In short, commodification (directly for men, indirectly for women) was a strong element of the system.

The failure of public efforts to help breadwinners in the 1960s and 1970s

While private employment and associated benefits, backed up by social security, worked well for most Americans, significant portions of the population were left out of prosperity (even as the coverage of occupations under social security was virtually universal by the 1960s). Responding to a diverse range of political forces, including the civil rights movement, President Lyndon Johnson in 1965 initiated the "War on Poverty," which encompassed a number of efforts to deal with those who did not enjoy the benefits of rising wages and employment and social insurance programs – prominently, the black and Latino urban poor (Weir et al. 1988; Weir 1992). Many of these efforts targeted men as

breadwinners (Quadagno 1994). Training programs and various public employment schemes were touted as ways to bring these groups into
the mainstream, attacking both persistent poverty and racial segregation.
Blacks were understood by many policy makers as suffering from dysfunctional families, and bolstering the position of men as breadwinners
and family "heads" was proposed as a cure. As Jill Quadagno (1994) documents, however, as these programs challenged whites' prerogatives in
favored employment, they ran into political opposition. While a number
of programs associated with the War on Poverty of the 1960s and 1970s
ultimately fizzled out, one unambiguous achievement of this period was
transformation of old-age insurance into a "retirement wage" and a significant decrease in aged poverty, particularly among retired male wage
earners.

Responding partly to concerns, perhaps most famously voiced in the
Moynihan Report, that AFDC encouraged marital break-ups and the
"pathology" of female-headed households since it was made available
principally to single parents – in other words, since it did not help families "headed" by men – President Richard Nixon authorized experiments
with a Negative Income Tax (NIT) in the early 1970s (Quadagno 1994;
Myles and Pierson 1997). But the NIT-type "Family Assistance Plan"
(FAP), which would have helped many two-parent families – and bolstered the position of poorer, especially minority male workers – was
politically damaged because it was found to be associated with an increased probability of "family break-up" (i.e. divorce). To counteract
the "anti-marriage" effect, policy makers might have considered targeting benefits only on male heads of household (as did family allowance
programs in more conservative countries, where benefits go to fathers
[Wennemo 1997]) – but they faced the legal requirement of gender neutrality. Probably more damaging was the opposition of Southern conservatives in Congress because of FAP's projected effect on local labor
markets – it would have bolstered the position of minority wage workers,
male and female, in the South too much; some Northern liberals joined
them in opposition because it would have meant lower payments to
their welfare constituencies (Howard 1997: 65–69; Myles and Pierson
1997).

Generally, the programs of the welfare state were made fully gender
neutral in the 1960s and 1970s. Provision in earlier periods was consciously premised on the ideal and material reality of gender differentiation in roles, but in this period legislation and court decisions shifted
social provision toward formal gender neutrality, although the underlying gendered division between family and labor market programs was
unchanged. Thus, for example, until 1977, dependents' and survivors'

benefits were available without question to female spouses, but, for male spouses to qualify, financial dependence had to be proven. In the wake of a successfully argued gender discrimination lawsuit (brought by a man who was denied a dependent's benefit), this double standard gave way to gender-neutrality in spousal benefits (Burkhauser and Holden 1982: 7). Similarly, benefits for surviving children were made gender-neutral in the 1970s.

Policy developments reinforced patterns in which welfare was reserved to the elderly, (some of) the unemployed, and very needy single-mother families, while other citizens had to rely on the market. With the exception of Food Stamps, a success due to an unusual configuration of social forces (Finegold 1988), failure was the fate of all initiatives which would have extended services or economic support to the working-aged population, whether male breadwinners (e.g. training, public employment), women workers (e.g. expanded day-care) or both men and women (universal health insurance – we got Medicare and Medicaid instead). Notably, this pattern of state intervention helped to solidify the racialization and (perhaps to a lesser extent) feminization of welfare (Quadagno 1994; Brown 1999), positioning (many) white men as "self-reliant" taxpayers and employees, rather than as worker–citizens or father–citizens. This helped to set the stage for the 1980s politics of backlash, in which many citizens set themselves against "welfare" – though not against the parts of the state, most notably Social Security, in which they had a stake.

In contrast to the welfare states of Europe, which "squeezed out" the market through the expansion of public labor market-related programs to near-universal coverage (Esping-Andersen 1990), the vast majority of the working-aged US population was not incorporated in the welfare state through public programs of benefits, training or services. Nor did care-giving work escape from the private sphere to which it was relegated in the New Deal; although legislation to expand day-care services was considered, it was defeated (Michel 1993). Instead, the United States limited public day-care to economically needy or educationally disadvantaged children. Private services have since expanded, with tax incentives as encouragement. Here, too, there is a contrast with at least some European countries; in this era, Scandinavian Social Democratic governments considerably expanded public day-care services and also began to support fathers' caregiving activities, as with paid parental leaves (Hobson and Bergman in this volume; Haas 1992; Leira 1992). Only Social Security (meaning contributory old-age insurance and medical coverage) provided visibly public protection to almost all citizens, and it retained its political popularity – but provided little political "cover" to other aspects of the US welfare state.

Reagan's attacks on welfare in the 1980s

The Reagan administration is widely perceived to have initiated the era of serious cutbacks in the welfare state (although retrenchment actually got underway under Carter). Reagan attacked social spending, and fundamentally challenged the politics of welfare expansion and state fiscal calculations. Cutbacks were held off in politically popular programs such as Social Security (Pierson 1994), but politically vulnerable programs such as AFDC were hit hard and the anti-state sentiments stirred up were useful in undercutting governmental fiscal capacities (Palmer and Sawhill 1984). Reagan Republicans promoted an ideology of the unfettered, deregulated market, of tax cuts and self-reliance as the road to well-being, appealing to those who saw themselves as free of welfare "dependency." An authoritarian–paternalist strain among conservatives argued that those who received welfare – and the fathers of their children – did not face structural barriers but were "behaviorally dependent" and should be forced to behave properly (see e.g. Working Seminar on Family and American Welfare Policy 1987). Deregulating labor markets exacerbated trends in which the economic position of less-skilled men deteriorated, and women continued to join the labor force for longer periods of their lives as families now saw their standard of living as dependent on two earners.

Much public attention focused on poverty among women, yet there was an initially less-visible erosion of the economic positions of many men, particularly men without college educations and poor men of color. Indeed, analysts such as William Wilson (1987, 1996) and Kathleen Neckerman (Neckerman et al. 1988) – foreshadowing the concerns of the "fragile families" wing of the Fatherhood Responsibility Movement (Gavanas in this volume) – linked poor employment prospects of such men to their unsuitability as marriage partners. If they could not be breadwinners – or at least economic providers – they could not marry. However, as would-be welfare reformers and the pro-marriage wing of the Fatherhood Responsibility Movement soon began to point out, these men still fathered children, who were provided for by social assistance. While not exciting as much opprobrium as "welfare mothers," "deadbeat dads" who did not support their children also garnered concern (Garfinkel and McLanahan 1986).

Without state-based protection for male workers and (male-dominated) trade unions, certain significant groups of men have been losing ground in terms of the quality of their employment (wages, access to privileged positions). Countless commentators note increasing income inequality over the 1980s and into the early 1990s, as well as the declining prospects of less-skilled men (see, e.g. Esping-Andersen 1999), although usually with little attention to gendered consequences. In the "golden age," many US breadwinners had their positions bolstered through *private* collective bargaining agreements, yet these were not guaranteed by the state. Once political and economic conditions changed, the unions were devastated, and market-based protections ("fringe benefits") for certain groups of formerly breadwinning men – particularly the less skilled – eroded considerably. At the same time, women's employment rates rose sharply with rising demand for women's labor, a well-developed gender-equity employment policy, the lack of support for women's unpaid caregiving, and the emergence of easily accessible divorce (Spain and Bianchi 1996). Along with the deteriorating conditions faced by some men, this has meant that a substantial number of women have been able to make inroads to "breadwinner" positions, or, at the very least, have gained the earnings capacities to support households. This has occurred even as other women are increasingly impoverished, while the men who might once have been their husbands have been economically marginalized – and seemingly, have lost their potential as "marriageable" males (e.g. according to Wilson). While trends in social politics from the 1960s and 1970s set the stage for the various backlashes of the Reagan era, arguably, this deterioration of men's position helped to elect Bill Clinton – even though he relied electorally disproportionately on the votes of women, especially unmarried ones, some of whom were also suffering the ill effects of Reagan-era increases in inequality and absolute declines in economic well-being. The problems of wage earners who could not "make work pay" was central to Clinton's political agenda, although policy initiatives to improve their situation were only unevenly successful (Ellwood 1996).

Current issues in restructuring

As a result of these historical developments, the welfare state in the United States has a very distinctive form: coverage is concentrated on the elderly, while the majority of the working-aged population must depend on employment (or marriage to employed persons) with very little safety net. The deleterious consequences of the stingy welfare system for single mothers and their children are often noted, since they are the explicit targets of social policies and their disproportionate poverty rates are well publicized. But it remains the case that little attention is focused on what Theda Skocpol (1996) calls "the missing middle" – working-aged, employed Americans, men and women. Men and women, unless desperately poor or retired, get little help from the US welfare state, which is, not surprisingly, comparatively ineffective against poverty among non-elderly groups (Ellwood 1988; McFate et al. 1995). Crucially, the distinctive American approach to employment has not changed – there is little public involvement in providing employment (e.g. through active labor market policies) beyond the workfare programs that target welfare recipients, sometimes including men with children (DeParle 1998); most fathers get no better or worse treatment than other men – or women. But there are important exceptions, in which men are targeted as (retired) husbands and (poor) fathers (of children on welfare): in Social Security, and in child support/paternity establishment policy linked to welfare. The gendered policy logic of Social Security is unlikely to be extended. But the targeting of poor men as "deadbeat dads" in child support and paternity establishment, linked to a politically volatile welfare program, may have a longer political life. Yet the gender logic of welfare/child support/paternity establishment is being challenged by the development of a gender-neutral program assisting employed parents through the tax system: the Earned Income Tax Credit.

Social Security – the premier program of the "top tier" of the US welfare state – does fairly well in providing protection to the elderly, especially elderly men. The system rewards those who have held steady life-long employment – disproportionately men. The basic structure of old age (retirement) and survivors' insurance was established during the New Deal, and has been changed only to make the system gender-neutral. The program institutionalized the policy thinking of the New Deal era: men were breadwinners, and the state should help citizens to provide for themselves when – but only when – private employment would not suffice. A contributory social insurance program providing for workers' retirement, and for the survivors of retired workers – assumed to have been non-employed – fit the bill. Today, male dependent spouses can claim as can female dependent spouses, but the policy-constituted positions of earner and caregiver/secondary earner remain. *De facto* the system continues to offer a bonus to "traditional" male breadwinner–female housewife marriages, since these are the overwhelming majority of marriages where there is a dependent spouse (Hobson 1994); this comes at the expense of dual-earner households and single people (Meyer 1996; McCaffery 1997). Explicit disentitlement through abolishing such benefits is unlikely, yet spousal benefits affect a declining proportion of Social Security recipients as more women work and pay taxes that in effect "pay for" these benefits. Retirement programs are changing in ways that will hurt marginal workers the most, but, while there is clear gender – and racial – bias in terms of who has access to "good" jobs, and who is more likely to be relegated to "bad" jobs, privileged positions are not entirely reserved for men, nor are all men protected from having to work in less-protected sectors of the labor market.

Among the working-aged population, it is only poor men who are being targeted as fathers – and only those whose children's mothers have applied for social assistance. But, while welfare reform has featured new initiatives to impose fatherhood and economic providing on these men, sometimes accompanied by services (DeParle 1998), other strands of policy, working through the tax system, would assist low-wage fathers and mothers if they are employed. While the first set of policies highlights gendered roles – (welfare, single) mother, (absent, "deadbeat") father – the second targets low-wage-earning parents, effacing gender difference in an attempt to assist families.

There is no debate among policy makers about men's role – they should be employed, pure and simple; and they should provide for children they father. But there are differences in emphasis as to what they need first: encouragement or mandates to become husbands if they are fathers, or economic support to become "marriageable" (e.g. the pro-marriage ver-sus the fragile families approaches, discussed by Gavanas in this volume). The Democrats have pursued the strategy of "making work pay," which was supposed to help low-income employed men as well as women, and allow both to be better parents and providers. In the influential version put forward by David Ellwood (1988), two-parent families would gain access to new benefits, including health insurance and expanded earned-income tax credits; single mothers on welfare would lose their exemption from the requirement to be employed, but would get services to help them to work for pay. This was an American version of an "individual model" of welfare – far more limited in coverage than the Scandinavian versions, but similar in the expectation that all would work for pay and dual-earner families would be the norm. Clinton did not succeed in leg-islating many of the elements of this package; welfare reform was taken over by Republicans and made far more deterrent. But there were a few policy successes directed at low-income employed mothers and fathers by which their capacities to contribute to family support were somewhat enhanced: the increase in the minimum wage, and the expansion of the Earned Income Tax Credit.

The Republican vision, which emphasizes the importance of marriage *per se*, offers little to men who are not successful in the labor market. Republicans favor traditional gender roles but they have been unwilling to use substantial state resources to supplement men's wages or support mothering and caretaking work directly (as have Christian conservatives in, say, Germany). They hope to curtail women's autonomy by promot-ing a traditional moral agenda and the restriction of access to abortion and to public services and benefits (in hopes that this will prevent women from having children out of wedlock or deciding to divorce). Men's providing will be supported materially through tax cuts only, and thus only men sufficiently well-off to pay substantial taxes gain from these policies, although the Republican-led "cultural war," valorizing traditional masculine virtues, may also be appealing to other (working-class) men.

Both visions of reform are premised on imposing the *logic* of the market on all citizens, although the Republicans – secondarily – also want to reimpose a traditional gender logic through law and exhortation. This reflects the residualism of liberal social policy, which has consistently featured in US policy history; what is novel is its extension to women. Those segments of the populace that do not receive any assistance from "welfare" programs (whatever other government largesse they may enjoy) – that is, a large majority of the non-elderly – depend on their capacities in the labor market to gain access to valued resources, including health benefits (indirectly, they are helped by public programs such as the home mortgage deduction, although, to benefit, they must have some income). There is widespread sentiment that mothers as well as fathers "must" work in order to have a decent lifestyle and to support children. It is this compulsion which is to be extended to welfare recipients. But little in the way of new resources has been forthcoming to help women or men to secure employment and support families. Economic good times have improved the situation of many men and women, but without any entitlement to assistance, and no government commitment to securing employment, one wonders what will happen in the next economic downturn.

Political attention has focused mainly on welfare reform, and on requiring mothers on assistance to work. Secondarily, there has been interest in getting "deadbeat dads" to pay child support (on the linkage between these areas, see Casey and Carroll 2001); however, there is relatively little emphasis on giving resources to men to enable them to play the role of breadwinner or provider (with the exception of the activists in the "fragile families" movement [Gavanas in this volume; DeParle 1998]). Biological fatherhood brings financial responsibility, not any kind of entitlement to employment or benefits to assist in heading a household or contributing to raising children. Child support enforcement and paternity establishment, significant components of welfare reforms for the last three decades, work to enforce "breadwinner" or at least "income-sharer" roles on men (and women without custody of their children; it is gender-neutral in its targeting of non-custodial parents, although the majority of these are indeed men) (Garfinkel et al. 1998). Provisions have again been strengthened in the 1996 Personal Responsibility Act which eliminated AFDC and established TANF (Mink 1998). Child support policy is framed in terms of public enforcement of a private, individual responsibility to support one's children. In this instance, the state does not dispense benefit dollars, but offers services, or, more often, requires mothers and fathers to accept its services and cooperate with its efforts to establish and enforce child support obligations. Paternity establishment policy has also gained a higher profile as never-married mothers, even more than divorced mothers, have been at the center of continuing debates over welfare reform (e.g. Garfinkel and McLanahan 1986; Ellwood 1988; Gordon 1994). A consistent theme in paternity establishment policy has been a long-standing concern about the financial burden on the state of supporting these non-marital children. Here is a clear example of the impact of policy liberalism on gender relations. Given that public sources of support – family allowances, for instance – are all but ruled out, there are few options to increase funds going to families other than forcing or encouraging women to work for pay and men to contribute support.

In both child support and paternity establishment, the state continues to assume the traditional gender division of labor and addresses men primarily as wage workers insofar as it requires them to pay child support, yet does not require them to feed, bathe or in any way directly care for the child; nor does it require them to marry the mothers. In effect, paternity establishment policy attempts to "make men accountable" for their non-marital heterosexual activity through a recapitulation of a traditional gender division of labor. And enforcing child support orders means that divorced fathers are not to be allowed to evacuate their provider roles. These policies can be seen as processes of "disciplining fathers into breadwinning," although they have been only unevenly successful even in their own terms of getting non-custodial fathers to contribute financially to their children.

Monson (1997, 2001) studied the implementation of these policies in Wisconsin, observing official interviews and court hearings, and conducting follow-up interviews with mothers and staff. The process begins with child support staff interrogating mothers of non-marital children receiving public assistance about the fathers' identity and whereabouts; they were required to cooperate with the paternity establishment and attempted collection of child support as a condition of receiving aid. Once legal paternity was established, fathers were required to provide materially for their children, and officials attempted to discipline fathers who were unemployed, working less than full-time, or who were self-employed but had low earnings into full-time breadwinning in a number of ways. They might have been ordered to conduct a job search, and appear at regularly scheduled follow-up court hearings to submit proof of their job search efforts. Some young fathers who fell behind in their child support payments were required to participate in a job training, search and placement program. Fathers who were receiving unemployment compensation had their benefits garnished to pay their child support. Fathers who failed to appear at a follow-up court hearing, cooperate with a court-ordered job training or placement program, or submit proof of their job search efforts often were subject to a "shirking order," whereby the court issued a child support order which assumed full-time work at minimum wage even if there was no evidence the father was employed (these often were used in cases where fathers were self-employed, worked for cash off the books, or worked in the underground economy). Due to the higher unemployment and underemployment rates of non-white compared to white men, all these disciplinary tactics disproportionately affected black and Hispanic fathers. In addition, bench warrants for arrest were issued for consistently missed court appearances or child support payments, but these were acted on only when a father was arrested on another charge. Here, too, this disciplinary measure fell disproportionately on black and Hispanic fathers due to their higher arrest rates.

Disciplining fathers into breadwinnerhood also took the form of persistent, detailed, sometimes intrusive questioning about fathers' employment, job history and living arrangements (Monson 1997). Family court personnel and attorneys for child support enforcement often closely questioned fathers about reasons for lost jobs, their prospects for future "good," well-paying jobs, their efforts to secure health insurance for the child, and how diligently they were searching for full-time employment. The underlying message of these questions was rarely lost on the fathers, who often responded with earnest, defensive or angry declarations of their adherence to the work ethic.

Although child support staff often obtain detailed information about men's as well as women's lives, the content of the information is quite different. Women are questioned far more extensively than men about their sexual practices and partners; women's accounts of their sexual practices and partners are used to evaluate their truthfulness and frequently their continued eligibility for public assistance; and the phrasing of the paternity summons and petition in effect requires an alleged father to state whether he is convinced of the mother's sexual fidelity. However, men are questioned in detailed, sometimes intrusive ways when child support orders are set and enforced – but about their employment and economic situation, rather than their sexuality and family living arrangements. Thus, in this case, the primary site for the state's intrusion in women's lives is their sexual privacy and autonomy, and the primary site for the state's intrusion in men's lives is their employment and income. If the custodial parent does not require public assistance, however, both parents are left alone – privacy and autonomy can be "purchased."

It is the relationship between legal custody, physical placement and financial support obligations which both undergirds and complicates (and sometimes undercuts) the state's enforcement of breadwinner fatherhood of non-marital children. In a standard paternity adjudication, the mother of a non-marital child is granted *continued* rights of sole legal custody (decision-making control over the child's religion, education and so on) and primary physical placement (where the child lives), since as the child's natural mother she had these rights at the child's birth. Because physical placement generally continues with the mother, unless the father is living in the household when he is declared the legal father he can (as the gender-neutral "non-resident parent") be required to pay child support. Thus the breadwinner father/caregiver mother model is fixed in place at the outset in most paternity adjudications. But, because legal fatherhood also bestows the right of visitation and the right to ask for legal custody or primary physical placement, fathers who want to reject or reduce support obligations can use these rights as a resource or rationale for doing so. Some men used threats of suing for custody, physical placement or increased visitation to coerce mothers not to identify them as the fathers of their non-marital children to the child support enforcement or welfare offices, or to say they did not know their whereabouts or earnings; conversely, some fathers stopped paying child support because they did not have as much access to their children as they wanted – a common reaction to disputes over visitation, and one championed as a reasonable reaction by mostly middle-class "fathers' rights" groups. Moreover, because the child support obligation is based on the gender-neutral principle that non-resident parents must share their earnings with their children, if a father was granted physical placement of the child in excess of 40% of the time his support obligation could be reduced accordingly (through a complex formula that takes into account the mother's income and expenses). On the other hand, some men cooperated with or even initiated paternity establishment (thus incurring formal support obligations) precisely because they wanted a legal tie or more access to their child, especially if informal arrangements of visitation or shared physical placement had broken down.

While the predominant thrust in paternity establishment/child support enforcement policy is collecting financial support for children dependent on welfare, some analysts associated with the "fragile families" approach to the "crisis" of fatherhood have begun to question the fairness and/or effectiveness of increased child support enforcement for some men, particularly men who are young and poor (see e.g. the research findings collected by the National Women's Law Center in collaboration with the Center on Fathers, Families and Public Policy in their 2000 publication *Family Ties*). Some small-scale programs have experimented with encouraging non-resident fathers' in-kind contributions to support (including regular visitation and parenting classes, as well as continued schooling and/or job training); these programs have had mixed results (see Gavanas in this volume). What is perhaps most interesting about these programs is a new focus (albeit tentative) on fathers' caring roles and the importance of fathers' presence, not simply fathers' economic support, in children's lives. However, researchers also note that encouraging emotional ties between fathers and their children, especially if these ties are direct (not mediated by fathers' relationships with the mothers), may have positive effects on non-resident fathers' likelihood of paying child support.

Rather than conclude that the US welfare state only addresses men as wage workers and not as family members, we might conclude instead that, in paternity and child support policy, men's status as family members necessitates their employment. Men's statuses as wage workers and family members are fused, such that a good father must be a good worker; the terms of the work ethic are, in fact, the terms of the family ethic for men.

Most Western countries recognize the burdens of childrearing for all families (Bradshaw et al. 1993). The United States, however, has had no universal family allowance, which has been a common way for governments to support childrearing. Countries have differed in terms of whether allowances go to mothers directly, or are paid to fathers (Wennemo 1994). Reflecting a trend toward greater targeting, family allowances in a number of countries have recently been made income-tested, and/or supplemented by tax credits for the working or non-working poor. Here, there is an American parallel. In the United States, parents who have earnings – the working poor, male or female – are eligible for a modest Earned Income Tax Credit (EITC), claimed through the tax system. The EITC, unlike other elements of the US system of social provision, has been expanded several times in the 1980s and 1990s, most recently and significantly in Clinton's 1993 budget package (Myles and Pierson 1997). Indeed, federal spending on EITC surpassed AFDC in 1992 ($12.4 versus $12.3 billion); by 1996, it was almost twice as much ($25.1 versus $13.2 billion) (Myles and Pierson 1997, Table 2). The EITC provided targeted benefits principally for the working poor with children. So parenthood is important, but eligibility is gender-neutral – there is no special help for men as fathers, and assistance is tied to employment (indeed, the majority of the funds are going to single mothers, although low-wage fathers are being helped as well; Orloff 2001). This bolsters the incomes of those parents in the paid labor force, thus complementing recent policies which are pushing (poor) mothers into paid work. It represents something of a departure *vis-à-vis* fathers, however, who had been basically excluded from state assistance under earlier policies. Changes in the labor market, notably the decline of jobs with "family-supporting" wages, have made purely private sources of family support harder for more people, including men, to rely on. Yet this help comes only to those fathers (and mothers) who are employed (have earnings); in giving gender-neutral help to employed parents, US policy here, too, links family roles to employment (now for women as well as for men).

The emphasis ideologically and materially on private sources of welfare – both cash and care – has been consequential for gender relations, and men's positions. The strong emphasis on private responsibility for all but the aged means that men's identities – as fathers, citizens, workers – are not forged within the welfare state, but outside it, or even in opposition to it. Retirees are a partial exception here – but, to some extent, gaining entitlement to Social Security is seen as parallel to market-based strategies for retirement investments, and does not necessarily undermine this market orientation, which means the dominant identity for many men and some women is that of employee. This also implies that the key gender identity of family provider also depends on employment, and gets little backing from state programs. For low-wage employees this may be beginning to change slightly with the expansion of the Earned Income Tax Credit, which supplements the earnings of low-income wage earners, both men and women, who are supporting children. But, since this is administered through the tax system, rather than being a welfare benefit, the employment relation continues to be underlined.

Conclusion

Today, as has been the case for most of the history of the United States, men must depend on markets (employment) for income and most benefits and services. They have little freedom *not* to engage in paid work – as we have long known, the US welfare state does not promote decommodification. (And, increasingly, women are also subject to commodification.) Moreover, class and racial stratification is reinforced in this system; one's status in the labor market largely determines the quality of one's health insurance, pension benefits and so on. Indeed, compared with other countries' systems, men (and women) in the United States depend most on their situation as *employees* of specific corporations (or other employers) rather than worker status *per se*, as linked to citizenship and contributions to public programs. Even the needy cannot get assistance unless they work ("workfare" in TANF [Tempory Assistance for Needy Families] or "real" work with earned income in EITC).

What about men's gender identities, and men's status as fathers? Parenthood receives scant support apart from what individuals can gain in the labor market, supplemented by tax credits for the poor, tax exemptions for the better-off. Thus, men are treated principally as workers and employees, and get little bonus from being family "heads." Social Security provides some advantages to "housewife-maintaining families" in that, when wage earners retire, their wives will get coverage – yet, given how many women now engage in paid employment at some point in their lives, this benefit will accrue to fewer and fewer people even if it is not phased out sometime in the future. To the extent that men have family households, they must earn the means to support them in the market; it is men's (on average) superior market positions that underwrite superiority in the family rather than direct state backing to breadwinners. Of course, it is important not to lose sight of *indirect* state benefits for household heads: the home mortgage interests deduction, for instance, the advantages of which accrue disproportionately to the affluent. (But again, crucially, this extends to employed women.)

The New Deal was something of an aberration in the history of the US gender regime (as it was in other ways as well). For this is the only period in modern history in which the state offered substantial direct material support to men as breadwinners during their prime working years as well as in retirement. But the lasting parts of the New Deal are those directed at citizens deemed not employable. Thus, policy decisions which gave old-age benefits to wage earners' spouses have lasted, although their importance is eroding as more women are employed and pay payroll taxes (Meyer 1996). During other significant periods of policy development, the Progressive Era as well as the 1960s and 1970s, the expectation that working-aged men would be employed and thus provide for their families without assistance from the welfare state has been sustained against suggested reforms which would have directed benefits or regulatory protection at men as breadwinners or workers.

Today, it may be that we are creating a limited departure from the policy legacy of treating men principally as workers or employees. To the extent that fathers are unable to sustain families on wages alone, they can be assisted through the EITC – as will mothers. Thus, the restructured labor market, with its expanding pool of low-wage work, in addition to its other social effects, may also be responsible for developing a policy the premise of which is that not all fathers can support families on their own with wages. It is also noteworthy that this policy is not limited to fathers. New lines of disadvantage now catch both men and women, while labor market participation remains the privileged form of entitlement in the United States. Without the kinds of state supports for families such as child allowances available in other developed countries, US fathers must depend on their capacities and luck in the labor market. Thus, one might well refer to a "crisis" in fatherhood for those men unable to contribute economically to their families' support, a part of an overall crisis of reproduction for marginalized groups of citizens and residents of one of the richest countries on earth, coexisting with continued privilege for many other men.

3 Compulsory fatherhood: the coding of fatherhood in the Swedish welfare state

Helena Bergman and Barbara Hobson

Feminist scholars have coined the term *women friendly* to refer to the Scandinavian welfare states.[1] Does this mean that these states are men unfriendly? These are societies with policies that have allowed women to combine work and family responsibilities, in which the male breadwinner wage ideology is weak. They are welfare states that are enabling for women in that they provide women with opportunities to organize households without husbands and to exit bad marriages or form families outside of marriage. From this perspective, we can say that the Scandinavian welfare states are unfriendly to men in that they undermine what Robert Connell refers to as the patriarchal dividend, the overall advantage that men receive from the overall subordination of women (Connell 1995: 79).

However, to say that Sweden, for example, typifies the weak male breadwinner model (Lewis 1992) does not imply that men are no longer the main earners in the family economy in these societies. There is no evidence for this either from the statistics on men's average work hours, the division of paid work as seen in time budget studies or the amount of earnings that women have after divorce (Hobson 1994; Hobson and Takahashi 1997; Flood and Gråsjö 2001; Takahashi forthcoming).

Rather than ask whether a society is men friendly or unfriendly, we might recast the question and consider how the policy framework has shaped the way in which societies define what is men friendly and in what spheres of life. This allows us to see explicit policy stances toward men as fathers, through the ideological framing of fatherhood, and the incentives to active fathering, and to make visible which fathers are recognized in law and practice. To ask the question in this way is to acknowledge that men are embedded in social policy in often contradictory ways; a point underscored in the research on the critical studies of men (Hearn 1998a; Hearn in this volume). The thesis that institutional features of welfare states enhance men's power (reproduce patriarchy) does not hold up under scrutiny when we begin to think about the different experiences of men as fathers, by race, ethnicity and class or by marital status (divorced men versus married men; gay men versus heterosexual men). All fathers in heterosexual couples are privileged in Western law and many countries do not permit gay couples to adopt children. In Sweden, gay couples have been given the right to marry in Swedish law since 1995, however the issue of whether gay couples can adopt children is still highly contested.[2] In most countries marriage confers rights to fathers, however, in Swedish law for the last three decades, there is no disadvantage to fathers who do not formally marry in terms of parental rights or custody after divorce.

Swedish policy-making with its emphasis on biological fatherhood, which has shaped its laws on paternity, marriage, cohabitation and custody after divorce, provides an interesting case from which to study the linkages in fatherhood, fathering and fathers. This policy stance has driven the questions: who is recognized as the father, who is privileged as the father, and what are the rights and obligations of fatherhood?

In this chapter, we trace the coding of fatherhood in Swedish law and policy, which has moved from a focus on establishing paternity and financial obligations (particularly in out-of-wedlock births) to the current-day laws and policy that seek to enforce fathers' caring responsibilities through compulsory joint custody arrangements. It is the case in which the shift from cash to care is perhaps the most dramatic. The ideological framing of fatherhood, and narratives and the public discourse on good fathers are reflections of these shifts in hegemonic masculinity, from men as breadwinners to men as participatory fathers in the care of their children. We make the case that the Swedish welfare state has had one of the most regulatory and highly interventionist policies toward men as fathers. Beginning at the first decades of the twentieth century, Swedish law made paternity compulsory – all children (including those outside marriage) were entitled to have a registered father.

Now at the beginning of the twenty-first century, both through court decisions and government policies, we see "compulsory" fathering carried out through mandatory joint custody arrangements. In many societies, there is a growing interest in fathers' caretaking roles in the family. The Swedish case represents the most institutionalized expression of this shift in fatherhood, which includes proactive policies for fathers to take a portion of the parental leave and joint custody laws that bind the biological father to his children after divorce.

Paternity

Very early on, Sweden began formalizing the rights and obligations of parents toward children born outside of wedlock. Whereas in many countries paternity was connected only to marriage, a Swedish law passed in 1917 formalized paternity establishment for children born outside of wedlock

(SFS 1917: 376). All Swedish children were entitled to parents in the formal sense, which meant a mother and father were both noted in the official registers, and both bore the economic responsibility for the child. This new policy ended a long-standing tradition that permitted even the mother to remain anonymous, dating back to 1778 when the Swedish king sought to prevent child murder by allowing unmarried mothers the right to remain anonymous, and not be named in the parish registers. However, it was not the mother's but the father's anonymity that the new law sought to end.

Behind the state's interest in establishing paternity and forcing fathers to contribute to their children's upbringing was a general concern about the situation of unmarried mothers and their children. Swedish illegitimacy rates were among the highest in Europe during the first decade of the twentieth century. More than one out of ten Swedish children were born outside of wedlock. A series of investigations about out-of-wedlock children conducted by the National Statistical Bureau showed that they were overrepresented at orphanages and foster homes, and that they often had to turn to the public poor-relief system for support (Kungliga statistiska centralbyrån 1914, 1916, 1917).

A solution to the problem of poverty among out-of-wedlock children, first suggested by the influential National Association of Social Work (Centralförbundet för socialt arbetet/CSA), was to formalize the maintenance obligation for out-of-wedlock fathers, and to give public authorities effective means to force men into fulfilling their paternal obligations (*Reformlinjer* 1907). The effort to minimize the use of public support among solo mothers was spurred by the fact that a new poor relief act, offering more generous poor relief, was on its way. Thus, the issue not only concerned men's/fathers' responsibilities toward their children and their failure to support their out-of-wedlock children, it also meant greater economic and social costs and higher public expenditures.

In early twentieth-century Sweden, a new category of man appeared in public discourse, the "negligent provider," which was applied to fathers who shirked their financial obligations toward their children. The methods for controlling these men were numerous and included measures such as the attachment of wages or property, and even a period of imprisonment in a workhouse. Fathers of children born outside of marriage could be prevented from leaving the country, and a 1927 amendment to the 1917 act made it possible to issue a description of "negligent providers" to public authorities nationwide, including the police, public relief and child welfare agencies (SFS 1927: 452). At the same time, a public social bureaucracy was created. The local child welfare authorities assigned a child welfare officer to each child born outside of wedlock in order to designate the father and to oversee the economic support of the child.

It is important to point out that there existed broad support for these types of interventionist policies against unwed fathers. The child welfare officer system was backed by those worrying over public expenditures, reform-minded liberals and Social Democrats concerned with citizens' responsibility, as well as various women's organizations focusing on the welfare of children and mothers (Sjögren 1997; Bergman 1999). As the editor of the journal *Vårdarebladet*, one of the leading Swedish social work journals, put it: "It is possible to say, as the Germans do: the woman alone must take responsibility for the child, because she knew the risk. But it is also possible to say, in accordance with Swedish legislation: one of these men must take the responsibility. He knew the risk" (Isberg 1919: 33).

The system of enforcing male breadwinning responsibility resonated in the male working-class ideology of the "steady worker." This ideology was taken up by reform-minded workers in order to distance themselves from the ways of rough unorganized workers. Policies which defined citizen norms, such as orderliness and independence, were filtered through the ideals of the organized working class, such as steadiness, propriety and responsibility – ideals that sought to make men into breadwinner fathers (Ambjörnsson 1988; Horgby 1993). Thus, the importance of the early Swedish welfare state in constructing legal and economic fatherhood was coupled to other hegemonic ideologies in the Social Democratic project.

The presumption of paternity in Swedish law was exceptional in the European context. It was not necessary to prove beyond a doubt that the putative father was the father. "Possible paternity" meant that in a court proceeding a man might be judged to be the father of a child if he had had intercourse with the mother near the time of conception. In Germany, England and the Netherlands (other cases in this book), the fact that the mother had intercourse with someone else other than the man summoned for the paternity trial, was a valid reason to waive paternity. Swedish legislators stated that it was enough that the man had "completed what according to the order of nature could have caused the child" (Lagberedningen 1915: 161). It was argued that it was far better to establish "possible paternity" than to leave the child without any father at all. Underlying this view was the belief that men had to take responsibility for their sexual actions.

Paternity and biology

In the 1920s and 1930s, the policy concerns around fatherhood shifted from stressing the importance of finding *a* father for each woman's child to emphasizing the necessity of finding the *right* father and to ascertain "the biological truth." In the years following the enactment, a reaction set in against the law, in which it was argued that it went too far and denied men legal rights and protections in paternity cases and did not insure that the named father was the *real* father. In 1933, the first law was passed that allowed blood testing of the child, mother and the presumed father (SFS 1933: 229).

Thus, the original strong presumption in paternity cases, which asserted that it had to be "obvious" that the child had not been conceived at the time of intercourse in order to waive paternity, was eased over the years. The revised Parental code, created in 1949, stated that the paternity presumption could be waived if it was considered "unlikely" that the man in question was the father. It was still regarded as being in the best interest of the child to establish paternity, but it was now also considered in the child's best interest to use all possible measures to minimize the risk of naming the wrong man as the father (SOU 1946: 49, 79–86).

Behind the quest for scientific and juridical measures to ascertain the biological father was a belief that men would be persuaded to take more responsibility for their children, either by marrying the mother or assuming their financial obligations. Why was ascertaining the biological father so important for the construction of fatherhood in a system in which the welfare state footed the bill for unwed mothers? In the majority of cases, fathers did not assume their economic responsibilities on a regular basis. Of course, not to be forgotten in the scientific determination of the "real" father is an ethical question: why should a man be economically responsible for paying for someone else's child? But there are many possible reasons for the centrality of biological fatherhood in Sweden. One was that it was viewed as a highly strategic policy; knowledge that a man was the real father might result in a man's decision to marry the mother. Another was concern over the declining population. During the period when the legislation was first enacted, population policy was on the public agenda and there were numerous commissions on population decline and low rates of marriage (SOU 1935: 6; Kälvemark 1980; Hobson 1993). Finally, the fixation with locating the real biological father can be seen as an extension of the social engineering of the thirties and forties, a period when experts, doctors, family planners and social workers were concerned about eugenics, social fitness and biological inheritance. In fact, there were thousands of parents deemed unfit (mainly unwed mothers) who were sterilized during this period (Broberg and Tydén 1996; Runcis 1998).

Even with the changing legal definitions of parenting, marriage and cohabitation, the rising divorce rates, and the emergence of reconstituted families, biological fatherhood remains crucial to the Swedish coding of men as fathers. The revision of the Parental Code in the 1970s begins with an unwritten set of assumptions that fathering a child entitles a man to contact with a child, visitation rights and even custody, regardless of whether the child was born in marriage or whether there is another man in the house who is the breadwinner for his child.

Implementing the law: economic realities

The child welfare bureaucracy created to implement paternity establishment produced an army of relentless social welfare officers to track down unwed fathers. The assistance of the child welfare officer was not optional: the assignment was obligatory for all children born out of wedlock, even for those couples who lived in stable non-marital relationships. The surveillance lasted until the child became of age, or was legitimized, either by the parents' marriage or an adoption.

The Swedish child welfare system existed for more than fifty years before it was finally abolished at the end of 1973, due to the changing norms around cohabitation and marriage, and feminist opposition to the labeling and stigma that such surveillance attached to mothers and children of non-marital relationships. By then, the Swedish welfare state had developed other measures to secure the welfare of children, such as the general child welfare committees, child and maternal health checks, medical supervision in kindergarten and at school – measures that did not discriminate between children born inside and outside of marriage (SOU 1972: 65).

The child welfare officer's primary task was to see that paternity was established for every child. As a rule, this was done by simple acknowledgement: the father signed a standardized form, which included both a paternity confession and a maintenance agreement. Approximately 80–85 percent of all paternity cases were established through voluntary acknowledgement between the years 1920 and 1970; later the figure increased to over 90 percent (Nordlöf 1997: 33). If the alleged father contested paternity, the child welfare officer would then initiate a court proceeding.

Once the father was identified, the child welfare officer monitored maintenance payments. However, enforcing paternity obligations often involved trying to extract blood from a stone. Working-class men without families could be highly mobile, moving from one job to the next. Many quit their jobs to avoid an attachment of wages; others left town with no forwarding address. According to a 1936 state investigation, approximately 50 percent of all children born out of wedlock, where paternity was established and the father was still alive, did not receive child support regularly (SOU 1936: 47, 40). Furthermore, the investigation showed that the various actions that could be taken against a father who failed to support his child were often not used. Only one-third of all fathers deemed as negligent were ever subject to the attachment of their wages or property, or a workhouse sentence (SOU 1936: 47, 76–83).

From our investigation of the Annual Reports of the Stockholm Child Welfare Office between 1930 and 1960, we found that many fathers who were supposed to pay back the advanced income maintenance paid to out-of-wedlock children, never did. Moreover, the fact that a man was sentenced to the workhouse did not mean that he actually "served time"; the sentence was revoked if he showed signs of improvement, which meant paying off part of his maintenance debt. For the majority of cases, child welfare officers just deemed it to be a waste of time to take legal action since most men had incomes that were too low to support themselves as well as their new families.

A child's right to know his or her father became a central tenet in Swedish family law; however, the assignment of paternity did not result in making the fathers economically responsible for children outside of wedlock.

The state guarantees payment

In 1938, Sweden passed the Income Maintenance Law for children of divorced or never-married mothers, in which the state guaranteed payment for child support and sought to collect the money from the father. In looking at the specific policy content of the Swedish income maintenance scheme, it is useful to keep in mind that it was one of many reforms during a period of welfare state expansion in the areas of family policy. Social reform during this period was closely integrated with population policy, which influenced the framing of social welfare legislation in such varied policy fields as housing, social insurance, child welfare etc. Swedish population policy was directed at the welfare of the family, and indirectly designed to encourage parenthood (Hatje 1974; Kälvemark 1980; Hirdman 1989).

With the institutionalization of the income maintenance scheme, non-married and divorced mothers were still tied to the fathers of their children (they were supposed to provide economic support), nevertheless, these women became less dependent on them. Thus, when fathers failed to provide support, a mother could claim a maximum advance of 250 crowns a year for each child. In 1953, the maximum allowed was raised to

600 crowns and in 1957 to 720 crowns. These payments were supposed to be advances to be collected from the father, but, in a significant number of cases, they were a cash benefit. According to various estimations, about 40 to 50 percent of these advances were never recovered. For instance, the Swedish National Board of Social Affairs (Socialstyrelsen) reported that only 48 percent of the maintenance advancements made during 1956 had been repaid by the end of the year (SOU 1957: 49, 57). In 1948, income testing was abolished, and after that the maintenance advance could be claimed irrespective of the mother's income. Children under the age of sixteen where paternity could be established were entitled to an advance payment, except when the parents were living together or the child lived with the father. In 1956, the law was changed, so that fathers with custody could claim maintenance advance if the mother stopped paying child support.

Even during the period when the income maintenance payment was means-tested, it was not dependent upon a social welfare officer's assessment of the respectability of a single-mother's household. But the key to receiving the benefit was naming the father. The mother had to cooperate in finding a father or she forfeited some benefits on behalf of her child. Only children with established paternity were eligible for the income maintenance program. Children without established paternity could draw a special child allowance instead, but only from the age of three. Until that age, they were denied this benefit in order to put pressure on unmarried mothers to reveal the name of the father. Cooperation in locating the father is still written into the law on income maintenance. However, since the 1960s the law has been modified so that women can receive income support if it is impossible to know who the father is, or if revealing his name would place the woman in danger (SFS 1996: 1030 §4; Bejstam and Wickström 1996: 32–46).

More and more exceptions in the law allowed fathers to opt out of paying, which also included for children in divorce cases as well as for children born out of wedlock. Wide variations existed in the amount of maintenance fathers had to pay throughout the post-war period, which was calculated on the ability to pay and the child's needs. However, it became a common practice to permit the biological father to reserve his income for his new family. Beginning in the 1970s, fathers were able to get approval for reducing support for many reasons. One notable court case allowed a father to discontinue his support because he took leave from his job to further his education, which the court construed as a valid claim since it could be interpreted as a response to labor market conditions (see NJA 1978: 362).

Despite the fact that the acknowledged fathers (sometimes through blood testing but mostly through confession of fatherhood) contributed very little to the support of their out-of-wedlock children and were often delinquent in their payments, this did not weaken the primacy of biological fatherhood in Swedish policy. In fact, after the 1960s reform period this position became even stronger, when contact with the biological father became part of the ideological construction of the best interests of the child in cases of divorce and when the parents never married.

The shift from cash to care

Before the 1960s, fathers of children born out of wedlock, even if they paid their support regularly, were rarely entitled to visit their children, or able to make claims for custody. The custom in divorce cases, true in every Western welfare state, is that custody was routinely awarded to the mother. In the cases we surveyed we found that, before the 1977 change in the Parental Code, divorced men were only granted custody when it could be proven that the mother was unsuitable, for example when the mother and her relatives in the home were found to be alcoholics (NJA 1975: C908). In one unusual case, the father was given custody because the mother was a Jehovah's Witness and the court reasoned that the child might be damaged by her association with the sect (NJA 1968: C861). The court denied a father's petition for custody in which he argued that the mother was a lesbian (NJA 1955: 63). There was no legal principle favoring the mother in custody cases, but it was considered "natural" that children remain with their mother.

A radical shift in the construction of fatherhood occurred in the 1970s, after the publication and debates from the government Commission on Family and Marriage (SOU 1972: 41), which altered the discursive landscape on the family. The Commission experts began with two premises: (1) that policy should be neutral in relation to family forms; and (2) how parents organize their relationship should not affect their rights and duties to their children. Policy recommendations from the Commission study resulted in a revamping of the laws pertaining to marriage and cohabitation. Not only did the legal distinctions between children born within and outside of marriage disappear, but also the distinctions between married and unmarried parents were blurred in law and withered away in practice.

The 1972 Commission recommendations were a response to broader societal shifts in ideologies and practice – changing patterns of marriage and cohabitation, the rise in women's labor force participation, and the numbers of women who were becoming wage earners. Embedded within the new family policies was a view of fathers' responsibility for care, even after separation and divorce, which was expressed in policies encouraging joint custody.

Joint custody

Joint custody, affirmed as the norm for divorced parents in the revised law (Proposition 1975/76: 120), gave non-married parents the same rights. The guiding principle in this policy was that it was to the child's advantage to have good contact with both parents, even if the child lived with only one parent. In contrast to earlier policy on the father's obligations, joint custody was taken to imply both cash and care responsibilities. What this meant in actual practice was that fathers had rights of decision-making, regardless of whether fathers were the actual residential parent. The courts have distinguished between physical custody (living arrangements) and joint custody (influence of parents with children). Even if the child spends all of his or her days with one parent, joint custody agreements give the other parent the right to influence decisions over education, religion and health care (SOU 1995: 79; Richardson 1997).

Implicit in the coding of fatherhood in joint custody were several assumptions. First, that the best interests of children were defined in terms of having contact with their biological fathers; secondly that joint custody would encourage men to participate in childrearing after divorce; and thirdly that household fathers were not responsible for financial support of children who were fathered by other men.[3]

Within Swedish law and policy on divorce and joint custody, there are unstated norms that shape legal practice. First and foremost, the policy assumes an amicable divorce, since joint custody is supposedly a consensual agreement; the divorced couple is expected to agree on everything. Although couples often write a formal agreement about the division of property and their economic responsibilities toward their children, which is a legal contract, their agreement on the division of care responsibilities is not legally binding since it is always a question of the best interests of the child. Only when individuals take the custody issues in divorce to court do the arrangements become binding. There is little place in this framework of consensual joint custody for dealing with individual disagreements and differences (Schiratzki 1997). Since the beginning of the 1990s, nearly a fourth of all divorce cases end up in court.

Studies of divorced men from different ethnic groups reveal how difficult it is to apply the consensual norms underlying joint custody, particularly among those immigrant couples who have different religious, social and legal codes in their native countries. One study showed that immigrant couples were more likely to turn to the courts in divorce cases (out of 113 judgments in Stockholm's District Court, 67 involved immigrants; Socialstyrelsen 1996: 126–128). Particularly those fathers who come from traditional Muslim cultures cannot accept the legal practices that allow women to initiate divorce and grant them rights to have custody of children.[4] Darvishpour (forthcoming), in a study of interviews with Iranian divorced men, notes that they often refuse to accept divorce in Sweden and seek revenge by trying to get sole custody of the children. Iranian men in this study believe that the higher divorce rate among Iranian families is a direct result of the men's loss of power and status in Swedish society. The reverse is true for women who have the opportunity to earn and keep their own wages, to divorce men without their consent (six months after filing for divorce even if it is not consensual). Counseling and mediation are recommended to couples that are unable to act in "the best interests of their children," who contest the basic principle of joint custody. But few immigrant couples take advantage of these services since they assume that the Swedish counselors will be prejudiced against them, particularly immigrant fathers whose beliefs are rooted in traditions of patriarchal authority (Richardson 1997).

In the most recent revisions of the Parental Code in 1998 (6 föräldrabalken kap S 5), joint custody has nearly become obligatory. The court can order joint custody if one of the parents is opposed to it. This is a logical step from earlier legislation, which presumed joint custody and the practice of the courts was to award joint custody if one parent showed "ambivalence." The reform poses a dilemma since joint custody assumes consensus that the couples agree to share responsibility and care for the child.

Two recent cases reveal the weaknesses in the practice of joint custody. In a groundbreaking case, the highest court overturned a lower-court ruling awarding custody to the mother and imposed joint custody against her wishes (Svea Hovrätt, nr. T 99/658). The lower-court decision followed the recommendations of the expert advisors, which has been standard procedure in Swedish custody disputes. After having interviewed both parents and children, the experts maintained that the parents appeared to have irresolvable conflicts, rooted in cultural differences, and therefore single custody was better for the children. The conflicts revolved around parenting codes: the father who was Chilean saw the mother's parenting as careless and lacking in discipline. The mother, alternatively, viewed the father's parenting style as too strict and uncompromising. This case represented the first time that the High Court imposed joint custody on a couple when one parent was opposed (in this case the mother since the father was willing to accept it). The rationale given for this departure from past practices was that, since both were fit parents, the principle of joint custody as in the best interests of the child should be followed. Nevertheless, the High Court concurred with the lower-court recommendation that the children remain in residence with the mother and that the children would spend every other weekend with the father, which was identical to the lower court's recommendation.

However, in another court case, the higher courts went further in defining the practices of joint custody by imposing residential joint custody. In that case the lower court ruled that, while both parents should have joint custody, the children should live with the mother and spend every other weekend with the father and his new partner. The reason they gave for the decision was that the father, who worked at the opera, had irregular working hours. In effect, the lower court did not depart from the earlier ruling of the Appellate courts. However, the Court of Appeal overturned that decision and ruled that both were fit parents and that the best interests of the child is realized through contact with both parents. In this instance, the Court ordered the parents to accept a joint custody arrangement in which the children should spend equal time with both parents (Svea Hovrätt DT 43: nr T 4467/99).

Obligatory joint custody is about compulsory fatherhood rather than compulsory fathering. Contact with the father can mean no more than having a father who has custodial rights, who sees the child occasionally (vacations and some weekends) or irregularly (with no set schedule). The central principle in the best interests of the child doctrine is therefore having access to two biological parents who are custodial parents, which can be seen as a means of perpetuating a stable family unit, an imagined community of father, mother and child. Yet this stable administrative family, constructed by the state, exists in a social context with highly dynamic sets of living arrangements involving single-parent families and reconstituted families from previous marriages (see Oláh, Bernhardt and Goldscheider in this volume).

Fatherhood, fathering and fathers

How do we understand obligatory joint custody and its ideological base, compulsory fatherhood? In some respects, it is a logical extension of the state's regulation of paternity at the beginning of the century. The primacy of biological fatherhood continues to be the main basis for men's obligations and rights as fathers. This privileging of biological fathers might be compared with the recent change in the Dutch law, in which judges consider how engaged fathers are with their children before determining whether a father who is not married to the mother has some rights to shared custody (see Knijn and Selten in this volume).

In the following section, we want to suggest that compulsory fatherhood can be best understood as a consequence of the ways in which men and fathers have been engrafted into social policy since the 1960s. The making of men into fathers in the Swedish context meant the unmaking of men as sole breadwinners. It is a process that grew out of the policy revolution of the 1960s and 1970s that resulted in the Scandinavian model of the dual-earner family. This policy was reflected in the policy logic of the Swedish welfare state, which coded family law and policy in gender-neutral terms. A gender-neutral policy frame did not necessarily alter gender-specific practices (who was responsible for the carework in families). What the policy did was to decenter the idea of naturalized motherhood. Equally important to this process of making men into fathers was the emergence of a politics of fatherhood, of men in public discourse speaking for men as fathers, and highly orchestrated state campaigns to promote active fathering.

The demise of the male breadwinner wage

In Swedish society, the shift from cash to care was mirrored in a new set of images of the active and participatory father, who was seen in the streets pushing prams and picking up children at the day-care center. In the popular literature, one found a new genre of children's stories of solo fathers raising children.[5]

The reimaging of fatherhood reflected broader ideological shifts in men's and women's roles in the family and paid work. Beginning in the late 1960s, a new discourse emerged on gender equality. The argument made in the major social policy investigation of sex roles, *Women's Life and Work (Kvinnors liv och arbete*; Dahlström 1962) was that gender inequality was attributed to both women's lack of participation in paid work and men's lack of participation in carework. Equality thus would result in deprivileging men who were supported by housewives and deprivileging women who were fully supported by husbands. However, altering the gendered division of labor was not seen in terms of conflict or power within families, but rather as an issue of re-education and socialization. Participation in the labor market would not only broaden women's horizons, but it would deepen men's emotional life (Dahlström 1962; Vestbro 1992; see also essays in retrospective, Visionen om jämställdhet 1992).

In order to understand what kinds of policy formulas were developed and their rationales, it is important to keep in mind that men were key actors in the debates on gender equality and policy-making bodies. Whereas in many countries men were not involved in the feminist debates on equality, in Sweden men have been key actors as both opinion builders and policy advocates for gender equality. Their presence in the equality debates has shaped the direction and the discourse on equality to include men's liberation. Equality meant equality between the sexes, emancipation meant emancipation of women *and* men.

Driving the policy agenda on gender equality was a belief that liberation for women meant changing men. Men became objects of the liberation project, which implied making the citizen worker of the 1930s into the citizen parent. In policy terms, this led to the end of marriage subsidies for male breadwinners and recasting gender-specific benefits for mothers to gender-neutral ones, such as parental leave and child sick leave.

According to Diane Sainsbury (1996), the weakening of the Swedish father role as breadwinner began in the 1940s when the child allowance was paid to directly to women. But the real turning point occurred in the 1970s when policies were implemented to redistribute benefits away from men as breadwinners. The tax advantage to men with non-working wives disappeared with the radical tax reform that treated all working persons as individuals. Under the old system, a wife's earnings were added on to the husband's and taxed at the highest possible rate. Under the new system, which treated spouses as individuals, only the most economically irrational men would seek to keep their wives out of the labor market. The last residue of the male breadwinner wage was the widows' pensions, which were phased out in 1989.

Beyond the disincentives for male breadwinner fathers, there were opportunities and incentives to take an active role in caring for children. Sweden was the first society in the Western world to denaturalize child leave policy. It became parental leave and the benefits were generous and the conditions were incredibly flexible: fathers and mothers could divide the leave up in any way that they chose and use the time up to the eighth birthday of their child. By 1989, parents could take up to one year and were compensated with 90 percent of their salaries up to a very high ceiling (about 32,000 American dollars per year) and a further three months with a flat benefit of about 8 dollars a day. The policy did not specify which parents should take leave or whether any of the leave should be reserved for the father, which is a recent policy innovation in the 1990s. However, when the Commission on Family and Marriage published their report in 1972, they not only recommended that the leave be gender-neutral, but also suggested that the leave be shared. This was meant to strengthen women's labor market position and increase men's responsibility for care (SOU 1972: 41).

In the 1970s, men did not mobilize to get a portion of the leave reserved for them. Women's organizations across the political spectrum were the political actors seeking legislation that would designate a portion of the leave for men. They reasoned that otherwise the reform would be meaningless and would perpetuate different wage and career prospects for women. Two parliamentary members of the Center Party proposed a twelve-month parental leave in which no parent would use more than eight months. Perhaps succumbing to the realities of policy-making, Social Democratic women insisted that one month be reserved exclusively for the father out of the eight months allowable (Bergqvist 1999). It took two decades before the daddy month was enacted, a time when men became the visible spokespersons for this reform; men in men's groups and men in key policy-making roles that had visibility and clout in political parties.

The weakening of the male breadwinner privilege and the rise of the dual-earner family was the impetus for wide-ranging policy formulas to protect parents' rights in the workplace and to promote active parenting: the introduction of gender-neutral parental leave and leave for child sick days, job security and rights to return at the same position after use of the leave. Five weeks of vacation for all workers was also a means of promoting parental involvement.

The dual-earner family model set in motion a host of expert discourses that connected gender equality to men's roles in the family and new masculinities. An array of experts was marshaled to re-educate parents in the late 1960s and early 1970s about equality in the family, and open up the debate about sex roles (Klinth 1999). Swedish radio and TV sponsored courses on gender equality. Family policy debates on public radio go back to the 1930s. Alva Myrdal in her writings and interviews argued that the modern family would only survive if men became more involved in child care and household work (Klinth 1999; Myrdal 1945). In the 1950s, many educational radio programs addressed the problem of the absent and uninvolved father and its impact on children, particularly sons. The experts on family policy in the following decades recast the debate and focused more directly on masculinities and men's roles as seen in the titles of radio programs, such as "It's About You: The Second Role of Man," which encouraged men to de-emphasize their commitment to full-time work and devote more time to active parenting. For women, this meant a widening of spheres; for men it meant a rediscovering of emotions. These discussions challenged hegemonic notions of masculinity and breadwinning. However, they accepted the primacy of the nuclear family and the biological parents' role in the emancipation project.

In some respects, the sex-role debate brought to the surface the questions that the massive entry of women in the labor market posed for families. In a society with a history of social engineering it is not surprising that the dual-earner family model would authorize experts to define new parenting styles and, with the loss of the full-time housewife, the construction of explicit norms for fathering.

In the 1970s, there were 74 government commissions that dealt with family issues around the raising of children, marriage and cohabitation, and gender equality (Florin and Nilsson 1999). Alongside the concern about parenting in families in the dual earner family, there was an anxiety over the rising divorce rate (the risk for divorce nearly doubled, partially explained by the liberal no-fault divorce law in 1974). Non-marital cohabitation rose by 12 percent in 1971 and continued to climb throughout the decade. In this context, joint custody can be seen as an attempt by the state to introduce explicit norms around fathering in response to the weakening of the marriage norm in Swedish society. As we discussed earlier, Sweden is a society with a history of low marriage rates up until the 1950s and also high rates of illegitimate births and cohabitation, especially among the working class (Matovic 1984). In the 1960s and 1970s the Swedish pattern of non-marital cohabitation became so widely accepted that one conservative family sociologist took it as the paradigm case of the de-institutionalization of the family (Popenoe 1988). But he falsely interpreted a weak marriage norm for a weak family norm. While it is true that couples often do not marry until after one or two children are born and a significant proportion of couples never marry (Duvander 1999), the nuclear family remains strong and obligatory joint custody is the legal instrument that keeps in place the idea of a nuclear family after divorce.

Reimaging fatherhood

The remaking of men's identities as participatory fathers was not primarily a grass-roots movement, as it was in many countries where men's consciousness-raising groups questioned macho images and styles of masculinities. Instead, in Sweden, the movement was orchestrated from above in government campaign literature and picked up by the media in the 1970s, featuring images of the soft, nurturing father (known as the "velour pappa"). The image of the velour papa was imprinted in Swedish culture in a series of posters of men with children: the most famous is one of a well-known Swedish weight lifter, Hoa-Hoa Dahlgren, holding a small infant in his arms (see visual). He is wearing a blue pullover with yellow crowns all over it, the colors of the Swedish flag and the symbol of the Swedish realm. The message was twofold: (1) fatherhood was masculine not feminine; the image of the weightlifter was used in order to reach working-class men, who were assumed to be the least likely to respond to the image of the nurturing and soft papa. (2) Participatory fatherhood was Swedish; to care for one's children was an important contribution to

society, and the practice of the good citizen. For immigrants who arrived in the 1960s, mainly from Turkey and the former Yugoslavia, acceptance in the new society meant adopting fathering practices that were more egalitarian and softer than in their own countries. Interestingly, the Swedish law that forbids parents to spank their children was also passed during the same period.

Throughout the 1980s, there was a growing awareness that gender-neutral policies did not lead to equal participation in family and work life as the experts had imagined (Haas 1992; Näsman 1995). Researchers from around the world who came to Sweden to study the dual-earner family model, concluded that, while women had changed, men had not. However, the statistical evidence that showed fathers were not taking a larger share of care work in the family did not in itself trigger a response, but rather the impetus for the revived campaigns to promote active fathering came about as a result of policy actors: men in the public policy arena, who became authorities on fatherhood and authors of proactive policies to provide incentives for men to become fathers. The proposal for a reserved daddy month came on the agenda again, but this time men were the key actors.

The daddy month

The passage of the daddy month was no surprise to Swedes who had heard the message of the importance of father–child contact for two decades, both from experts on commissions as well as from journalists who published articles by fathers who confessed that they had been too busy for fathering and by sons who missed their fathers. The only question raised in the daddy month debates was whether the month would be in addition to the existing twelve-month parental leave, a thirteenth month, or be a part of it, a reserved month of the existing twelve. The legislation came in 1994 during a period of economic crises in the Swedish welfare state, so the question of an extra month was not an option, particularly since the conservative parties were in control of the parliament, and the prime minister was a fiscal conservative. As was true of the law forbidding gender discrimination in the workplace passed in 1980, the Liberal Party initiated the mandated daddy month. The main advocate of the daddy month was the Minister of Social Affairs, the Liberal Party leader, Bengt Westerberg, who himself had been a father on parental leave with his children. Ironically, the passage of the daddy month was passed as a result of a deal made with the Christian Democratic Party (also in the ruling coalition) who wanted to fulfill a campaign promise for a care allowance for mothers. Clearly these were measures that worked across purposes since the care allowance was not a wage replacement benefit like parental leave; which meant that fathers would have to invest more time in paid work in order to be able to support mothers who chose to be full-time carers. Claiming that the care allowance would threaten the gender equality goals of their party, Social Democratic women placed the repeal of the care allowance on the top of the agenda, and it was one of the first pieces of legislation when the Social Democrats returned to power the following year. The daddy month, on the other hand, aroused no opposition.

The daddy month once again put Sweden in the forefront of gender-equality policies. Though the policy was couched in gender-neutral terms, it was understood that it was a policy for fathers. Two months of the leave would be set aside for each parent at the highest benefit rate (now at 80 percent of one's salary) and the rest could be divided according to the preferences of individual family members. In the public debate the law has not been characterized as intervention into the private lives of families or as compulsory fatherhood. In Sweden, proactive fathering has been presented as enabling fathers to bargain with employers and their wives.

Fatherhood and fathering: a consensus movement

Fatherhood has been a consensus social movement in Sweden supported by women's groups within parties and a male minister of social affairs as well as men's consciousness-raising groups and feminist organizations. Whereas the original debate on the absent father in the 1960s and 1970s focused on delinquency and the lack of a father figure, the main thrust in the discourse on fathering in the 1990s (DS 1993, 1995) was that men were prevented from taking up their rights as fathers because of structural constraints, family dynamics and age-old patterns that prejudiced society against men as caregivers. The blameworthy were recalcitrant employers, wives who refused to share the parental leave, and society in general (DS 1995: 38).

Most prominent in this discussion has been an advisory group mandated by the government in 1993 to study fatherhood "Arbetsgruppen om papporna, barn, och arbetslivet (Working group on fathers, children, and working life)" to investigate the question of why men have not taken up more of the parental leave. Interestingly, the men appointed to the government group were not experts on gender roles, nor psychologists or sociologists who had done research on men and masculinities. They were professional men who were fathers: a TV program director, a vice-president of a Swedish company, a consultant and writer, a secretary of the Culture Department, and one local and national politician. They were all committed to fathering and to reimaging masculinities (DS 1993).

Though members of the papa group admitted that structural reasons (attitudes of employers and co-workers) were the main reasons why men did not take up their rights to parental leave, they also pointed out that men felt disempowered in the family. They faced hidden discrimination by mothers who patronized them or derided their competence as fathers. They argued that men needed to take their share of leave in the first year of childrearing in order to gain experience as fathers, to have total responsibility on a daily basis with care – for the diapers and feeding – which is not only a period of bonding, but also a time when gender roles in the family are often formed.

The idea of men's rights for custody and care is implicit in the papa group's stand on joint custody. They were the strongest advocates in government studies arguing that joint custody should be a basic principle in law and policy that should be followed whether parents have lived together or not and whether the mother refuses to recognize the biological father's rights to custody or not (Promemoria 1998: 06.05). Still the papa group differs from other men's rights groups in that they do not perceive of fatherhood as a power issue between men and women or between divorced men and policy-making bodies favoring women (see Gavanas; Municio-Larsson and Pujol Algans in this volume).[6] They are actors in a context of consensus, mandated by government support, and employing a discourse of the best interests for the child, parents and society.

New campaigns emerged after the passage of the daddy month, and the government offered large sums of money to governmental and non-governmental agencies that developed educational programs. The main beneficiary was the National Board of Insurance, who produced packets of materials for every worker taking as its slogan "Papa Come Home"

Me and my boss
(when I was going to take daddy leave)

from a song by Evert Taube, a famous Swedish twentieth-century trouba-
dour. A special packet was sent to employers. A change in the message
reflects the fathers who are being targeted and the images of recalcitrant masculinities. The tough weightlifter who was meant to appeal to
working-class images of masculinity has been replaced by the image of a
man in business suit set on a career track (see visual).

The information packets that were sent emphasized that men did not have to take the leave during the first year of the baby's birth (an issue that the papa group felt strongly about, as it is central for bonding and for understanding the daily demands in caring for babies). They underlined the fact that the days were flexible, the leave did not need to be used consecutively and men could take the leave up until the child was eight years old.

The soft sell on the daddy month seemed to work against the rationales underpinning the original framers of the reform and discourse on fathering that led to its passage. For feminist groups, the impetus for a daddy month was altering gender relations in the family. For the papa group, the daddy month was a means of reconstructing masculinities and father identities. Making men into active fathers and equal parents was the standpoint of the architect of the law, Bengt Westerberg, head of the Liberal Party.

The image of the father as caregiver became an icon in Swedish society, promoted by policies such as the daddy month. There have been active recruitment policies to attract more men to work in day-care centers. Finally, new laws on obligatory custody (that courts can impose joint custody) are strategies to extend the project on making men into fathers after divorce or separation.

Policies and father practices in the 1990s

How much did the policies and discourse on fatherhood and fathering alter the practices of fathers? To ask this question is to confront the standard chicken-and-egg problem in social policy: what comes first, the policy or the change in behaviors? The question also spawns others, such as how do we measure the success of a policy change and over what period of time? To analyze this relationship is to unpack the complex sets of relations in the institutional triangle of state, market and family and the domestic triangle of mother, father and children.

Being a father has become a crucial part of men's identity in Sweden. A survey in 1991 replicating a study in the 1960s showed that men increasingly had become family oriented (cited in Björnberg 1998). When asked: what lies closest to your self-identity? over 50 percent of the male respondents in the 1990s answered family life, 32 percent said work and family, and only 9 percent responded labor market work (Björnberg 1998). However, the gap between the ideological layering of fathering and the practices of fathers underscores the fragmentation in the institutional triangle: state policies to promote fathering confront market realities that place men, who exercise their rights as fathers, at risk, and family negotiations around paid and unpaid work interface with a highly gendered labor market and wage structure.

Moreover, these attitudinal changes are not reflected in the actual division of household work. Among the architects of the dual-earner model, there was an expectation that men's and women's roles would converge as more and more women entered the labor market. Policies were purportedly enabling for men and women to be equal participants in the spheres of market, work and family. Time studies of households provide the hard facts that reveal the *naïveté* behind these assumptions. According to the figures on division of paid and unpaid work, women and men work about the same number of hours per week: 60 versus 61 hours. But women spend more time in unpaid housework, 33 hours, as opposed to 27 in paid work (Flood and Gråsjö 2001). Swedish men tend to devote more time to household work than men in other Western welfare states and it has been increasing since the 1980s. If we consider time spent with young children, time budget studies show that men with small children are devoting more hours to fathering; in 1993 the average time spent was 9 hours and 5 minutes, an increase of 4.5 hours per week from the previous decade (Flood and Gråsjö 1997 and 2001). Despite these figures on the increasing number of hours fathers spend caring for their children, there is little evidence of a shift in the practices of fathering that corresponds to a shift in attitudes toward a stronger commitment to family over employment. For example, one study found that, whereas 87 percent of mothers said that they had restricted job involvement after they had a family, only 62 percent of fathers claimed to have done the same (Björnberg 1998). These differences are most evident in how much men make use of their rights to care.

Parental leave

Men's use of parental leave has steadily increased, particularly in the number of men who take advantage of their rights as parents. From the early 1980s, this rose from less than 20 percent to over 50 percent after the passage of the daddy month. However, these dramatic figures are misleading, since the proportion of days fathers use remains low and has not changed much, despite the passage of the daddy month. In 1987, fathers' average share of the parental leave was slightly over 6 percent; in 1997, three years after the daddy month policy was in place, there was only a slight increase in this figure (9.9 percent of the 360 days). The 50 percent figure highlighted in all the press releases of the National Insurance Board to affirm the success of the reserved leave for fathers is calculated over a four-year period (Sundström and Duvander 2001). If one looks on a yearly basis, about 30 percent of fathers are on leave, and there has been very little change from the early to late mid 1990s (Figure 6).

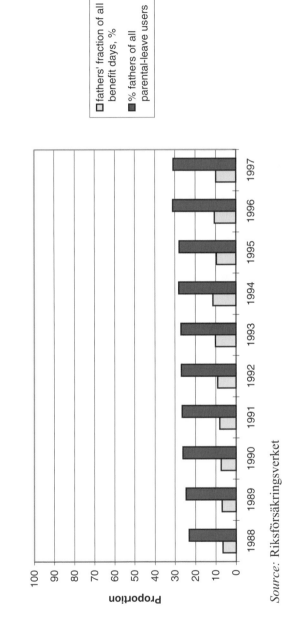

Legend:
☐ fathers' fraction of all benefit days, %
■ % fathers of all parental-leave users

Source: Riksförsäkringsverket

Figure 6 Proportion of fathers who took parental leave. Proportion of days taken by fathers, 1987–1997.

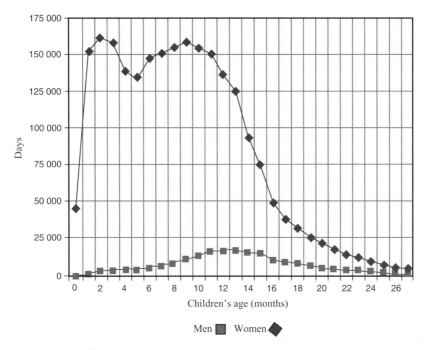

Source: Riksförsäkringsverket

Figure 7 Men's and women's use of parental leave by child's age.

As Figure 7 suggests, fathers tend to spread out their proportion of the leave over a period of time. The flexibility of parental leave enables parents to use the time any way they choose up to the child's eighth birthday. So, half days, long weekends or longer vacations can be taken. Statistics on when men use the parental leave (Figure 8) suggest it is concentrated in the summer months, which could be an extension of a summer vacation with the mother – an outcome that undercuts the ideological component in the policy to enhance men's role as caretakers of children, to empower men as fathers with competence (DS 1993).

The division of the parental leave suggests that men are still expected to be the main breadwinners and that interruptions in male careers are perceived as most costly (Albrecht et al. 1999). A study of parental leave in three municipalities in Sweden found that 80 percent of parents claimed that the division of the parental leave was driven by economic concerns. Families in which there were great differences in the mother's and father's incomes, the higher earner (nearly always the father) took less leave, as the income replacement is at 80 percent of one's

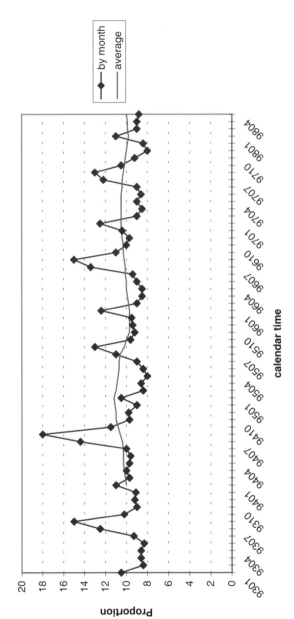

Source: Riksförsäkringsverket

Figure 8 Fathers' proportion of parental leave days during the calendar year, from 1993 to 1998.

income and there is an income ceiling of 22,000 per month (approximately 2,200 dollars). Female students took more leave than male students, suggesting that women were assumed to be the ones to put a brake on their careers. However, there were other gendered outcomes that could not be explained by a pure cost analysis of lost earnings. For example, unemployed men tended to take less leave (see Riksförsäkringsverket 2000). Education is the predictor for parental leave use rather than market earnings (Sundström and Duvander 2001).

From a comprehensive study of parental leave published in 1993 (*Vilka Pappor Kom Hem* 1993) we can construct a composite of a father who would be most likely to take the highest proportion of leave (Riksförsäkringsverket 1993). He would have a fairly high education, beyond secondary school, and he would work in the public sector. This is most likely his first child. Most interestingly, he is not necessarily a native Swede. In the study, fathers from Iran have the highest average use of parental leave days (80), while Swedish fathers have the lowest average number of days compared to other nationalities (48.9). However, if we take those fathers who took any parent leave, Swedish fathers score highest (48 percent). Active and participating fatherhood has become hegemonic in Sweden, but labor market options and opportunities determine how much leave men take. Iranian men, who have a weak position in the labor market, can afford to take advantage of their rights to parental leave. Swedish men, at the high end of the earning scale, are more likely to use the parental leave than men with less education and income, despite the fact that they have the greatest to lose in economic resources, since there is an income ceiling of 80 percent of one's salary. The resistance to parental leave is among highly paid men in the private sector. Despite the fact that two of Sweden's large corporations, Ericsson and the Wallenberg Group, offer to subsidize fathers who take leave, with 80 percent of their regular monthly salary above the ceiling, the take-up rate remains low.

Divorced fatherhood: divorced fathers

The current debates around joint custody take a proactive stance toward fathers' rights to fatherhood. The most recent commission of joint custody puts forward a new principle in the Parental Code, the notion of automatic custody (Promemoria 1998: 59). All fathers will be given joint custody at the birth of a child unless the mother brings the case to court within three months, and, even then, the court has the prerogative to grant the father joint custody against the will of the mother. Fathers who have had no contact with the mother after the child was conceived can claim their rights to fatherhood. Even in situations where a father has lost contact with his child and the mother has remarried, the biological father who has automatically been given custody can return and demand his rights to shared custody of his child. Thus, this change in the law reaffirms the primacy of biological fatherhood and the status of the biological father in the family. Conversely it delegitimizes social/household fathers, men who live with, support and care for children who are not their own.

Obligatory joint custody most likely will empower fathers against the general practice of social workers and other mediators in contested divorce cases who have tended to recommend sole custody to the mother. There are very few studies of preferences of parents in divorce cases, but we do know the outcomes of contested custody cases, which provide some evidence that the mother has tended to be advantaged in these cases (Richardson 1997), even though the Parental Code explicitly states that it is gender-neutral, that neither of the parents is considered to be more suitable to exercise custody on the basis of gender only.

Care

In the 1990s biological fathers have gained more rights with the widening powers of the state to enforce joint custody and the hegemonic ideology that children need equal access to both parents even after divorce. But does this mean that more divorced fathers are co-parenting? Sweden has some of the highest proportions of couples in the world that hold joint custody. But what does that mean in practice? Who is the care provider? What are the obligations of the non-residential parent? We know that there are very few sole-parent custodial fathers, less than 3 percent of the sole-parent families (who were 16 percent of all families in 1991). There are no reliable statistics about the time divorced fathers who have joint custody spend with their children. Since all children must be registered at one address, even if they live with both parents, we have no idea how the parents share daily care or divide the time between them. The common pattern has been that children in joint custody spend every other weekend with their fathers and some portion of holidays, which is mirrored in the decisions of the lower courts in the two contested cases described earlier. Some surveys suggest that there are fewer fathers who have no contact with their children after divorce (Jalmert 1994; Jalmert and Olsson 1997). Furthermore, there is some evidence that some divorced fathers are becoming more active; fathers who are remarried or living with another partner take a much larger share of the parental leave than fathers who are married to their children's biological mother. Particularly fathers who are remarried take on average 197 days, over four times that of men who are living with their children's mother (see figure p. 6 in *Vilka Pappor Kom Hem* 1993).

Has the expansion of men's rights in fathering after divorce as reflected in obligatory joint custody and automatic custody been followed by demands that fathers take a larger share of the economic responsibilities for child support?

Cash

Since the 1960s, fatherhood in Swedish policy discourse and practice has become more and more linked to care and not cash, despite the periodic reports and commissions warning of the rising costs of support for solo parents. In fact, throughout the 1980s the policy formulas and calculations about the father's ability to pay revealed the tendency of the state to pick up more and more of the financial slack in the economic support of children who were no longer living with both parents. For example, in 1994 among persons registered in the state system, 35 percent of them were unable to pay anything at all. The average support payment was assessed to be 366 SEK per child (about 46 dollars in 1994). Only 22 percent of child support allowances were set at 900 SEK or more per month (112 dollars in 1994) (Jalmert 1994; Jalmert and Olsson 1997).

Having contact with the biological father was considered so central for a child's well-being that it overrode all other rationales for changing the current system of child support. The basic principle in all policy discussions was that fathers should not be socially excluded from families because of high child support payments (SOU 1977: 37). This principle has shaded out all other pleas for equality across classes, which was a powerful argument in other debates that governed Swedish policy and held sway in policy discourse. For example, in various commissions and government studies in the 1980s, it was argued that the current system was biased against working-class men whose wives had a lower income, since they had to pay more in income support than middle-class men who made less income than their wives. One commission study recommended either means-testing or equal contributions regardless of relative income (Winkler 2001). These proposals were all rejected since they might result in less father contact with children. If fathers had to pay more, they might have to work more hours. Moreover, they might resent children in former marriages who took resources away from their resident children (SOU 1983: 14).

In the 1990s, the question of economic support in divorce once again became a primary concern in public debate. Two government studies, back to back, considered the question of who held the responsibility for covering the costs for children in divorce. The debates in the 1990s did not challenge the 1977 reforms of the Commission on Marriage and Family; that choice of family forms was not a concern for the state, and joint custody was the preferred solution in divorce. Rather, the issue was how to reduce the state's costs and cut back expenditures.

In the first Commission study on income maintenance and alimony (SOU 1995: 26), a recommendation was made that the income of a partner living with the custodial parent (almost always the mother) should be included in evaluating the costs assessed to the non-custodial parent (almost always the biological father). In practice, support for children in divorce was not seen as a duty, or a reflection of equal parental responsibility, but rather a question of household incomes. This has always been the working assumption in the implementation of income maintenance, since the calculation of benefits took into account the father's new families and his costs for a household and a new partner. However, a storm of protest arose over the Commission's recommendation that new partners should be paying for the costs of children from other biological parents. LO, the blue-collar union, and TCO, the white-collar union, saw the new proposal as a rejection of the principle that a child has two parents. Women's organizations across the political spectrum opposed the proposal. The Social Democratic Women's Association and the Liberal Women's Association denounced the proposal in their official responses since it denied a basic part of Swedish family policy: that we have children for life and that new spouses and partners should not have responsibility for someone else's child (SOU 1995: 26: 6).

Deeply imprinted in Swedish law and norms was the belief that a biological father was *the father* of a child, and therefore responsible for his or her support. That principle had powerful play in the Swedish debate – more than the question of the constraints against women repartnering (an argument that could have been made), and more than a belief that cash payments make the father feel more responsible and involved with his child (which was not put forward either).

Immediately after the Commission published its report, it was replaced by a new Committee under the auspices of the Ministry of Social Affairs, headed by a powerful Social Democratic woman, who herself had been a solo mother. The policy formula that was brought forward from this Commission represented a total reversal from the former. The new law stated (1) that all parents had to pay regardless if one parent did not need the money, and (2) that, while new families would be taken into consideration, the father's living costs would not be an excuse for not paying.[7] The essence of the reform is to increase the share of child support paid by the non-resident partner, most often the father and the earner with the higher income (DS 1996: 2).

Has the reform, which has been in effect since 1997, achieved its goals – to increase the proportion the non-residential parents pay for child support? Before attempting to assess the effects, a caveat is in order. As we discussed earlier, we can only look at those families who are registered with the social insurance board, in which the residential parent has applied for income maintenance or support from the state. A recent study estimates about 45 percent of children are registered in the system. All other agreements are private agreements.

Another consideration is that assessment of cost is not necessarily the amount paid. Since the reform, we can see that the proportion that the non-residential parents (most often fathers) are expected to pay back to the state's advanced maintenance scheme, has increased, on average from 35 percent to 43 percent. But, in fact, the proportion of what the state managed to recover from the non-residential parent has remained fairly stable around 80 percent. The state's share of costs for child support has hovered around 30 to 35 percent, with the exception of 1995, a year of high unemployment (Riksförsäkringsverket 1998). The figures suggest that rather than changes in the law, it is the economic situation of fathers that has had the greatest impact on how much of the advanced payment is collected.

Finally, one unintended consequence of the reform is that it has created intense conflicts between couples with shared residential custody (referred to as split living in policy discourse) around the division of the cash benefit for child support. The new system brings to the fore all the dilemmas in joint custody since it is totally based on earnings and disregards care.

In the past, if the children spent half of the time with each parent, the higher earner, most often the father, did not have to contribute to the state benefit, which was most often given to the mother. The parent who could receive the benefit lived at the address where the children were registered (most often the mother). Even though the father was supposedly taking the children 50 percent of the time and was covering costs for their clothing and activities, he was not entitled to the benefit. Instead he was expected to negotiate with his ex-wife/partner to recover the costs that he believed should be shared. When residential fathers were required to pay part of the benefit during the time children stayed with the mother (Proposition 1998/99: 78), they began demanding part of the state benefit, an acknowledgement of their fathering. In 1999

(DS 1999: 30), there were several proposals that were framed in terms of gender inequality in the law, against residential fathers. The new proposal, which recently became law (SFS 2000: 1397) allows both parents to receive up to 50 percent of the benefit, which can reach up to 1,153 SEK a month per child (about 100 dollars). This is both a recognition of the weaknesses in the assumption of consensuality within the joint custody norm, and, more importantly, an attempt to reconcile cash and care. There is also a proposal being discussed to divide the child allowance, which currently is paid to the mother and has been since the 1940s.

Conclusion

At the beginning of the twenty-first century we see a disjunction between policy goals and the realities of labor markets and family economy. The valorization of fatherhood and the incentives to fathering have emerged in a period of high unemployment and tenuous economic circumstances for many families. The daddy month was a proactive policy to seduce more men into being primary caretakers. But, during the period the reform was enacted, there was a drop in benefit levels (from 90 percent in the 1980s down to 80 percent), and a ceiling on the replacement levels.

Obligatory joint custody became even stronger in the 1990s (and recent changes in the law made it even harder to deviate from this standard). However, the Swedish legal framing of fatherhood rooted in the principle that children shall have access to both parents is counterpoised by other cuts in public spending that place greater pressure on divorced fathers to earn more income, particularly those who are supporting two families. The benefit for children's travel between parental homes, once covered by the state, is now to be shared by the parents.

Returning to our original question of whether Sweden is men-friendly, we have provided the contextuality to assess its import. In Sweden, men-friendly has come to mean father-friendly, which follows the same lines and the normative assumptions that underlie the notion of a women-friendly state: the ability to combine labor market work and caring responsibilities in a dual-earner family model. Swedish policy and discourse has shaped men's identities and interests around participatory fatherhood and gender equality. However, all men do not embrace this hegemonic masculinity; it may be perceived as men-unfriendly by immigrant fathers from countries that retain laws supporting patriarchal rights. Men-friendly in the Swedish context implies a father-friendly state in a dual-earner family model, which presupposes gender equality.

Given this construction of fatherhood, we can say that Sweden is men-friendly in the following ways: men's rights to care are recognized in law and policy, which is most visible in proactive policies toward fathering, such as the daddy month; men can make a stronger case to take some of the leave since, if they do not, it is a benefit lost. Moreover, the discursive and ideological support for active and engaged fathering can also be seen as a resource for men who confront employers and workmates with their claims to care for children: these include parental leave, child sick days and school conferences.

An important consideration for evaluating whether divorced fathers are favored in the Swedish context is that we are talking about biological fatherhood. Household fathers are in a weak position legally and socially to try to influence the lives of the children in their household whom they often provide with economic support. The law and policy discourse recognize the biological father. In fact, household fathers are invisible in debates about children after divorce. True, they are not formally responsible for supporting children fathered by someone else, but in practice fathers in reconstituted families are supporting the children under their roof.

From the perspective of divorced and never-married fathers, Sweden is perhaps one of the most men-friendly societies. Both obligatory joint custody and automatic custody are instruments that tip the balance in the direction of the biological father. Since mothers tend to be favored in cases where joint custody is contested, this turn in the law toward compulsory fatherhood has strengthened men's position in divorce. The law itself and the social insurance bureaucracy who administer it have placed little pressure on fathers to support children economically after divorce. This is partly because women are assumed to be earners in their own right, but also because of the hegemonic ideology concerning the best interests of the child: contact with the father after divorce has been the guiding principle in policy over the last two decades. Though there has been some attempt to force men to pay a greater share, the state is still picking up the tab (around 70 percent of the costs for child support) and providing other social benefits for divorced mothers, such as housing allowances and social assistance (Hobson and Takahashi 1997). Men face few economic constraints against repartnering (see Oláh, Bernhardt and Goldscheider in this volume). Compulsory fatherhood in the Swedish context implies the obligation to care rather than the obligation to be the mainstay of economic support.

If we phrase the question another way, and ask whether the policy response to fatherhood and fathering has been transformative for gender relations within the family, then the issues appear more ambiguous.

Sweden has been cast as a parent–citizen or parent–worker model in comparative research on gender and welfare states (Hobson 1994; Hobson and Takahashi 1997; Siim 2000). Within this framework, both men and women are expected to be active labor market participants and active parents; nearly all policies are gender-neutral. But what does this imply for gendered subjects, in this discussion of men? Men who wish to succeed in careers cannot share equal parenting. In fact, studies show that men who take advantage of their rights as parents are penalized more in their careers than women (Albrecht et al. 1999). Making men into fathers has meant celebrating participatory fathering, while at the same time not disturbing the division of labor within the family or the gendered inequalities in the labor market.

4   The problem of fathers: policy and behavior in Britain

Jane Lewis

Fathers entered the policy agenda in Britain, as elsewhere, at the end of the 1980s. Superficially, the debates in many Northern European countries and in the United States look somewhat similar, revolving mainly around the responsibilities of fathers to maintain and to care for their children. However, there have been real differences in what has driven the policy debate in the different countries and in the nature of the policy response.

In respect of the policy debate, the balance between concern about fathers' roles as providers and as carers has been different in the different countries. In Scandinavia, where the dual-earner model is firmly established and where adult citizenship is tied to participation in the labor market, the focus has been more upon the care provided by fathers, and has been part of the debate about achieving greater equality in the division of unpaid as well as of paid work. In Britain, which has historically adhered to a strong male breadwinner model in terms of its social policies, more emphasis has been put on the obligation of fathers to maintain. Care has been secondary in the debate, although there has been considerable concern about the effects of father-absence on children (whether as a result of divorce or unmarried motherhood), which has filtered through from the American as well as the British psychology literature. As will be argued in the last section of this chapter, policies affecting fathers have been concerned mainly about their role as breadwinners and about their role as carers only insofar as it can help secure their obligation to maintain. With the rapid increase in lone-parent families during the 1980s (from 7.5 percent of all families with dependent children in 1979 to 23 percent in 1998) and the concomitant rise in the cost of supporting (mainly) lone mothers and children to the state, British governments of the late 1980s and early 1990s sought to shift the responsibility for supporting their biological children to individual fathers. This attempt to shift the balance within the family, market and state triangle also entailed changes in the meaning of fathering, although not in fatherhood. Indeed, the legislation encouraged the perpetuation of an essential link in the minds of fathers between cash support and care. There has been little recognition given to the need to develop the caring role of fathers independently of mothers and independent of the provider role.

On the whole, the British state has always adopted a hands-off stance toward the organization of work between men and women in the family, which contrasts greatly with many continental European countries. The tendency has been to draw a firm line between the private and public spheres, with the result that there has been little positive legislation forthcoming in Britain to enable either men or women to "reconcile" paid and unpaid work. One of the main hallmarks of the British debate over fathers compared to its European neighbors is its negative character. Fathers' commitment to their families has been seen as increasingly fragile and the concern is about their failure to maintain and their failure to provide good role models for their children. Indeed, the discourse around fathers in Britain (as with that around lone mothers) has many similarities to that in the US (see Orloff and Monson in this volume). However, it is notable that the trends in policy are not so different from some other European countries, especially the Netherlands (see Knijn and Selten in this volume), where the discourse is much more positive.

The nature of the policy response to the debate about the role of fathers has also been affected in the different countries by the previous shape of legislation. For example, as Meulders-Klein (1990) has pointed out, the UK has been distinctive in historically denying the unmarried father any rights in respect of his child. Under the early nineteenth-century Poor Law, unmarried mothers were forbidden from seeking maintenance from the fathers of their children. The fear was that if mothers could get money for their children this would only encourage both immoral behavior and the naming of rich men as putative fathers. On the other hand, until relatively recently married fathers had full parental authority over their children. A famous legal judgment of 1883 awarded the father the right to bring up his child as a Protestant and to deny access to the mother because to do otherwise would "be really to set aside the whole course and order of nature . . . and . . . disturb the very foundation of family life" (cited by Collier 1995: 187). Equal guardianship rights were not secured by mothers over their children until 1973, even though the child welfare principle was interpreted in terms of the importance of the mother/child bond from the 1920s. All European countries have historically given patriarchal authority to the father, but the form that this has taken and the speed and degree to which it has been modified has varied. As the other authors in this book show, the reconceptualization of masculinity has differed substantially in different countries.

The role of fathers was conceptualized in terms of financial provision, and it was marriage that activated the male breadwinner for policy-making purposes. As lone mothers became much more numerous in the late twentieth century and the role of father could no longer be automatically linked to that of husband, then policy began to address the issue of fathers' responsibilities explicitly. Marriage law could no longer be relied on to secure parental responsibility. The practices of fatherhood were thus linked to marriage and to the role of provider, which has made it difficult to develop a set of independent fatherhood practices centered as much on care as on cash.

Variation in the nature of family change during the past two decades has also influenced the policy response in different countries. Britain has the highest divorce rate in Europe and has had one of the fastest growth rates in unmarried motherhood over the past decade. Together these have served to fuel the prevailing climate of fear about fathers' commitment to their families and legislation that tends to be punitive rather than enabling. As this chapter shows, we know little about changes in the behavior of fathers, but what evidence we have suggests that trends toward both more caring and more distant fathering may coexist. The central issue would seem to be the issue of care and unequal division of unpaid work, but, as this chapter argues, this has not been a priority for policy makers.

Fathers as a focus for policy

The focus on fathers from the end of the 1980s was new in comparison with the rest of the post-war period, but in fact it repeated some much older concerns familiar to commentators at the beginning of the century. In 1906, Helen Bosanquet, a leading member of the Charity Organization Society and influential spokeswoman on social action, clearly described the characteristics of the stable family. It required the firm authority of the father and the cooperative industry of all its members, the wife working at home and husband wage-earning. She made the connection between the stable family and the national importance of maintaining male work incentives particularly forcefully:

Nothing but the combined rights and responsibilities of family life will ever rouse the average man to his full degree of efficiency and induce him to continue working after he has earned sufficient to meet his own personal needs . . . The Family, in short, is from this point of view, the only known way of ensuring with any approach to success that one generation will exert itself in the interests and for the sake of another. (Bosanquet 1906: 222)

Thus Bosanquet tied together the importance of the male breadwinner model family for both the welfare of the individual family members and for the wider nation.

Bosanquet believed that such a family sheltered young and old in one strong bond of mutual helpfulness (making old-age pensions, then under discussion, superfluous) and rendered the development of a political residuum (an underclass) impossible, by training its young in the habits of labor and obedience. She made the point that families at both ends of the social scale failed to conform to this model of family life. However, much more concern was generally expressed about the working-class family, and as much or more about the working-class father as the working-class mother. Bosanquet was not alone in suspecting working-class fathers above all of unwillingness to shoulder their economic responsibilities. Other Edwardian investigators firmly believed that married women's employment merely provided their husbands with the opportunity to be idle. The economist, F. Y. Edgeworth (1922: 453) quoted approvingly the comment that a social worker made in 1908 to the effect that "if the husband got out of work, the only thing the wife should do is sit down and cry, because if she did anything else he would remain out of work." Only the advent of mass unemployment in the inter-war years modified this view somewhat. The value of family life as a means of making men "useful" members of society re-emerged in the late twentieth century.

In the wake of World War II there was much greater sympathy with the father than previously. Several commentators felt actively uneasy about the father's position, believing that the changes in the legal status of women – for example, toward a more equal divorce law and guardianship rights over children and in respect of the suffrage – posed a threat to the father's authority. Bertrand Russell, who took a consistently radical line throughout the early part of the century in demanding marriage and divorce law reform, also deplored the decline in power of the father. He felt that the paternalist state and the caring professions were removing his *raison d'être* by providing his children with free school meals and medical attention and usurping his authority via the school and the juvenile court (Russell 1929).

After World War II, the cooperation of fathers tended to be assumed. The work habits of working-class men, who had proved themselves in battle, were no longer regarded with such suspicion, and experts focused their attention firmly on mother and child, whether in terms of the studies of maternal deprivation or of maternal "adequacy." The literature of the 1940s and 50s gave little space to the role of the father. In a 1944 radio talk, entitled "What about Father?," the leading child psychologist, D. W. Winnicott (1957) said that fathers were needed to help the mother feel well in body and happy in mind and to give her moral support especially in matters of discipline. The father's role was of marginal importance when it came to the care of his children. As Mitchell and Goody (1997) have recently noted, the mother/child families that were the focus of the

1940s psychology literature actually came into existence during the 1980s and 1990s. In the case of unmarried fathers, they were constructed in the increasingly dominant "expert" psychoanalytical social work literature of the day in a similar manner to unmarried mothers: as abnormal and as victims. The unmarried mother was described in pathological terms and the unmarried father was the "counterpart of the neurotic personality of the unmarried mother" (Young 1954).

Fathers were largely absent from the policy-making and academic discourse until the late 1980s. Lone mothers became the center of attention during the early 1970s because of the dramatic rise in the divorce rate, and a government committee was appointed to look into the circumstances of one-parent families. However, its focus was very much the lone mother and not the father, the emphasis switching to the way in which all lone mothers, whether divorced or unmarried had "extra needs" and the extent to which these would have to be met by the state (Cmnd. 5629 1974). The Finer Committee did not deny the responsibility of men to maintain. However, it shied away from the degree of effort necessary to determine paternity and trace fathers, believing that the greater confidentiality of personal information in Britain, than in the Scandinavian countries, for example, would make this impossible (Lewis 1998). It was also inclined to respond pragmatically to male behavior, believing that it was impossible to dictate who a man should live with and support in a democratic society. The Committee recognized that public law assumed that a man would support the family he lived with. Private law tried to insist that he support his "first" family, often with conspicuous lack of success. Hence the pragmatic view that the state would have to support lone mothers. In the early 1970s, male responsibility to maintain was recognized, but not problematized.

Fathers re-entered the policy agenda of the late 1980s because they were seen to be increasingly absent and because their failure to maintain was resulting in a large burden on the social security budget. In their review of the literature on fathers and fatherhood, Burghes et al. (1997) commented that fathers had achieved new visibility. Since the beginning of the 1970s in Britain there have been marked changes in marriage patterns, involving older marriage and substantial declines in marriage rates – trends that continue to the present; a dramatic rise in divorce rates that has plateaued from the 1980s; and the emergence of widespread cohabitation. The proportion of never-married women who were cohabiting more than trebled between 1979 and 1993, from 7.5 to 23.5 percent. Additionally, in 1993, 25 percent of divorced women were in cohabiting unions. By 1994, 58 percent of extra-marital births were registered by couples living at the same address, but studies of cohabitants with children have shown them to be at considerably greater risk of breakdown than married couples (Buck and Ermisch 1995). From the late 1970s, the proportion of births outside marriage began to increase slowly at first and then rapidly throughout the 1980s, with signs of stabilization in the early 1990s at about one in three of all births. Between 1970 and 1990 the percentage of lone-mother families more than doubled to 18 percent. The anxiety of the 1980s and 1990s was therefore about the separation of marriage and parenthood, and the main concern regarding men centered on how to tie them into families, enforcing parental responsibility, both for the sake of their children and in order to protect society from their feckless and possibly anti-social behavior.

Many American New Right political commentators of the 1980s both deplored the reliance of lone mothers on the state (most notably, Murray 1985) and stressed the importance of their children having the example of a breadwinner to follow, even if that person happened to be female. The United States was first to introduce workfare programs, which treated lone mothers more as workers than as mothers. However, to the more traditional American Right such a policy merely created more of the problem. Gilder (1987) deplored the idea of more mothers entering the labor market. In his view, the problem was lack of paid work for young men; more women working could only exacerbate the problem. In Britain, as late as 1990, the National Audit Office reiterated the government's official policy of neutrality regarding lone-mothers' employment, although this changed in the mid-1990s, when first the Conservative government and then the new Labour government stated their aim as encouraging more lone mothers into the labor market. However, as strong a desire in the British context at the end of the 1980s was the enforcement of the parental responsibility of fathers to maintain those mothers who otherwise would be a burden on the Exchequer.

Many British polemical commentators on the political right and left have followed the example of Gilder in the United States. Morgan (1995) argued that policies to encourage lone mothers to become breadwinners are "the solution to the wrong problem." As Michael Howard, then Home Secretary, said in a speech to the Conservative Political Center in 1993:

> If the state will house and pay for their children the duty on [young men] to get involved may seem removed from their shoulders...And since the state is educating, housing and feeding their children the nature of parental responsibility may seem less immediate.

This was very similar to both Gilder's (1981) claim that the father "has been cuckolded by the compassionate state" and Helen Bosanquet's fears expressed in 1906. The father's duty to maintain was argued not only on the grounds of the importance of the role model it provided for children, but also in terms of fairness to the taxpayer:

when a family breaks up, the husband's standard of living often rises whereas that of his wife and children falls, even below the poverty line. Taxpayers may then be left to support the first family, while the husband sets about forming another. This is wrong. A Father who can afford to support only one family ought to have only one. (*The Economist* 1995)

Such views stood in stark contrast to the attitudes expressed some twenty years earlier in the Report of the Royal Commission on One-Parent Families (Cmd. 5629 1974), which recognized the difficulty in a liberal democratic society of determining who had the right to procreate and which, in the absence of the capacity to stop further reproduction on the part of men, was bound to support the mothers and children they left behind.

The prime concern of political commentators about men's obligation to maintain was often allied with what might be termed a "masculinist backlash" during the 1990s, which insisted that men have been alienated from society because women and/or the state have stripped them of their role. For writers such as Morgan, but also for those on the political Left, such as Halsey (1993) and Dennis and Erdos (1992), and for politicians (Hansard, Commons, 3/12/93, *c.* 1283) and the media (e.g. BBC "Panorama," 20/9/93) concerns about families with absent fathers ranged more widely than the obligation to maintain. All argued that the successful socialization of children requires the active involvement of two parents. Dennis and Erdos (1992) sought to trace the rise of the "obnoxious Englishman" to family breakdown. Their chief concern was the effect of lone motherhood on the behavior patterns of young men. This was new. Commentary up to this point had not problematized the fathers. Lone motherhood was, in the view of commentators like Dennis and Erdos, responsible for at best irresponsible and at worse criminal behavior in the next male generation. In fact such convictions about the link between absent fathers and rising crime rates have not been tested for any large-scale British sample. Halsey (1993) stated his belief that "the traditional family is the tested arrangement for safeguarding the welfare of children and that only a post-Christian country could believe otherwise." In his view, the greed and individualism engendered during the Thatcher years were largely responsible for the disintegration of the traditional family. Morgan (1995), while not blaming individualism, would like to provide more incentives, for example in the form of tax allowances, to two-parent families.

The assumption behind this literature is that men are instinctively uncivilized and that family responsibility is the only thing that ties them into communal living. Dench (1994: 16–17) has argued strongly that family responsibilities are an indispensable civilizing influence on men:

if women go too far in pressing for symmetry, and in trying to change the rules of the game, men will simply decide not to play...If women now choose to...withdraw the notion that men's family role is important, then they are throwing away their best trick. Feminism, in dismantling patriarchy, is simply reviving the underlying greater natural freedom of men...Many women are now setting great store by the coming of New Man...the current attack on patriarchal conventions is surely promoting almost the exact opposite, namely a plague of feckless yobs, who leave all the real work to women and gravitate toward the margins of society where males naturally hang around unless culture gives them a reason to do otherwise. The family may be a myth, but it is a myth that works to make men tolerably useful.

This kind of view had much in common, in terms of its diagnosis of the problem of male flight, with some feminist analysis. However, it differs profoundly in terms of its favored solution, which seeks to turn the clock back to something approaching the 1950s with clearly segregated roles between men and women within families. The responsibility of being a breadwinner is seen as vital to the wider society, to men's identity as social beings and to the successful socialization of children. The influential journalist Melanie Phillips (1997) has also concluded that it is the erosion of the male role that has created "yobbish men."

The academic literature has also fed similar lines of argument. Social psychologists in the United States supplied the first and most influential evidence of the detrimental effects on children's well-being of lack of contact with their fathers after divorce (Wallerstein and Kelly 1980). British research followed American in providing evidence of the impact of divorce on the educational achievement, employment and personal relationships of children and young adults, but the precise nature of the impact of father-presence as opposed to absence has proved difficult to measure (e.g. Lewis 1996), and it has also been difficult to unravel the effects of conflict before and during the divorce process from the effects of loss of contact with fathers. What is noteworthy is that, even though the evidence regarding the effects of children's contact with fathers was mixed when Wallerstein and Kelly published their influential research in the United States, the other side of the argument made no impact (Piper 1993). Rather the policy debate seemed disposed to overturn the long-held stress on the importance of the mother/child dyad as fundamental to the child welfare principle (reiterated as late as 1980 by Goldstein, Freud and Solnit) in favor of bringing fathers back in. The attention to the psychological problems arising from "broken homes" does, of course, stretch back considerably further. Police court magistrates raised the issue in the 1930s (Cairns 1934) and in the 1950s (Mullins 1954), although in the post-war period (in keeping with the focus on the mother/child dyad) the problem was more likely to be conceptualized in terms of "latch-key children."[1]

The political concern was focused firmly on what American feminist Barbara Ehrenreich (1983) had termed the "flight from commitment." Sociologists have argued that there has been a substantial change in values in respect of personal relationships in the twentieth century. Giddens (1992) has suggested that we have seen the emergence of the "pure relationship," a social relationship entered into for its own sake and for what can be derived by each person from it in terms of material, but more usually emotional, exchange. Love has thus become contingent, rather than "forever." Beck and Beck-Gernscheim (1995) have also pointed out that it is no longer possible to say what family, marriage, parenthood, sexuality and love mean. All vary in substance, from individual to individual and from relationship to relationship. The collective norm seems to be that there is no norm. What has emerged from these studies is a picture of ever-increasing individualization.

Indeed, many sociologists have noted a growing decomplementarity between men and women (for a review, see Burns and Scott 1994). The basic premise of this theory of behavior is that men and/or women have adapted rationally to a changing economic climate affecting work and welfare, and have become more independent of each other. In Fukuyama's (1997) analysis, the individualization of women, achieved through increasing economic independence and control over fertility, has had the effect of making men irresponsible. This analysis is not dissimilar to that of Dench: men are identified as a problem, but it is the increasing independence/individualization of women that is identified as the root cause. The idea of female economic independence can easily be overemphasized. De Singly (1996) is surely right to see this as more the case for men than for women given the unequal gendered division of paid and unpaid work. But the merits and demerits of ideas about increasing independence and individualization are not so much the issue as the fact that the fear of these trends has influenced policy makers. This became crystal clear in the parliamentary debates over the 1996 Family Law Act, during the course of which many members of parliament sought to make the legislation more of a vehicle for saving marriage. In the House of Lords, Baroness Young said that: "for one party simply to decide to go off with another person . . . reflects the growing self-first disease which is debasing our society" (Hansard, Lords, 29/2/96, c. 1638). Policy makers during the 1990s have clearly expressed their fear of increasing individualization which they have automatically assumed to be selfish and to be the natural antithesis of interdependence (Smart 1995a). In the words of an influential American polemicist: "People have become less willing to invest time, money and energy in family life, turning instead to investment in themselves" (Popenoe 1993: 528). Given that 90 percent of lone-parent families are headed by women, this concern has focused increasingly on men. Legal commentators, feminist and non-feminist, and economists have blamed no-fault divorce (partially introduced in Britain in 1969) for an increase in opportunistic behavior on the part of men, because of the way in which it permits easier exit from a marriage (Weitzman 1985; Cohen 1987).

Fathers' behavior

But what do we know about the behavior of fathers? In 1974 a new pressure group was formed in Britain called Families Need Fathers, formed to campaign for greater access by men to their children on divorce. How far the motives of these men had to do with any genuine desire to undertake the day-to-day care for their children has been subjected to sharp questioning (see below), but there is considerable evidence in Britain as in the United States to suggest that there are two populations of fathers, one seeking more contact with family life and one becoming more distant (Moss 1995). As Furstenberg (1988) has added, men may actually move between these two modes within their own life cycle.

Increasing female economic independence has proved the most popular explanatory variable for the increase in lone motherhood (Oppenheimer 1994), however, the changing fortunes of men are also significant. William Julius Wilson (1987) was among the first to suggest that more attention should be paid to the deteriorating economic position of black men in the United States. In Britain, too, the proportion of income contributed to married couple families by men has fallen sharply (Harkness et al. 1996). Gary Becker's (1991) idea that marriage should be understood in terms of two individuals maximizing their utility by men looking for a good housekeeper and care and women looking for a breadwinner, no longer matches the social reality of the vast majority. In Ann Phoenix's (1991) qualitative study of young unmarried mothers, the vast majority of the young fathers were unemployed. There were certainly few economic reasons for these women to marry the fathers of their children. To re-read some of the "angry-young-men" novels about working-class life in the 1950s is to enter a different world, where male school leavers were assured of well-paid factory jobs and could very soon start thinking about marriage and children (e.g. Sillitoe 1970).

The sociology of the 1970s was very optimistic about the increase in dual-earner families in Britain and assumed that this would inevitably lead to a more equal division of unpaid work and a more "symmetrical family" (Young and Willmott 1973). The reality has been somewhat different. The 1980s were marked by the re-emergence of high unemployment rates and the 1990s by a shift toward a more flexible labor market in which employed men were working the longest hours in Europe. The National Child Development Study (NCDS), a longitudinal birth cohort study tracing the lives of all those in Britain born in a specific week in 1958, reported that, in 1991, 39 percent of fathers worked more than 60 hours a week and 34 percent between 30 and 39 hours (Ferri and Smith 1996). Recent research has revealed the emergence of "work rich" and "work poor" households, that is, a rise in the proportions with either two earners or none, and a corresponding decline in those with just one adult in employment (Gregg and Wadsworth 1995). Men without jobs may be adjudged poor marriage material by never-married mothers and are also more susceptible to divorce. Men with long working hours are also likely to give rise to tensions in respect of their lack of contribution to unpaid work at home, which, in turn, is a major reason for women's dissatisfaction with marriage.

Gershuny, Godwin and Jones (1994) have shown, via time-use studies, that men increased the amount of time they spent on household labor between 1975 and 1987 by a small amount in the case of men married to part-time employed women and housewives, and by a more substantial amount in the case of those married to women employed full-time. Furthermore, cooking and routine housework has been proportionately the fastest-growing sub-category of domestic work, and "odd jobs," such as gardening and care maintenance, the slowest. Nevertheless, the rate of change has been relatively slow, something Gershuny et al. (1994) attribute to intergenerational transmission, although many studies note that the relatively small group of men who do perform substantial amounts of household labor have consciously rejected their fathers as role models (Coltrane 1996). Indeed, in their report on the 1991 NCDS data, Ferri and Smith (1996) conclude that men's identity lies more outside the home and family than within it.

The qualitative literature has emphasized the extent to which men's failure to change in respect of the amount of time they devote to household labor is responsible for women's dissatisfaction. As the sociological literature of the 1980s revealed the extent to which women had changed in terms of their relationship to the labor market and men had not in terms of their participation in unpaid work, attention focused on how the division of work between men and women had become apparently irrational, *pace* Becker. Social scientists have been forced to conclude that gendered meanings influence the allocation of household work. Housework and child care are not necessarily allocated efficiently to the person with the most time to do it (unemployed men have been shown to do very little household work), and Hochschild (1989) found that American women working full-time would often try and do more housework in order to bolster their husbands and assuage their own guilt. Hochschild also found what she called "an economy of gratitude," whereby the wife invested more in household work and both expected and valued support from her husband, which she interpreted as "sharing." Thus a profoundly unequal situation was understood as equitable. Backett's (1982) study of British mothers also showed the lengths to which women were prepared to go to interpret their husband's words and deeds favorably. Indeed, most studies have shown that women do not report discontent about the unequal division of unpaid work *per se* (e.g. Thompson 1991), rather their dissatisfaction is caused by the absence of appreciation for their labor. However, while there is little evidence that men have changed the degree to which they contribute to unpaid household work, the profound changes in the labor market during the 1990s, whereby the security of men's jobs has been undermined, may have produced a change in "mentalities," such that men are more willing to acknowledge the tensions arising from the gender division of labor. This more open acknowledgement may have performed the same role as myth for couples in the 1970s and early 1980s in serving to defuse conflict (Lewis 2001).

Gerson's (1993) qualitative study of men in the United States developed a typology of autonomous, breadwinning and involved male partners (married and cohabiting). The autonomous man was the genuinely individualistic, who might encourage his female partner's economic independence, but who did not either share the work of the household or contribute to it economically. Such attitudes have been shown in other American studies to be more typical of men who cohabit (Lye and Waldron 1997). The sole breadwinner in Gerson's study was in a minority and often tended to a traditional view of male/female relationships, but nevertheless saw himself contributing to the welfare of the household economically. Men who were "involved" (40 percent shared fully, the rest "helped") had usually either started on a fast track at work and decided to quit, or had hit a dead-end at work. In other words, their position owed much to period effects. Coltrane's (1996) research on fathers found that their contribution to housework depended mainly on their female partner's position in relation to the labor market, but their contribution to child care depended more on their own working hours.

Certainly Fassinger's (1993) fascinating study of divorced American men with care of their children showed that they did not see housework as part of parenting and did not see it as their responsibility.

Gerson (1993: 284) wrote of the "Scylla of male dominance" and the "Charybdis of obsessive individualism": the breadwinner model upheld male commitment at the expense of women's rights, while the autonomy model offered independence at the expense of interpersonal commitment. The issue is a real and pressing one. Women have radically changed their labor market behavior, but men have not changed their patterns of unpaid work to anywhere near the same extent, which has been shown to cause major dissatisfaction among the women they live with. While qualitative British data are lacking, Ferri and Smith's (1996) report on the 1991 NCDS data showed that men who did least at home were the most optimistic and happy, while their female partners were the least happy. This evidence adds to a picture that suggests that it is men's pursuit of autonomy within relationships that borders on the selfish. It seems that it is men's lack of contribution to household work that is the problem.

Recent policy toward fathers

However, this is not quite how policy makers have seen it. The concern about fathers focused on their flight from commitment, which was interpreted as their failure above all to maintain their children. Not only had the proportion of lone mother families increased, but the percentage dependent on state benefits had also risen from 20 percent in 1961, to 40 percent in 1979 and 66 percent in 1987 (Bradshaw and Millar 1991). In addition, by the late 1980s only one out of three lone mothers was receiving regular maintenance. The well-publicized discovery by Leonore Weitzman (1981) in California of men's substantial financial gains on divorce and women's and children's losses (and subsequent analyses of men's opportunistic behavior under no-fault divorce) fuelled concern in all the English-speaking countries about fathers' support (Maclean 1994). A Conservative government committed to reducing public expenditure was bound to want to do something to counter these trends, and in 1990 the then Prime Minister, Mrs. Thatcher, stressed the obligations of parents toward their children and said that the government was "looking at ways of strengthening the system for tracing an absent father and making the arrangements for recovering maintenance more effective" (*Independent* July 19, 1990).

Maintenance payments had always been set at a low level by the courts; even in the 1930s no persisting obligation to maintain was placed on men. Furthermore, in Britain private legal decisions enacted by the courts made certain assumptions about the role of social security law in reaching its decisions. This was recognized in the 1974 Report on One-Parent Families (Cmnd. 5269 1974: para 4.49), where it was admitted that the burden of support would inevitably fall on the state given that it was well-nigh impossible in a liberal democratic society to control marital and reproductive behavior:

Once it is conceded that the law cannot any longer impose a stricter standard of familial conduct and sexual morality upon the poor than it demands from others, it follows inexorably that part of the cost of breakdown of marriage, in terms of the increase of household and dependencies, must fall on public funds.

The Report believed that there was "no method consistent with the basic tenets of a free society of discharging the community from this responsibility" (para. 2.22), because it was impossible to restrict the freedom to divorce, remarry and reproduce. The Report concluded firmly that "the fact has to be faced that in a democratic society, which cannot legislate (even if it could enforce) different rules of familial and sexual behavior depending on the ability to pay for the consequences, the community has to bear much of the cost of broken homes and unmarried motherhood" (para. 4.224).

There was nothing therefore especially new about the recognition at the end of the 1980s that men tended to move on and to procreate again in a second family. As Gillis (1997) has pointed out, men who leave their children may be condemned as "bad dads," but that in and of itself is not a threat to their masculinity. What changed in the 1980s was that ever-increasing numbers of fathers were behaving in this fashion and it was becoming more explicit that it was expected that their ex-wives would rely on state benefits. This was in part because legislation was passed in 1984 (the Matrimonial and Family Proceedings Act) that contained a number of provisions designed to direct the court's attention to the principle of self-sufficiency and to facilitate in appropriate cases the making of a "clean break" between husbands and wives (Davis et al. 1994). In reaching their decisions about the arrangements for divorce, the courts began to make more explicit reference to the possibility that a wife would be entitled to state benefits. In Delaney v. Delaney, the court held that the fact that the wife could claim state benefits in the absence of maintenance payments, which would allow the husband to establish a home in which he could see the children justified a nominal maintenance order. The judge said:

the court deprecates any notion that a former husband and extant father may slough off the tight skin of familial responsibility and may slither into and lose himself in the greener grass on the other side, nonetheless this court has proclaimed and will proclaim that it looks to the realities of the real world in which we live, and that among the realities of life is that there is a life after divorce. The ... husband is entitled to order his life in such a way as will hold in reasonable balance the responsibilities to his existing family which he carries into his new life, as well as his proper aspirations for that new future. ([1990] 2 FLR 457)

Thus the 1984 legislation resulted in "decomplementarity" (see above) being seen in a positive light by the courts and it was openly acknowledged that men were being freed from lifelong obligations to their first families. At the same time, the Department of Social Security (DSS) reduced the resources it devoted to pursuing "the liable relative" – usually the absent father – for maintenance. When maintenance accounted for so low a proportion of lone mothers' income it is easy to understand the DSS's lack of enthusiasm in the face of its own budget cuts.

However, later in 1990, Mrs. Thatcher was to state firmly that "parenthood is for life" (*Independent* July 19, 1990). In face of the growing fears about fathers' failure to maintain, it was decided in 1991 (by the Child Support Act) to require all fathers, divorced and unmarried, to support their biological children, regardless of their current social arrangements. In many respects this may be interpreted as an effort to bolster the male breadwinner model family in the absence of stable marriage. No longer able to rely on the obligations of men as husbands, the state legislated to enforce their obligation to maintain as biological fathers. The 1991 child support legislation also contained an element of support for mothers, again in line with the male breadwinner principle. The 1984 legislation had overturned any notion of a persistent obligation to pay spousal maintenance, but the 1991 legislation justified maintenance for mothers in terms of the impact of caring on women's ability to enter the labor market (Maclean 1991, 1994). Some compensation on divorce for the unequal division of unpaid work has been argued for fiercely in the American literature, although what precise form it should take is a matter for dispute (e.g. Cohen 1987; Brinig and Crafton 1994). Feminists remain split on how far they feel such compensation is a matter for the individual father and how far it should be transformed into a collective responsibility. There was, nevertheless, broad support for the idea that men should support their children financially; problems arose mainly from the way in which the 1991 legislation was implemented.

The policy goal of the controversial child support legislation was to shift responsibility for the support of lone-parent (overwhelmingly lone mother) families from the state to men as fathers by increasing both the number of fathers paying child support and the amount they paid. Anything collected from the father of a child whose mother was drawing state benefits went straight to the Treasury. The underlying purpose of the legislation was to persuade men to have only as many children as they could financially support, in other words fundamentally to change the way in which men have come to assume that they can reproduce and move on. In so doing, the policy rejected the long-accepted idea in public law that men support the families they live with, something that has more recently achieved a large measure of acceptance in private law, in favor of making men pay for first and second families insofar as there are biological children present in both. Thus the 1991 Child Support Act also set out to change men's ideas about fathering. However, in the main the underlying ideas about fatherhood remained traditional.

As many have observed (e.g. Collier 1995), the legislation was sold in terms of doing something about the problem of "feckless, absent fathers." Men who were already paying something (no matter that it was in all probability a fairly small amount) and middle-class men did not think of themselves as "feckless" and did not expect to come into contact with the new Child Support Agency. However, the legislation was made retrospective, thus potentially drawing in those who believed they had made "clean break" agreements. In addition, the agency was given very stiff performance targets, which meant that it had an incentive to focus its attention on men who were already paying something and who were thus easier to trace. The targets for benefit savings were set at £530 million in the first year (Millar 1996). The legislation employed a complicated formula to establish the amount of child support to be paid by the "absent parent." The idea was to replace the discretion exercised by the courts by a rule-based system. The formula used allowed for the absent parent's living costs based on social assistance allowances, which are far from generous. Many more separated, divorced and unmarried mothers had ended up drawing social assistance than had their male partners. The size of the assessments made by the agency was therefore bound to be a shock for many men and was additionally unacceptable given that the mother's income was not investigated.

The agency began to operate in April 1993, and complaints from fathers followed swiftly. These were expressed by individuals and through the pressure group the National Association for Child Support Action, which quickly moved toward campaigning for the complete repeal of the legislation. By the end of 1993, the Social Security Select Committee had given its support to the view that the formula allowed fathers too little by way of basic protected income, and that the element in the maintenance payment designed to support the carer (mother) was too high. Early in 1994, the carer's element was reduced by 25 percent when the child reached the age of eleven, and the amount of basic protected income was increased. However, the size and vigor of street demonstrations by fathers and their second families, organized to coincide with the first anniversary of the implementation of the legislation in April 1994, were extremely impressive. The fathers' case was aided by the appalling record of the Agency. In October 1994, the first Annual Report on adjudication standards of child support officers found that of 1,200 cases only 14 percent were correct in terms of assessment and adjudication. By August 1994, there were 2,412 appeals waiting to be heard, compared with 414 in January of that year (Barnes et al. 1998).

The child support legislation of 1991 was radical in intent. It aimed to change men's behavior. While there is a long tradition of direct intervention by the state in the family aimed at mothers, fathers have not been targeted in this way. In face of the massive protests by fathers and manifest administrative failure of the agency, the government's response took three forms. First, while the agency had always targeted cases in which the parent-with-care was drawing state benefits (in line with the explicit aim of shifting responsibility from the state to fathers), its work increasingly became explicitly confined to these cases. Late in 1994, it abandoned plans to re-assess non-benefit claimants who were in possession of a court order. By 1997, 88 percent of parents-with-care on the agency's caseload were drawing benefits (Davis et al. 1998). Thus, the UK has reverted to a two-tier system whereby those with enough money to avoid the benefit system altogether use the courts and those who cannot must use the Child Support Agency. This eased the workload of the agency[2] and also removed well-off men from state surveillance.

Secondly, the scheme was progressively modified to lower the level of payment required. Following the tinkering with the formula in 1994, another piece of legislation was passed in 1995. This allowed "departures" from the formula in special cases; it permitted past property and capital settlements to be recognized; made greater allowance for fathers' travel to work costs; and set a maximum limit to the amount of support and to the proportion of net income that could be required to be paid. The average full maintenance assessment fell from £23.83 in mid-1995 to £20.26 in mid-1998 (CSA 1998). The New Labour government's 1998 consultative paper on child support proposed changing the nature of the formula altogether, making it a much simpler straight percentage scheme, which would result in an average payment of £29 per week from those in employment (Cm. 3992 1998). The tone of this document was much more conciliatory, symbolized by the rejection of the term "absent parent" in favor of "non-resident parent."

Thirdly, and possibly most significant in the long term, in the face of male opposition policy makers switched their attention back to lone mothers. When after the 1995 legislation the performance of the agency failed significantly to improve, the Social Security Select Committee began to suspect that mothers and fathers were colluding to avoid the

Agency. In fact, recent studies have found that the agency becomes a central part of the bargaining between mothers and fathers. Bradshaw et al. (1999) and Davis et al. (1998) offer evidence of manipulation and coercion. Thus fathers may threaten that they will charge that their ex-partners are claiming social assistance fraudulently in order to persuade them not to apply to the agency; mothers may threaten to use the agency if the man does not make a lower, privately agreed payment regularly. Despite the lack of evidence as to deliberate collusion, in August 1996 lone mothers who failed to cooperate with the Agency by refusing to name the fathers of their children found their benefits cut by 40 percent. In addition, the whole focus of policy began to change. Given the aim to shift the burden of child support away from the state, and given that there are only three main sources of income for lone mothers: the state, men and the labor market, it is not surprising that government attention began to focus on the last of these. First the Conservative government in 1996 and then the New Labour administration set up schemes under the broad banner of "welfare to work." New Labour's consultative paper on child support proposed that the state should guarantee maintenance for low-paid lone mothers drawing in-work benefits in recognition of the threat that irregular maintenance payments posed to work incentives, and early in 1999 it was announced in the Budget that lone mothers receiving in-work benefits would no longer be required to cooperate with the Child Support Agency. This means that the agency will work almost entirely with cases where the parent-with-care is living entirely on social assistance payments.

At the end of 1998, only one in three lone parents was receiving child support payments, the same proportion as prior to the implementation of the new legislation. The levels of payment had also fallen back to the pre-Child Support Act level (Barnes et al. 1998). The level of debt reported by the agency amounted to over a billion pounds (Knights et al. 1999) and more than half of this was reckoned to be uncollectable. The state had therefore failed to make fathers pay, but why had fathers refused?

In 1990, the British Social Attitudes Survey asked respondents whether they thought a father should pay for his children after divorce. Ninety percent of men and 95 percent of women said that he should (Kiernan 1992). However, the quarterly statistics of the Child Support Agency published at the end of 1998 showed that 45 percent of non-resident parents were paying the full amount of the assessment, 24 percent were paying part of it and 31 percent were paying nothing. There are many possible reasons for this. First, the high level of inefficiency on the part of the agency cannot be ignored. The amount of error was bound to result in hostility on the part of fathers. Secondly, it is likely that large numbers of non-resident fathers cannot pay. Widening inequalities in Britain during the 1980s and again in the late 1990s have meant that there are more low-paid people earning lower wages in real terms. About 9 million workers earn less than the "decency threshold" set by the Council of Europe and only about three-quarters of employed men are now in full-time jobs. The 1974 Finer Committee recognized the impossibility of making a low male wage stretch between two households. As Millar (1996) has argued, the 1991 child support policy relies on the existence of a "family wage." In Bradshaw et al.'s (1999) sample survey of non-resident fathers, it was found that 63 percent of the non-payers could not pay.

Nevertheless, there has been enormous hostility to the legislation from middle-class men who can pay. This may be the product of simple hostility to state surveillance, but irresponsibility and/or selfishness may also play a part. Davis et al. (1994) have drawn attention to the results of the Child Support Agency's weakness in respect of investigative and enforcement powers, something that becomes particularly evident in the case of self-employed fathers. The agency's quarterly statistics for the end of 1998 showed the average weekly assessment for employees to be £38.85, while that for the self-employed is £23.23. The agency does not investigate the returns made by non-resident parents. The lack of effective enforcement means that little is done about those who refuse to pay, which may in turn encourage non-compliance.

However, the more complicated issue, about which we have little evidence, centers on the meaning of child support for fathers and how they have interpreted the legislation. In face of the attempt to portray the legislation as a proper attack on "feckless fathers," fathers' pressure groups were able to marshal impressive street demonstrations by respectable, middle-class men who claimed that they were the victims. The voice of the lone mothers was rarely heard. In any case, the vast majority of lone mothers on the caseload of the agency did not benefit from the legislation because they were drawing social assistance and thus anything collected went into the government's coffers. There have been only two qualitative studies that have interviewed non-resident fathers (Bradshaw et al. 1999; Davis et al. 1998). Bradshaw et al. found that most of the nineteen fathers they interviewed in depth identified as male breadwinners and viewed money as a more important contribution to their children's welfare than time. This is consistent with Gershuny, Godwin and Jones' (1994) findings that male behavior in the family has shown relatively little change. Other findings in terms of attitudinal change, especially on the part of younger men, toward participation in other aspects of family life (e.g. Lewis 2001) is important, but not incompatible with the relative lack of behavioral change. Much testimony regarding child support that is reported by these studies shows a remarkable degree of confusion. Davis et al. (1998: 203) summarized the views of the fathers in their study as showing an "ill-thought-through conception of where their responsibilities should end and those of the state, through the benefit system, should begin." Some of the men in Bradshaw et al.'s sample agreed that "feckless men" should pay, but did not necessarily pay themselves. This distinction is reminiscent of that found by Mansfield and Collard (1988) between "my marriage" and "marriage in general." One interviewee paid for the children of his second failed marriage, but not those of his first.

It is far from easy to work out what the precise rationale for fathers' behavior is. Bradshaw et al. suggest that child support can be seen by fathers as a gift, as compensation (for past bad behavior) or as an entitlement. They point out that most non- and partial payers in their sample made informal payments or gifts to their children averaging £15.99 per week. This is probably in line with pre-Child Support Act behavior. As Davis et al. (1998) comment, in the past men paid very little by way of child support but could persuade themselves that they were generous by gift-giving. However, it is important to understand why these men are prepared to give something directly to their children and yet not to pay child support. Child support payments go either to the Treasury or to the mother. In either case, as Bradshaw et al. point out, they are probably invisible to the child. These men identified as male breadwinners, but the child support system required them to contribute to their children financially from a distance without being able to exercise any control, which many found intolerable. Gift-giving allows control. The father could give shoes and not have to rely on the mother's good sense to buy some. Gift-giving also allows the father direct contact with the child, who would see him as a benefactor. Older men in intact relationships have been found to identify themselves as "good family men" having spent very little time with their families but having handed over virtually all their wages (Gerson 1993; Warin et al. 1999). These men trusted their wives to make good use of the money and to maximize the family's welfare, and were happy with their breadwinner status. But in cases of family breakdown that trust has, by definition, vanished. In these circumstances the absence of the control, which the "good family man" did not usually exercise but which was nevertheless his to deploy were he to feel it necessary, together with the absence of status as the breadwinner, can become a problem for some non-resident fathers.

Maclean and Eekelaar (1997) concluded that, while mothers favored biology as a basis for child support, men put more emphasis on the social construction of parenthood. Certainly, men have always been more willing to support the family they live in, while women rarely leave their biological children. However, the biological/social divide does not fully explain how fathers reach decisions about whether and how much to pay in respect of their children. Fathers who do not pay child support are unable to separate the needs of the child from their own position or lack of it, *vis-à-vis* the mother and the family as a whole. They resent payment to a household in which they can exercise no control and receive no recognition as the provider. Not surprisingly, Bradshaw et al. found that fathers were particularly unwilling to pay child support to mothers who were living with new partners but were dependent on social assistance. The child support legislation seeks to perpetuate the traditional gender roles of mothers and fathers beyond the point of relationship breakdown. Many fathers have little quarrel with the behavior associated with those roles, particularly the idea that they should be the primary breadwinners. However, the legislation requires them to perform this role without the traditional rewards.

The problem that responsibility without power and status poses for some fathers may also help to explain their approach to care as opposed to cash. Fathers' pressure groups have argued strongly that obligations must be socially based and that financial support should be concomitant with the right of access to the child. As with the issue of financial support for mothers alongside that of children, this has raised difficult issues for feminists, who have questioned the investment in care that men appear to be willing to make on divorce when there is little evidence of any major shift in the division of unpaid work between men and women prior to divorce (Smart and Neale 1999). The point is that the nature of the relationship between cash and care is different for men and women. Women are used to separating the two and taking responsibility for care in the absence of direct control over cash. Men are not. Access to a child means the opportunity to make direct provision for him or her, for example by gift-giving, as well as caring for the child.

In regard to the arrangements made on divorce or in respect of unmarried mothers and fathers, British policy in respect of fathering has sought, above all, to enforce the father's obligation to maintain, and it has been understood by government that fathers are more likely to pay if access to the child is granted. But there has been little effort to change fathers' approach to care. Indeed, there is clear evidence that this has taken precedence over any obligation to care. One aspect of the child support formula that was subjected to severe criticism was the lack of regard for traveling expenses incurred by fathers who maintained contact with their children. The ministerial response agreed that such expenses could be heavy, but insisted that it was not right to give them precedence over the child's right to maintenance from its father (Garnham and Knights 1994). Thus, care by fathers was subordinated to financial support and in addition was seen as being more a luxury in the interests of the father than in the interests of the child.

This does not mean, however, that policy makers have been impervious to arguments about the importance of the caring role of fathers. But, until very recently, recognition of this was more evident in the courts than in public law and was influenced directly by the re-conceptualization of the child welfare principle by academic psychologists to mean the child's right to have contact with its father as well as its mother. There has therefore been an increasing tendency to stress the importance of fathers maintaining contact with their biological children. From the point of view of successive governments, this has been influential insofar as it has been seen as part and parcel of securing fathers' obligation to maintain.

Paralleling the influential American research that purported to show the importance of continued contact with fathers for the welfare of children, British research investigated court decisions about fathers' access to children after divorce. The evidence was mixed as to whether or not the courts favored mothers. Eekelaar et al. (1977) pointed out that only 6 percent of cases were contested, although some argued that fathers did not ask for custody over their children because they did not expect to get it. Maidment (1984) argued strongly that judges tended to abide by the status quo and, after the 1973 legislation liberalizing divorce, custody and the right to stay in the matrimonial home tended to be decided together in favor of women. This debate in the 1980s on the care of children after divorce was couched in terms of the effect of father-absence on children, however, as Smart (1991) has argued, this masked the fact that fathers' claim to rights over their children were, in the name of child welfare, beginning to take precedence over mothers' claims based on an ethic of care. By the mid-1990s, virtually any mother who opposed contact between their child and its father for whatever reason was labeled "implacably hostile" (Smart 1997). Thus, developments in private law have assumed both that continued contact with fathers is good for all children and that all fathers want contact. However, evidence as to the increasingly polarized population of fathers (see above, p. 133) makes such a universal assumption unlikely to hold.

In the public policy arena, the issue of what constituted welfare for the child met government's primary concern to reduce public expenditure throughout the 1980s and for most of the 1990s, and, as Eekelaar (1991) convincingly argued, the concern to encourage parental responsibility came to assume a double meaning: responsibility toward the child, on the one hand, and a preference for parental responsibility over state responsibility, on the other, with the latter taking precedence over the former. The 1989 Children Act set out parental responsibility as individual responsibility, and thus as something that cannot be voluntarily surrendered to the state. It remains undiminished when the care of the child is shared with the state; only adoption ends it. The aim is that parents rather than the state should provide care for children with the minimum of state intervention. Unmarried fathers were brought into the picture first by the 1987 Family Law Reform Act, which eradicated the status of illegitimacy for children and made it possible for the courts to recognize the parental rights of unmarried fathers. The 1989 Children Act then permitted these fathers to share parental responsibility by private agreement, just as the 1996 Family Law Act expected parents to reach their own solutions about their post-divorce arrangements with the help of mediators.[3] Under the banner of encouraging all parents to exercise responsibility for their children, the Labour government has proposed giving unmarried fathers the same rights as married fathers, with possible exceptions in cases where the child was conceived as a result of rape or where the father has a history of violence (LCD 1998). A similar proposal was strongly opposed by women's groups in 1980, because it did not address the reality of the gendered division of labor (ROW 1980).

As in the case of the child support legislation, the main concern of policy makers has been to perpetuate family relationships beyond divorce, or indeed to create traditional relationships among the unmarried where quite often none had ever existed. Changes regarding the care of children embodied in the Family Law Reform Act and the Children Act were framed around the central concept of parental responsibility, which was also at the heart of the child support legislation. There is little to suggest that government was thinking about the day-to-day business of care in making these changes. Rather, the primary emphasis was on attaching children to fathers in order to secure their maintenance, something that fathers' pressure groups agreed was necessary if they were to be persuaded to pay.

Conclusion

British policy toward fathers for most of the last two decades has been driven by the fear that they are increasingly unwilling to maintain their families, and by the allied concern about the anti-social behavior of young men who are not tied into families. It has focused on the responsibilities of fathers to support their families and has sought to reinforce traditional gender roles. It has thus been characterized by *negative* considerations rather than by a more *positive* approach to enabling fathers to become more involved with their families, and in this more closely resembles the policy rhetoric of the United States, with its attack on "dead beat Dads," than other Northern European countries. In 1992, the UK adopted a European Council Recommendation on child care, Article 6 of which stated the importance of promoting the participation by fathers in household work in order to promote both equality at home and women's position in the labor market. However, in 1994, the UK refused to accept the European Directive on parental leave. The issue was subjected to ridicule in parliament, while the press showed how little understood the idea of parental leave was by repeatedly confusing it with paternity leave. Demos, a think-tank close to the Labour government, made a strong case for parental leave, citing the "time squeeze," the parenting deficit (which in the case of fathers exacerbated juvenile delinquency), and poor child-care provision in the UK (Wilkinson 1997). The lengthening of working hours for British men who are in full-time work made it additionally difficult for them to share unpaid work.

Public policy regarding fathers and care has been substantially revised by the New Labour government, elected in 1997. Labour has sought to promote the employment of all adults and to move men and women off welfare benefits and into work. In so doing, it has had to take into account the UK's historical lack of any policy regarding child care. Child-care provision has been promoted via tax credits and cash injections into public/private "child care partnerships," although the effort has not been as coherent (or large) as policies on the employment side. Labour has also had to face the issue of parental leave, in part because of increased pressure resulting from the explicit assumption that all adults will be in the labor market, and in part to fulfill the UK's obligations in respect of the European Commission's Directive on parent leave. Tony Blair faced personal publicity on this issue when his fourth child was born. Since 1999, British parents have been entitled to 13 weeks parental leave, compared to 18 months for Swedes, a year for Austrians and 10 months for Italians. Furthermore, the leave is unpaid and a recent government consultation paper (DTI 2000) has proposed changes that are very conservative in comparison to the continental European countries.

British policy has responded to the profound change in family structure by seeking to reinforce men's traditional obligation to maintain. This is not without merit, although it is doubtful how far such privatized solutions can go in solving the huge rise in child poverty in the UK. Between 1979 and 1991, the number of children living in households with below 50 percent of average income trebled to 3.9 million. In addition, such a response constitutes something of a "knee-jerk" reaction designed to re-establish older patterns. Just as successive British Conservative governments were reluctant to do anything to recognize and to help to reconcile the problems that mothers have in combining paid and unpaid employment, so they did nothing to promote the involvement of fathers in the care of their children, despite research evidence that suggests that the lack of such involvement at home is a prime cause of family breakdown in the first place. The stress on "parental responsibility" did not include care when it came to fathers. The New Labour government has begun explicitly to address both the issue of child poverty and the reconciling of family and workplace responsibilities. Its consultative paper on child support stated that "fathers need help to be good fathers and regular payers" (Cm 3992 1998: 14) and tries to locate the issue of child support in the wider context of "supporting families" more generally (Home Office 1998). However, much more needs to be done to address the huge gendered care gap in the UK, as the issue of parental leave shows.

5   A new role for fathers? The German case

Ilona Ostner

Fatherhood and fathers are imprinted in the German landscape, in the collective memory of the Nazi past. Yet there has been remarkably little discussion of contemporary fatherhood or fathering, or debates concerning new roles for fathers. Divorce rates in East and West Germany have steadily increased, nearing those of other Western European countries. German divorced fathers, too, often lose contact with their children or do not fulfill their financial obligations. However, one does not find the same moral discourse on absent fatherhood as in the United States or Britain (Curran and Abrams 2000; Orloff and Monson in this volume). Instead, public attention has focused on low birth-rates, costs of living and, recently, the poverty risks of lone mothers and their children (Ostner 1997). The parental leave and the custody law reforms directly concern fathers and fatherhood. Yet they are not framed in terms of fathers' interests, but in terms of labor market needs and the best interests of children.

To understand why there has been so little debate about how to transform men into "responsible dads" in both Germanys, one has to turn back to the legacies of fatherhood from Nazism. But to fully grasp the impediments in the search for a new role for German fathers, one cannot ignore the unification of two countries with radically different social politics of fatherhood. The first part of this chapter considers these legacies: (1) the symbolic father–son conflicts rooted in the Nazi past; and (2) the different constructions of fatherhood and fathering in the two Germanys. Then I turn to the question of the search for a new role for fathers and address the changing policies toward fatherhood around cash and care. I concentrate on specific policies, such as flexible parental leave rights and the expansion in divorced fathers' custody rights.

The authoritarian personality and the fatherless generation

Discourses on fatherhood are ever-present in Germany, bound up with the history of Nazism and its intellectual and political legacies. In order to comprehend the ambivalences about fatherhood and fathering that impede the search for a new role for fathers, one has to turn back to the first generation of critical theorists and their analyses of the authoritarian personality.

The founders of Critical Theory linked what they called the "authoritarian personality," and mass support for Nazism, to men's weakness as fathers and husbands (Fromm et al. 1936, Adorno et al. 1969). The extension of the market and commodification of labor, they argued, seriously eroded men's status in society and their authority in the family, and thereby jeopardized male identity.

Habermas extended critical theories about the family to the ongoing process of democratization in West Germany. He viewed the family as a part of this process, although legal reform was still lacking behind cultural change. Looking for potential origins of the 1968 protest movement in Germany, Habermas (1969: 33) identified two parental milieus, both "bourgeoisie" or middle class – and two distinguishable student generations: the "liberated" and the "fatherless generation." The latter concept he borrowed from the left-wing psychoanalyst Alexander Mitscherlich. Struck by what he called the "Unfähigkeit zu trauern," the incapability of mourning the Nazi past and its losses, Mitscherlich had written about the "invisible father" and "fatherless" generations first during the 1950s and later presented in a book that was very much debated during the 1960s (Mitscherlich 1955, 1963; Stein 2000: 52).

In a recent issue of the periodical *Kursbuch* devoted to "Väter" (fathers) (*Kursbuch* 140, June 2000), the discursive links between fatherhood and Nazism are rehearsed in a series of articles on father–son conflict and the 68-generation. In one article, Christian Gampert (2000) recalls the story of the disempowered father. For Gampert, it began with the devaluation of everything that referred to fathers in reaction to the Nazi period. Those born after World War II had fathers who were active culprits or complicit fathers. If sons were lucky, their fathers had been too young to be deeply involved in Nazi crimes. Other articles in the special issue on fatherhood also reveal the psychological/social dimensions of the 1968 protests: connecting the civil disobedience toward the state and the sons' rejection of their fathers, whom they accused of having blindly obeyed the state (Stephan 2000).

The 1968 protest movements revisited the sins of their Nazi fathers, confronting the crimes and "fathers" involvement. In the unified Germany, debates on fatherhood and the authoritarian personality re-emerged in a new context with the return of elements of the Nazi past. Xenophobic attacks of East German youth have revived the concept of the "authoritarian personality" coined by the post-war generation. For a short period, the authoritarian socialist state was held responsible for significantly higher right-wing voting and violence of young males, which were aimed at ethnic and other minorities in post-unification East Germany. Socialist child-care facilities were also part of the scapegoating (Pfeiffer 2000). Parallels were made between the "fatherless society" (Adorno et al. 1969) in which the Nazi state took command of essential family functions and assumed the parental role (mainly the father's role) and, to some extent, that of the breadwinner husband, and the totalitarian socialist state. The argument was made that children had experienced forms of child care that did not respond to individual needs and develop self-confidence. Hence, in later life, they would turn against weaker people or groups. These theories have been widely tested and contested during the 1990s (for an overview: Oswald 1998). The research findings show that East and West German parents' childrearing practices and values did not differ significantly when the wall came down. Nor do East German adolescents show more "rightist" attitudes than West German adolescents. Education and degrees of deprivation, such as unemployment, matter in both parts of Germany.

As these debates reveal, fatherlessness is a symbolic configuration, bound up with discourses of the sins of fathers and forefathers. Real fathers and their fathering, their attitudes toward their families and their practices, do not have the same visibility. The ambivalence toward fatherhood and fathers has inhibited research that would have laid the base for policy debates in a search for a new role for fathers after unification, a point that will be returned to in the final section of this chapter.

Before turning to the question of the search for a new role for fathers, it is important to recall the different policy logics in the two Germanys and how these shaped the construction of fatherhood.

Two logics of family policy

The German Democratic Republic (GDR) and the pre-unification Federal Republic of Germany (FRG) clearly belonged to two different welfare and family policy regimes: the Western model privileged husbands and husband–fathers, not fathers. The socialist model focused on children and child-related policies that aimed at helping mothers to combine child care and paid work and thereby also to participate fully in the building of a socialist society. Each model in its way treated fathers unfavorably: in the West, the non-married father was overtly discriminated against and the married father as carer was given little play in the strong male breadwinner society. In East Germany, married, divorced and never-married fathers were marginalized from their fathering by state policies.

East Germany: the socialist state as "surrogate father"?

While West Germany strengthened young women's personal dependence on a husband and breadwinner, the East German regime identified emancipation with economic activity and expected women to be both workers and mothers. Such ideas contributed to women's independence from male partners and shifted remaining forms of dependence to the state (Ostner 1998: 90). The socialist "providential state" took command of essential family functions, assuming a parental role and to some extent that of the breadwinner husband.

In 1950, the GDR established the Law on the Protection of Children and Mothers and on Women's Rights, which formally abolished women's economic dependence on men. (In West Germany, husbands' decision-making in the family – whether married women could enter paid work – did not disappear until 1977.) The socialist GDR required women's full-time employment, which was promoted in fierce ideological competition with West Germany. Trappe (1995) distinguishes six stages of child-centered policies which also reveal the relationship between men and women as workers, and the remaking of fatherhood and motherhood. The *first* and *second* stages removed legal barriers from women's employment by reforming the marriage and family laws. The *third* stage promoted positive action with respect to women's training and retraining and by extending public child care. Faced with rapidly declining birth-rates, the *fourth* stage sought to extend the new Family Law by emphasizing men's obligation to promote women's work outside and within the home. However, this was more of a symbolic than real campaign, which did not increase birth-rates – which, in fact, declined further. The *fifth* stage was marked by a rhetorical shift toward explicitly natalist concerns. The *sixth* stage from 1976 onwards eventually introduced various paid leaves and work-reduction options – albeit for mothers only. The last three stages indicate that social entitlements given to mothers – especially since the 1970s – served many purposes of the socialist state, including regime competition and gender equality, but this did not imply giving any role to fathers.

According to Kerstin Bast (an economist from the former East Germany), on the surface East German society consisted of a gender-neutral world of *Werktätige*, working people, of *Erwachsene* and *Kinder*, adults and children, sometimes of mothers and fathers, but not of women and men, girls and boys. Despite the gender-neutral language, the state-planned feminization of caring and teaching created a gender division of work that rendered care a solely female task; men as fathers who cared and provided for their children were marginalized in this framework (Bast and Ostner 1992).

As discussed above, child-centered policies became more openly natalist from the 1970s onwards. Such policies gave priority to the objective of increasing the number of children irrespective of family forms and marital status. This, in turn, reduced the costs of out-of-wedlock births, divorce or separation for both women and men; a trend that was increasingly criticized by GDR officials. It also enhanced the role of social/household fathers (Winkler 1989) in the reconstituted families.

At the time the wall came down, the socialist state paid directly or indirectly for 80 percent of the costs of children, through all sorts of subsidies, including public child care and holiday facilities, and additional benefits given to single mothers. Supported by the state, mothers could form their own households without the risk of poverty. If one applies the dimensions of a "woman friendly state" developed by feminist researchers, "defamiliazation" – the extent to which the state rid mothers of cash and care obligations toward their children – and "economic independence" (Orloff 1993a; Hobson 1994; Lister 2000), East German women would have been at the top of the scale.

The state became a main provider for its children and shared this task with the working mothers by facilitating their work through state services, temporary leaves and work-time reductions. Dennis (1998: 52) speaks of a "semi-privatization" of family life, the other side of the providential state, which tried to politicize family affairs: in the highly politicized GDR system families could not avoid intrusion and steering by the state.

West Germany: strong husband breadwinners, marginal fathers

According to comparative welfare state research, the German welfare state has been described as a paradigm case of a conservative–corporatist regime, as a familiast welfare state (Esping-Andersen 1990, 1996). "Conservative" refers to, among others, the principle of "subsidiarity," which in a Catholic ideological frame, assumes that the higher levels of social organization should be subsidiary to the family. Thus, for example, state supported full-time child care goes against the essence of this principle, which seeks to promote the self-help capacities of the family. In the Fifth Family Report in 1994, the Federal government drew a clear boundary between public responsibility and the privacy of the family. It underlined "subsidiarity," the priority of the smaller unit, comprising couples, parents, mothers and fathers; hence the priority of transfers over publicly provided social care services.

The "relational" aspect of the German welfare state provides a corollary to the principle of subsidiarity. According to Catholic social teaching, which shaped West German social policy, people are embedded in relations (e.g. gender and generation relations), and "relational" obligations take precedence over individual rights. Hence social entitlements follow a "relational" logic. They are attached to status and relations – to couples, parents, children, employees, retirees etc. – not to individuals. Individuals and groups can, however, rely on solidaristic redistribution of the wider community, state or society to become or stay self-reliant. Solidarity precedes subsidiarity and explains the generosity of many benefits or allowances. Parents, for instance, can claim rather generous cash benefits, since cash, in contrast to care, supports but does not replace families' self-help.

This logic may explain why Germany still expects husbands and wives, parents and children by law to mutually take care of each other if necessary and for as long as necessary. From one perspective, one can speak of "strong" (highly institutionalized) "marital and family obligations." From a feminist research perspective, West Germany scores low with regard to "defamiliazation" or the "right to form an independent household," since policies have favored the male breadwinner until recently. Lone mothers outside the labor market have faced a high risk of poverty in West Germany (Hobson 1994) in contrast to their Eastern sisters who, supported by the state, regularly worked full time.

Whereas gender relations in the socialist East meant a highly individualized dual-earner family, in West Germany the idea of gender difference permeated the construction of equal and complementary roles: husband and wife, father and mother, men and women. West Germany has traditionally supported marriage and the family via marriage-related entitlements and benefits representing what has been called a "strong" (marriage-centered) "male breadwinner regime."[1] The German welfare state defines marriage as a mutually supportive relationship – wives support men by taking care of the children and domestic chores, husbands support wives and children by breadwinning. The mutuality justifies the lifelong splitting of income and resources or strong marital obligations.

West German family policy was deliberately designed to prevent what was seen as natalist intervention of the socialist state for two reasons: (1) it valorized the privacy of marriage and the family; and (2) it recalled the abuses during the Third Reich. Instead, West German family policy supported strong male breadwinning and children through the male breadwinner wage, and through tax advantages to single breadwinner families. Family benefits provided incentives for women to stay at home and take care of the children rather than take up labor market work. Transfers were aimed at horizontal rather than vertical redistribution, and have influenced opportunities rather than outcomes.

Consequently, the 1994 Family Report (296) notes that redistribution from childless people to families, not vertical redistribution from high-to low-income families, has been a priority of German family policy. German family policies have long provided cash rather than care, as most fully realized in steadily increased child benefits or in the parental care benefit. They have slowly moved toward a combination of cash and care, as evident from the German Care Insurance or the right to part-time child care which were both established in 1996. However, these measures still provide incentives for (married) women to reduce working hours or to fully exit employment. As a consequence, women in West Germany work predominantly part time or quit employment while having children; men, in contrast, invest even more time into employment when they become fathers. However, over the last decade, mothers' employment has steadily increased, thereby eroding the strong breadwinner norm.

Fathers and fathering in the two Germanys

West German fathers

Compared to the vast literature on mothers, working and non-working, motherhood, married or lone, and mothering in (West) Germany, we know little about what it means to be a father, how fatherhood is shaped by institutions and legal procedures or about fathering practices (Döge 2000). Serious social studies about fathers are rare, and most of what one reads about fathers can be found in manuals on norms about fathering.

Helge Pross (1978) pioneered with her study "Männer" (men). She used "equal sharing of housework," including child care, as a measuring stick for men's involvement with the family and the meaning of fatherhood in West Germany. Her research became famous – less for the results, they just confirmed the strength of the male breadwinner model in Germany and the norms of complementary gender roles, than for its novelty (being the first study aimed at dealing solely with men). It also received a lot of attention because it was financed by the popular fashion journal *Brigitte*. When Sigrid Metz-Göckel and Ursula Müller (1986) replicated the Pross study ten years later, they found only a slight change in fathering practices. Men in the first study had almost no involvement with fathering; ten years later fathers showed a slight involvement in child care and other domestic activities, mainly playing with children and shopping (see also Busch et al. 1988). In the research on families, men as carers remained largely invisible, their non-wage contribution to parenthood minor.

The various studies suggest that the majority of (West) German fa-thers still interpret fathering in terms of male breadwinning (see also

Blanke et al. 1996). One study of husbands six years after marriage (Schneewind and Vaskovics 1996) showed that they spent on average 44.5 hours per week in the labor market. Becoming a father, or the number of children they had, did not alter their work times very much. According to the authors, some interviewees worked more than 45 hours, while only one-third had hours that followed the standard working time made in collective agreements of 37.5 hours per week (Schneewind and Vaskovics 1996: 199). Admittedly, time for caring is costly for both men and women in the German competitive high-skill/high-wage employment system (Ostner 2000). In the many male-dominated industries – most of which are exposed to global competition – workers can be obliged to work 10 hours per day, 6 days a week for a period of 6 weeks. Overtime has become standard for the qualified worker in the new economy. It has always been normal for those in top positions. Obviously, fathering and globalized market competition do not work well together (Sennett 1998; Connell 1998).

East German fathers

Fathers have not been studied explicitly in East Germany, either before or after unification. The GDR, which urgently needed qualified workers, became increasingly interested in time spent by women on housework and child care. In this context the gender division of domestic labor gained some importance. The 1990 Women's Report (Winkler 1990: 128), which presents one of the rare studies of the division of household tasks, used data from 1988. These data showed that typical domestic chores and child-care activities, such as preparation of meals, cleaning, washing clothes, feeding and bathing children, and caring for a sick child, were to a large extent performed by women only. Other tasks like bringing children to or getting them from day-care were done by both mothers and fathers. Household repairs remained a male activity (Winkler 1990). The Women's Report published in 1990 reveals the "high tolerance among women of their multiple roles" (Dennis 1998: 46) and women's readiness to put their career behind that of men. Looking back at the GDR and family life, Gysi and Meyer (1993: 160) recalled that the traditional gender division of household labor was reproduced among children in which boys were shown to have more free time than girls due to house- hold tasks assigned to girls. After unification, opinions on dual earning, especially those of men, and, in general, of the younger cohorts have be- come more gender specific (Kurz 1998: 214). While very few men would speak against women's employment, an increasing number of men sup- port part-time work for mothers. Approval of part time versus full time varies with household income, social background and education.

Dennis (1998: 47) quotes from a study that was conducted by the Institute for Sociology and Social Policy in 1984. Despite the various forms of maternal leave, East German parents worried that they devoted too little time to their children: 52 percent of the mothers and 66 percent of the fathers of children under the age of twelve years stated that they spent less than two hours with their children during the working week. Time spent for child care at home did not change between 1990 and 1996 despite the significant decrease in the workforce and the loss of child-care services after unification. Rather the demise of the provider–socialist state has had the effect of a dramatic decline in birth-rates (Berger et al. 1999: 124).

Fatherhood had been of little importance in socialist East Germany. The state acted as a "parent surrogate" by providing benefits and services. Although nearly all mothers worked full-time, the few existing data suggest that East German fathers did not equally share child care and other domestic activities (Winkler 1990: 129). They behaved very much like West German men (Schneewind and Vaskovics 1996: 149). When the wall came down, East German women asked for many things, predominantly, job security; they did not ask for a new role for fathers. Unification, however, became a catalyst for a transition from one- to two-earner households in West Germany, which has recently redefined rights and responsibilities between mothers and fathers; parents and children; and state and parents.

A new role for fathers?

Since unification, the state has played a more active role in helping parents to combine employment and family life, framed in the best interests of the child. Changes in the parental leave legislation are one example of the father's new role, but this is more a result of increased female labor market participation. Another example is the weakening of the maternal preference in custody after divorce (Mason 1994). Both of these reforms, cast in terms of the best interests of the child to have access to two parents, have had the effect of improving fathers' rights.

Parental leave reform

One of the most famous gender equality cases brought before the European Court of Justice concerned discrimination against fathers in maternal leave benefits. It came from a West German father who felt that the German maternity leave legislation was a form of unequal treatment of men as fathers (Hofmann v. Barmer Ersatzkasse (Case 184/83[1984]

ECR 3047). Although the European Court of Justice did not recognize Mr. Hofmann's complaint, since it refused to hear cases concerning the division of responsibilities between parents, only two years later the West German government responded with a change in the gender-specific law.

In 1986, the Christian–Liberal government entitled both fathers and mothers to three years paid leave and means-tested flat-rate benefits. However, only 0.68 of those on leave were fathers in 1987. During the 1990s, the proportion of fathers increased to nearly 2 percent. These were highly educated working fathers or partners of highly qualified women. Very few combined part-time work (the original law conceded up to 19 hours per week) and partial parental leave: a total of 2.6 percent of parents chose this option, of which 9.5 percent were men in 1987. The latter doubled during the 1990s (Statistisches Bundesamt 1985–1998; Vaskovics and Rost 1999: 26).

In 2000, the German government passed a major reform of the Parental Leave Legislation. While the old law strictly ruled that the three-years leave had to be taken immediately after the child's birth and the parent on leave was only allowed to work a maximum of 19 hours per week, parents are now given various options: they can share the up-to-three years of leave; they can care for their child at home together for some time, or utilize their leave in one year only and thereby be entitled to a 30 percent higher (income-tested) parental leave benefit. Parents can decide to split the leave, for instance, take two years after the child's birth and then take the remaining year of parental leave when the child enters school, which is not a full school day in Germany. The leave has to be taken, however, before the child reaches eight years of age. Finally, most important for fathers, who are more often the higher income earners in the family, thresholds for income testing of the parental leave benefit have been raised. Moreover, an important part of the reform for employed fathers and mothers is that they are allowed to work up to 30 hours per week which, in fact, equals reduced full-time employment in Germany, and are still entitled to the benefit. Though the benefits are low, the flexibility in the reform opened up new possibilities for men to become carers.

The proposal primarily aims at adapting the existing rules to the needs of *employed* parents, of both, mothers and fathers, who increasingly work flexible jobs, by giving them more options; it also reacts to employers' needs by providing incentives for parents to stay in (reduced full-time) employment while being eligible for parental leave; and, as is explicitly stated, the reform wants to increase fathers' take-up rate by flexibilizing eligibility rules and providing incentives better tailored for men. Taken together, these changes constitute major shifts in the earlier logic of parental leave. Working men are being recast as caring fathers, mothers as workers, households as two-earner units that share their resources, be they time or money. In effect these changes represent a move away from the strong male breadwinner earner and – at first glance – the marginal father.

The logic of the parental leave reform becomes more evident if related to another law, which from 2001 onwards allows everyone a right to be employed part time. In addition, those opting for part time have the corresponding right to go back to full-time work. Employers must put forward good reasons for denying full-timers any reduction in their hours. The Minister of Family Affairs who drafted the law argued that employers often made it difficult for men to reduce their work hours to part time in order to share child care at home. She also assumed that an equal sharing of child care will raise mothers' employability, while other politicians expect an increase in the birth-rate.

Custody reform

Men as divorced or separated fathers were disempowered in West Germany. Before the reform in the law, the court's pro forma gave mothers sole custody after divorce. The abolition of the automatic maternal preference in the courts, followed by changes in custody law in 1998, has meant that joint custody after a divorce is now established as the norm in Germany. It was argued that joint custody provides an incentive for fathers to stay in touch with their children, and that access to both parents is in the best interest of the child.

Since the reform, a parent seeking sole custody has to apply to the courts and give just cause. If one parent objects to joint custody, the courts provide mediation to achieve a consensual solution "in the best interest of the child." Non-married (including cohabiting) parents can obtain joint custody by signing a respective declaration (*Sorgerechtserklärung*). If the parents have been married, the family courts do not intervene. Such intervention was seen to represent undue distrust toward the mother who decides in favor of joint custody.

The 1997 custody and child support laws, following a ruling from the Federal Constitutional Court, provided cohabiting fathers with new custody rights. The court stated that discrimination of out-of-wedlock children had to be eventually abolished and the status of children of married and non-married mothers equalized. The reforms affected custody, visitation and child maintenance issues. The law took as its starting point the 1989 UN Convention on Children's Rights, which maintained that children be given access to both parents and their parents' resources. However, Article 6 of the German Basic Law provides a barrier to equal treatment of married and non-married fathers, since it explicitly states that the Constitution protects (heterosexual) marriage and the family, which implicitly prohibits the same treatment of marriage and cohabitation.[2]

Care and cash: rights and obligations

Care: the disempowered father

Basic German law in the early twentieth century assumed out-of-wedlock children to be fatherless; otherwise – it was argued – men would have married the mother and thereby "recognized" their children. Not until 1969 did the Law on the Legal Status of Illegitimate Children move toward granting the non-marital father the status of "a father." Nevertheless, he was given a legal relationship to his child, albeit only through economic obligations, not rights, since the mother retained sole custody rights and decisions over contact between the father and his children. Fathers regularly had to pay maintenance for the child and the non-employed mother, and give some of their inheritance to the child.

Even after the current 1998 reform, non-marital fathers have weak rights. They are weakest for fathers who never lived with the child and the mother. The new law allows non-marital cohabiting fathers the rights to joint custody, but these are dependent upon the consent of the mother. Even if the mother agrees to grant sole custody to the non-marital father, the court requires an examination of the case. The non-marital father is not given automatic custody if the mother dies or loses child custody.

Christian Gampert (2000), in his contribution to the special issue of *Kursbuch* on The Father, characterizes present-day forms of fathers' disempowerment by relating the story of the non-married father, whom he calls A, who cared for his child after the child's mother, K, re-entered employment. When the mother fell in love with a colleague, A moved out of the flat. Even though the father regularly took care of the child, the mother was unwilling to give up her right to sole custody. Since custody issues in the case of non-married parents are exclusively decided by the mother, A's claim was rejected by the court. During all these years A not only paid regular child support, he also took care of the child with the mother's consent.

Fathers like A have brought their cases to the Constitutional Court. The decision on their rights to custody is still pending. An article in the weekly *Der Spiegel* (1997), whose English version was entitled "The disenfranchised father," presented cases similar to A.'s, but in a highly polemic tone. Men's groups have been active in this struggle. There is support among legislators who have argued that the weakened commitment of fathers after a divorce can be attributed to deficient custody rights, fathers' disempowerment.

Cash

Germany stipulates strong family obligations. Parents have to provide for their children through either cash or care. The parent who does not live in the child's household has to pay maintenance for the child as well as for the mother since her care obligations prevent employment. Divorced fathers are obliged to continue to pay child support until the children finish school or become employed.

Maintenance payments have become increasingly standardized and enforced by legal procedures. Monthly payments increase with the age of the child and with the father's earning capacity. The *Düsseldorfer Tabelle* provides guidelines for family courts. Support for small children (age 0–5) of low-wage earners (up to 2,400 DM after taxes) amounted to a minimum of DM 355, for high-earner earners (7,200–8,000 DM) to a minimum of DM 675 in 1999.

New rights for divorced and non-marital fathers imply obligations. Alongside their improvements in custody rights, non-marital fathers have increased financial obligations. If a non-marital father's income exceeds a particular threshold, he now has to pay for child support as well as a "care maintenance" to the child's non-employed mother (*Betreuungsunterhalt*) for a minimum of three years (this was formerly one year). The period corresponds to that of parental leave. Since nobody expects married mothers to enter the labor market before the youngest child has reached the age of eight, further extensions of non-marital fathers' obligations are pending. The payment to the mother is legally defined as a payment to the child who is said to need full-time care.

Obviously, such an extension would correspond to the principle of subsidiarity, since fathers' contributions relieve the state from social assistance payments. The extension of non-married fathers' obligations also follows the marriage-centered logic of the German welfare state. As has already been said, the German welfare state defines marriage as a mutually supportive relationship – wives support men by taking care of the children and domestic chores, husbands support wives by breadwinning. In the case of non-married parents who are separated, the logic is as follows: the non-married mother takes care of the father's child, and through his financial obligations to her, he has to keep a steady job in order to provide for his child: care versus cash and care for cash. However, in contrast to married and divorced non-employed mothers, she does not have any rights to his pension. This can be interpreted as remaining discrimination of the non-married mother in a male breadwinner regime (Büttner 2000).

The studies that exist on child maintenance and enforcement consist of heterogeneous data. We do not know the total of entitled children, nor the amount or the frequency of payments. Conclusions are often drawn from data that only include children who are entitled to advance payments or children in households that receive social assistance. The last study, which calculated the number of entitled children, dates from 1977 (EMNID-Institute 1978). At that time 70 percent of non-marital and 90 percent of marital children could claim payments. One-third of the mothers indicated that they either did not receive or only irregularly received money. Kirsten Scheiwe (1996), looking at different studies, found that the compliance rate for spouse maintenance ranged between 18 and 40 percent. According to a study which focused solely on the Land Brandenburg (East Germany) 30 percent of children of a total of 490 did not get any payments, another 20 percent received them only irregularly (Großmann et al. 1998). The study found no differences between marital and non-marital fathers. It is difficult to interpret these findings, but the high levels of lone-mother poverty in Germany suggest the difficulty of applying the marriage-centered logic of mutual obligations to divorced and non-marital fathers.

A new role for fathers?

To what extent have these new rights for fathers as carers, which include the changes in custody laws and the parental leave reforms, resulted in a new role for fathers? First of all, it is important to recognize that policies in themselves do not necessarily alter practice. Moreover, as the chapters in this book suggest, reconfiguring the fatherhood triangle is highly dependent on changing the relationships in the domestic and institutional triangles.

How much has the change in the custody law meant a new role for divorced and non-marital fathers after separation?

The new law has improved fathers' access to their children, in the form of visitation rights for both divorced and non-marital fathers after separation. The law also includes mediation for parents who cannot agree about visitation rules. Non-marital fathers can have their rights to access to their children enforced by involving the police. Such a practice, however, may further deteriorate the relationship between the father, the mother and the child.

The new law also increases the decision-making of non-residential fathers with joint custody. In practice, joint custody does not mean joint residential custody, since most children remain with the mother. The law does give some decision-making to fathers who are not residential parents, involving important questions, such as choice of school, education and health problems. Nevertheless, the parent with whom the child resides (most often the mother) does not have to abide by the decisions or influence of the non-residential parent (most often the father) in everyday issues. Finally, when there are conflicts between parents after divorce or separation, litigating mothers get sole custody; maternal preference still exists. Many argue that this asymmetry violates the Constitution.

Costs of fathering and the problem of "collective action"

Will the changes in the parental leave law encourage a shift from cash to care, from the father breadwinner to the father carer?

Studies of men's use of parental leave (Vaskovics and Rost 1999) reveal that men's stronger labor market position, that is the high opportunity costs and income losses, explain part of the low proportion of fathers who take parental leave. Employers' prejudices must also be included in the calculation. Finally, research shows that mothers – be they East or West German – only half-heartedly support male parental leaves.

As in Great Britain and the United States, German companies now require longer hours to compete in the global economies (Soskice 1999). Asking fathers to work less constitutes therefore a typical "collective action" problem (Olson 1971; Offe and De Deken 1999). Why should a father work less in order to be a good father (or mother), if other fathers (and the many childless men and women in Germany) still work full time or even overtime? And, how can a father risk the opportunities and forgo the income, particularly during a period of growing unemployment, income insecurity and greater demands for overtime work? Opinion polls increasingly mirror this sort of reasoning.

For parents, especially for fathers, working-hour reductions are a prerequisite for time to care. New panel data (Holst and Schupp 1999) show a significant change in men's, but also women's attitudes, toward working-time reductions between 1993 and 1997, which seems to be due to the increasing competition and related insecurity of job and income prospects (Bell and Freeman 1995). In 1993 (West) German men who already had the lowest annual working hours in the OECD still wanted further reductions; West German women were content with the number of hours they spent in employment. East Germans, in general, wanted to work more, especially those in part-time employment. However, in 1997, only West German women were still content with their working hours. German men, in general, wanted to work more. Especially, single-earner fathers resented the working-time reduction policies of large firms like Volkswagen or Ruhrkohle AG (Promberger et al. 1996).

Persistence of the male breadwinner norm in unified Germany

The German man and father is, above all, a worker and breadwinner – an *Arbeitsmann*. A recent representative study revealed the extent to which men (and women) stick to the male worker/breadwinner norm (Zulehner and Volz 1998). Four questions were asked: (1) should the female partner or mother stay at home? (2) Should she stay at home as long as children were below school age? (3) Should women do paid work to the same extent as their partners/spouses? (4) Will all profit when the mother/female partner is fully employed while the man/father stayed at home and cared for the children and the household? (Zulehner and Volz 1998: 143). Only three of a total of 1,200 men interviewed and one of 814 women approved of question 4. The others gave varying degrees of a positive answer to the remaining three questions. More men than women preferred the temporary-leave solution for women (question 2); more women than men answered equal sharing (question 3). While strong breadwinning is fading and dual earning emerging, East as well as West German men stated their preference to remain the main breadwinners, especially when their children are small. As Blanke et al. (1996: 6) emphasize, men define their involvement in paid work as their male version of care. Many increase their working hours when they become fathers.

Zulehner and Volz distinguished four types of men and women: the "traditional" breadwinner (19 percent of men), two mixed types, the "insecure" (37 percent) and the "pragmatic" (25 percent); and finally the "new" men (20 percent). "New" men are highly qualified and have good occupations; they are active fathers and like to be good partners. "Insecure" men cognitively accept women as equals but do not know how to meet this standard in reality. "Pragmatic" men are traditional and self-centered, but, at the same time, they often out of necessity take on caring roles. All interviewed men, regardless of type, held stereotypical (often dichotomous) views about male and female qualities (e.g. man as rational, the leader, woman as the one who needs loving care).

It may not come as a surprise that the authors found more "new" women than "new" men (Zulehner and Volz 1998: 145). What is surprising is the similarity of East and West German men. The authors discovered nearly the same distribution of the four types among men from the East and West, though East German men characterized themselves as slightly less "traditional," more open to "new" masculinities, but equally "insecure." The same numbers of men and women – whether East or West German – belonged to the "pragmatic" type.

A new agenda for fathers, fatherhood and fathering

Clearly the search for a new role for fathers must begin with making fathers visible in public discourse. A prerequisite is a new discourse on fatherhood, decoupled from its Nazi past, and grounded in a research agenda on fathers.

In Germany, fathers have been rarely talked of in positive terms. Until very recently, it was mainly (West German) feminists who studied men, and men as fathers (Hagemann-White and Rerrich 1985; Kavemann and Lohstöter 1985). In this literature, issues, such as male domestic violence, child abuse and gendered power relations dominated. Some feminist analyses of the gender division of domestic labor also searched for "new" egalitarian men.

Little research has been done by men on men. In his recent review of the international state of the art, Peter Döge (2000), one of the very few German social scientists who have specialized in men studies, maintains that, in contrast to Anglo-American countries, critical men's studies hardly exist in Germany. They have not yet been established in universities, respective courses are rare.

There are, however, some institutes where researchers are now producing research on men as fathers. The Bamberg Institute for Family Research headed by Laszlo A. Vaskovics, a sociologist of Hungarian origin, has studied the status, attitudes and daily practices of parents, for instance, mothers' and fathers' attitudes toward fathers who have taken parental leaves (Vaskovics et al. 1997; Vaskovics and Rost 1999). Ministries and politicians sought the advice of his institute before drafting new legislation on family policies. The joint custody and parental leave reforms, or the part-time legislation draw upon his insights. The Greek psychologist Wassilios Fthenakis who works in (West) Germany published two volumes about the importance of having and being a father. He is one of the fiercest fighters for the improvement of fathers' rights and the equalization of fathers' legal and social status with those of mothers (Fthenakis 1988).

Another precondition for a new agenda for fathers is a shift in the focus of policies from husbands to fathers. Family policies in the West were constructed around husbands, not fathers; the GDR largely ignored both. Fatherhood and fathering practices are in the background of much of the new legislation. None of the reforms were drafted explicitly to help fathers. They either focused on labor markets' or on children's needs. If conflicts between divorced and separated parents arise, the courts generally rule in favor of the mother, with the rationale that it is in the best interest of the child. The child's best interest also allows for greater financial obligations of non-marital fathers that are not matched by corresponding rights. Nevertheless fathers are expected to be providers of support, not only breadwinners. Yet the structural constraints, job insecurities and global pressures make it difficult to search for a new role for fathers.

Given the framework of this book, one can view the new policies and laws on parental leave and custody rights as interventions in the fatherhood/fathering/fathers triangle, initiatives that could alter the practices of fathers and shift the meanings of fatherhood from strong breadwinners to father breadwinner carers. Yet, without disturbing the relations in institutional and domestic triangles, these reforms will not lure men into fathering. Market realities, gender differences in full- and part-time work, and the division of paid and unpaid work among married and divorced families all suggest otherwise.

6 Transformations of fatherhood: the Netherlands

Trudie Knijn and Peter Selten

Introduction

Fatherhood has taken center stage in the Netherlands. One finds a new emphasis on a father's role as carer, not just as provider, articulated in public discourse, law and social policy. This shift can be illustrated by three striking examples privileging fathers, which reveal the importance of the caring role of fathers. First, the most visible is a media campaign launched by the government to persuade fathers to become more involved in the upbringing and raising of their children. Take, for instance, a television spot, initiated by the Ministry of Social Affairs (and Emancipation) which shows an old-fashioned family with haircuts and clothes reminiscent of the 1950s. The intention of this depiction is probably to remind us of the traditional family form of that period, one which we are all familiar with. The picture shows the following scene:

A father, two daughters and a son are sitting around the table in the dining room. No one says a word. Suddenly, a woman, obviously the mother, enters the room and offers a plate with meat to the father who cuts the meat. At that moment, a voice representing the thought of the son, says, "who is this man who cuts the meat every Sunday?" Then, a written text appears: "Men are as indispensable at home as they are at work."

The campaign highlights the care responsibilities of men from a relational perspective. The message is that fathers should not be estranged from their children, that children need to know their fathers, and that fathers can only be known when they are more involved in the lives of their children. The campaign is striking because of its impact and momentum. A decade ago, a similar media campaign was abandoned because an experimental target group of fathers rejected the message. Now, in the late 1990s, the climate has changed. The Dutch government thus encourages men to be involved with their family and be caring fathers.

The second example is found in a section of the new Civil Code, which came into effect in 1998. It concerns many issues that address fatherhood, fathering and fathers: joint custody after divorce, the naming of children,

168

the inquiry into fatherhood in the case of unmarried parents, the denial of fatherhood within marriage, and the equalization of children born inside, and outside, of wedlock. Laws, such as the right of parents to give their child either the father's or the mother's last name, have been accepted in most Western societies. However, in the Netherlands it has taken about fifteen years to get this bill passed. Until January 1, 1998, parents who did not want to give the child the father's last name were doomed not to marry and to deny fatherhood; only then could the child bear the name of the mother. The new law makes it possible for about 20,000 children to be legitimized by their fathers while getting their mother's last name.

The third example addresses innovative policies that encourage the reconciliation of work and family care for both fathers and mothers. In 2000, the parliament passed a law that contains the right for workers, male and female, to reduce or extend their working time. This law, called the Adjustment Working Hours Law offers employees working in the private, as well as the public, sector a legal claim to adjust their working hours. The arguments in support of the law are based upon developments in the labor market – internationalization, flexibilization and a shortage of employees – as well as on developments in family life – a wish for the reconciliation of work and family among women and men (Tweede Kamer der Staten Generaal 1998–1999: 26358, no. 3).

What is happening in the Netherlands, as reflected in the changing discourses, practices and laws concerning fatherhood, fits into the pattern of re-emphasizing and redefining the role of fathers and the position of fatherhood in many other Western countries. The tendency toward compulsory co-parenthood after divorce in several Northern European countries clearly reflects a movement in laws and policy to redefine the position of fathers toward their children and their former wives. However, the Child Support Act in Britain (Smart 1995b; Lewis 1997b) represents a renewed emphasis on the support obligations of the father. The "daddy quota" in parental leave legislation in Sweden and Norway (Hobson and Bergman in this volume; Leira 1998) suggests a shift toward the care responsibilities of the father.

In this chapter, we analyze new laws and social policies from the perspective of the shifting parameters of cash and care. We ask: in what ways has the provider role of fathers changed in the Netherlands and to what extent is caring integrated as an aspect of fatherhood? In the following section, we focus on the shifts in the construction of fatherhood in the Netherlands and the reaction of the Dutch to these changes as seen in social policies and legislation. We will distinguish the description of the fathers' role as provider and Dutch social policies concerning fathers as breadwinners from the fathers' judicial relationship *vis-à-vis* their children. Because marriage is a crucial distinction in the legal relationship of fathers, mothers and children in the Netherlands, we will compare these two aspects of fatherhood for married and unmarried fathers.

Changes in fatherhood in the Netherlands

Changes in fatherhood reflect other transformations, which can be analyzed in terms of the interdependencies within the domestic and institutional triangles, outlined in the Introduction of this collection. Inner-familial changes in the position of fathers are constituted within the "domestic triangle," which encompasses the relationships between fathers, mothers and children. Beyond the inner-familial changes there are those located in the "institutional triangle": the family, the market and the state. Together, these three institutional domains give shape to the "welfare mix" responsible for the well-being of citizens (see also the Introduction in this volume). Within the domestic triangle, processes of individualization and democratization have influenced the relationship between the sexes and the generations, which has put new demands on fathers. In the Netherlands, as is true in some other Western countries, most notably the Scandinavian ones, these processes resulted in the discourse of the "caring father." This discourse is inspired by at least three, not always easily compatible, ideologies. First, feminist perspectives state that men should be as responsible for caring as women are. Secondly, the fathers' movements claim that men are as capable as women of caring for children. Thirdly, the familialist claims of the Christian Democrats, family sociologists and pedagogical experts stress the importance of father–child bonding as well as working toward an involved and caring father. Both the feminists and men in the fathers' movements share the belief in father–child bonding, though not its familialist base.

Since the late 1980s, caring fatherhood has become a "hot issue" in the media; it has been a topic of many round-table discussion programs, promoted by groups who represent a "caring fathers" movement, which is warmly welcomed as an alternative to the traditional father-as-breadwinner model (Knijn 1995; Duindam 1997). Caring fatherhood was presented in numerous educational programs: fatherhood videos, young-father groups and courses for teaching fathering skills were given all over the country (Grunell 1997). The media campaign of the Dutch government, mentioned in the beginning of this chapter, was part of this process, but similar campaigns were also found in the trade unions.

This promotion of caring and involved fatherhood might be viewed as an expression of, as well as a reaction to, transformations within the domestic triangle of fathers, mothers and children. On the one hand, it expresses the greater value of egalitarian and democratic relationships within the family, which no longer assume that fathers are the heads of the family. Rather, fathers are expected to take equal responsibility for the construction of family life and its daily tasks. On the other hand, the promotion of the caring father can be seen as a reaction to the individualization of women and children (e.g. the rising divorce rates), which creates a sense of urgency around the commitment to, and involvement of, all members of the family, including fathers. Although these concerns reflect processes which may not appear that dramatic in comparison with those of other countries, they are issues that play a significant role in debates within the Netherlands. The increasing divorce rate does not sound as alarming as it does in some other European countries (an increase from 3.3 per 1,000 marriages in 1970 to 10.4 per 1,000 in 1994). However, the number of children born to unmarried mothers has certainly increased at a much faster rate – of all lone mothers in 1971, 10 percent were both unmarried and not cohabiting, in 1993 this percentage rose to 25 percent – and the percentage of children born out of wedlock also increased – from 2.1 per 100 new-born children in 1970 to 15.7 in 1995 (van Praag and Niphuis-Nell 1997). Most of these children, though, are born to common-law couples – parents who cohabit (CBS 1995). From these demographic figures we may conclude that the relationship between fathers, on the one hand, and mothers and children, on the other, is weakening, although not dramatically.

The realization of caring fatherhood, however, depends not only on the fathers' commitment to mothers and children, but also on processes in the institutional triangle that connect the family with the market and the state. Demands of the labor market, however, do not fit easily with the ideologies for caring fathers. These demands can produce constraints on the possibilities for fathers to care, as well as introduce policies, directly or indirectly, to encourage caring fathering. Both labor market developments and welfare state policies influence the way caring fathering can be put into practice. The decline of regular working hours to an average of 36 hours a week in the (semi-)governmental professions and 38 hours a week in private companies can have the effect of giving fathers more time with their children. At the same time, many companies extended their work weeks by creating flexible work patterns and new shifts or compressed work weeks (four days of nine hours each). As a result, the regular (five days, eight hours a day) work week has been disrupted with severe consequences for households. However, it is still too early to tell whether these flexible work weeks are either a stimulation or a constraint for realizing caring fatherhood. Probably they are both; they may create opportunities for scheduling caring days for some groups of fathers and disrupt caring shifts for others. Figures show that, to date, most men, and especially fathers of young children, work full time, while only a small proportion work part time for reasons linked to parenthood. The percentage of all working men with part-time jobs increased from 8 percent to 10 percent, although this was often for reasons linked to study and illness (Plantenga 1996).

The rise in women's labor participation can also be another reason behind the discourse and policy on caring fatherhood. The Netherlands, compared to other European countries, has had one of the lowest proportions of employed married women. In the 1970s, only 30 percent of all Dutch women above the age of 16 participated in the labor market, while only 20 percent of mothers with children younger than 17 years, and 10 percent of the mothers of siblings were employed – often part time (de Hart 1995; van Praag and Niphuis-Nell 1997; SCP 1998). Nowadays 51 percent of all women (with and without children) are employed (Keuzenkamp and Oudhof 2000). Most of the new working women are young and well educated, though the labor participation of mothers of young children (below 6 years) still lags behind the participation of women of their generation who do not have children, or who have older children (de Vries 1998). Alongside the increasing labor participation of women, the fragmentation and flexibilization of jobs has to be taken into account; full-time jobs are replaced by part-time jobs as the preferred choice of mothers. In 1992, 53 percent of all working women had a part-time job. In 1999, this increased to 67 percent (Keuzenkamp and Oudhof 2000). Moreover, flexible and temporary jobs are increasing more than regular jobs; from 12 percent in 1992 to 14 percent in 1997 among women, and from 5 percent to 7 percent respectively among men (CBS 1997).

We might conclude that the shift to the caring fatherhood discourse is inspired by an amalgam of different, and sometimes competing, ideologies. These reflect, as well as respond to, the processes of individualization and democratization within the private triangle. Feminist movements, fatherhood movements and experts each developed their own assumptions about the responsibilities, rights, capabilities and commitments of fathers. Developments in the labor market may encourage, or discourage, the tendency toward caring fatherhood. The increasing needs of the labor market for female employees and the desire of mothers to work (part time) without doubt promoted the longing for shared parenthood among men and women. This is also a practical strategy, since there is still a huge shortage of child-care facilities in the Netherlands. Still, the labor market is full of constraints for men working part time; and thus the polarization between the market of full-time jobs for men and part-time jobs for women is increasing. The implication is that, to date, the one-and-half-earner family is the dominant pattern among parents. In practice, the majority of fathers do not have the opportunity to do anything more than some additional caring during their leisure time. The domestic triangle and the institutional triangle are therefore both shifting, though not necessarily in the same direction. Within the relational triangle, fathers, but not all of them to the same degree, are increasingly becoming interested in being more involved with their children, within or out-of marriage. This tendency is, theoretically and practically, supported by the government, pedagogues, other professionals and also by many mothers. However not all fathers, and maybe even not a majority, show a real commitment to increasing their share of carework. Although 68 percent of all men agree that men and women should share carework equally, only 8 percent of fathers with children under eighteen want to reduce their working hours (van Praag and Niphuis-Nell 1997).

Tensions concerning fathering within the domestic triangle, such as the father's claims to remain involved in the life of his child after divorce or a parent's problems with scheduling care and work, form the background of new legislation and provisions to improve the involvement of fathers in family life and caring. Within the institutional triangle, tensions occur from changes in the labor market, the increasing labor participation of women and the attempts of the Dutch welfare state to facilitate the combination of work and family life. With the new "Adjustment Working Hours Law" (2000) the Dutch government intends to develop family policies which suit labor market developments and vice versa. However, companies still have a great deal of decision-making to do on whether this legal right can be implemented since they have the right to make exceptions to the law when they can prove that the company's interest is at stake. Such limitations show that the Dutch government places a great deal of trust on the co-operation of social partners in the development of family policies. In the following section we will focus on the specific developments in welfare state policy concerning the position of fathers in cash and care in the Netherlands.

Transformations in the father's role as provider

Concerning the provider role of the father, the Netherlands was, and in some respects still is, a strong breadwinner regime (Lewis 1992). This model reached its climax after World War II when the Dutch welfare state developed. All kinds of arrangements, which were organized in these post-war decades, confirmed, as well as benefited, the pre-war position of the male breadwinner. However, from the 1970s onward, the Dutch welfare state transformed into a "breadwinner–motherhood model" by supporting the mother without a husband/breadwinner.

The breadwinner–motherhood model financially supports motherhood in several ways. Mothers have an equal status within marriage and the family as well as an exit-option based upon specific citizenship rights related to motherhood, for instance by social assistance and widows' pensions. The implication of the breadwinner–motherhood model for fatherhood is that the father's role as provider within the marriage is strongly supported, while it is almost totally ignored when he is no longer married. While almost all fathers were fully responsible for maintaining their wives and children during marriage, only a small minority of non-married fathers retained their financial responsibility for their children. Current transformations are reshaping this gap in the financial responsibility of married and non-married fathers, however not by enforcing the role of fathers as providers in the case of divorced or unmarried mothers, but by modifying the father's position as sole breadwinner. The provider role of a married, male breadwinner endures and is not easily weakened. It remains distinct from the provider role of a divorced or never-married father.

In situating post-war Netherlands at the end of the spectrum of male breadwinner models, three characteristics are crucial. (1) Fathers were strongly supported for the costs of supporting families. (2) Labor legislation and the tax system explicitly privileged men as workers above women. (3) Public services or benefits for married working mothers were not available (Sainsbury 1994: 156–157). Two aspects of the Dutch welfare state, a combination of egalitarian Social Democratic principles and Christian Democratic principles of subsidiarity, worked in tandem to support the position of the father as the one and only provider of his family. Wage policies intended to minimize poverty – such as welfare benefits, pension benefits, unemployment benefits and child allowances – were exclusively paid to the "head of the household," that is the father/provider. The same was true for the contributions to the increasing welfare system; premiums for compulsory health insurance, taxes and social insurance were paid by the male breadwinner of the family, not by married women.

The privileged position of male breadwinners was also bolstered by the tax system. Husbands lost tax privileges when wives earned their own income. In addition, in 1947, the "Stichting van de Arbeid" put in place a policy that standardized the minimum wage at a level sufficient to provide for a married man, his wife and two children below the age of 16. Female workers were defined as "girls" and their minimum wage level was set at 60 to 80 percent of male wages. In 1971, the Netherlands was, in fact, the last European country to ratify the European directive to equalize wages between men and women (Cuyvers, de Hoog and Pott Buter 1997).

The Dutch welfare state was, until the 1970s, a strong male bread-winner model in all its work-related policies. Not only its social policy, but also the Dutch family law, codified the dominance of the father in decision-making within the family. The law gave fathers preeminence in all decisions concerning the education of the children, the housing and the financial affairs of the family (Holtrust 1993). Although the mother was given equal responsibility for parenthood in 1949 and married women's "incapability of acting" was abrogated in 1957 – until then, she was not even allowed to have her own bank account – the father kept the final authority. The husband maintained his status as the economic head of the family (Gastelaars 1985: 116; Holtrust and de Hondt 1997: 247).

Family life slowly changed. Increasing prosperity offered fertile ground for the individualization of women and children, and the rising educational level of women stimulated their ambition to get a job. The availability of contraception reduced the size of families and the divorce rates increased. These transformations had consequences for the provider position of fathers.

In the 1970s, a process of equalizing the rights of fathers and mothers began and the Dutch welfare state weakened the dominance of male breadwinners through changes in policy and law. This was expressed in daily life patterns as well as in the welfare system and family law. The introduction of the new Civil Code in 1970 (which replaced the Civil Code of 1838) implied a transformation of the father's (financial) rights *within the family*. Under the old Civil Code, family law gave all power to the husband and father. An important alteration in the new Civil Code was the disappearance of this absolute power of the husband. But, the position of the man remained dominant. The new principle that gave the husband and wife control over the possessions they had brought into the marriage, or bought themselves during the marriage, worked out in favor of the man. Because he received an income for his work, most consumable goods were legally his property. Nevertheless, there existed some provisions in the law to protect the family against potentially harmful decisions made by the father. Each spouse, for example, needed the consent of the other to buy or sell the house (Holtrust and de Hondt 1997: 253). Nevertheless, the father had sole authority on the capital of his minor children. A mother could not open a savings account in the name of her child, nor take money from it. The authority for the children formally rested with both parents, but, in case of disagreement, the father had the veto. It was not until 1985 that the disparities between husband and wife disappeared in family law. In case of disagreement, the dispute on authority over the children could now be submitted to court (Holtrust and de Hondt 1997: 268).

The introduction of the new Divorce Law in 1971 made divorce easily accessible. Under the new law, married people could proceed to divorce if a so-called "lasting disruption" had occurred, while in earlier periods adultery had to be proven. At the same time, the Social Assistance Law came into effect, which provided lone mothers with economic support. This, alongside the new Divorce Law, was followed by an increase in the divorce rate. It also contributed to the increase in *fatherhood outside marriage*. Until the 1970s, divorce rates were rather low. Between 1945 and 1967 approximately 2.5 out of 1,000 marriages ended in a divorce. From 1969 onwards, these rates increased to 3.3 in 1970, 6 in 1975, 7.5 in 1980 and 10 per 1,000 in 1985. Since then, it has steadily declined, mainly because of the increasing tendency toward (separation after) co-habitation (CBS 1994).

Before the 1970s, the break-up of the domestic triangle of fathers, mothers and children did not mean that the state stepped in as provider for the remaining family. While in many other countries a widow's pension was enacted in the first decades of the century, it was not until 1959 that the Netherlands finally implemented a comprehensive financial provision for widows. This Algemene Weduwen en Wezenwet (General Widows and Orphans Law) guaranteed widows with children a whole-life income at the minimum wage level, without means-testing. However, a widow would lose her pension upon remarriage (and, if she was very young and had no children, she got a limited pension). The Dutch welfare state in the 1970s gave means-tested, but generous, support for all mothers without a breadwinner. This policy allowed lone mothers to form their own households without the financial obligation to work, but these welfare benefits, in combination with a rather diffuse alimony policy, also weakened the financial responsibilities of a father toward his children as well as to his former – often unemployed – wife (Knijn 1994; Bussemaker et al. 1997).

One of the main consequences of the specific social policies concerning divorce is that they hardly placed any financial burden on the man to support his former wife. The new Divorce Law included an option, the "nil-condition," in the law that allowed both former partners to deny reciprocal financial responsibilities, even when that resulted in a need for social assistance for one of the partners. Under the conditions of the 1970s, this was the norm. Divorced women applied for social assistance while divorced men were freed from paying alimony. This resulted in a marked increase in the number of social assistance benefits, and, at the same time, the income of municipalities paying benefits decreased, which meant that they lost their right to enforce fathers to pay their financial share (see also de Regt 1993). In the decades after the introduction of the

Social Assistance law, a majority of all divorced mothers received social assistance (see also Bussemaker et al. 1997).

During this period of the golden era of the welfare states, few changes in the work pattern of fathers took place; the main changes occurred within the relational triangle of the family connected to change in the institutional triangle through family policies and laws. A new Civil Code, the Divorce Law and the Social Assistance Law supported the position of mothers within, and outside of, marriage. Although fathers remained the main providers of the family, their financial supremacy within marriage declined. Outside marriage, many fathers were freed from financial obligations toward their first families; the welfare state became the main supporter of lone-mother families.

Fathers between cash and care

Since the end of the 1980s, the Dutch government has recognized the need to modify the strong male breadwinner model and its support for single mothers. A strong shortage of labor in a booming economy and demographic developments (in particular the relative growth in the number of elderly) has resulted in policies to stimulate the employment of women and to decrease welfare benefits. These policies fit with the long-standing feminist claim for enabling policies to support the entrance of women into the labor market (Ministerie van Sociale Zaken en Werkgelegenheid 1997). The increase of women's labor participation is, however, restricted by the preference of many parents to care for children within the family as well as by structural constraints. For example, day-care is available for 15 percent of all children below school age (five) who, on average, attend 2.5 days a week, and after-school care is available for only 2 percent of all schoolchildren (Keuzenkamp and Oudhof 2000). In addition, tax advantages for sole breadwinners still discourage less well-educated married women from obtaining paid employment. A strategy for combining work and care by mothers, as well as fathers, is therefore ideologically supported by the government, as well as by many parents. Such a strategy might also create flexible family patterns that facilitate flexible work patterns, and presumes that parents co-operate to share family responsibilities. For these reasons, the government has tried to persuade fathers to take care of their children in the broadest meaning of the word (see the aforementioned media campaign).

In practice, families in which the man is the single breadwinner are still not exceptional in the Netherlands in the 1990s. Figures from 1994 show that this type of family usually has either children below the age of 12 or children who have left the parental home. In the latter, the mothers of these families are above the age of 40. Dual-earner families hardly exist among families with children; such couples are young, highly educated and have no children, and 70 percent of them are under 35 years of age. Among families with children, three patterns are found: the male bread-winner/female housewife type, the one-and-half earners of which the woman works part time, and the "both parents working part time" type, where both parents work less than 35 hours each a week (Hooghiemstra 1997: 60). It can be concluded that, although women's labor force partici-pation rates have increased rapidly in the Netherlands since the 1970s, this resulted in mothers working part-time, whereas the ideal of many parents, that is both working part time, is only realized by 3 percent of all couples in 1999 (Keuzenkamp and Hooghiemstra 2000). Therefore, fathers are still, more than in many other European countries, the main breadwinners in two-parent families. The implications of women's labor participation for the net income of the family are rather limited, due to women's part-time jobs, the gender wage gap, and because women have lower positions in organizations than men, even when they have simi-lar levels of education (Plantenga 1996, 1998). Besides, partner-related income policies – like taxes, premiums and benefits – reduce women's contributions to the family income to such an extent that women have to work a lot to balance the loss of tax advantages for single-earner fami-lies. Calculations of the incomes of different categories of families made by Hooghiemstra show that one-and-a-half earners work 1.5 times more than single earners but earn about 1.3 times more. Dual earners work twice as much as single earners but earn not more than 1.4 times more income (Hooghiemstra 1997: 67). Social policies intending to equalize single- and dual-earner families in the Netherlands are not very success-ful. In particular, less-well-educated wives are not employed. This widens the income gap between dual and single-earner families as well as between higher and less-well-educated families.

The slow shift toward dual-earner families with children forms the background of the fact that women still do three-quarters of the care work in the family when they have children, even though fathers are increasingly taking responsibility for some portion of the housekeeping and care for children. This is a general tendency among all fathers, in particular those who have children under five years of age. These fathers of young children spend significantly more time on housekeeping: 21 hours a week in 1995 in comparison to 16 hours in 1975. They also spend more time caring for the children; this increased from 4 hours a week in 1975 to 8.5 hours in 1995 (van Praag and Niphuis-Nell 1997). In general, we can state that the increased employment of mothers of young children did not result in a reduction of caring time by parents. In contrast, the significance of the emotional and affective relationship between parents and children – fathers as well as mothers – increased during the last decades and forms the background of the growing involvement of fathers in the daily lives of their children (Knijn 1997).

Fathers' rights and obligations

In the 1980s, the government tried to re-establish the obligation of divorced men to pay alimony. The government had now decided, for both pragmatic and ideological reasons, that alimony should be paid for a limited period, for twelve years following the date of divorce. One argument that led to the proposed change in policy was the cutback in social assistance and the desire to reduce inequalities between municipal policies, some of which were rather strict in obliging fathers to pay their share, while others never tried to get fathers to pay anything. The Secretary of State who introduced the new law put ideological reasons forward. She stated: "Marriage is an economic contract, loving each other can do without marriage . . . [In the Civil Code] it is stated that the obligation for mutual support also lasts when one isn't married anymore" (quoted in de Regt 1993: 50).

The proposed law was highly contested and was never put into practice throughout the country. Older divorced women, the majority of whom were not employed during their marriage, resisted because it decreased the period in which they could claim an additional income from their ex-husbands. In addition, younger women, as well as the majority of divorced men, opposed the law for reasons of financial independence after marriage. At that time, divorced women were rather satisfied with social assistance as an alternative to dependency on their former husbands. Fathers, in contrast, envisioned the law as an attack on their autonomy and their ability to start a new family. Both groups expressed their interest in financial autonomy after marriage via the mass media. Another reason for objections against the law was the practical difficulties involved in attempting to enforce former husbands to pay their share. Ultimately, only about 25 percent of all divorced mothers received child allowances, while courts have obliged about 40 percent of fathers to pay for their children in 1993, and only 7 percent of lone mothers receive alimony for themselves (CBS 1994; Niphuis-Nell 1997: 97; van Wel and Knijn 2000). Divorced men developed different strategies to evade their obligations – for example, making irregular payments, decreasing formal income and threatening former wives. Divorced women rarely try to obtain their rights with respect to alimony; mostly because they are afraid to disturb the very fragile relationship with the father of their children. Although the official policies are in place to enforce the financial obligations of former husbands and have been more stringent since the end of the 1980s, in practice payment still depends on the goodwill of fathers.

While the policy to enforce the financial obligations of fathers for their former families has not succeeded, the policy to reduce the costs of benefits for lone mothers has resulted in a New Social Assistance Law. Since January 1, 1996, lone mothers with children above four years of age have the obligation to find a paying job, which may reduce their ability to form an autonomous household because they now have to combine work and care. Together, the alimony policy has not increased men's financial responsibility, but the obligation to work for single mothers has reduced the costs of divorce for the state. In this respect, the Netherlands differs from some other European countries, such as those described in this volume, which have much stricter rules for the financial obligation of fathers to children born outside marriage. The Netherlands did not enact a Child Support Act like Britain to enforce the financial obligation of a father for all of his biological children. Nor is there much effort to pressure fathers to pay alimony by reducing the tax-credits of their wages, as in Germany, or by deducting the payment directly from their wages, as is the case in Sweden.

Improving the legal position of fathers

Social policies and legislation concerning the role of the father as the provider are mirrored by family policies defining the relationship between fathers and children. In this respect, issues of guardianship after divorce, the recognition of children by biological parents and the legal relationship between children and unmarried fathers are now being reconsidered in the Netherlands. Since 1998, a new set of legal provisions on the family came into effect. In some respects, these legal provisions represent a sharp break with former codes and regulations. There is a tendency toward regulating the judicial relationship between fathers and children in accordance with their social relationship to their children. At the same time, there is a strong emphasis on biological fatherhood. In the following section, we follow some of the debates that have led to new legislation and policy concerning non-marital fatherhood.

Father's recognition

The Family Law system, which was in effect until January 1, 1998, was developed at a time when cohabitation and divorce were still exceptional. It was built upon the dominant view that the protection of the

prevailing relationship between mother and child, especially when involving lone mothers and widows, was paramount. Unmarried cohabiting fathers hardly existed, and divorce rates were low. No special legal arrangements were available for unmarried, though present fathers. In cases
of divorce, the children were usually awarded to the mother. Divorced
fathers were more or less in the same position as deceased ones. They
should pay for them and the children could inherit, but policy makers
felt no need to arrange a more formal role with respect to the care and
education of children. Family Law confirmed this position. A distinction
was made between children born within marriage (legitimate children)
and children born out of wedlock (illegitimate children). If a child was
born within a marriage, the husband was automatically the legal father,
even if he was not the biological father of the child. A married man could
recognize a biological child of his wife, born before marriage, as his own.
The child would then, like all legitimate children, carry the name of the
father and inherit from both parents. If one of the parents died, the other
one automatically became guardian over the child.

Biological, though unmarried, fathers could recognize a child at the
registry office. A man only needed the written permission of the mother
to become the legal father. This recognition, however, did not give him all
of the legal rights and duties that a married father possessed. A recognized
child got the family name of the father and the father was financially
responsible for the child. A recognized child could also inherit from its
father. The recognizing father, however, had no formal parental authority
over the child. The parental authority was automatically entrusted to the
mother. The father could only hold co-custody, but again only if the
mother gave her permission. Besides, the only way a co-guardian could
have influence on the education of the child was by approval of the mother
(Holtrust 1988: 57; Raad voor het Jeugdbeleid 1988: 16).

When cohabitation outside of marriage became more popular, the system seemed outdated. In 1970, only 2 per thousand children were born
out of wedlock, in 1993 there were 13 per thousand (CBS 1994). Unmarried fathers began to claim their rights. Most importantly, they raised
the question of whether the need for a mother's permission to recognize
a child was not in conflict with the interests of the father and of the child.
In 1981, the Minister of Justice still answered this question in the negative: "From the position of the mother it is unacceptable that a man puts
himself in some legal relation to the child against her will. The establishment of such a relation requires the free permission of the mother and
this man" (quoted in Holtrust 1993: 108). Two comments were made
on this position: the pedagogical experts stressed family life, saying that a
child needs both a mother and a father. The juridical position emphasized

the fundamental rights of the individual, be it a man, woman or child. "Why should an unmarried woman have a right a married woman does not have?" This was the rhetorical question of the Amsterdam Professor of Youth and Family Law, Doek (quoted by Holtrust 1993: 109).

This debate, of course, was a highly charged one when the cohabiting couple broke up. The lack of legal clarity and guidelines suited to the new forms of parenthood led to numerous court cases during a period of about twenty years. For example, in 1985, the Amsterdam Court of Justice for the first time ruled in favor of an unmarried father who had been denied recognition, because the mother refused her permission. The Court was of the opinion that the need for a mother's consent conflicted with the European Agreement on Human Rights, especially the articles on the right of respect for family life. The Supreme Court passed a comparable judgment in 1988. However, the Court determined that the mother's refusal could only be overruled if there had been a close personal relationship between the father and the child, for instance if the father actually had taken a major role in caring for the child (Holtrust 1993: 109–117). Being the biological father in itself was not sufficient. These conditions have been recorded in the new Civil Code, which came into effect in 1998.

Another important innovation of the new Civil Code concerns judicial paternity. As far back as 1901, the law had explicitly forbidden any inquiry into paternity. One concluded that fatherhood and filiation by definition were legal concepts, tied to marriage. Maintenance was seen as a duty of the procreator, but only on a voluntary basis (Sevenhuijsen 1987). As late as the 1990s, the Supreme Court judged that it was not the task of the courts to force a man to recognize a child, but of the legislative power. In 1995, a court denied the claim of a young girl to get a DNA test to prove that her father had become – by rape – the father of her child. Under the new law, such an inquiry into paternity is possible. The now proven biological father will be appended to the birth certificate of the child. There are only two conditions: there must be no other legal father present and only the procreator can be recognized as being the legal father (de Boer 1998: 7). Probably, the Netherlands is the last European country in which the opportunity to apply for an affiliation order has finally been accepted in law.

Therefore, a general characteristic of the new Civil Code is that biological fatherhood has gained more weight than social fatherhood within the formal rules. A striking illustration of this is that the terms "legitimate" and "illegitimate" child have been crossed out. The question of recognition is crucial for the recognition of a father's rights and duties. A father who has recognized a child also has a right to see the child and can ask for co-guardianship. In doing so, he acquires financial responsibility for the child. The legal provisions on paternity in the new Civil Code stress the importance of biological fatherhood, and strengthen the legal relationship between fathers and their biological children.

Guardianship

Traditionally, guardianship mainly concerned divorced fathers and widowers. A widower automatically became guardian over his children after the mother died. When a couple divorced, the court appointed one of them as guardian. The other became co-guardian, a position lacking influence. Until the 1980s, in 90 percent of divorce cases the mother was appointed guardian on the grounds that she took daily care of the children. Only if the mother had left the children or was evidently incapable of taking care of the children (for instance because of mental illness) was guardianship given to the father. Sometimes the court also decided that the father could offer the children a better, or more stable, family life than the mother, for instance if he was re-married and when the mother was employed (Bonnekamp 1988). In such cases, images of proper gender roles and proper family life overruled the past performance of mothers as carers.

As more couples cohabited and had children, the range of guardianship practices was broadened. The mother who gave birth, automatically became the guardian. If the father recognized the children born out of this relationship, with the consent of the mother, he could be appointed co-guardian. Many fathers felt this arrangement was discriminatory toward unmarried couples and went to court. In response, since the end of the 1980s, judges have been increasingly willing to allow shared custody on the condition that both parents agree. This rule also became widely established in cases of divorce. In 1995, shared custody also became possible (Holtrust 1993: 122–123; Holtrust and de Hondt 1997: 271; de Boer 1998: 5–6).

However, the condition of mutual consent meant that each of the parents could still veto the arrangement. The new Civil Code that came into effect in January 1998 reversed this principle. The new law states that, after divorce, joint custody is compulsory unless one of the parents succeeds in convincing the court that such an arrangement is harmful to the well-being of the child. The tendency is to equate non-marital relations with marital relations. Moreover, parenthood is distinguished from partnership and the relationship with the child has to be continued when marriage or cohabitation ends. Women's organizations have objected to this reversal; they fear that fathers will interfere with the daily life of the family, something that they do not partake in themselves (Holtrust and de Hondt 1997: 272). The net-effect of these measures is that the rights of fathers, especially when they are no longer married to the mother of the child, have been strengthened. However, it is doubtful if the changes in law have consequences for the actual conditions of education. Most children of divorced parents continue to live with their mothers. Struggles between divorced or separated parents, then, have to do with visiting rights.

Visiting rights

Under the Divorce Law of 1971, children were assigned to one of the parents, almost always the mother. The court could establish a visiting arrangement between the father and child. There was, however, no provision made on the implementation of this arrangement. In practice, this meant that such an arrangement depended on both parents' willingness to cooperate. In 1979, the Minister of Justice presented a new bill, in which a visiting arrangement was seen as a reciprocal right between parents and children. There were pedagogical and judicial arguments for this point of view. From the pedagogical point of view, the Minister stated that birth created an affective relationship and a particular commitment between the child and both parents, something that could not be broken down by divorce. From the judicial point of view, a visiting arrangement was seen as a fundamental right, not only in the interests of the parent, but also in those of the child. Only in exceptional cases could such an arrangement be refused. This bill was subject to intense debate. On the one hand, several groups, such as pedagogues and magistrates in juvenile courts, doubted whether such visiting arrangements should always be "in the interest of the well-being of the child." Others, especially fathers who after divorce had been deprived of the right to meet their children, were of the opinion that this bill was not far-reaching enough. They asked for co-custody instead of visiting rights to guarantee that the non-guardian–parent could participate in important decisions. In addition, they claimed sanctions in cases where a mother did not cooperate. Beyond this, legal experts argued that the bill was in conflict with the so-called Marckx-arrest of the European Court of Justice of 1979 and Section 14 of the European Treaty on Human Rights; the right of family life.

Although in 1981 this bill was rejected, courts acted in accordance with a view that a visiting arrangement was a right of the father as well as in the interests of the child. In 1995, this practice was passed into law. As cohabitation without marriage increased, similar regulations were made for cohabiting couples who separated. From 1977 onwards, several judgments were passed in which fathers, who had recognized their children, were granted a visiting arrangement. The courts made two conditions: a father had to have recognized the child (which could only have happened with the consent of the mother) and a kind of family relationship had to have existed between father and child (Holtrust 1993: 245–246).

The new Civil Code of 1998 does not change this judicial practice. The shared custody assumes that both parents agree about visiting arrangements whether it be after divorce or after separation. Increasingly, however, professionals as well as lawyers and judges are calling for obligatory divorce mediation on behalf of the child. Similar to other European countries (e.g. Norway, Sweden), preparations are being made for compulsory courses for divorcing parents who need support in maintaining the relationship between the child and both biological parents.

During the 1980s and 1990s, a number of judicial adjustments have been made. They have all pointed toward a growing tendency to strengthen the legal rights and the pedagogical significance of fathers – children should know and have contact with their fathers. The assumption is that, while a divorce might mean that the relationship between the father and the mother has ended, it does not end the relationship between a father and his child. This rule has been laid down in the sections of the new Civil Code of 1998 that maintains shared guardianship, by both the father and mother, as the norm after divorce. Unmarried fathers, nevertheless, still need the permission of the mother to recognize the child, but their chances to overrule a refusal have increased. Being the procreator is not a strong enough argument in itself; judges consider the father's actual involvement with his children, as well as his former and future relationship with the child and his commitment to family life important. This is in line with the growing dominance of the ideal of the committed father as well as with the increasing valuation of the relationship between the child and both its parents. By the end of the 1980s shared guardianship by unmarried fathers was made possible and, as is the case with divorced parents, the possibilities for the father to keep in contact with his children after separation have also increased.

Conclusion

Discourses, practices and legislation concerning fatherhood are in a period of flux in the Netherlands, as they are in many Western countries. These changes privilege both the caregiving father and the biological father. The governmental media campaign to encourage a father's commitment to family life fits well with the discourse on caring fatherhood and tries to persuade fathers to take their part in the carework within the family. The policies toward the reconciliation of work and family care support fathers who want to take responsibility for their share of family care. Through the implementation of parental leaves, short-term paid care leaves for both mothers and fathers, and the right to part-time work, the Dutch government hopes to create better conditions for parents who combine work and care on an equal basis.

These shifts in discourses, social policy and law are both expressions of, and reactions to, transformations in the relational as well as institutional triangles. The efforts to stimulate involved and caring fatherhood express the desire to strengthen the commitment of fathers to their children, at a time when families are fragmenting and the division of tasks is no longer self-evident. Alongside the policies that encourage cooperating parents and flexible work patterns, there are the laws that have strengthened the legal position of divorced fathers in relation to recognition, visiting rights and joint custody.

When we compare developments concerning fatherhood in the Netherlands to what is going on in other countries, there are two striking differences. The first concerns the emphasis on recognition according to the past performance of the father in terms of commitment and care. This emphasis fits with the overall tendency to promote caring fatherhood, and differs from the privileging of biological fatherhood in, for example, Britain and Sweden. As is not uncommon, the involved father is not always the biological father, which can potentially lead to struggles between the biological and the caring father of a child. When the birth of a child is the result of artificial insemination, there may be few claims made against the caring father. Where we can expect the most conflict is between the biological father and the resident or household father cohabiting with the mother. However, this is not likely to happen, given the law and the practice of the courts, who rarely have privileged biological fatherhood above involved fatherhood and certainly not against the consent of the mother. The second striking difference between the transformations in fatherhood in the Netherlands and those in other Western countries concerns the financial obligation of fathers outside marriage. While the male breadwinner within marriage in the Netherlands is still supported by tax advantages, family based social security and pension systems, the financial obligations of biological fathers is not enforced, even when unmarried or divorced mothers are receiving social assistance. A weak alimony and child allowance policy undermines a father's cash responsibilities at a time when families are fragmenting.

In emphasizing caring fatherhood, Dutch policy encourages the voluntary commitment of fathers to their children under the assumption that the relational triangle can develop in harmony even when the parents are living separately. In the same way, the voluntary commitment of fathers to the daily life of their children is supposed to be the major force behind the equalization of work and care among fathers and mothers. This assumption may appear naïve in the face of conflicts over work and care between married parents, or disputes over visiting rights and guardianship between divorced and unmarried parents. In these cases, the assumption of the best intentions of the father results in a severe economic inequality between divorced mothers and fathers. It also results in a stronger position for the visiting, divorced father over the caring mother. Finally, it reflects the widening gap between those fathers who show strong cash and care commitments to their (former) families and those who do not.

Part 3

Resisting and reclaiming fatherhood

7 Making sense of fatherhood: the non-payment of child support in Spain

Ingegerd Municio-Larsson and Carmen Pujol Algans

During the transitional years toward Spanish democracy, encompassing the time from the death of Franco in November 1975 to the electoral victory of the socialists in October 1982, legal reforms affecting the family were made. There are two important moments in this reform process. The first was in 1978 with the promulgation of a democratic Constitution, where equality between women and men was explicitly stated as a fundamental family value. The second was in 1981 with the Civil Code reform in which equal rights between women and men in marriage were recognized. In addition, the distinction between the rights of children born in wedlock and those outside of wedlock disappeared. These rights were already designated in the Constitution. Finally, the termination of marriage through divorce, which had also been acknowledged in the Constitution, became specified in a new law, where the procedure and the rules for separation and divorce were outlined.[1]

According to a study of the development of family law in Spain, these reforms aligned Spanish legislation, "with the most advanced western legislation." In spite of the scope of these reforms, they were carried out "with highly reduced political tensions and with little social protest" (Iglesias de Ussel and Flaquer 1993: 64–65). The obvious exception is the law on abortion (Higuera Guimera 1997). The absence of public protest and political debate during the period of this legal renewal seems to indicate a broad consensus on these issues. However, during the implementation of these new laws, the spirit of consensus that guided the legislators of the time has been replaced by a spirit of conflict. This conflict revolves around issues of cash (who should be responsible for supporting children in divorce) and care (whether divorced fathers should have greater access to their children).

Legal changes in an era of political consensus

The family reforms were part of a democratic transition that was made up of deep political, economic and social change, in which "the goal of

191

change" was part of "the path to the utopia of a better society" (Tezanos 1989: 65). Based upon accounts of the Spanish transition, it is generally assumed that the changes of this period were brought about in a "spirit of agreement, compromise, and consensus," something quite different from other periods of transition in Spanish history (Cotarelo 1989: 318).

Within the general social atmosphere of the transition to democracy, expressed in the rhetoric of change, successive legal reforms were introduced. These reforms aligned civil legislation with the principles of civil rights and equality, promulgated in the 1978 Constitution, and were perceived by wide sectors of the Spanish public as necessary steps for the completion of the democratic transition. These included the vision of "integration into the modern, liberal and democratic continent," of which Spain was geographically a part. This integration required "full equality with the criteria of Western Europe," in reference not only to political liberties, but also to public and private ones (Menéndez del Valle 1989: 716).

How can one explain the fact that these reforms were passed in the parliamentary chambers, in spite of overturning norms that previously governed the social arena? The explanation lies in the incredible receptivity to unconditional change in this period. It was generally accepted that Spain would not be recognized as a country worthy of full participation in the European political cooperation without these changes (Menéndez del Valle 1989: 731). Thus, by underlying this openness to change, there was a belief that Spanish integration into the European Community was an essential condition for the development of economic and social welfare – something that was expected after years of dictatorship. Even after the democratic transition, the European Union continued to be an engine for the reform of family policy (see e.g. Thiebaut Luis 1992). Given the democratic government's explicit ambition to break with tradition and appear modern and European, family relations became a window of opportunity for formulating new ways of viewing obligations and rights and allowing for new demands upon the welfare state.

Conceiving Spain as "European" did not necessarily mean that age-old practices in marriage and separation were altered. The circumstance of the impetus for change came from abroad, which may explain why these changes were, in fact, more symbolic than real. Thus, this cleavage between symbolic changes and actual practices is illustrated by the fact that the consensus that apparently supported family laws was lost in their actual implementation.

Conflicts in the practice of the law

An often-proclaimed goal of legal change is to introduce new norms into society. It is not possible to judge either the success or the failure of this purpose until the moment of actual implementation. Thus, laws are tested as they are applied to real-life situations with real actors (Hurstel 1997: 296).

In Spain, the process of marital separation, more so than that of divorce, involves conflicts between the persons that constitute the family unit. While a divorce is reached only after at least a one-year period of separation, the rules that guide the judicial process required for a legal separation make provision for the possibility of conflict.

The conflict is most apparent in the payment of child support, and the courts are the contested arenas for the different parties to interpret, justify and oppose the legal process. This chapter documents these conflicts through narratives of the involved parties, which attempt to define how the responsibility for the children in question is to be divided between the mother, the father and the state. What is the fairest way to distribute obligations of cash and care between the parents, and what are the responsibilities of the welfare state?

In this quest for the right to define the situation, the state is clearly the most powerful party in that it has the right to finally decide what is a just settlement in each case and to prosecute cases of non-compliance by means of a criminal procedure. In view of the fact that the judgments reached by judges establish the conditions which are to regulate the future tripartite relations of the mother, father and children, it is of the utmost importance for each of the involved parties to be able to focus upon their own arguments while downplaying those of their opponent. Each case touches on the broader questions beyond the individual parties. Thus, the change in a particular family situation that separation entails reflects the broader changes of Spanish society since it questions the ways in which the idea of family is generally conceived.

A twofold transition

Thus, the narratives of fatherhood studied in this chapter are related to the twofold transition that Spanish society is experiencing today. The first of these transitions refers to the demands of citizens for social reform, something that the political reconstruction has made possible. Other European welfare states provide a reference model for these demands. The second transition emerges from the redefinition process of the patriarchal and hierarchical traditional family into a modern family characterized by equality and democracy.

Separation, divorce and non-payment of alimonies

In focusing upon divorce, we realize that we are studying a case with comparatively low rates of marital dissolution. The simple incidence of separation and divorce, in itself, would not make Spain a case for studying marital dissolution, since this incidence is lower in Spain than in most other European countries.[2] During the years since divorce was made possible in 1981, the number of divorce and separation suits filed in the judiciary increased more than fivefold.[3] In spite of this, demographic data from 1996 show that of 11.8 million households that consisted of more than one person, only 1.6% were headed by a separated individual and only 0.9% by a divorced individual.[4] But, our decision to study separation and divorce, specifically with regard to non-payment of child support, is based upon our interest in revealing the competing narratives of fatherhood in this period of transition around family policy.

In 1989, the article that regulates the non-payment of child support and/or alimony was introduced into Article 487, section 2, of the Criminal Code. Non-payment was classified as an offence and included under the category of "family abandonment." This article reflects the successive numerical increase of separations and divorces after the ratification of the family law act of 1981. Furthermore, in the following years, it became apparent that there were many difficulties regarding the enforcement of payment of economic benefits as ordered by the courts. According to the Secretary of Social Affairs of the former Popular Party government, half of the fathers did not pay child support.[5] This resulted in impoverishment, for many women and children, following marital breakdown. Of course, this impoverishment is related to the difference between women and men with regard to their participation in the labor force. Women constitute 40.3% of the work force and 58.8% of the unemployed, and earn 76% of men's annual wages.[6]

A contested and modified article

Several of the conflicts experienced within Spanish society today revolve around the second section of Article 487 of the Criminal Code. The parties involved in these conflicts are, first and foremost, separated women, their children and the lawyers who represent their cases in the legal separation and divorce processes. The party in direct opposition consists of men organized in several, special-interest associations. The third party is the Spanish state, represented by the judges, who pass judicial judgments under the direction of this article.

The fact of the matter is that the modification of Article 487 was originally derived from the struggles of separated women and their special-interest associations,[7] as well as the Association of Women Jurists (Themis). The goal of this struggle was primarily to attract attention to the economic problems related to separation and divorce, as well as to find solutions to the problem of non-payment of child support and, where appropriate, alimony to the ex-spouse. During the years following the 1981 law of separation and divorce, the Association of Women Jurists brought numerous complaints concerning this situation to the attention of the Ministry of Justice, where the problem was finally acknowledged. The result was the 1989 modification of the Criminal Code.

Similarly, the most recent modification of this article, in the new 1996 Criminal Code, includes a response to demands from both the special-interest associations of separated women and women lawyers. These demands were based upon the experience of actual problems encountered during the years that this article was in effect. The modification implies the shortening of the period required for non-payment to qualify as a crime and the coupling of the judgment of non-payment with an obligation to pay the due balance. The period of non-payment previously required was three consecutive months or six non-consecutive months. It is now two consecutive months or four non-consecutive months. The women lawyers have also drawn attention to other inconsistencies concerning this article. An example is the fact that the previous law did not cover the non-payment of child support to children born outside of wedlock. This has now been modified (Jurisprudencia Tribunal Constitucional No. 441. 1997).

The second party in these conflicts, the separated fathers and their special-interest associations,[8] have also formulated their demands in response to this. As they see it, the article reveals what they refer to as the disadvantage of men in cases of separation and divorce. Whereas the non-payment of child support is qualified as a crime applied to husbands, the non-compliance in granting visiting rights, in which wives are responsible, is not correspondingly criminalized. However, they recognize that some of their demands have been partly appeased. One example is the alteration, in 1996, of the penalty for non-payment of child support. Before this modification, this was "imprisonment from one month and a day to three months" or "a fine from 100,000 to 500,000 pesetas." This was changed to "jail during weekends." Thus, the penalty of imprisonment due to non-payment of child support was removed from this article. The special-interest associations had used the possibility of imprisonment as a focus point for their anger, as well as to gain support for their cause. It is worth noting that during the interviews the arguments evolve as if this modification had not been made.[9] According to them, another example of their success is that, in general, judges have reduced the monetary amounts of child support during the last two years.

The state, on the other hand, reaffirms in court decisions the duty, without exception, of both mothers and fathers to assist their children economically. Thereby, it exposes the practical non-existence of social benefits established for families, which illustrates the rudimentary character of the Spanish welfare state.[10] In reference to cases of non-payment of child support, there have been various attempts to partially remedy this problem. The former Popular Party government initiated the preparation of a bill for the creation of a fund guaranteeing child support and alimonies in such cases. The goal was to "meet the needs in situations of absolute necessity." The state would be responsible for a certain amount of child support and alimony in cases of families with a very low income or no income at all. The person obliged to pay child support and alimony was expected to eventually reimburse these sums to the state.[11]

The outline of the following

In the text that follows, the arguments presented by judges are contrasted with those of the concerned fathers, which are, in turn, complemented with arguments given during interviews with the associations of separated fathers. We have condensed the arguments in the studied documents, as well as in the interviews, into two conflicting views on fatherhood. Then we consider whether the claim of a new model of fathering, put forward by the associations of separated fathers, corresponds to what we know about the participation of fathers in child care within nuclear families. Finally, we reflect upon the scope of the changes introduced into family law since 1981 and the extent to which the new legislation is marked by continuity or change.

Conflicting views on the rights and duties of fathers

As we have noted, the changes in the Criminal Code toward the fathers' non-payment of child support and alimony was a response to demands by women lawyers working with separation and divorce cases. Many of these lawyers were organized in Themis, the Association of Women Jurists. This association was formed in 1987 with the aim of ensuring that the legal rights, given to women in the Constitution, as well as in the laws that changed accordingly, were in fact implemented by the Courts.

Since 1989, when the non-payment of child support was included into the Criminal Code, the interest of women lawyers has focused upon the implementation of the new article. Consequently, Themis has organized a program concerning this article. This program was originally financed by the former Socialist government's Ministry of Social Affairs and was extended by the Popular Party governments. The original strategy of the women lawyers was to bring many cases of non-payment to the Courts, in order to ensure that the law was implemented.

The Association has evaluated the program and the material analyzed here is from their report (Herrera Rivera 1994). It consists of statements made by judges in sentencing, as well as arguments used by fathers who answer charges of non-payment of child support. This documentation covers a total of 176 Civil Code decisions and 243 Criminal Code judgments concerning accusations of non-payment of child support. These are from lower and higher courts all over the country. They represent all of the cases where lawyers associated to the Themis program have been involved, and where a judgment has been rendered. The quotes that follow in the text are from this report. In our analysis, we expose the conflicting narratives of fatherhood presented in these texts. The arguments used by the fathers are placed in the context of fathers' associations by information taken from interviews with representatives of two Madrid-based associations of separated fathers.

We assume that these situations of conflict reveal broader discursive conflicts on fatherhood in Spanish society. In these cases, the concerned parties are forced to explicitly formulate their perceptions of reality, and through their narratives they express wider concerns about conflicts concerning fathers' rights and duties.

How judges interpret state discourse

The changes made in 1989 to the Criminal Code introduced the non-payment of financial support to both the spouse and the children into the article referring to family abandonment. This offence consists of the non-payment of alimony and child support, but only when the amounts have been previously decided upon in separation or divorce agreements. An additional condition for this offence to be subject for trial under this precept is that the spouse, who is obliged to pay, fails to do so for three consecutive months, or for six non-consecutive months. The punishment for such an offence was, until 1996, a fine or imprisonment for from one month and a day to six months.

The judicial narrative is expressed in the legal decisions that refer to this code. This narrative, on the one hand, justifies the judgments in each case and, on the other hand, formulates the social function of this law.

A recurring pattern in sentencing is that the judges go further than what is required in the strict interpretation of the law. Thus, they do not limit themselves to verifying or proving that non-payment has occurred. Instead, many judges characterize the offence as "maliciousness." Equally negative terms including "especially bad faith," "lack of solidarity," "caprice," or "selfishness" are applied to the ex-spouses who claim insolvency. The judges also refer to what they call a "mockery" of the economic duties toward a family, and a "contempt" for the warrants and decisions of the judicial administration.

So, why do they justify their decisions in such value-laden language, offensive to those indicted? In addition to establishing the relatively objective facts of non-payment and imputing this to a person, the judges evidently feel the need to explicitly express their distaste for the debtors' behavior.

One explanation for the use of this critical language is the difficulty in proving that "an intention of non-payment" exists. What in some cases the judges call "rebellious and reluctant conduct" refers to the many ways of eluding the public control of income and wealth, not only by individuals but also by companies. The conduct of those obliged to pay alimony, which the judges are aware of, is described in a number of the sentences. For example, it is stated that ex-spouses opt for voluntary redundancy or negotiate dismissal with their employers, "in order to no longer present oneself as a worker with a stable income available for seizure." Furthermore, it is noted that, in spite of these circumstances, those persons involved "maintain the same standard of living." In another method, the ex-spouse "turns to friends and relatives in order to register his property in their names, so as to appear to be living in utter poverty, while in fact he enjoys a comfortable standard of living." Cases are also cited where an ex-husband registers his company in the name of his new female partner, resulting in the income of the company appearing to be her income, not his.

In order to understand the charged language, it is also necessary to consider the context of the legal decisions and agreements. Most importantly, the article concerning family abandonment has been strongly contested, particularly by the fathers in separation and divorce cases. Their attacks on this law are frequent, both individually and collectively, and the media has reproduced it. The main argument used against this law is that it implies a return to "imprisonment on the grounds of debt" and that this is an archaic practice that does not belong in a modern and democratic society.[12]

The fact that many judges are uncertain as to whether or not to apply the law seems to be another reflection of this critique. According to the evaluation by Themis, the refusal of the judges to execute the sentences is expressed in two ways. First, some judges "resist treating the non-payment of alimony under criminal law," and, secondly, the judicial processes are unnecessarily prolonged (Herrera Rivera 1994: 71, 78). Consequently, only approximately half of the cases that reach trial have been concluded with a "favorable" solution, while one fourth of them have been delayed for more than two years without reaching a decision. The reasons given by the judges for dismissing cases of non-payment vary from an explicit rejection of the new law to an acceptance of an ex-husband's right to decide when to pay and how much to pay for child support (Herrera Rivera 1992).

This may somewhat explain why judges, who actually apply the law, find themselves compelled to justify their decisions in terms which indicate a strong reproach for the action that they pass judgment upon.

Disorganization of the state

When judges justify their decisions, they not only directly rebuke the debtors, but also condemn the state for its inability to control its citizens' financial declarations. The comments made by the judges disclose a situation that Spanish society currently suffers from, which has not been solved by the democratization of the state. First, there is an abundance of black-market labor and it is quite socially acceptable to work in that market in order to evade the payment of state tax. Secondly, it is well known that the public administration lacks the means to eradicate this market. As an example, in one case the judge commented upon the fact that the income-tax returns, presented with the intention of proving a lack of means, were in fact "unilateral declarations of dubious control by the Ministry of Finance." In another case, a judge supported his decision by stating that, when an ex-spouse is self-employed, it is very difficult to evaluate his income since this is "a field that allows the concealment of income."

In these individual cases, the judges echo declarations made at the government level. An example is the statement by the government's expert on taxation declaring that fraud is the main injustice of the present taxation system (Martín 1998). Thus, the judges' statements only reproduce something that is already publicly "known."

Despite the fact that the judges have additional evidence in these types of cases upon which to base their decisions, it seems questionable to apply knowledge of a general social phenomenon to individual cases. The fact that this occurs is probably best understood in the context of the rudimentary character of the Spanish welfare state. Thus, public authorities do not yet offer any specific economic support to single-parent families and, as we shall see, the social assistance to low-income families is truly limited.[13] Therefore, the judges know that there is no alternative to fathers' provision for their ex-families. This is different from other cases described in this volume, where the fathers' failure to pay is, at least to some extent, compensated by state benefits.

The social function of the new law

The comments above offer some insight into the judges' language of reproach of "rebellious and reluctant conducts." The judges seek to condemn both the failure of fathers to accept their duty to pay child support, and the practice of concealing income and wealth from the state. However, they also qualify the conduct of the debtors as in "contempt" of the judiciary. Thus, this conduct implies a rejection of the state's fiscal, as well as judicial, control of its citizens. At the same time, the judges' critique also indirectly addresses the state authorities, because of their deficient measures of control, which allows for the claims of "apparent insolvency" of the persons indicted in these cases.

In some of the condemnatory judgments, the social functions of the new law are explicitly formulated. As an example, in one decision from the High Court, it is stated that the non-payment of alimony is "a crime of multiple offences," and therefore the law has "three well-defined protective intentions." The first of these is "the security of family members," which should continue "even after the family's dissolution." The second intention is "the right to the dissolution of marriage," which is said to depend upon "the possibility of effectively enforcing economic contributions." Finally, it is stated that the third protective intention is "the State's interest" in maintaining the respect of citizens for the legitimate authority and dignity of the civil service. In these statements, neglect of fathers in their parental duties is described as a threat to the overall well-being of Spanish society.

Fatherhood and fathers

In their narratives of fatherhood, judges work hard attempting to make sense of their view that fathers, even after separation, should comply with their obligations as the main providers for their families. In the sermon-like speech that these judges deliver to negligent fathers, we recognized themes of the discourse of good and bad fathers, which is expressed in varying forms in other countries. In this narrative, fatherhood is identified with the practice of fathering, which is, in turn, defined as the fulfillment of the "cash" part of the responsibility of fathers.

The derogatory language that plagues this narrative both reflects upon and consolidates the atmosphere of confrontation that characterizes these judicial processes. This language may also reflect a certain frustration amongst judges when faced with the impossible task of resolving pressing social problems by means of a judicial process, rather than legislation or stronger administration at the state level.

The fathers' defense

When fathers summoned before the courts contest the narrative describing them as "malicious," their prime goal is to prove that the non-payment of alimony is unintentional and therefore not punishable by law. The fathers often claim that their inability to pay is caused by financial problems of various origins, the most frequent being unemployment.

The high level of unemployment is recognized as one of the most pressing problems in Spanish society and constitutes the general context of the individual cases of alimony non-payment. The 1990s began with a strong recession and the moderate economic recuperation of recent years has only marginally resulted in increased job opportunities. Therefore, the unemployment rate that was 20 percent during the first years of this decade had increased to 24 percent at the end of 1994, but decreased during the following years to reach 14 percent in 2000. We have also noted that the problem of unemployment affects women to a much greater extent than men. Consequently, unemployment may aggravate the problem of the single-parent family, when it is already affected by non-payment of child support and alimony, but it may also be a cause for non-payment.[14]

In cases where the evidence presented by the ex-husbands is rejected by the judge, the decision of the Court is based upon two different types of argument. The first refers to the documentary evidence brought forward by ex-wives, which shows that their former husbands actually work, and therefore should have an income. The second refers to the fact that ex-husbands have not requested an adjustment in the first alimony agreement in order to accommodate the alimony to their present income or lack thereof.

Alternative support

An argument, sometimes used by fathers in order to justify the non-payment of alimony, is that they have given their children presents or bought them clothing and shoes. In the Court decisions, these gifts are generally estimated to represent a smaller financial value than the alimony that should have been paid during the corresponding period of time. However, on occasions, judges accept this, qualifying it as a proof of goodwill, and therefore a reason for dismissing the case.

This argument manifests an attitude on the part of the fathers that implies that they have chosen an alternative relationship toward their children. Instead of providing regular support, they occasionally appear with presents. A study of households without a father distinguishes four possible roles for men in the family. One of those described is precisely that of a "Rey Mago" (or Father Christmas), a father who is absent most of the time, but brings presents whenever he returns home. After separation, this role of a "clandestine" father provides a possibility for men to maintain a positive relationship with their children, without accepting their traditional role as a breadwinner (Rojas Marcos 1995: 195f.). Underlying this fathering practice is a strategy that makes sure that the father's economic contribution is used only by his children and can in no way benefit his ex-wife.

Men mobilize as fathers

The fathers' defense and rationales for non-payment are reflected in our interviews with separated fathers' associations. There are many such associations in Spain, the first of which was founded in 1992.[15] Representatives of two associations, both based in Madrid, have been interviewed for this study.

In Asociación de Padres Separados, called Separated Fathers in the text that follows, the president was interviewed on two occasions. This association seems to be the more established one of the two, and it has lately expanded its office facilities and personnel. This association seems to be perceived as the most representative of separated fathers. Thus, they are contacted on occasions when a spokesperson for separated fathers is required. Its president, Carlos Herraiz, has frequently participated in TV debates about separation and divorce. According to him, they no longer participate in spectacular actions, like chaining themselves to the doors of the Courts, in protest at non-compliance with visiting rights, or demonstrations in public squares, in demand of joint custody. Instead, they devote time and effort to lobbying and attempting to influence public opinion in favor of legal changes, as well as of state allowances to families that live under these circumstances. On his own initiative, the president also participates in a task force, consisting of judges, prosecutors and lawyers of family courts in Madrid. Their aim is to "facilitate the work of all those who are involved in family court processes," by clarifying the procedures to follow in these processes (*OTROSÍ informativa* 1999).

The other association, Asociación de Padres Separados y Maltratados, called Mistreated Fathers in the following, was more reluctant to give an interview. Their president altogether refused to be interviewed, alleging lack of time. The member who was finally interviewed was in charge of receiving visitors on that day. Another member, who arrived during the interview, intervened in the last part of it, commenting on what he considered to be the increasingly unfair relationship between women and men in present-day Spain. This association has currently refrained from participating in actions intended to influence public opinion or demand legal changes. The interviewees suggested that changing laws is "much more difficult than it seems" and that "men have no power," due to the fact that they, in contrast to the women, "are not united" (interview February 24, 1998). This refers to conflicts, both within associations as well as between them, which have made it difficult to unite the associations of men into one federation. Instead, the activities of this association mainly focus on individual assistance to its members, and occasionally demonstrations to draw attention to what they consider to be an unjust treatment of men, in court cases of separation and divorce.

Both associations offer services to men who are going through the process of separation or are already separated. Legal services, as well as the services of psychologists and private detectives, are provided. The fact that the processes of separation and divorce occur in the courts explains the need for lawyers and legal services. The services of psychologists are not primarily meant for the men, but instead are meant for their children and are used in cases where children refuse to visit their father. The services of the private detectives are required for purposes similar to those that have appeared in the previously studied legal decisions. Women also employ private detectives to prove that their ex-husbands do indeed work, despite their denials. In the same manner, men require the services of detectives in order to show that their ex-wives work, and therefore do not need alimony. Another motive may be to prove that an ex-wife lives with another man who therefore should contribute to the household expenses (*Diario 16* 1996: 12).

In our interviews, we mainly discussed the confrontation between fathers and the courts, but we also discussed their demands that the Spanish state alleviate their situation. This also gave us the opportunity to discuss the relationship between a biological father and his children, when he no longer lives with them. Throughout our interviews, an overriding theme was the belief that the current divorce and separation law, as well as its application in the courts, benefits women and is prejudiced against men. Linked to this perception was their analysis of the changing status of women in Spanish society.

The spokespersons of Mistreated Fathers often referred to the changing relationships between women and men during the last decades. They meant that women's increasing participation in society, as well as the state's attempts to improve the status of women, had undermined the authority of men. Their position is summarized in the statement that "you may observe the extremes that this has reached." For example, they cite a legislative bill in parliament offering the possibility for parents to choose whether to give priority to the surname of the father or the mother when deciding the order of their children's surnames (Rodríguez 1998; *El País* 1999b). They were particularly indignant about an advertisement in the Madrid newspapers that gave a telephone number for the local police, which was specifically designated for women who wanted to report their spouses for wife battering.

During the last two years, the mass media has called attention to the problem of battered women. In view of the fact that the conflicts concerning the sharing of rights and duties in the family realm are won or lost, not only in the courts, but also in the battle of public opinion, the associations of fathers perceived themselves to be at a disadvantage in defending their cause. This is because, as formulated by the president of Separated Fathers, the image given by the mass media when attracting attention to the numerous cases of battered wives was "the man is the bad guy in the movies" (interview March 6, 1998). The spokespersons of both associations did indeed denounce men killing their wives, but they considered it normal that in "a confrontation between couples, a moment is reached when it may come to blows and there may be a point when one kills the other" (interview March 25, 1999). In the association of Mistreated Fathers, they also attempted to play-down the issue of battered wives, by saying "there have been four or five cases," and setting these cases against cases of "men who have gone years without seeing their children." This ambivalence toward violence against women seems to reflect the attitude conveyed by the law. Thus, the law punishes only those who "habitually" exercise physical violence against their spouse or children (Pujol Algans 1992: 309).

The president of Separated Fathers also stated that Spain "has progressed from a patriarchy to a matriarchy." Contrary to the spokespersons of Mistreated Fathers, he based his assessment not on the actual position of women in society, but on what he judged to be a favorable treatment of women and an unfavorable treatment of men in the court cases of separation and divorce, and the judgments in cases dealing with child support and alimony non-payment. A similar rhetoric of victimization, focusing particularly on the loss of power and control by men over their former families after separation and divorce, seems to be expressed by men's rights movements in other countries as well (cf. Orloff and Monson; Gavanas in this volume; Bertoia and Drakich 1995).

Fathers' narrative in interviews

The issue of a father's economic obligations toward his ex-wife and children has given occasion to verbal attacks by spokespersons of Separated Fathers. These attacks have been directed particularly toward separated women, conceived as a group with common interests, which are unjustifiably defended by the courts. In a TV debate in 1995, a spokesperson of Separated Fathers characterized women who demand alimony after separation as "social parasites." However, neither he nor other representatives of Separated Fathers who participated in the debate explicitly rejected the fathers' obligation to pay child support. What they unanimously complained about was the monetary amounts decided by the courts ("Los unos y los otros," *TVE Internacional*, January 31, 1995).

This is parallel to the narrative exposed by the spokespersons of fathers' associations interviewed. Thus, in neither of the two associations do they attempt to justify the non-payment of child support after separation. However, both associations are opposed to judges imposing alimony payment upon fathers who claim to have no income.

The president of Separated Fathers stated that the monetary amounts of child support awarded by the courts were generally too high. Furthermore, he stated that the courts did not take the possibility that the father may have a new family to support into consideration. On the other hand, he admits that these monetary amounts have been reduced during the last two years. However, he claims that there are large differences in the amounts imposed between the courts and judges within the same court. According to him, this adds to the insecurity and defenselessness of men in this situation. Therefore, another important demand is the establishment of fixed criteria, decided upon at the state level, for standardized monetary levels of alimony.

He also protests against a modification of the law passed in 1991. Before this change in the law, child support was paid until the coming of age, and after, child support was to be paid "until the child attains economic independence." This may partly reflect the fact that in Spain the emancipation of young people is attained later and later in life. The president of Separated Fathers states that it is extremely difficult to define "economic independence" when applying the law, leaving fathers defenseless. Simultaneously, this rule corresponds to tax reductions allowed for dependent children that are extended beyond the coming of age for children who do not support themselves. This modification also somewhat reflects the guiding principle of Spanish family law, as will be commented upon later, which establishes economic solidarity between relatives, including adults and minors.

A demand supported by men and women in cases of separation is one for a state fund guaranteeing the payment of child support and alimony in cases of non-payment. As has been already stated, a Bill with this intention was prepared by the former Popular Party government. However, at the end of 2000, it has still not passed the legislative process. In addition, it is uncertain whether the reform, if enacted, would be comprehensive enough to solve the problems associated with non-payment. In the economic report coupled to the project, only 25,283 cases affected by non-payment were anticipated, while the 1997 report of the State Prosecutor indicates that there were 7,896 cases of non-payment, registered in Court, for that year alone, a figure which represented an increase of 40 percent in comparison to the preceding year (*El País* September 16, 1998). Furthermore, the possibility of receiving state allowances would supposedly encourage single parents to declare cases of non-payment, which do not currently reach the courts.

Fathers' demands on the state

In a fashion that parallels the democratization process that followed the fall of the Franco dictatorship, Separated Fathers paraphrases its demands for support from the state or other official entities in a rhetoric of *change*:

We are not the fathers of times gone by, the Spanish man who did not concern himself with matters of the family, who had two mistresses ... We are different, we are born with democracy, we believe in democracy. Almost all of us accept that the State has to make laws that should be obeyed. We pay taxes ... You comply with the law, but when you appeal to the courts in order that they comply with you ... (Interview March 6, 1998)

It asks why traditional attitudes are reproduced in the separation and divorce agreements, while the rest of society focuses upon political and social change. These traditional attitudes lead the judges to place financial responsibility upon the father, without conceding him equal responsibility in the care and custody of his children.

As is common in political debate, representatives of Separated Fathers use the countries surrounding Spain as a reference point for what they consider fair demands. They ask why their country, which defines itself as a welfare state, has "the worst services of all the countries in the European Community" (interview February 24, 1998).

In this matter, which is in addition to the state's fund guaranteeing child support and alimony, they demand other state measures, such as social mediation services in the process of separation and divorce, as well as in cases of non-compliance with visiting rights, which they claim follows an English model. They demand the services of social assistants and family-therapy psychologists in cases where children do not want to visit their father, which they claim exist in other countries of the Community. Finally, they want a new divorce law that is not punitive. They claim that in a civilized society divorce should be considered normal, that the current legislation does not need to be "patched up," but that a completely new family law should be written. The president of Separated Fathers specified in detail what the new law should include. He mentioned, for example, the right of adoption for homosexual couples, as he claimed was the case in the United States, as well as the regulation of the cohabitation of unmarried couples, joint custody and care, with Sweden used as a case in reference. The demand for a new divorce law has repeatedly been posed by representatives of Separated Fathers, in TV debates and demonstrations.[16]

A new model of fatherhood

During the 1990s, the possibility of a more equal share of paid and un-paid labor between women and men has been a recurring theme in the public debate in Spain. The request that men take their share of car-ing and housework is probably mainly a reflection of women's increasing participation in the labor market, but also in part a response to policy documents issued by the European Commission (Deven 1994: 4). How-ever, it is doubtful whether the recommendations of the Commission have had much impact, either on the actual distribution of caring and housework or on how the responsibilities of women and men in the fam-ily are generally conceived. In Spain, surveys of attitudes show that men's equal participation in caring and housework is widely accepted, while the actual distribution of this work remains the traditional one (Menéndez Alvarez-Dardet 1994: 56–86; Ventimiglia 1995: 26). Similarly, a study of the most important daily papers, in seven countries of the Community, concludes that positive images of men as caring fathers were represented less frequently than negative images of fathers, as not paying child sup-port or as "monsters," based on anecdotal evidence of family tyrants, child abusers, etc. On the other hand, stories describing good fathers also seem to be based on anecdotes (Deven 1994; Laleva 1999).

   In spite of this, the possibility of a new model of fatherhood is suffi-ciently well articulated in Spanish society to serve as a focal image for the narrative of separated fathers. The way this model is used may well illus-trate the "spread of global images of fatherhood" (see Hearn in this vol-ume). Thus, in their demands for change, Separated Fathers frequently refer to fathers' rights to participate in care. They mean that in order to live up to a new model of fatherhood, their demand for joint care and custody must be recognized. This would result in measures for achieving a higher compliance with visiting rights that are agreed upon in the legal process of separation and divorce. In separation agreements, joint custody has lately become more of a rule than an exception, while, in decisions of where children should live, it is usually specified that care is left up to the mother. Visiting rights may be specified, for example, to every second weekend and one afternoon a week. According to Separated Fathers, this will not provide room for complying with the new father ideal.[17] As the president of Separated Fathers claims:

> You can't be a real father. I do not bring up my son. I am not really his father. Instead I am a friend of his. I have noticed that in this situation... the father figure disappears totally and instead a friend is created, one who once lived with his mother. Many times he doesn't even call me dad.

This reflects a wish to create a new relationship between father and child, different to the one that he himself experienced with his father. It is expressed in the desire to take part in the daily life of the child:

> I live near my son and I could go and pick him up at his school, he could stay overnight with me, if [visiting rights] were less restricted.

He claims that a closer relationship between father and child would also implicate the father's participation in decisions regarding aspects of the daily life of the child that the fathers considered important. These decisions may span everything from civil or religious education to dentist visits.

In this desire to share more closely in the life of the child after family dissolution, and to create a new model of fatherhood, another more traditional theme is concealed. This theme is men's control of women, which traditionally has been a man's right. Hints of this are caught in the expressed opinion that it is unjust that an ex-wife does not need to provide evidence to her former husband of the expenses incurred, complete with receipts, on behalf of their children. It is more clearly revealed in the opinion that even violent men, who have been sentenced for battering their wives, should be granted visiting rights to their children. This reveals the belief that a woman's right to physical safety is less important than a man's right to visit his children.

Fatherhood and fathering

In men's narrative of fatherhood, *care* is emphasized, while *cash* is given less prominence. They object to the judges' main view of fathers as providers and instead construct an image of a father who is as close to his children after separation as before. In their rhetoric, the meaning of fatherhood is participation in the life of your children on a day-to-day basis. They claim that in order to be a "new" father, joint care is indispensable in separation agreements. In a demonstration by Separated

Fathers on Father's Day in 1999, the demand for joint care was further specified, suggesting that the children remain in the matrimonial home after separation, and that each parent lives with them, during alternate months or years (*El País* 1999a; Deven 1994: 13).

As seen from our interviews with fathers' associations and from the many cases of non-compliance with court orders of child support, fathering, in the sense of financially providing for their children, is rejected by many fathers after separation. Does this imply a shift to providing care for one's children, and is this visible in studies of fathers in intact families?

A study of 250 families with underage children living in the Barcelona area shows a mean of 37 hours a week spent in child care, 23 attributed to the mother, 11 to the father and the rest to other family members or hired help. Furthermore, more than half of the time that the fathers did dedicate to their children was on weekends, while the opposite was true for the mother. In families where the mother was gainfully employed, the father's participation somewhat increased, particularly during weekdays (Carrasco 1991). Another national survey presented an even more unequal sharing of the workload, especially concerning the care of the youngest children, where mothers accounted almost exclusively for the work. Only amongst the couples with the youngest fathers, those between 25 and 34 years, was the proportion of shared care slightly higher (Durán 1998: 254–255, 272–277).

This illustrates a difference between fathering, the fathers' actual participation in child care, and the abstract ideas of fathering, as reflected in the Separated Fathers' narratives on fatherhood. Thus, the ideal image of a father is constructed without the restrictions imposed by everyday life. Studies of nuclear families describe fathers who participate in child care during weekends as opposed to during the week, doing specific tasks more than taking overall responsibility for the child's well-being. This is similar to how care is usually specified in legal separation agreements.

The rhetoric of the "new father," as well as the demands for joint custody, seem best to be understood against a background of mothers' responsibility for the everyday care of the children being taken for granted. Thus, the fathers' demands for joint custody are generally specified in terms of unlimited access to their children and continued control over decisions in their former families, and not in terms of a shared responsibility for everyday care.

In the fathers' narrative, the *cash* aspect of fatherhood is deferred partly to the state and partly to the mothers. They expose a narrative of injustice in their complaints of how they are treated by the courts. They claim that both the state and the mothers are more successful in evading economic obligations toward children than they are. The cognitive context of this narrative is reflected in their references to the loss of their privileges in different spheres, a fact they interpret as signaling the coming of matriarchy. In this respect, their narratives echo those of men's movements in other countries. In this view of reality, the tradition of male hegemony in relation to women and children is used to make sense of, and normalize, even such acts as wife battering.

Change or the continuation of tradition

The legal context surrounding sentences for non-payment of child support is a mixture of change and continuity. Change is represented by the recognition of separation and divorce. However, the fact that the law still considers it necessary to determine guilt in a separation process hints at traces of legal continuity. Another trace of continuity is reflected in the fact that the responsibilities of the traditional extended family are maintained. This implies the strengthening of the links between the biological father, the discourse of fatherhood and fathering, where fatherhood is conceived as the fulfillment of economic obligations toward his children. The admission of paternity investigations breaks with a privilege that the law has traditionally given to men, a tradition that provided the choice of which children to father. The traditional discourse of fatherhood is also changed in respect to the supremacy of men within the family, but maintained in its reference to fathering as principally involving the provision of cash.

This last feature of continuity is revealed in the successive legal changes, which represent reactions to the common occurrence of non-payment of child support after separation. It is in this context of the traditional extended family, with financial obligations extending beyond the nuclear family, that the opportunity to criminalize the evasion of these obligations exists. Consequently, in Spain, formal legal language labeling fathers as deviants is used to deal with a phenomenon that in other countries appears in the policy discourse of "deadbeat dads." In Britain, more severe penalties, including jail, for fathers who refuse to pay child support are presently considered by the Child Support Agency. In Spain, the new law that classifies the non-payment of child support as an offence is an important break with tradition due to the fact that it criminalizes a behavior that was previously ignored by the legal system.

However, these instances breaking with tradition do not include the possibility of forming a new family after divorce. Thus, when judges comply with demands to defend the interests of those who are in the greatest need of protection, only members of the first family are considered. This implies that old family codes remain in questions of repartnering. This was also the case in Britain, until a policy change in 1994 (see Lewis in this volume). To modify this would be to admit that women and men may meet new partners, even remarry, and to revise rights and obligations in view of this situation.

Deficient adaptation to the new situation is also reflected in the rigidity of the court processes where the relationships between the members of a dissolved family are to be continually defined. Firstly, a divorce is not obtained directly, but is instead preceded by a court judgment of separation, which, in turn, may be preceded by a court decision where provisional measures referring to child custody, the use of common housing, and economic benefits are settled. Similarly, each modification of child support or, where appropriate, alimony payments, requires a new court decision and therefore additional expenses. This rigidity is aggravated by waiting periods, caused by the continual accumulation of cases in the Civil Courts.[18]

Welfare provision

Another context of the legal decisions referring to the non-payment of child support is the previously mentioned "rudimentary" character of the Spanish welfare state. There are currently no specific allowances for single-parent families. Instead, family policy is largely limited to tax reduction. However, only families with incomes exceeding 7,215 euros per year benefit from these. Specific deductions for large families are also provided for, but fewer and fewer families are actually entitled to these. In addition, there is a means-tested child allowance of 200 euros per year within the social security system for families with low, or no, income (Valiente 1995: 103).

In some of the larger municipalities there are also so-called social integration programs which, in addition to job creation and other social services, include economic support for families with low or no income. However, the monetary amount of this support is much less than the minimum wage.

Contesting parties and narratives

The Spanish Constitution holds the promise of a welfare state for those who are in need. As the state recedes from this promise, these needs have to be met by other means. In the case of non-payment of child support, this withdrawal is described by judges who formulate a narrative of individual fathers' responsibility that reinforces the private character of welfare provision. In this context, separation and divorce are allowed by law, but are at the same time based upon the perpetuation of the traditional extended family.

For the other party in this contest, the men, *change* is the key word of their narrative. They distance themselves from traditional obligations by repeating the promises of sweeping changes in society, which characterized the entire democratic transition. They remarry more often than women do, and they thereby defend their right to conceive family relations in new ways that suit them (Solsona, Simó and Houle 2000). However, many of them still exercise their traditional privilege to abandon their wife and children without the inference of the courts by simply not complying with court orders. Similarly, they side with tradition as they defend the right to maintain control of their former families, even after divorce.

Here the voice of the third party in this contest – that of the women – is silent. In spite of this, the issue of non-payment of child support and alimony affects them more directly than it affects the other two concerned parties. Women and children are those who ultimately suffer the consequences of the state's failure to either provide welfare or force ex-husbands and fathers to comply with court orders. Women continue raising their families as single mothers, despite their lower wages and their more precarious position in the labor market. The extended family becomes their last resort, as the welfare state and their ex-husbands deny their obligations to those who, in the wording of the law, "are in the most need of protection."

8 The Fatherhood Responsibility Movement: the centrality of marriage, work and male sexuality in reconstructions of masculinity and fatherhood

Anna Gavanas

During the past few years, liberal and conservative politicians and policy makers alike in the United States as well as in European welfare states have increasingly identified fatherlessness as a social crisis of top priority. A crucial set of actors in shaping and reframing this debate in the United States defined themselves as belonging to the Fatherhood Responsibility Movement. Within this "movement," one may discern a range of groups with competing masculinities and contesting claims and grievances. Nevertheless, there are apparent convergences of strategic, or real, points of agreement. The constituencies of the different organizations have different social locations in relation to the state, and they consequently, but not predictably, have different agendas for reform. In public demonstrations, the Fatherhood Responsibility Movement seeks to overcome barriers of income, race and politics. It includes men's organizations as diverse as fathers' rights groups, pro-marriage groups, mythopoetic men's movements, fatherhood programs for low-income minorities, and faith-based grass roots manifestations such as the Promise Keepers and the Million Man March (see Horn et al. 1999). By highlighting contesting masculinities within US family politics, this chapter illustrates the ways notions around marriage, work and male sexuality shape the debate on father responsibility.

"The family" is a contested cultural and symbolic concept in many countries; it is perhaps more fiercely contested in the United States than in many other countries. Notions of "the family" are a matter of profound social and emotional tension in American politics. The family has become the point of intersection between gender, sexuality, hierarchy and social problems, and a point at which the state may legitimately move to influence all of these phenomena (see Rainwater and Yancey 1967; Berger and Berger 1983; Davidson Hunter 1991; Stacey 1996). Many of the contentions involve race, which has always played an intricate and integral part in US family policy-making. Associations between African American males, family breakdown and absent fatherhood have a long history in US policy, and images of African American "dangerous," "promiscuous," and unmarriable young men are carved into the American landscape (Marsiglio 1995; Collier 1996). "Family pathology" and "juvenile delinquency," especially among African Americans, were a national public policy concern in the 1950s and 60s. Since the 1960s, there has been an ongoing academic discussion about African American families (see e.g. Hannerz 1969; Billingsley 1992; Hill 1993, 1997). In 1965, the nationally debated Moynihan report[1] warned about the disastrous consequences of "family breakdown." One of the biggest examples of the dangers in this development was the "tangle of pathology" Moynihan found in African American communities, which included notions that re-emerge in today's discussions around fatherhood – the absence of fathers, "illegitimacy," female-headed families, welfare dependency, crime, low school performance, and violence (Rainwater and Yancey 1967). "Broken homes," working mothers, and "erratic" or "effeminate" fathers were some of the assumed causes of poverty among African Americans (Hannerz 1969: 72; Ehrenreich 1989: 23).

At the time when the Moynihan report was published, national policy on the "family problem" and fatherlessness was highly influenced by the emerging Civil Rights Movement (Rainwater and Yancey 1967). Although the political context is different today, notions of racial and socioeconomic difference are still central issues in policy-making around fatherhood. One wing of the Fatherhood Responsibility Movement consists of the fragile families groups,[2] who are primarily concerned with labor market opportunities for poor- or low-income minority men. The ideal of marriage is central to the other Fatherhood Responsibility Movement wing: the pro-marriage groups. This chapter analyzes the impact of *competing* notions of race, socioeconomic class and gender relations within the Fatherhood Responsibility Movement and relates this to the positions of different constituencies.

This chapter is based on semi-structured and recurrent or single interviews with about fifty leaders, directors or other staff of the most influential fatherhood responsibility organizations at all levels,[3] as well as participant observation during the years of 1997 and 1998 at major conferences, workshops and demonstrations.[4] The chapter begins with a presentation of the types of organizations involved divided into clusters. This is followed by an analysis of some of the crucial similarities and differences in the interviewed representatives' views of marriage, work, government policy, gender relations, and the roles of race/ethnicity and socioeconomic class. Throughout the analysis, the focus is on the role of religion within the Fatherhood Responsibility Movement. Finally, the role of notions of male sexuality in the construction of masculinity and fatherhood is analyzed.

Standing divided: the field of the Fatherhood Responsibility Movement

We're in the same circuits but in slightly different camps.
We all work for the same cause but for different constituencies.
(Statements made by pro-marriage and fragile families interviewees)

Since the early 1990s, there have been a number of bi-partisan federal initiatives to strengthen fatherhood that describe fatherlessness as "one of the greatest social evils of our generation" and "an engine driving our worst social problems" (see Horn et al. 1999). Organizations like the National Fatherhood Initiative and the National Practitioners Network have worked to put fatherhood responsibility at the center of the national agenda, and since 1994 there have been presidential and vice-presidential federal initiatives to strengthen the role of fathers in families. There has been an enormous allocation of resources and attention to fatherhood issues, and the field is growing and evolving rapidly – much to the surprise of fatherhood organizations, such as the Institute for Responsible Fatherhood and Family Revitalization, and the Fatherhood Project at the Families and Work Institute, that had been around for decades. The current Fatherhood Responsibility Movement has seemingly been able to establish a consensus that the key to attacking most social ills – including the federal deficit – is fatherhood responsibility.

Today's fatherhood politics is responding to changes in the demographic profile of families and changes in the nature of work and employment patterns. In addition, the positions of contemporary fathers are affected by (white) women's increased labor force participation and the related issue of parents' division of household labor. The contemporary context is also affected by recent debates over child well-being, welfare and single-parent households (Marsiglio 1995; Donovan 1998). When parties in the Fatherhood Responsibility Movement approach all of these changes and issues, they explicitly or indirectly emphasize the perspectives of men who are asymmetrically positioned in relation to one another and the state. Accordingly, masculinity and fatherhood are constructed out of different viewpoints and concerns within the Fatherhood Responsibility Movement. Whereas the fragile families wing represents low-income minority fathers, and emphasizes paternity establishment and breadwinning, the pro-marriage wing promotes marriage as the key to fatherhood responsibility for all types of men.

To understand the Fatherhood Responsibility Movement is a very complex task, and it is often problematic to consider the participant organizations in terms of a "movement" for two reasons. First, it is a movement dealing with different levels (local, state, federal), organizational aspects (coordination, training, policy-making, research, "hands on" working with fathers) and societal sectors (employment, the faith community, health care, education, recreation, the juridical system...). Secondly, the movement label is problematic because, despite a few general convergences, the organizations within the Fatherhood Responsibility Movement deal with separate issues. There are injustices and concerns that some organizations bring up and others do not, because the men or fathers they represent simply do not face the same problems. Despite these problems and complexities, this chapter approaches the Fatherhood Responsibility Movement in terms of a "field" consisting of strategic alliances between pro-marriage and fragile family oriented groups.[5] They have a mutual interest in expanding the field through the increase of political and public attention, public and private funding as well as local activity around fatherhood issues.

There are difficulties in defining the Fatherhood Responsibility Movement in terms of masculinity politics because most representatives say that their goals and concerns are not necessarily specific to men, but may also benefit women and/or children too. Actually, most representatives throughout the Fatherhood Responsibility Movement often pointed out that they are *primarily* about children. However, the Fatherhood Responsibility Movement can be analyzed in terms of masculinity politics, defined by Connell as, "those mobilizations and struggles where the meaning of masculine gender is at issue, and, with it, men's position in gender relations. In such politics masculinity is made a principal theme, not taken for granted as background" (1995: 205). The meaning of fatherhood and masculinity are contested by, and within, the Fatherhood Responsibility Movement.

In order to get an impression of the types of actors and levels involved in the Fatherhood Responsibility Movement, one may divide the different organizations into clusters (see Figure 9). However, there are overlaps within the Fatherhood Responsibility Movement in terms of both constituencies and the types of grievances they express.[6] Actors from the different clusters belong to the same networks and work on the same campaigns. Importantly, there is a lot of variation of opinions and predispositions *within* the single organization. Many of the groups involved in the Fatherhood Responsibility Movement are active in social policy, public and judicial/legislative arenas.

The Fatherhood Responsibility Movement as described here mainly consists of two types of groups: pro-marriage and fragile families. I use

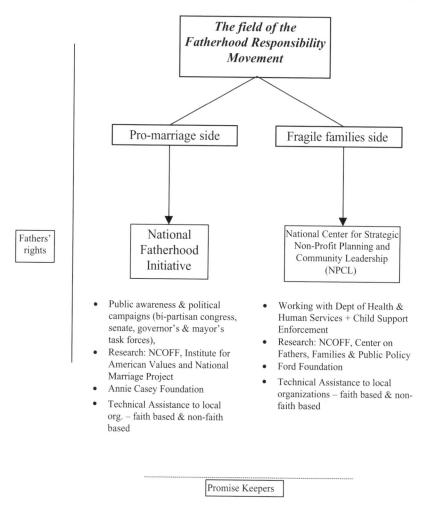

Figure 9 Fatherhood Responsibility Movement (NCOFF = National Center on Fathers and Families).

these labels to simplify the extremely complex Fatherhood Responsibility Movement field. Within the pro-marriage wing, the National Fatherhood Initiative is the most influential organization. Other prominent pro-marriage organizations examined in this study include the National Center for Fathering and the Institute for Responsible Fatherhood and Family Revitalization. The latter is a unique case of a pro-marriage organization that works directly with fragile families. It sends married couples into low-income communities with the mission to live there as role models. Within the fragile families wing, the Partners for Fragile Families, National Center for Strategic Non-Profit Planning and Community Leadership, National Practitioners Network, and the Ford Foundation Strengthening Fragile Families Initiative are the most significant groups. I also talked to other well-known fragile families oriented organizations such as The Fatherhood Project and the Baltimore City Healthy Start Men's Services.

Pro-marriage groups focus on social consciousness and promote marriage and a "culture of fatherhood." These groups maintain that men need to be (good) husbands in order to be good fathers. Organizations in this cluster look primarily at men as custodial and biological fathers and (preferably) husbands. They explicitly talk about all kinds of fathers, but do not usually focus on agendas or government programs for low-income and/or minority men. The leaders and representatives of the largest and most well-known organizations – the National Fatherhood Initiative, the National Center for Fathering, and the Institute for Responsible Fatherhood and Family Revitalization – are of main focus in this study. The National Fatherhood Initiative tries to involve all social sectors (education, business, civic, faith-based, private social service, public policy, media and philanthropy) in a mass movement of social consciousness. The National Fatherhood Initiative has started bipartisan task forces at a range of political levels: congressional, governoral and mayoral. It also helps run state-based initiatives and is very connected with political figures and legislators. The National Fatherhood Initiative works closely with David Blankenhorn from the Institute for American Values and David Popenoe at the National Marriage Project, which are research institutions with the goal to put marriage on the national agenda as a "natural progression" of the Fatherhood Responsibility Movement. Although these individuals may prefer other labels, they, and their organizations, are generally considered conservative within the Fatherhood Responsibility Movement. In addition, the pro-marriage groups are mostly funded by foundations that are considered moderate to conservative.

The most common discursive lines among representatives from pro-marriage groups are fatherlessness and related social problems, a lack of recognition of men's unique and irreplaceable contributions as fathers, and the gender-specific roles of fathers other than as breadwinners. Other grievances are divorce, out-of-wedlock childbearing and the "deculturation" of marriage. Most pro-marriage interviewees also link the "decline of fatherhood" to changing gender roles, and point to a current confusion about men's roles that is perceived as extremely harmful to society. As a counter strategy, they stress conceptions of *difference* between women and men and translate these into differences in the "roles" and "natures" of mothers and fathers. The Fragile Families oriented groups, the second cluster within the Fatherhood Responsibility Movement, are mainly concerned with poor or low-income unmarried African American and other minority fathers as well as their "fragile families." The organizations in this cluster look primarily at men as welfare recipients or unskilled, low-paid workers, and as never-married, non-custodial, social and/or biological fathers. The leaders and representatives from the largest and most well-known organizations – the National Practitioners Network and the National Center for Strategic Non-profit Planning and Community Leadership – are of main focus in this study. These organizations work closely with Child Support Enforcement and the Department of Health and Human Services, and are funded by the Ford Foundation, which is generally considered liberal. In comparison to the National Fatherhood Initiative, which focuses on the public arena, the fragile families organizations consider themselves to be more "hands on," working directly with fathers, or, in the words of one leading National Practioners Network interviewee, "we're kind of getting our hands dirty working with the guys." In working with non-custodial fathers, the fragile families organizations promote "team parenting" in order for children to have both biological parents in their lives, with marriage as an optional end goal – not a priority.

Fragile families interviewees located the problems of fatherhood from the perspectives of low-income and poor African American, and other minority, men, and they often mentioned racism, as well as racial discrimination. As opposed to the marriage proponents, the reference point for fragile families interviewees was not primarily women and mothers, but *other men*. They made distinctions between masculinities in terms of race and socioeconomic class and tended to stress *similarities* or interchangeabilities in parental features, rather than differences. Most fragile families representatives identify with the men they represent, and often point out that they are the same race and come from similar socioeconomic backgrounds. They do not primarily focus on the concerns of upper/middleclass white men/fathers. Interviewees brought up problems they see in African American communities, such as unemployment, poverty, out-of-wedlock birth, disconnection, that "angry young men" are driven to the streets and that fathers are "driven underground" by "the system." Some interviewees also touched upon a lack of recognition of, and understanding for, responsible but poor fathers, "non-traditional" fragile families and the negative impact of stereotypes about African American men and fathers. Like the marriage proponents, fragile families representatives also pointed out that the governmental view of men and fathers is restricted to that of a breadwinner. In addition, many interviewees lamented that men (as opposed to women) have not had access to public benefits and parenting programs.[7]

In addition to the pro-marriage and the fragile families groups, I bring up additional types of organizations, who draw upon, and have certain impact on, fatherhood and masculinity discussions and politics. Actually, some of these groups preceded the 1990s movement around fatherhood and masculinity politics and in some ways anticipated it by seeking to unite men around common interest and grievances.[8] Unlike the fatherhood responsibility movement, their groups have a more single-issue focus. The Fathers' rights groups are mainly concerned with the legal rights of divorced upper- and middle-class fathers. They constitute a response to family law and child support policy and mostly work in the legislative/judicial arena and offer legal advice and support to individual fathers involved in divorce and custody cases. These organizations have a very ambiguous relation to both wings within the Fatherhood Responsibility Movement; there is both (limited) cooperation and tension. Fathers' rights groups are sometimes represented at conferences put on by the Fatherhood Responsibility Movement and primarily view men as citizens, ex-husbands and professionals from a legal standpoint. They may be distinguished from the fragile families groups for their oppositional approach to child support enforcement, and from the pro-marriage groups for their emphasis on rights as opposed to responsibilities. I interviewed organizations like Fathers United for Equal Rights of Maryland LTD, American Coalition for Fathers and Children, and the American Fathers Coalition. Fathers' rights interviewees framed their grievances in terms of discrimination against men and lamented that men in divorce are stripped of their property and their children by feminists and the state. For them, men have become the weaker party (they are often abused by women and have no rights or protection) and some interviewees even claimed that men are discriminated against in the labor market by getting the dirty and difficult jobs. Finally, men are driven out of the home, while state policy privileges women.

Secondly, there are other contemporary men's movements, some of which are unrelated or stand in opposition to each other (see e.g. Hearn 1993; Schwalbe 1996). For instance, there are faith-based grassroots manifestations and pro-feminist groups. At one end of the spectrum, you have faith-based groups who seek to involve fathers in the upbringing of children and view fatherhood as the expression of traditional[9] family and god-given gender roles. At the other end of the spectrum, you have pro-feminist groups who seek a more active and participatory fathering role based on non-sexist models of the family. The interviewees within the

Fatherhood Responsibility Movement claimed to be non-sexist and were opposed to a patriarchal and oppressive model of fatherhood and the family. Nevertheless, they were generally more influenced by the faith-based end of the spectrum than the pro-feminist one. For instance, one significant and influential faith-based group is the Promise Keepers, which consists of Christian men and a large national network of churches. The majority of interviewees within both wings of the Fatherhood Responsibility Movement spoke very highly of the Promise Keepers, who were represented at the National Fatherhood Summit in June 1998, organized by the National Fatherhood Initiative. The Promise Keepers primarily view men as husbands and "spiritual leaders." They consider men to be fundamentally different from women, and to have different god-given roles in the family. Furthermore, they maintain the importance of men holding each other accountable for, among other things, the responsibilities of fatherhood. The primary grievance of this movement is spiritual poverty, which is causally linked to "the breakdown of the family" and other problems that the representatives identify. Another main concern is the failing of men to be good husbands and fathers and to be the self-sacrificing "servant leaders" of their wives and children. They have also failed to build strong marriages as well as "intimate relationships" with other men.

One example of a pro-feminist organization is the National Organization of Men Against Sexism (NOMAS), which largely consists of white, middle-class, middle-aged men who are often part of academic and activist circles. Pro-feminist men's groups are not involved in the Fatherhood Responsibility Movement whatsoever. However, such groups participate in an ongoing discussion about masculinity and fatherhood, and their approach here serves as an interesting contrast. Contrary to the Promise Keepers and pro-marriage groups such as the National Fatherhood Initiative, the National Organization of Men Against Sexism is concerned with the reconstruction of masculinity and fatherhood into less differentiated and less hierarchical gender roles, and seeks to de-emphasize the differences between men and women from a non-essentialist approach. As opposed to the Fatherhood Responsibility Movement, fathers' rights or the Promise Keepers, the National Organization of Men Against Sexism includes gay and bisexual men in their discussion of masculinities.

Interestingly, both main clusters of the Fatherhood Responsibility Movement described earlier – the pro-marriage groups and fragile families oriented groups – consistently emphasize the importance of spirituality (as opposed to religion) in the Fatherhood Responsibility Movement and want to recognize the moral and spiritual dimensions within the issue of fatherhood. Of central strategic and rhetorical significance to the Fatherhood Responsibility Movement are the many churches and religious/spiritual organizations and leaders involved in working with fathers and communities. Religious/spiritual leaders and organizations are often represented at workshops and conferences organized by both fragile families and pro-marriage organizations, and spiritual discourses and rhetoric (in most cases Christian) permeate the Fatherhood Responsibility Movement at all levels – from national public manifestations to the everyday work of local programs. Involving and working with the faith-based community is crucial to work with all types of constituencies, but, throughout the Fatherhood Responsibility Movement, churches are traditionally thought to be of particular importance to African American communities and thereby key to affecting those communities (see e.g. Hill 1993, 1997; Billingsley 1992).

Commonalties and lines of controversy: the explosiveness of marriage

There are a number of basic commonalties shared by the pro-marriage and the fragile families wings of the Fatherhood Responsibility Movement: (1) a concern for child well-being; (2) a view of "the family" as foundational to society; (3) an attribution of importance to the father, and a subsequent link between his absence and social ills (although causes, consequences and the fixedness of this link differs between organizations); and (4) an agenda to redefine the role of the father in the family, labor market and government policy *from* primarily a financial provider, disciplinarian and breadwinner *to* including a notion of an emotionally involved, nurturing mentor. Interestingly, the first three of these common concerns resonate in the Moynihan report of 1965. However, current promotion of responsible fatherhood, child well-being and the strengthening of families takes place within shifting economic, legal, moral and social conditions for the construction of fatherhood, and Fatherhood Responsibility Movement representatives express different opinions of these changes (Williams 1998; Knijn 1995).

Uniting around "the family" and child well-being fits into American core beliefs that any US citizen would subscribe to. Who could say that responsible fatherhood is a bad idea? Who is going to disagree if one says that everybody should love his or her child? On the surface, the Fatherhood Responsibility Movement presents itself as based on a national consensus. In public and political campaigns, a concern for fatherhood responsibility, child well-being and the family is often presented by spokespersons involved in the Fatherhood Responsibility Movement as politically neutral and "beyond ideology" (See Horn et al. 1999). When analyzing such rhetoric, one should not forget that history and current politics show a variety of agendas under the banner of family and children (Beisel cited in Donovan 1998). A focus on fathers may appear logical to both liberal and conservative welfare reformers in the face of welfare state cutbacks. However, the internal divisions within the Fatherhood Responsibility Movement are an illustration of how the banner of children and family masks opposing claims, grievances and stakes. Fatherhood policy contestation has implications for the politics of men and fathers divided by race, sexuality and socioeconomic class who have differing positions *vis-à-vis* the state. Fatherhood politics and family policy can be compared to a minefield where powerful political agents are setting off highly charged issues.

Marriage seems to be the most divisive issue within the Fatherhood Responsibility Movement. This is where the pro-marriage and fragile families wings strongly disagree while simultaneously sharing the same, sometimes contradictory, principles.[10] Many *pro-marriage* interviewees even look at the Fatherhood Responsibility Movement as the first stage of a marriage movement, but feel that they have been silenced and cannot even bring up the issue of marriage, or use the "M-word." The pro-marriage wing of the Fatherhood Responsibility Movement, as well as the marriage movement,[11] who both feature the same leading figures (e.g. David Popenoe and David Blankenhorn), feel that the government should not be neutral on the issue of marriage. Most of the *fragile families oriented* interviewees think that marriage is a good thing but point out that it does not guarantee "positive child outcomes." Their priority is to work with a range of socioeconomic problems for families and communities and, in turn, increase the marriageability of men. On the other hand, marriage proponents regard marriage as an ideal, but do not say that less than ideal families necessarily result in "negative child outcomes." Their priority is to re-establish marriage, which they regard as a social norm and institution that is dangerously in decline. They maintain that marriage is primarily about securing the well-being of children. Although they say that marriage might not solve everybody's problems, they believe that marriage can serve as an incentive to increase employability and the responsibility of fathers. These might seem like small differences in views, but the issue actually reflects fundamental ideological divisions and fierce discussions within the Fatherhood Responsibility Movement. According to the pro-marriage wing, men need to be married before they have children in order to be responsible fathers, whereas the fragile families wing points out that marriage is often unattainable for their low-income, poor and minority constituencies, and maintains that unmarried "team parenting" and meeting the needs of non-custodial fathers could equally foster responsible fathers. The fragile families wing is opposed to the idea that marriage should become a policy goal, which may end up making conditions worse for their constituencies.

It is not the legitimacy of marriage as a traditional and heteronormative[12] institution that is discussed within the Fatherhood Responsibility Movement, but rather how, and to what extent, it is viable to obtain it. There are many different opinions on the positions of men and women within marriage – is a man supposed to be a "servant leader," a "captain of his ship" or a "team partner"? You often hear marriage proponents talk about the ways men and women are "wired" differently and have different innate "natures" and "behaviors" as parents. However, when you ask them to elaborate on these notions, they also acknowledge the impact of culture and change and demonstrate a "looser" essentialist approach. Michael Schwalbe (1996: 64) defines "loose essentialism" as "an assumption of an essential, internal difference, yet it is non-specific or 'loose,' with regard to claims about how this difference will be manifested in personality and behavior." The *pro-marriage* interviewees tend to emphasize loose essentialist gender difference and parental features, often according to socio-biologist, biblical or pop-Freudian notions. Leading *fragile families* oriented interviewees tend to emphasize flexibility and similarities in their notions of gender and parental roles, although many fragile families representatives also expressed loose essentialist ideas. In describing the current positions of men in (heterosexual) families, interviewees from both wings often accounted for recent processes of change into more equal divisions of breadwinning and caretaking between men and women within (heterosexual) households, and pointed out that they consider these to be positive developments.

Masculinity, work and government policy

Practitioner: We have to learn to conform: nobody wants to change nobody. Like Dr. Jekyll and Mr. Hyde, you can be how you want. To be in the hood. But, we have to stay at a legitimate track. The majority of people who have a job are white. That's my understanding. We have to go to them and be like them in order to get a job.

Participant: They run the country: white supremacy! . . . To get a job to support a family: why do you have to have what they have? (From field notes taken at local National Practitioners Network related father's program)

Whereas marriage is a key issue for the pro-marriage wing, work is a key issue at all levels within the fragile families wing of the Fatherhood Responsibility Movement, and particularly for African American, as opposed to white middle-class men's, access to the labor market. The pro-marriage wing acknowledges the importance of the employment situation for certain populations of fathers, but does not bring this up as a primary issue. Most interviewees concerned with low-income African American fathers point out that a lack of jobs results in barriers to fatherhood involvement. The relationship and relative importance between work and fatherhood responsibility is contested within the Fatherhood Responsibility Movement. The approach of the fragile family oriented interviewees usually corresponded to a "money matters approach" in the sense that economic and educational possibilities affect the ability to form and support a family, or whether men are "marriage material" (a term used within the fragile families wing). According to this perspective, the "failures" of poor African American men to get steady employment and marry the mothers of their children are related and attributed to a lack of opportunities for education and socialization into professional skills and discipline, rather than to a cultural attitude (see e.g. Wilson 1996). In the words of a fragile families representative:

The stereotypical definition of man in this society is to be able to care for his family, to be a provider. And when a man can't be a provider, he does not engage in that process as a full player – it does not mean that he won't have children. But he refuses to accept the vow of marriage, in a holistic sense, because of his own instability, and I think that could be directly correlated with the lack of labor market participation of men of color, particularly African Americans, over the last thirty years! (quotation from interview)

Within the fragile families wing of the Fatherhood Responsibility Movement, one talks on all levels about discrimination of poor/low-income African American and minority men, in contrast to the privileged positions of other men, in the labor market. One of the leading fragile families figures said in an interview, "employers generally hire people who look like them, who live in the same neighborhoods being like them and the majority of employers in this country are white!" A practitioner at the local level discussed the same situation in the following terms during a workshop:

Ain't nobody's gonna give you nothing – there's still racism and discrimination. Keep your earrings, keep your ways ... but keep it in the hood – to get a job you have to modify. Ain't nobody's trying to change you. What does it mean: *when in Rome, do as the Romans do?* You've got to conform ... I'm not saying it's *right*. I'm a black man just like you. In order to get what you want, that's what you've got to do. We have to learn to do what The Man wants us to do. And The Man can be black, white, Korean ... But, you have to get that job to feed your family. (From field notes taken at local National Practitioners Network related fathers' program, original emphasis)

Obviously, poor/low-income African American and minority father-hoods and masculinities are conditioned by scarce opportunities for se-cure employment and breadwinning (Wilson 1996). Subsequently, work becomes a crucial issue in constructions of masculinity and fatherhood, whereas it is closer to a non-issue on the pro-marriage side, where the majority of representatives do not address questions of socioeconomic class, poverty, race or discrimination as structural (as opposed to psy-chological or cultural) reasons why men do not take responsibility as fathers.

Overall, Fatherhood Responsibility Movement representatives believe that men should be entitled to emotional (in addition to financial) involve-ment in their families, although different men face different work-related, legal or cultural barriers to this goal. The main barrier that hinders poor (African American) fathers' involvement is the lack of employment prospects, which makes it harder to fulfill breadwinner responsibilities, whereas the problem of working- and middle-class fathers is too much work obligation, which makes it harder to fulfill caretaker responsibili-ties. Another key issue that conditions responsible fatherhood within the fragile families wing is child support enforcement and paternity estab-lishment. Both the pro-marriage and the fragile families wings of the Fatherhood Responsibility Movement envision the ideal role of govern-ment to be as small as possible. This may be seen as a specificity of the US case, where private grounds of provision are assumed (see Orloff in this volume). Overall, the Fatherhood Responsibility Movement has ambigu-ous relations to the government. One example of this ambiguity is the fragile families oriented networks' recent cooperation with child support enforcement, which is seen as an enemy at the local level. When practi-tioners and advocates cooperate with child support enforcement, they are seen as "snitches" by colleagues and program participants. More strik-ing is the attitude toward welfare for African American men and women, which is seen as an oppressor rather than a helper by many of the fragile families practitioners. It was not uncommon for practitioners to believe that welfare creates dependence and worsens unemployment for men, thereby crippling men as breadwinners (Wilson 1996; Cornell 1998).

There is little consensus in the Fatherhood Responsibility Movement concerning the possible impact of government on social processes and changes in the family. Although, throughout the Fatherhood Responsi-bility Movement, the government is not considered to necessarily work in the interests of its citizens, and especially fathers, there are still different strategies in dealing or not dealing with the government. Most intervie-wees from pro-marriage groups thought that government policy has little effect on "the culture of fatherlessness" and that there is a danger in letting the state replace the role of fathers rather than to hold the individuals themselves accountable. There is a feeling, throughout the Fatherhood Responsibility Movement, that the government has treated men and fathers unfairly in welfare policy during the last thirty years. Women are often described by interviewees from both wings as the protégées of government and the recipients of programs and support. There is a general feeling within the Fatherhood Responsibility Movement that government policy has *rewarded* single-mother households and "feminized" the family, although spokespersons are careful to point out that they are not bashing single mothers. There is also a general perception that men have been stereotyped as deadbeats, abusers, predators, etc. within government policy.

Another general critique toward government from the whole Fatherhood Responsibility Movement is directed toward the view of fathers as merely breadwinners, or "walking wallets," and the neglect of men to be nurturers and caretakers as well as moral and emotional fathers. Another way in which men were pictured as victims of misguided government policy, mostly by fathers' rights interviewees, was in terms of legal rights to custody and visitation. Fathers' rights interviewees were the most fierce critics of government and felt that the state deliberately discriminated against men in various areas, including custody, visitation, child support, abuse cases, etc. They maintain that the state profits from the way these things are arranged, by robbing men of their resources and pushing them away from the family.

In a situation where the financial possibility to marry and raise children has become a privilege that many men can not afford, low-income, poor and minority men seek equal opportunities and recognition within the labor market, as well as governmental and educational opportunity structures. Interviewees concerned with fragile families maintain that poor and minority men basically have the same ideals of masculinity as white, upper- and middle-class men – to be a successful breadwinner, to be able to form a family, possibly marry, and to become "responsible fathers." While most organizations of the Fatherhood Responsibility Movement want to re-establish the father's involvement as an individual responsibility, the fragile families wing points out that low-income, poor and minority fathers need support systems to "catch up" with white middle-class men as breadwinners. On the other hand, the pro-marriage wing endorses policy incentives for people to get, and stay, married as a *motivator* for responsible fatherhood and breadwinning. These differences in approaches to government policy reflect that the constituencies of men that the organizations represent have asymmetric relations to the welfare state as citizens and/or recipients.

At first glance, it may seem like the organizations involved in the Fatherhood Responsibility Movement are dealing with the same problems (such as father absence, and the social ills they perceive as being related to this: "negative child outcomes," drug abuse, crime, teen pregnancy, etc.) and have the same basic goals (to encourage responsible fatherhood in breadwinning and care). However, upon closer examination, different representatives approached causes, consequences and solutions to fatherlessness from fundamentally different angles. One pro-marriage interviewee said that there are three possible approaches: a focus on economic structure, a focus on misguided government policy or a focus on cultural values. He attributed importance to the latter. The approaches of the interviewees can be divided roughly into emphases on the following root causes: (a) spiritual or cultural poverty, (b) income distribution and racism (and government and business conspiracy, scapegoating, and general profiting from the poor), or (c) a government/radical feminist conspiracy (meaning that male irresponsibility is the government's fault and that government and feminists/"gender terrorists" profit at the expense of men). Perceptions of the root causes of the increasing rate of fatherlessness are discernible by the ways in which interviewees frame social processes and problems. Some pro-marriage interviewees thought that *fatherlessness* itself caused poverty and all other social problems, and that problem communities are *driven* by fatherlessness, whereas many fragile families interviewees thought that *poverty* causes fatherlessness as well as related problems. Pro-marriage interviewees sometimes regarded poverty as more of a psychological and social problem – a way of life, and said that money is not going to change this problem, whereas it was common within the fragile families wing to maintain that money is a very big part of the answer to poverty and fatherlessness. Most of the approaches above correspond to the structure versus culture debate where fragile families representatives tend to focus on structure and marriage proponents on culture (see e.g. Gans 1995, Valentine 1970). On the one hand, *structuralists*, common within the fragile families wing, focus on economic processes and the labor market as the major causes of poverty. On the other hand, *culturalists*, common within the pro-marriage wing, rather focus on attitudes, norms and values. This line of controversy was played out when interviewees brought up the question of choice and whether it is the "choice" of poor people to raise children in bad neighborhoods or the "choice" of women to have low paying jobs.

Reclaiming and reconstructing notions of masculinity

The male role as nurturer and mentor is largely debatable. And I think that it's at the very core of a lot of social and policy issues around families . . . the role of men has been largely marginalized ... To me that's the crux of everything. (From interview with fragile families representative)

Although the stated purpose of the Fatherhood Responsibility Movement is not to push for any particular gender politics, the movement still implicitly addresses the conditions, constructions and positions of men, women and families. Here I examine gender politics mainly in terms of the fatherhood policy for *men* and *fathers* – not women or children. The efforts of the Fatherhood Responsibility Movement have resulted in small-scale achievements such as putting diaper-changing tables in local men's public rest-rooms, to large-scale achievements such as federal presidential initiatives and government proposals. The Fatherhood Responsibility Movement as a whole has indirectly shaped public debate and social and juridical policy discourses in three major ways. First, as mentioned above, its representatives push for a *redefinition* of the father's role from merely a financial provider to an emotionally involved nurturer and mentor. Secondly, they help introduce men and fathers as a focus in gender rights issues as well as in academic and policy *discussions* on gender and the family. And thirdly, within the Fatherhood Responsibility Movement there is an emerging discussion of the notion of *difference among men* in terms of the conditions of social groups, as well as fathering styles and cultural traditions. However, a fine line distinguishes the ways in which difference among men is discussed within the Fatherhood Responsibility Movement. Generally, marriage proponents point to similarities between the situations of men while acknowledging difference, whereas fragile families interviewees generally point at differences between men while acknowledging similarities.

At a certain level, the fragile families wing of the Fatherhood Responsibility Movement is about the empowerment of men who, in various historical contexts, have been disadvantaged, or discriminated against, by government policy, the legal system and the labor market. In these arenas, fragile families representatives primarily compare themselves, or their constituencies, to *other men*. More specifically, in constructing their gendered outlooks they tend to differentiate themselves from white middle- and upper-class men in assuming low-income, poor or minority men's perspectives. Empowerment may imply advocacy at a federal or state level, community mobilization, public awareness campaigns, legal, financial or social support or developing skills, self determination and esteem among individual men.

Marriage proponents, on the other hand, neither position themselves, nor primarily distinguish, between men in terms of race/ethnicity or socioeconomic class. When discussing masculinities and fatherhoods, they generally express loose essentialist notions of innate universal male capacities such as aggressiveness, "promiscuity" and competitiveness. Furthermore, men are supposed to be innately career-oriented, rule-oriented, instrumental in their relations to others and reluctant to emotionality, according to leading marriage proponent interviewees. These gender notions inform pro-marriage distinctions between masculinities in terms of *"constructive"* versus *"destructive"* masculinities. Constructive masculinity focuses the innate male capacities above on "productive" goals on behalf of the family and society, such as marriage, father involvement, monogamy and law-abiding citizenship. Unless the society/culture encourages a man to be constructive according to these goals, his "masculine energies" may transform into violence, "masculine excess," or "protest masculinity." "Androgynous" or "soft" masculinity is another unproductive and distorted type of masculinity according to pro-marriage interviewees. This new type of "sensitive" masculinity erases masculine traits and makes men more like women, which is unnatural and impossible in both theory and practice according to the pro-marriage approach.

Pro-marriage interviewees emphasized *gender difference* as an important value in developing responsible fatherhood. I was often told by marriage proponents that mothers and fathers parent differently according to "innate behaviors" tied to the loose essentialist notions of gender described above. Since there are such essential differences between men and women, only fathers can truly model masculinity to their children and be a credible source to sons in approving masculinity. To sum up from the pro-marriage interviews and speeches, father roles constitute being a risk-taking, "hard" but fair disciplinarian to children, and a self-sacrificing protector of the family. Fathers also tend to be more physical and rough with their children and encourage independence, but simultaneously show limits and teach self-regulation. As a contrast, mothering is characterized by the binary opposite: cautious, "soft" and comforting child-rearing practices. Hence, the pro-marriage argument that children need both and that the father is irreplaceable. Being a nurturing father should not imply that a man is less of a man and more like a woman according to pro-marriage constructions of gender difference. As one of the leading figures within the pro-marriage wing said in an interview:

A lot of people say there's nothing wrong with a guy being a father as long as he does it the way mothers do it . . . You've heard people refer to stay at home fathers as Mr. Moms. That's pretty insulting! I mean, why don't we call mothers that stay at home with their kids Mrs. Dads?

There is an ongoing internal and wider debate around the gendered relational positions and roles of heterosexual men/fathers in their families that is crucial to the Fatherhood Responsibility Movement. These discussions both challenge and reinforce traditional notions of gender and the breadwinner/caretaker constitution of motherhood and fatherhood. Whereas the groups in the Fatherhood Responsibility Movement might disagree with feminist or social constructivist ideas of gender and families, they share the feminist intention to reveal the impact and power implications of gender stereotypes within social policy. For instance, they demand programs for men and fathers – not just for women and children – and seek to redefine the family within social policy to reinclude the father as equally important. While organization representatives are uniting around the agenda to increase men's responsibility/involvement as breadwinners and caretakers, their conceptions of gender relations and practices may still differ completely. However, the entire concept of the Fatherhood Responsibility Movement is built upon the notion that men/fathers have gender-specific, indispensable and irreplaceable contributions to make not only to their families and children, but also to their communities.

In addition, some representatives even say that fatherhood responsibility is important to the nation and "civilization." At the National Fatherhood Initiative's second national summit on fatherhood, on June 15, 1998, it was concluded that nothing could replace the male father figure. Fostering good masculinity is dependent on involvement of the father, and masculine excess, or "hyper masculinity" of rebellious young men reflects fatherlessness. Then vice-president Al Gore, who is a front figure for the Fatherhood Responsibility Movement, said at the summit that fathers getting involved in their children's lives is the single most powerful civilizing force in human history and the glue of a civilized society.[13] The Mayor of Washington DC (where the summit was held), Marion Barry, said, "anybody can make a baby, pigs do that, dogs do that, but it takes a man to raise a son." Such statements seem to assert that there is a consensus on gender differences, and that fathers are fundamentally different from, and complementary to, mothers and there should therefore be gender-specific roles in heterosexual families. Apparently, according to Barry's statement above, the difference that (heterosexual and responsible) fathers make would separate us from the animals.

Interviewees throughout the whole Fatherhood Responsibility Movement often described the redefinition of masculinity and fatherhood as a response to a redefinition of femininity/motherhood. Generally, policy that is motivated by child and family well-being is also said to indirectly benefit women and mothers. Fatherhood Responsibility Movement representatives often point out that they are fighting for what feminists always have promoted in terms of getting men to take responsibility for care and breadwinning. While the pro-marriage wing constructs its politics in adversarial relation to what they call "radical feminists," there is a strategic ambition within the fragile families wing to collaborate with organizations within family policy concerned with women and children. There is a particularly complex relation between the fragile families wing and African American feminists. One of the reasons for this is that the African American women's relationships to the labor force, as well as to their families, have always been different than the ones of white, middle-class feminists, and their claims and demands may both converge with and diverge from African American men's in specific issues (for further discussion see Hill 1997; Staples 1993). For instance, according to one of the leading figures within the fragile families wing, the main goal of African American women, whose labor force participation already is higher than that of African American men, might not be to function independently from men but to make "their" men more family and community oriented.

When describing historical processes affecting fatherhood in America, most pro-marriage and fragile families interviewees brought up the feminist movement as an important factor that has helped to push away fathers from the family, although they accepted feminist accomplishments as facts that they had no intention of undoing. However, the fragile families and pro-marriage responses to those processes were different. Marriage proponents wanted to reinforce notions of gendered and parental difference and cement those differences within the institution of marriage. One of the developments pro-marriage interviewees held the feminist movement partly responsible for was an attempt to erase what they saw as naturally founded differences between mothering and fathering. They framed current changes into less-differentiated gender roles as "androgynization" which works against the "natures" of men and women and only "confuses" and alienates men. Aware of the feminist critique the pro-marriage wing has received, the fragile families interviewees claimed to be less "traditionalist" than the marriage proponents are in their responses to changing gender roles and family forms. Their responses are explicitly conditioned by strategic concerns not to alienate feminist decision makers within organizations that they are financially dependent on, such as the Ford Foundation or the Department of Health and Human Services. Local fragile families groups are thus encouraged to form strategic alliances with women's groups in order to maximize opportunities in various agencies. In the words of Ronald Mincy, program officer of the Ford Foundation Strengthening Fragile Families Initiative:

There's no way in the world that you or I can do the work that we have to do in ways that are insensitive to women's issues. As a consequence, those of us who are working on behalf of low-income fathers and families, on behalf of fragile families,

I never say the word *father without families* – doesn't make sense! . . . You have a window of opportunity to walk through to engage people who care about children, women and community, in order to say *yes, fathers are critical to the development of children, and we're going to work with you in some ways that make sense to you in order to build the capacity of fathers to be who they are.* (Mincy, Keynote speech at the Baltimore 5th annual Male Involvement Conference, June 18, 1998, original emphasis)

In contrast to the strategically collaborative stance of fragile families representatives and the cautious gender politics of marriage proponents, fathers' rights groups openly declare "radical feminists" the enemy and speak against the type of feminist politics they call "gender terrorism." Importantly, however, fathers' rights groups are considered marginal to the Fatherhood Responsibility Movement by pro-marriage and fragile families oriented groups. These two latter groups do not have explicit counter-feminist agendas and want to distinguish themselves from fathers' rights groups in order to maximize their wide-based, political appeal. However, the fatherhood responsibility movement shares a concern with fathers' rights groups in wanting to remove barriers to the involvement of fathers within the child support system.[14]

Another case of gender controversy is the clashes between the Promise Keepers and the National Organization of Women over the role of the father in the family. The National Organization of Women strongly opposes the Promise Keepers' position that women would benefit from the re-establishment of the father as the "servant leader" in the family. Whereas some Fatherhood Responsibility Movement interviewees objected to the patriarchal and religious connotations of the Promise Keepers, they were generally positive about the Promise Keepers' activities at a mass, grass-roots and spiritual level, about their efforts to promote responsibility to men, and to "restore" masculinity and fatherhood or "moralize masculinity into self sacrifice on behalf of women, children and community."[15] Only one Fatherhood Responsibility Movement interviewee was generally critical about the Promise Keepers. In contrast, the pro-feminist National Organization of Men Against Sexism was highly critical of the Promise Keepers, and one of the seminars at their annual conference claimed that the Promise Keepers had a neo-fascist agenda.

The notion of the father as a "protector" is tightly connected to the more controversial notion of the father as a "servant leader" within the mutually reinforcing masculinity politics of the Promise Keepers and the Fatherhood Responsibility Movement (and particularly the pro-marriage wing). Marriage proponents sometimes claim that both they and the Promise Keepers have been misunderstood in what they mean by the father as "protector" and "servant leader" – especially by feminists. In speeches and interviews, marriage proponents rarely fail to point out that they are driven by concern for child well-being rather than self-interest *as men*. This is the defense the Promise Keepers use when explaining their biblical notion of servant leadership; it is about men assuming *responsibilities* for the sake of women and children. This notion is one example of the ways in which the Promise Keepers inspire many representatives within the Fatherhood Responsibility Movement. Marriage proponents especially, see men, as opposed to women, as particularly apt to serve as the protectors and self-sacrificing leaders of their families.

The term that's usually used is *servant leader*, and people who don't like that model focus on the word *leader*. People who like that model focus on the word *servant*. So, where you put the accent makes a great deal of difference. Servant leader means you lead by example, you lead by serving others. It comes from the Bible, and it comes from the reference that men should lead their families as Christ lead the church... What he is really saying is: *if need be, your job is literally to die for your family, you know, if that's what it takes to keep your family safe* – now, I mean, is that a horrible idea? Is it a terrible idea?... It's a much more self-sacrificial form style of leadership. Now there are clearly those people who believe in, you know, the man ruling... with an iron fist... And I disagree with those people, I think that that is **not** what the biblical prescription of servant leaderhood is all about. I believe that servant leaderhood is: *what can I do for you?* – not *you have to do what I say*. (Quote from interview with a leading marriage proponent within the Fatherhood Responsibility Movement – not a Promise Keeper representative)

Among the fatherhood responsibility representatives, there were a variety of approaches to gendered division of labor ranging from loose essentialism in the pro-marriage wing to more flexible approaches in the fragile families wing. Fragile families interviewees tended to emphasize similarities in parenting between mothers and fathers. For instance, many fragile family oriented speakers and interviewees said that fathers basically could do everything mothers can do except give birth to the children. However, both pro-marriage and fragile families interviewees explained gender difference in biological terms by referring to genes or a "biological formula." One pro-marriage interviewee explained by saying that men's and women's genes are complementary, but men have both x and y chromosomes, whereas women have only xx, and subsequently men can do what women can do, but women cannot replace the role of men (thus, single-father families are "better" than single-mother families). He was one of the marriage proponents who also maintained that fathers should be the "servant leaders" in the family. Many interviewees from both the fragile families and the pro-marriage wings talked about gender relations in biblical metaphors.

There was only one interviewee within the Fatherhood Responsibility Movement, from the fragile families wing, who made a point of stating s/he was pro-feminist. Pro-feminist interviewees, who were not part of the

Fatherhood Responsibility Movement but still participated in US masculinity politics, offered a critical view of sexist, biblical and sociobiologist ideas that flourished within fatherhood politics. One profeminist interviewee from the National Organization of Men Against Sexism argued, "there are things that either men *or* women can do that women have traditionally done, and if men want to be better fathers, what they really need to do is to do what women have done for a long time." This interviewee maintained that the Fatherhood Responsibility Movement is ultimately founded in ideas of hierarchical gender difference. Similarly, the pro-feminist fragile families representative, Michael, critiqued the Fatherhood Responsibility Movement and maintained that both the fragile families and the pro-marriage wings fundamentally believe in male leadership but at the same time use disclaimers to say that women are important.

Michael [Local fragile families organizations] may say the correct things about *treat your women with respect*, and they say stuff like that, but fundamentally, when they use those rites of passage programs, most of them – not all – reinforce the idea of men that, once they get themselves together, once they get themselves in a job and they're making money, they have a responsibility to their families. And hence, that responsibility is to be the moral leader of that family . . . what they mean by *take care of your family*, they mean like, *be a man, take the leadership role, save your family* . . . To me it's pretty simple . . . it's that when you say something like *men are hardwired different*, you're implicitly saying there's something unequal. Because when you say there's difference between me and you beyond biological, I mean beyond the waist, right, [laughs] then to me what's implicit in making that assumption is that then you're going to place value. Once you're saying that there's difference, you're going to place value on which is more valuable than the other. And once you do that, you go right back into the situation that we're trying to get rid of; of a society where sexism is rampant, racism is rampant.

Author   And both sides – fragile families and pro-marriage – are saying that men and women are wired differently?

Michael Yes, I strongly believe that. I strongly believe that they believe that that's true.

Author   Are you alone among your colleagues in thinking about things this way?

Michael Past me and [my co-worker Paul] you'd be hard pressed to find someone who's in the work, who's doing this type of work who would agree with this. Other than the women's groups that we've talked to. (Quotes from interview with fragile families representative)

A Congressional fatherhood hearing may further illustrate the issue of male leadership within the Fatherhood Responsibility Movement (Committee of Ways and Means, House of Representatives 1998). Charles

Ballard, from the pro-marriage Institute for Responsible Fatherhood and Family Revitalization (IRFFR) stated in his testimony that: "Just as the family is the nucleus of a community, a father is the nucleus of a family." When asked whether the mother could be included in the nucleus as well, Ballard maintained:

In any corporation, and the family is the same way, there has to be a final decision maker and sometimes when two people cannot agree, *someone* has to make the final decision, and in many cases that is the father ... Women are the equal partners in *relationships*, but again the decision has to be made by *someone*. (Emphasis in original)

In comparing the pro-feminist fragile families statement and Ballard's quote above – the former critical of male leadership in families and the latter promoting it – one gets an impression of the breadth of gender ideologies within the Fatherhood Responsibility Movement. Most interviewees position themselves somewhere in between these two extremes – public representatives of large organizations especially take the middle road in order to maximize their appeal to grant-giving agencies and political constituencies. But, regardless of how mainstream organizations like the National Fatherhood Initiative and the National Practitioners Network are at a national level, there is considerable variation among the practitioners they assist and the men/fathers that these serve.

In dynamic ways, masculinities are contested and reconstructed from the situations and views of local practitioners and program participants which both challenge and appropriate national rhetoric. At the local level, issues that the Fatherhood Responsibility Movement are trying to affect are applied to the experiences of real men, and discussed from their approaches. The issues that are covered include relationships with relatives, mothers, girlfriends, children and friends. Participants and practitioners also deal with issues such as sexuality, male identity, religious values, employment, drugs, child support and the criminal justice system. Here the central themes of the national Fatherhood Responsibility Movement rhetoric become less clear, and there are oftentimes as many views as there are practitioners and participants. One example comes from a local fragile families organization on the east coast I visited around twenty times, which ran a fathers' workshop for poor/low-income (mostly African American) men. In one workshop, one of the practitioners promoted the fragile families notion of team parenting:

Many of us have difficulties in sharing leadership and responsibility with our women. Many of us try to *dominate* them. There's something very wrong with that. That has a direct impact on my children. They have to see us being able to disagree and work it out. We dominate our women and our children too. Because we get pushed around outside the home, the only place we feel that we can dominate is in our home. I say: take care of your lady, and your lady will take care of you. What they see you do, they're going to immolate. (From field notes taken at local fragile families fathers' program)

A very agitated discussion followed, where the fathers who participated in the workshop expressed different views. One of the participants maintained that the man is the stronger part and should be the head of the household, whereas the woman should be subject to the man, according to God. There was a storm of protest, critique and ridicule of this view among participants and practitioners. The most prevalent view the practitioners promoted in these workshops was that men/fathers should listen to, and assume equal positions to, "their ladies" and the mothers of their children, but different guidelines were expressed by different people in various contexts. In contrast, at another workshop at the same fathers' program, there were no protests from either practitioners or participants when guest lecturers throughout their lecture maintained that the father is "the captain of the ship" and the "leader of the family" – or else "the devil would take over."

Although parts of the Fatherhood Responsibility Movement in some instances seem to reinforce traditional notions of male dominance in heterosexual families (Collier 1996; Cornell 1998; Donovan 1998), this field (*including* the pro-marriage wing) also challenges notions of the authoritarian father. Fragile families representatives especially contest stereotypes and expectations that men can handle anything on their own and can, by nature, support their families. In many cases, interviewees stressed that men need each other in brotherly as well as governmental support, which may also be exemplified by the Promise Keepers' search for "accountability" and "intimate relationships" between men.

Notions of male sexuality in construction of masculinities

While Fatherhood Responsibility Movement representatives occasionally challenge stereotypes of men as testosterone-driven predators, both pro-marriage and fragile families representatives still conceive of masculinity as "naturally" constituted by a gender-specific sexuality that has to be harnessed or else men will run berserk. Men's sexual practices are under the spotlight, and a central part of the Fatherhood Responsibility Movement agenda is to hold men responsible for managing their perceived insatiable heterosexuality according to universalizing notions of masculinity.

Fatherhood Responsibility Movement representatives, and especially the practitioners who work directly with fathers, are expected to be "role models" and limit their own sexuality to marriage and/or monogamous relationships (see Anderson 1990; Duneier 1992; Wilson 1996). Speakers at conferences and workshops often give examples from their own lives when talking about fatherhood and masculinity issues. Fatherhood responsibility is supposed to be founded in the personal lives and experiences of practitioners – they are supposed to "walk their talk" and practice what they preach. The issue of practitioners and program participants managing their sexuality has been discussed frequently in the fragile families wing lately, and a speech given by one of the leading figures may exemplify this:

> Studies from all over the world [show] that men have greater frequency for sex than do women – basic... And it is all around this question of: *how* are men going to *manage* their sexuality so that, as they grow up, they can remain faithful to their partners and to their children, and they can keep their wealth within their household and not pissing away – excuse me – on child support and maintaining two households... And you remember Solomon, David and Abraham, and what was the one thing, the *one thing* that took these kings and tore them down? It was their failure to manage their sexuality! (From recording of regional fatherhood conference, original emphasis)

Another main figure from the fragile families wing spoke at another conference about teaching men to control their sexuality in terms of managing a stock account, with a reward at the end. Not unlike the pro-marriage view that men have an innate "promiscuity" that needs to be harnessed into pro-social goals, fragile families representatives base fatherhood responsibility strategies on notions of universal male sexuality. In a sense, the entire Fatherhood Responsibility Movement may be analyzed in terms of efforts to harness heterosexual masculinity as constructed by loose essentialist notions of gender-specific sexuality. Men are considered unable to control their own sexual urges unless controlled by someone or something, such as a higher power (God) or social institutions (marriage). Fragile families organizations generally use economic motivations, whereas marriage proponents, to a larger extent, use religious or moral motivations in maintaining that a responsible father waits until he is married before he has children. For instance, one of the leading marriage proponents spoke of the control of masculinity in religious/moral terms:

> We [men] need a *good reason* to keep those base instincts in, you know, check. Well, faith is one of them – you know, if you're connected, if you feel that you can be held accountable by a higher authority... I think that the most powerful contract to keep men's behavior in check is not the contract between the *woman* and the man, but the contract between the man and God... It's a lot more powerful motivator to keep my baser instincts in check if I know God is going to hold my eternal

soul accountable than if my wife is. (Laughs) You know, OK that sort of has that bigger ring to it, and that's why I think faith is a more powerful motivator than just the sort of contract between men and women. (From interview with leading marriage proponent within the Fatherhood Responsibility Movement)

One hallmark of masculinity, as constituted by notions of male sexuality within the Fatherhood Responsibility Movement, is its implicit heterosexual nature.[16] For example, notions of heterosexual complementarity within marriage or "team parenting," as well as in terms of parental roles, may indicate heteronormative presumptions.[17] The representatives' talk of children's need for "the complementarity of the parenting equation" is one example of such heteronormative notions. For another example, one interviewee within the pro-marriage wing argued for the value in maintaining gender difference, founded in the idea that sexual attraction and complementary parental roles, are based on sexual difference. Thus, the pro-marriage "androgyny" concept reveals not only the fear of distorted gender identities, but also a fear of distorted sexualities.

Thus, in this view, fatherhood responsibility within family and marriage is centered around the "problem of managing male heterosexuality." A responsible father is someone who does not have more children than he can afford to raise, and who is committed to one monogamous heterosexual relationship. As opposed to women, men are thought to need incentives in order to become responsible parents. This is one of the junctures where the pro-marriage and fragile families wings converge in loose essentialist constructions of gender and families. However, they diverge in their approaches to the nature and solutions to "the problem of male sexuality." The fragile families wing frames the problem in economic terms, whereas the pro-marriage wing focuses on culture and moral commitment.

Changing the political terrain and constructions of father responsibility

This chapter has analyzed voices of the Fatherhood Responsibility Movement primarily in terms of the ways masculinity politics is played out among the competing constituencies of men that the two wings of the Movement claim to represent. I do not intend to analyze the ways in which the Fatherhood Responsibility Movement impacts the positions of women, mothers, children or social groups that are not explicit concerns for the Fatherhood Responsibility Movement. My aim is to map out the field and analyze the ways the Fatherhood Responsibility Movement representatives construct the issues and politics at stake. Although real power asymmetries do exist among men, particular constructions of masculinities emerge in tandem with historically located *perceptions* of equality, inequality and deprivation (Cornwall and Lindisfarne 1994). As apparent above, interpretations of power are always *contested*, and deprivation may be considered as *relative* to the position one finds oneself in at different points in time toward the welfare state, one's family and the labor market as a husband, welfare recipient, citizen, etc. There are claims and grievances that unite the different groups of the Fatherhood Responsibility Movement. One may, for example, conclude that the Fatherhood Responsibility Movement as a whole struggles for the recognition of men as fathers in terms of caretakers, and legal *or* economic possibilities to nurture their children. In addition, the Fatherhood Responsibility Movement seeks to redefine masculinity to include nurturing – not just breadwinning.

Within the organizations of the fragile families wing, constructions of masculinities are conditioned by opportunity structures in the labor market and the judicial system, social oppression, and governmental and public stereotypes that undermine poor and minority masculinities. The point of departure is an adversarial socioeconomic environment dominated by middle/upper-class white men as differentiated from low-income/poor and minority masculinities and fatherhoods. A general counter strategy of fragile families groups is to empower and support "positive" notions of masculinities through role models in African American, mixed or race/ethnically specific groups of socioeconomically disadvantaged men. Furthermore, fragile families organizations offer practical support in terms of helping fathers to get jobs, skills, education and assistance in dealing with child support enforcement.

This is to be compared with the approach of pro-marriage groups, who primarily differentiate masculinity and fatherhood from femininity and motherhood – not other men – and mainly distinguish between masculinities in terms of "constructive" versus "destructive." One explanation marriage proponents give to the difference in perspective between them and fragile families groups is that the latter only focus on specific and limited groups of fathers, whereas they work with *all* fathers – not just one target group. From the perspective of most marriage proponents, it does not make sense that marriageability is an economic question, because, as far as they can see (and we are not talking about people who claim to have experienced poor conditions), if you put your money together within marriage, you will live above poverty level. Furthermore, if you are a married father, your breadwinner motivation and earnings are likely to rise according to pro-marriage interviewees.

Marriage proponents generally located the decline of responsible married fathers in an individualist *culture* – not in terms of the *race or class positions* of fathers, but in terms of people's shifting ideas and values.

Pro-marriage interviewees consider feminists to be part of a cultural change that undermines rather than celebrates gender difference according to their loose essentialist notions of masculinity, fatherhood and the necessity of marriage. If the father's perceived unique and irreplaceable contribution to the family is unrecognized, and the institution of marriage is devalued, then the legitimacy of fatherhood disintegrates. Subsequently, according to this view, social and moral order breaks down. However, if you ask marriage proponents what exactly constitutes the male characteristics they attribute such essential importance to, they are often pretty vague about it or reluctant to talk about it at length. From what I could gather, non-androgynous masculinity is marked by traits like "aggression," "competitiveness," "rule orientedness," "instrumentalism," and "promiscuity," whereas androgynous, "soft," or femininized masculinity is characterized by less of these things.

The contestation over the positions of men and fathers within families reflects broader tensions around breadwinning, caretaking and gendered divisions of labor. While conditions and expectations on fathering and father practices are changing in American society at large, the Fatherhood Responsibility Movement both reclaims and reconstructs notions of gender difference. Compared to the other men's movements in this volume, such as the openly contested Fathers' Right Movement in Spain and the Swedish Consensus Movement, the US Fatherhood Responsibility Movement is exceptional in its breadth and visibility. Beneath the unified image of national consensus, there are complex tensions between pro-marriage culturalists and fragile families structuralists who represent different claims and constituencies of men.

Although there is a wide range of approaches to gender difference and parental roles within the Fatherhood Responsibility Movement, both the pro-marriage and the fragile families wings depart from loose essentialist notions of innate male heterosexuality. One major way to achieve "responsible fatherhood" in both wings of the Fatherhood Responsibility Movement is through managing male sexuality by "taming men to the domestic yoke."[18] This is done by means of different strategies to control men's "naturally" relentless heterosexuality through economic, moral, religious or institutional restrictions. Thus, the Fatherhood Responsibility Movement seeks to domesticize masculinity while masculinizing domesticity by reinforcing notions of gender/sexual difference. The efforts of the Fatherhood Responsibility Movement to control male sexuality is manifested by race and socioeconomic class; on the one hand, by restricting white middle-class men's sexuality to monogamous marriage. On the other hand, by promoting monogamy and the channeling of men's sexual "energy" into breadwinning and one affordable family among poor/low-income minority men. Many of the conceptions about the "violent" and "promiscuous" qualities of poor/low-income African American men and fathers, as well as the belief in the centrality of the two-parent family to social order, have been prevalent since the Moynihan report.

Low-income/poor, African American and minority responsible fatherhood is threatened *vis-à-vis* other men in the sense of their declining opportunities, on the one hand, to provide for themselves and their families, and, on the other hand, to manage their sexuality in an affordable way (as to not have more children than they can support). In contrast, the marriage proponents feel that masculinity is threatened *vis-à-vis* mothers and women who might misrecognize their perceived unique and irreplaceable role as fathers and the importance of marriage in connecting men to families and children to fathers. Consequently, fragile families representatives construct low-income/poor and minority masculinities in comparison to *other*, more privileged, *men* (in most cases white middle/upper-class men) – whereas pro-marriage representatives construct notions of universalizing masculinity in differentiation to a generalized notion of *women*. Both wings of the Fatherhood Responsibility Movement want their version of responsible fatherhood to be recognized by the state and by the public, and to become a model for masculinity and fathering.

The Fatherhood Responsibility Movement is responding to and constructing a second crisis in fatherhood within a changing economic and cultural climate that redefines good and bad fathers. Today's participants in fatherhood policy-making are trying to make sense of changing gender relations as well as changing roles and conditions for men and fathers in family, labor market and state policy, although they interpret such processes differently, and approach them from the perspectives of differently positioned men. Within the same "movement," there are also contradictory claims for justice, as well as different perceived sources for the problems of fatherhood. These differences are particularly reflected in the fundamentally divergent key issues of the two wings of the Fatherhood Responsibility Movement; the pro-marriage wing stresses marriage, and the fragile families wing stresses work. Subsequently, although the Fatherhood Responsibility Movement exercises and affects masculinity politics, it is misleading to talk about a unified "men's interest" in promoting fatherhood responsibility, considering the diverging strategies and approaches of the asymmetrically positioned constituencies involved.

Part 4

Theorizing men, masculinities and fatherhood

9 Men, fathers and the state: national and global relations

Jeff Hearn

Debates about fathers and fatherhood need to be more explicitly gendered and more explicitly about power. Fathers need to be understood as gendered and *as men*, and fatherhood needs to be understood as an institution, historically constructed as a form of certain men's power. Fathers and fatherhood are social, rather than "natural" or biological, constructions and institutions (O'Brien 1981; Hearn 1987), intimately connected with the social production and reproduction of men, masculinities and men's practices. In particular, the relationship of fathers, "the family" and the state is a matter of the relationship of *men*, gendered families and the gendered state.

This chapter addresses this basic problematic, and as such builds on recent work within Critical Studies on Men. This has emphasized the importance of questions of men's societal and structural dominations within patriarchies; the pluralizing of masculinity to masculinities set within relations of power, and the analysis of the interrelations of unities and differences between men; and men's specific practices, identities, sexualities and subjectivities. In particular this analysis of fathers, fatherhood, families and the state follows earlier work on the changing historical relations of men/fathers to the state and the welfare state within public patriarchies; the complexity of men's power and the extent of men's (often fathers') violences to women; and the interrelations of social oppressions and institutions.[1]

These genderings are partly about changing forms of identity, organization, welfare, state, nation and global relations – particularly in the transitions from what might be called modern to late modern social relations. Similarly, the gendering of fathers as men does not suggest any kind of essentialism or inevitability. Social realities, such as fatherhood, may be characterized as social centers of dominance, yet should not be seen a priori as solid, unified or singular; more usually, they are multiple, dispersed and sites of contradictions. Tendencies in dominant centers to dispersal and fragmentation are constantly being both reinforced and yet countered and supplemented in the formation of new centers of dominance. These paradoxes are important in focusing on fatherhood and the state within the context of gendered globalization and global patriarchies.

While throughout this chapter I focus mainly on "Great Britain" and the UK, I also use some examples from other countries, particularly Nordic countries. This is partly simply because England is where I have lived and Finland is where I am currently living, but it also serves a more general comparative purpose to highlight the *very peculiar* nature of the British case in the development of the state and the welfare state. The first part of the chapter introduces some of the debates within Critical Studies on Men as a framework for rethinking fathers and fatherhood. This is followed by a general critique of men's and fathers' changing relations to welfare, the welfare state, citizenship and the nation-state. There is then a more focused discussion, within their historical contexts, of contemporary constructions of men as fathers, and fathers as men, in relation to the nation-state. The next section is on men's and fathers' relations to transnational and global social organization, beyond the nation-state, as part of the analysis of "world" or "globalizing patriarchies" and a critique of such concepts. It is not appropriate to be simply "for" or "against fatherhood," or to assert a fixed positive or negative meaning to it. Fatherhood changes massively across time and space; this is a dialectical, not an either/or, matter.

Fathers in the context of critical studies on men

Debates on fathers and fatherhood can be usefully considered in the context of recent, more general Critical Studies on Men. This recent growth of interest in the study and theorizing of men and masculinities has derived from several directions and traditions. First, there have been various feminist critiques of men – including liberal feminist critiques of men's unfairness and privilege; Marxist and socialist–feminist critiques of men's economic class advantage; radical and lesbian feminist critiques of men's sexuality and violence; and black feminist critiques of (white) men's sexism and racism. Secondly, there have been critiques from (male) gay studies, and to an extent queer studies. Gay scholarship is not necessarily complementary to or reconcilable with feminist work (Edwards 1994), not least because gay perspectives are premised on the assumption of desire for men and the desirability of men rather than the direct critique of men. Queer theory and practice have problematized dichotomous thinking on gender and sexualities even more profoundly, and argued for activist, constructionist and fluid approaches (e.g. Beemyn and Eliason 1996). Thirdly, there have been some men's specific and explicit responses to feminism. These include those that are specifically pro-feminist or anti-sexist; there is also work that is ambiguous in relation to feminism or even anti-feminist in perspective. The idea of "men's studies" remains an ambiguous development: it is often unclear how such studies relate to feminism, and whether they refer to studies by men or of men (Hearn 1997). In addition, there are a wide range of other critical, and more or less gendered, perspectives that have directly or indirectly problematized understandings of men and masculinities, and thus fathers and fatherhood. These include black studies, studies on race and racism, cultural studies, poststructuralism, postmodernism and studies on globalization and localization.

These critiques of men together make up Critical Studies on Men. They have brought the theorizing men and masculinities into sharper relief, making men and masculinities *explicit objects* of theory and critique. Often these studies have involved searches for the center of men and men's power – in biology, the self, identity, "masculinity"/"masculinities," subcultures, institutions, nation-state, social system, culture, capital, community, even fatherhood. One strand of conceptual and political change that may be identified in the progressive development of these critical studies is a movement from the non-recognition of men's power, to its recognition, then the search for a center to that power, and thence to the deconstruction of possible centers (Hearn 1997). Among the many areas of current debate in the theorizing of men and masculinities, I introduce just three that are particularly relevant to the analysis of fathers and fatherhood: societal questions around the usefulness of the concept of patriarchy; middle-range questions around varieties and differences between men and between masculinities; and experiential/structural questions around sexuality and subjectivity. In each case, there are tensions between generalizations about men and masculinity and specificities of particular men and masculinities, which may assist understanding the social construction of fathers and fatherhood.

The central political and theoretical place of the concept of patriarchy within Second Wave feminism was subject to both feminist and pro-feminist critiques in the late 1970s (e.g. Atkinson 1979; Beechey 1979; Rowbotham 1979; Barrett 1980; also see Alexander and Taylor 1980; Walby 1989; Waters 1989). While the understanding of patriarchy had shifted from the literal meaning of *the rule of the father or fathers* to that of social, economic, political and cultural dominations of men more generally, it was still critiqued as being too monolithic, ahistorical, biologically overdetermined, and neglectful of women's resistance and agency.

Despite these critiques, the concept has not gone away. On the contrary, the debate has continued and remains unfinished – in three principal ways. First, there has been particular attention to the historical movement from private patriarchy, with men's power located primarily in the private domain as fathers and husbands, to public patriarchy, with men's power primarily in public domain organizations as capitalist and state managers and workers. This sets the framework for revisiting fathers and fatherhood but now as increasingly constructed within the powers of men in the public domains. Secondly, the various sites or bases of patriarchy have been specified more closely. Walby (1986, 1990) has analyzed six patriarchal structures: capitalist work, the family, the state, violence, sexuality and culture. I have identified a slightly different set of structures: reproduction of labor power, procreation, degeneration/regeneration, violence, sexuality and ideology (Hearn 1987). Patriarchy may thus be understood as diversified and differentiated rather than unified and monolithic; it may be more accurate to refer to (public) patriarchies rather than patriarchy (Hearn 1992). Thirdly, structural commentaries on men and patriarchies are increasingly being developed in relation to debates on globalization (Connell 1993, 1998) and glocalization (the simultaneous occurrence and intersection of globalization and localization, see Robertson 1995). While concepts such as "world" or "global patriarchies"(Mies 1986, 1998; Hearn 1996a) are not unproblematic, there is a growing concern with the implications of globalizing tendencies on the changing form of patriarchal relations. These debates also have very fundamental implications for the power of fathers and fatherhood. The concepts of patriarchy, patriarchies and patriarchal relations facilitate a focus on men in terms of not only interpersonal relations but also *structural relations*, and the ways men and different groups of men, whether local, national or transnational, may act as power blocs, with their own, sometimes contradictory, interests. Patriarchies are historically specific forms of societal organization, with their own particular characteristics, dynamics and structural tendencies, not a principle of universal social organization.

A second area of development in Critical Studies on Men has been around difference and multiplicity, as is clear in the pluralizing of masculinity to masculinities. This has been partly a means of recognizing both power relations between men and women *and* power relations between men (unlike much of the earlier sex-role theory on masculinity in the singular) and masculinities (Carrigan et al. 1985; Connell 1995), for example, between hegemonic, complicit and subordinated masculinities. This is not any kind of simple turn toward difference. On the contrary, there has been a parallel concern with the analysis of both unities and differences between men and between masculinities (Hearn and Collinson 1993). Just as a major issue within feminism has been the relationship of commonalities and differences between women, so, too, men can be usefully analyzed in terms of commonalities and differences, mirroring the debate on the diversification of patriarchy and patriarchal arenas. Men's power in patriarchy and patriarchal social arenas is maintained in part through men's commonalities with each other. Men are bound together, though not necessarily consciously, by dominant sexuality, violence and potential violence, social and economic privilege, the power of the father, and political power more generally. Just as there may be a gender class of women, so there may be a gender class of men, whether in terms of biological reproduction (Firestone 1970; O'Brien 1981), sexuality (MacKinnon 1982, 1983), household relations or work (Delphy 1977, 1984). All these, and indeed other, social relations might be possible bases of the gender class of men (Hearn 1987, 1992). However, the idea of a unity of men is *also* a myth. Men's collective power is maintained partly through the assumption of hegemonic forms of men and masculinities – often white, heterosexual, able-bodied men (WHAMs), as well as often fatherly and breadwinning, too, as the most important or primary form – to the relative exclusion of other kinds of marginalized and subordinated men and masculinities. Instead, different kinds of men, dominant or otherwise, are reproduced, often in relation to other social divisions. In many social arenas there are tensions between the collective power of men and masculinities and differentiations amongst men and masculinities, defined through other social divisions, such as age, class, disability, family status, generation, race and sexuality (Hearn and Collinson 1993; Collinson and Hearn 1994).

A third area of development and debate has been around sexualities and subjectivities. Tensions between unities and differences can apply to the realm of sexuality; while sexuality may be individually experienced, it simultaneously operates transindividually, not least through structured discourses. Critical studies of sexuality/subjectivity have pointed to the dominance of men's heterosexuality and male (hetero)sexual narratives, and the close interrelations of dominant forms of men's sexualities and men's violences. Yet such heterosexual dominance often coexists with homosociality and even homosexual/gay subtexts. Within these contexts, resources and instances, there are recurring tensions: between the domination of heterosexuality and homosociality/homosexuality; asexuality and the sexualization/eroticization of dominance and hierarchy; coherent identity and fragmented identity; and essentialized experience, felt as one's own, and deconstruction. These issues are again important for a reconsideration of fathers and fatherhood – in terms of possible and often taken-for-granted connections with sexualities and violences; tensions between the power of individual fathers and the relations of fathers to each other as men; and the fragmented experiences and identities that may, for some men, accompany being fathers.

R. W. Connell (1998) has summarized contemporary themes in these critical studies on men and masculinities as: plural masculinities; hierarchy and hegemony; collective masculinities; bodies as arenas; active construction; contradiction; dynamics. Each has clear implications for rethinking how we understand fathers and fatherhood. Finally, the very concept of "masculinities" has itself become more actively critiqued for its ethnocentrism, historical specificity, false causality, possible psychologism and conceptual vagueness (McMahon 1993; Hearn 1996b). Instead there is a growing concern with the more precise specification of men's individual and collective practices within gendered glocalization.

Men, fathers, welfare, citizenship and the nation-state

Mainstream or malestream (O'Brien 1981) debates on citizenship have usually ignored gender relations and have instead through their own practices reproduced patriarchal social relations. Until the development of feminist scholarship on citizenship (Pateman 1988; Lister 1997), debates on citizenship usually meant debates by men on men. So to gender citizenship more fully certainly does not mean increasing the presence of men in theorizing, but making the theorizing of men more critical and more explicit. Changing this certainly means increasing women's presence within such analysis, as theorists, actors and subjects of analysis. However, gendering citizenship also means considering the relationship of men, including fathers, welfare and citizenship. However, to focus on men can lead to reaffirming men and men's power, and a further reduction of attention to women and women's interests. Thus here the attempt will be made to simultaneously name (Hanmer 1990), yet decenter men (Collinson and Hearn 1994).

The nation-state and national politics have been intimately and dominantly associated with the construction of men as fathers, and both men and fathers as citizens, and the nation-state has itself been characteristically patriarchal. This applies in men's relations to state formation, governmental centralization and expansion, the "national economy," the national military–industrial complex, state–capital alliances, political participation and the political enfranchisement of both women and men. The nation-state has been a powerful center of men's actions. Political development of the nation has often been men's preserve (or at least profoundly dominated by men until relatively recently), as in the "award" of suffrage by men to women, men's domination of the law, military, the police, the civil service, the state machinery, parliaments and autocracies and so on (Hearn 1992). Men's relations to citizenship, state and nation are, however, far from uniform: we might note men as controllers of the state, as the dominant group in the reproduction of political regimes, as adult male citizens, as fathers and as those (immigrant, black, young, homeless, prisoners and so on) excluded as citizens.

The growth of the modern state is fundamental to the construction of fathers' relation to the complex relation of country (space), state (political, legal and administrative authority) and nation (culture and ideology) (Yuval-Davis 1997). The state, through civil, family and property law, population registration and numerous other policy regulations and procedures has, especially and increasingly over the last 200 years, devised, sanctioned, constructed, constrained and determined what fathers are and what a father is. Men's and fathers' actual, potential or absent citizenship has been developed and maintained in relation to women. Above all there has been a pervasive assumption, influence and power of the enfranchised, autonomous, adult, heterosexual, married, fathering, family-heading, individual, male subject: the "collective individual" within and outside the state.

A major trajectory in the construction of men, fathers and citizens has been in relation to welfare and the welfare state (Hearn 1998c). The primary focus of the modern Western European welfare state has been represented as the agendered citizen, even though this has been implicitly gendered, being based on assumptions of the nuclear family, the unpaid work of women and the rights of fathers and husbands (see Wilson 1977). Feminist analysts have articulated models and understandings of welfare and welfare states that place gender relations at the center of analysis. Lewis (1992), for example, distinguishes strong, modified and weak "breadwinner states," exemplified by Ireland, France and Sweden respectively. Welfare state development can thus be linked to assumptions about the social position and responsibilities of men as fathers, husbands and "breadwinners." Welfare theory, whether gendered or not, can be interpreted as implicit theory about fatherhood. Gendered conceptualizations of welfare have usually spoken about men in three main ways – in families (particularly heterosexual ones), in paid work (particularly full-time employment), and in the state (particularly as managers and decision makers). Less usual in these gendered models are commentaries on men managing the institutions of capital, men outside the heterosexual family (for example, gay or lone young men) or men as "users" of welfare. While it as been relatively unusual for feminist analyses of social policy to focus primarily on fathers or men, recent feminist studies increasingly include men, but now as gendered actors (see, for example, Bryson et al. 1994; Daly 1994; Popay et al. 1998).

In rethinking fatherhood–state relations, we may note that different feminist perspectives have different implications for the analysis of men/fathers. For example, approaches that critique the patriarchal and/or capitalist welfare state as opposed to women's interests are implicitly at least also presenting an account of men/fathers. First, in emphasizing the patriarchal interests of the (welfare) state, men are implicitly understood as having patriarchal interests as a collectivity, and as occupying different positions in relation to the state – as managers, policy makers, users and so on. Secondly, in emphasizing the capitalist interests of the (welfare) state, other distinctions are suggested, most obviously men's different locations in the class system. In contrast to these approaches, some feminist perspectives have focused on the structuring of care and caring. The critique of community care may direct attention to both women's paid/unpaid care and men's paid/unpaid care, including fathers' uneven performance, avoidance and control of care. To understand men's and fathers' relations to welfare, it is necessary to broaden "work" and "labor" from so-called "productive" labor to "reproductive" labor, care, emotions and violence. Gendering welfare and welfare states involves taking more seriously social relations other than those of employed, paid labor.

Historically, men have often acted in their own collective interests as husbands, fathers, workers and managers, and occasionally against those interests, placing women's interests as a higher priority. Histories of welfare/state development can be re-read not just in terms of extending a gendered or women's citizenship but as accounts of men with different locations, positions and interests – as citizens, politicians, workers, managers, professionals, fathers, welfare recipients and so on. This suggests both synthetic analyses of broad patterns of different men's relations (as, for example, fathers, husbands, workers, managers) to welfare, and specific analyses of the variability of those relations over time, between societies, and by other social divisions, such as age, class, disability, race, sexuality.

Contradictions derive from the historical changes in welfare and the state. Just as mothers and women have contradictory relations to welfare, so, too, do fathers and men. Welfare systems can involve the redistribution of resources from fathers'/men's control, even if men are in control of system policy and operations. However, such systems can increase fathers'/men's control of women, even if women run the system day to day. The relationship of fathers and men to the actual provision of welfare services can also be contradictory. In some situations, fathers may receive preferential treatment over women, for example, at times of "family crisis" or when it is assumed that men cannot cope (although women might be assumed to be able to). On the other hand, men may tend to use some welfare services less than women, as is most clearly seen in the case of health services. Fathers and men thus have quite diverse relations with welfare and welfare services. These relations involve sometimes needing care from others, say, around depression or addiction; sometimes needing control, say, around violence; sometimes absence from or avoidance of contact with care and/or control (Hearn 1999). All these can occur simultaneously for particular welfare agencies and individual fathers/men. Patriarchal relations can persist and be reproduced through combinations of fathers'/men's control of welfare, fathers'/men's need for and sometimes avoidance of care (both of themselves and by others), fathers'/men's need for and sometimes avoidance of control (both of themselves and by others). Fathers'/men's power can also indirectly involve damage to men, for example, in suicide and lower life expectancy. Damage to individual fathers/men and even whole groups of men may paradoxically assist the maintenance of fathers'/men's collective power.

Welfare and the welfare state are, of course, also organized through different policy arenas, with their own institutional traditions, arrangements, rules and procedures. Each arena provides not just services but also social spaces for workers, managers, policy makers and users, for different kinds of men, masculinities and fathers, for the reproduction of and occasionally opposition to masculinism. Fathers/men may ally with each other, and indeed oppose, compete with and distance themselves from each other. Alliances, oppositions, continuities and discontinuities between men also operate *across* boundaries between public and private domains. Fatherhood, whether or not "in crisis" (Knijn 1995), has increasingly become a disputed terrain across those boundaries and between policy arenas. Such contestations in and around the state are part of more general problematizations of men and masculinities (Hearn 1998a; Williams 1998).

With all these discussions on the shifting relations of men, fathers, welfare and nation-state, there is the recurring question – which men and which fathers are we talking about? Sometimes it is men in the state; sometimes employed "breadwinning," "family men"; sometimes fathers, present or absent; sometimes "violent men"; sometimes men who are not employed; sometimes black men, men of color, immigrant men and ethnic minority men. Men's relation to welfare may be determined, affected or mediated by legal nationality and by racism in and around the state, where questions of "race" and nationality may be bound up with sexuality. The state frequently defines citizens, especially new and potential citizens, in reference to their sexuality, actual or perceived, and their "marital/parental status." Men, especially black and (potential) immigrant men, along with their relatives, may be defined by the state in relation to the presence or absence of "his" children and heterosexual marriage. "Gay marriage" and "gay fatherhood" are not easy routes to citizenship for men not legally national citizens.

Contemporary constructions of fathers and the state

Reassessing contemporary social relations of fatherhood and the state may become clearer by looking back at historical change, and the long-term movement from private to public patriarchy. For many centuries early modern relations of fatherhood and the (incipient) state were sanctioned by local religious institutions along with local forms of governance. Fatherhood was assumed to be a biological fact, part of the social associations of marriage, taken for granted, part of the definition of the "head of the household" and reinforced by legal, quasi-legal or communal practices. While fatherhood concerns particular men's relations with particular children, it is historically difficult to separate it from marriage arrangements and gender relations more generally. However, having said that, it is important to acknowledge the great variability in both patriarchal social forms and family forms that existed before nineteenth-century state interventions. Indeed the patriarchal family cannot be equated with the bourgeois or petit bourgeois family in any simple way, though they may be among the clearest statements of patriarchal legal ownership of wives, children and other relatives as property (Stone 1977; Elshtain 1981). The absolutist individual patriarch is one model of profoundly gendered social relations for society that may act as a confluence of familial, communal, religious, monarchical and state powers. Fatherhood has historically been an institution of power, often an unspoken social problem (O'Brien 1981, 1986; Hearn 1983, 1987).

Though the modern British state intervention in the family can be dated from at least the mid-eighteenth century, early state intervention in fatherhood was dispersed and minimalist. Men in the state engaged in minimal management of young lives, leaving that responsibility mainly to mothers or fathers; unhygienic conditions, social neglect and physiological deterioration took their toll. Religion, medicine, science, law and welfare reforms have all stipulated "correct" forms of fatherhood and the patriarchal family. State interventions have increased in both biological fatherhood (especially the recording of paternity and population censuses) and social fatherhood (especially the assignment of authority as "head of the family," ownership of children and financial responsibilities). The state has become involved in an increasing range of ways in the construction of fatherhood, as part of transformations of (increasingly public) patriarchies.

While there has been an historical shift from fathers having automatic rights to fathers having both rights and duties, fathers are still very much dominantly defined in terms of rights (in relation to children and women); in contrast, mothers continue to be defined through the notion of responsibilities (in relation to children) (Williams 1998). The absolute rule of the authoritarian Victorian paterfamilias may now be much less usual, but the status of "father" still involves getting something, some power, status and certain rights, for (almost) nothing. Interestingly the logics of government policy on the family, and fathers within it, have often become quite inconsistent on these issues. Contemporary constructions of fathers and fatherhood are far from stable. They involve increasing diversification and increasing contradictions. These include paternity; birth registration; legal and social sanctioning of patriarchal property, ownership and control; and state intervention against fathers' violence; the separation of "the biological" and "the social" in the construction of fathers, and thus the notion of "social" rather than "biological fatherhood" through fostering, adoption, stepfatherhood; changing relations of cash, care and responsibility; and state sponsorship of "family planning," involvement of fathers at childbirth and in children's education, and even fatherhood classes. These diverse relations are becoming even more complex, partly with the growth of transnational social forces beyond the nation-state.

Contemporary contradictions may be partly because of confusion around whether it is "fathers" (or "mothers"), "the family" or "marriage" that is to be the focus of state policy and practice. The UK Children Act of 1989 emphasized the importance of "*parenting*," of both mothers and fathers. The 1991 Child Support Act shifted financial responsibilities from the state to fathers. The 1995 Family Homes and Matrimonial Act failed to give protection from men's violence to cohabiting women. The 1996 Family Law Act sought to reform the divorce law in notoriously inconsistent ways, including the abolition of fault, the introduction of longer delays and conciliations, and pension-sharing. There has also been a growing range of contemporary commentators, across a wide political spectrum (including liberal and socialist feminists, older men formerly of the left but now of the center, civil servants, state administrators and men from the new right) who argue that some, many or too many fathers are not being fathers the way they should be – in particular that they are too absent and/or too distant (Williams 1998). These emerging worries are part of the continuing historical "paradox of patriarchy" (Lewis and O'Brien 1987), whereby fathers exert power and authority at least partly through absence. There is now a greater variety of ways of being fathers, of alternative modes of fathering and supposed "new fathers," mirroring the mythical "new man."

In order to elucidate these growing complexities, the remainder of this section focuses on three particular and important arenas of fathers–state relations within public patriarchies: violence; rights and responsibilities; birth and sexuality. These three are clearly not the only important aspects of what might be called "public patriarchal fatherhood," but they do point to the diverse ways in which fathers, and indeed mothers, as well as potential fathers, are constructed through state relations.

Violence – home and away

First, let us consider fathers–state relations through the perspective of violence. This provides a case study of the complex movements from private patriarchy toward public patriarchy. Collier (1995) has argued, it is marriage rather than paternity *per se* that has generally determined the legal conditions that constituted fatherhood (also see Williams 1998). This is particularly relevant in considering the question of men's/husbands'/fathers' violence, for the construction of fathers often occurs in the context of marriage or marriage-type relations. Until recently, the state has frequently, perhaps characteristically, condoned men's violence to women. This is very important in understanding how men's, often husbands' and fathers', violence to women has been accepted, condoned, normalized and ignored by individuals and institutions, and generally seen as a "private matter." British legal reforms around violence introduced in the nineteenth century included the 1853 Act for the Better Prevention and Punishment of Aggravated assaults upon Women and Children, but this "did very little to deter husbands from abusing their wives and children" (Steiner-Scott 1997: 127). In the late nineteenth century, the state was becoming more active in the construction of fathers through limited intervention against men's violence in the family (Hearn 1992, 1996c).

At a meeting of the 1882 Liverpool Society of the Prevention of Cruelty to Animals, the suggestion was made to form a parallel society for the prevention of cruelty to children, which was instituted in 1883. In 1889 a further Poor Law Amendment Act gave Poor Law guardians powers over children in their control on all matters except religious upbringing. Also in 1889 the National Society for the Prevention of Cruelty to and Protection of Children (later to become the National Society for the Prevention of Cruelty to Children [NSPCC]) was established, and in the same year the Protection of Children Act was passed – in effect the first "Children's Charter." This made it a misdemeanor to *willfully* ill-treat, neglect or abandon a boy under 14 or a girl under 16 in a manner that was likely to cause *unnecessary suffering or injury to health* (Eekelaar 1978: 68). The NSPCC grew rapidly with locally managed branches; by 1909,

250 inspectors operated nationwide as a buffer between local committees and clientele; "drunkenness, accompanying dirt and squalor, accounting for a large share of the neglect" (Ferguson 1990). State intervention into child welfare in the family was codified with the 1908 Children Act, leading to the appointment of infant life protection workers and the formal delegation of state powers to the NSPCC, as part of Liberal government social reforms.

Fathers' relations to the state have been strongly affected by national crises, particularly war, and collective willingness to develop state welfare. Constructions of men's/fathers' violence in and around the state, country and nation have often been very closely allied to national militarism, and the reproduction of men's violence more generally. Fathers'/men's relation to the state, country and nation, has been strongly mediated by the performance and control of violence; the construction of, obedience to and breaking of the law; and the commitment to defend the country. The modern relationship of men, fathers and nation derived in part from the movement to modern welfare and the creation of national mass male armies, in Britain, first with the Boer War and then with World War I. Recruitment campaigns appealed to men's responsibilities to defend "King and Country," and fathers' responsibilities to defend "their" women, children and families. They also revealed the parlous state of British men's health, leading to military interest in the control of soldiers' drinking and the creation of their institutional eating facilities. World War I brought further concern for "human resources," with the recognition of "shell-shock" and the more general health problems of men as workers and soldiers. In 1919, the Ministry of Health was introduced to respond to these problems of men workers as efficient bodies, and fathers as reproductive bodies. After World War I, public housing provided "homes fit for heroes," reaffirming the strong associations of men, fatherhood/manhood and the nation-state. For some men, these connections involved particular senses of imperialist fatherhood/manhood/nationhood, mediated by age, class, ethnicity and sexuality (Mangan and Walvin 1986).

The impact of World War II on new forms of citizenship, state planning and welfare is well established (Thane 1982). These processes were clearly gendered, with men's movement to and return from war; women's involvement in munitions, engineering and other new work and their then loss of such employment; and the evacuation of women and children to new living areas and then their subsequent return (Riley 1983). The experience of British men/fathers/soldiers often involved being away from "home"; their Finnish counterparts were more occupied with fighting on the home front – first against the Russians then the Germans. Finnish men and women lost much; they could be said to have lost the battle but won the war against rejoining the Russian Empire, though large border areas were ceded to the then Soviet Union. Peacetime often brought a return of the father in more senses than one. Interestingly, this pattern was not repeated throughout Europe in the same way. Jaana Kuusipalo (1990: 16) notes: "During the war women took the main responsibility for farming and the production of industry as well as for the continuity of civil life and thus they were breaking the division of labor between the sexes. At the end of the Second World War women comprised more than half of the Finnish industrial labour force." Furthermore, after the war Finnish women kept these jobs and did not "return to the home" (Rantalaiho 1997: 26). Compulsory conscription was abolished in the UK in 1957, but continues in Finland along with community service.

In recent decades, the British state, like many others, has challenged and changed fathers through its responses to Second Wave feminism. This has often been indirect, through responses to men's violence and abuse, rather than to controlling fathers directly. Fathers' and the state's authority has, like men's authority more generally, become problematized, admittedly in rather limited ways. With men's (often husbands' and fathers') violence to women and children, often labeled "domestic violence," the state has been challenged and at the same time has been urged to increase its powers and involvement against husbands and fathers. Increasing recognition of the problem by state agencies has followed the actions of the Women's Movement, particularly Women's Aid. However, even in 1967, when the first Matrimonial Homes Act was passed, "matrimonial violence was a non-subject" (Freeman 1987: 38). Following the establishment of the Women's Aid Federation in 1974 and the Parliamentary Select Committee on Violence in Marriage in 1975, the Domestic Violence and Matrimonial Proceedings Act was passed in 1976, giving additional powers of injunction, including for the unmarried, and arrest. Subsequent reforms strengthened the power of the ouster order, yet failed to produce fundamental state reform freeing women from violence.

The 1970s and 1980s saw a heightened awareness and intervention around child abuse. This was clearly relevant to the powers of fathers, including social fathers, but rarely presented as such. One indication of this increasing concern has been a negative one – in the shape of a series of official inquiries into child deaths and the (mis)conduct of social workers and other professionals. Between 1970 and 1985 there were no less than thirty-five such inquiries. The late 1980s saw the high-water mark of "scientific" risk assessment, and the growth of more proceduralized state responses to child abuse – often in effect fathers' violence and abuse. There has also been a growing concern for child sexual abuse, informed particularly by an increased awareness of sexuality, survivors' accounts, and feminist theory and practice more generally. In 1986, Childline, the national telephone helpline, was set up in close association with the national television program Childwatch. In 1987, the Cleveland controversy erupted, with large-scale social work and police intervention against parents suspected of sexual abuse. This highlighted the possible widespread scale of sexual abuse in what were portrayed as "ordinary families," but also led to a backlash against social workers' intervention in families and with fathers. The Butler–Sloss Report followed in 1988. Seven governmental circulars were issued in 1988 in the wake of the controversy, dealing mainly, though not only, with child sexual abuse. In 1989, the Children Act, together with the nine volumes of guidance issued to supplement it, consolidated policy and practice, and gave local authorities a general duty to safeguard and promote the welfare of children in their area, through Area Child Protection Committees. The Act also emphasized the desirability of maintaining social and emotional ties with both parents, including fathers, after separation and divorce.

Since 1988, police reforms around violence to women have included "domestic violence" pro-arrest policies; force rules on treating violence equally seriously regardless of the relationship of the parties; and the creation of special units. State agencies, controlled by men, have made a series of concessions in response to men's violence to women. The state has sponsored particular social forms within the private domains. Increasingly, if gradually, the private violent powers of men – individual husbands and fathers – have been brought more fully into the view, sometimes the control, of the state. Legal and other state constructions of violence have generally served to play down its significance, whilst at the same time there has been a gradually increased awareness and recognition of the problem in law, policy statements and, to an extent, implementation, by the police, the prosecution service and probation.

In the Finnish case, the supposedly (and apparently compared with the British) "woman-friendly" welfare state has been developed around employment, family, education and care, and much less against violence and abuse. The 1983 Finnish Child Welfare Act embodied the principle of children's welfare being paramount – in social work, education, health, environmental planning and other state functions. "Family support" has been the focus rather than "child protection," though striking children is illegal. Men's violence to women has been seen rather separately and not as a high-profile problem until relatively recently. The Sub-committee on Violence against Women in the Council for Equality between Women and Men was created in 1990, and the national and regional Project on the Prevention of Violence against Women was set up from 1998 to 2002 by the Ministry of Social Affairs and Health.

In both Finland and the UK, state procedures for (fathers') violence to children and (husbands') violence to women have largely developed separately, with the former located in Social Services child protection systems or child welfare services, and the latter in the criminal justice system. Yet the latter (both the violence and the responses to it) often provide the context of the former. While public patriarchal relations now seem well established in the formation and limited control of men's/fathers' violence, this still entails state sponsorship of private patriarchal families, powers and violences, and limited public intervention against fathers' "private" violence, pointing to the close interconnections of public patriarchal structures around violence and the family (Hearn 1998b).

Rights and responsibilities – cash and care

A second set of state relations in the construction of fatherhood are changing patterns around employment, the family and fathers' rights and responsibilities, particularly in the provision of cash and care. In mapping the contemporary rights and responsibilities of fathers, fundamental contradictions have persisted between "the ideology of change" (Lewis and O'Brien 1987), whereby it is assumed that fathers are becoming more involved in family life, and the slow rate of change in fathers' actual involvement in families and child care. Many studies report alarmingly low amounts of time spent by fathers in personal family tasks, and the relative rarity of fathers taking *prime* responsibility for them, as opposed to "helping out." Sue Clarke and Jennie Popay (1998) conclude from their survey of the literature that, "[d]epending on household type, women's employment status, [and] age of children, men's contribution to parenting labor alternates between a quarter and a third," whilst "[t]heir contribution to overall responsibility has been reported as negligible" (Clarke and Popay 1998: 200). There are also national variations, with Nordic countries showing slightly more active participation by fathers. While these "contributions" appear to be slowly increasing, many fathers continue to specialize in specific tasks, such as doing the main shopping, washing up, taking children out, putting them to bed, rather than the continual series of everyday work/care that comprise family life. Fatherhood is thus not just social construction or ideology, but specific material practices whereby women generally do more work and have less leisure than men.

The historical context is again important in understanding the contemporary picture, both of which are characterized by state underwriting of (respectable) fathers' rights and rather limited responsibilities. In the late nineteenth century, the respectable British working man was obliged to be *prudent*, requiring him as a father and husband to take active steps to secure himself, his family and his dependants against future misfortune – joining insurance schemes provided by trade associations or friendly societies, personal involvement in benefit selection and making regular payments and so forth (Defert 1991).[2] These associative relations were soon displaced by private insurance schemes run for profit; then at the turn of the century the state intervened with national compulsory social insurance schemes (Rose 1996: 341). From about the 1890s, the division between the father as breadwinner and the mother as child carer was strongly reinforced, especially in families "headed" by skilled workers.

Around the turn of the century, and especially during and after the Boer War, the British state, that is certain men in the state, asserted a much greater recognition of women as mothers; mothers became a state policy question rather than strictly a private matter or the preserve of fathers or husbands (Lewis 1980). While women were constructed as mothers, men were meanwhile constructed more explicitly as workers and soldiers, and rather implicitly as fathers, potential fathers or disposable (in war) fathers. Men's status as fathers was necessary but taken-for-granted and, by contemporary standards, low profile. To be a good father generally meant providing not much direct caring. Indirectly at least (men in) the state was devising the means to be relatively uninvolved in the process of active fathering, instead creating the detached father, through reliance on active mothering. Throughout the twentieth century, the norm of the "working man," the so-called "family wage" and the "family man" (Collier 1995) have continued, perhaps until relatively recently, to be central in the construction of fathers, often through an alliance of government and organized trade unionism. As Nikolas Rose (1996: 338) puts it: "In the strategies of government . . . over the twentieth century . . . [e]conomic activity, in the form of wage labour was given a new set of *social* responsibilities, seen as a mechanism which would link males into the social order, and which would establish a proper relationship between the familial, the social and the economic orders." Such market-based distributions have been allowed to persist in their own rather *laissez-faire* way until recently.

Somewhat paradoxically, this "free market" situation has itself been reformed through (the former Conservative) governmental reforms in the 1990s around financial "child support," particularly following separation and divorce but also with non-cohabiting parents. The state has directed the enforcement of individual fathers' responsibilities, ideologically and financially. The 1991 Child Support Act focused on financial responsibilities neglected by fathers, thus complicating the broad distinction between rights and responsibilities. It could be argued that fathers are being placed increasingly in a position of responsibilities, both morally and financially, through the actions of state officials. The Child Support Agency (CSA) can also represent part of a state withdrawal from responsibility in relation to fathers and fatherhood, and part of a rationalization of state apparatus, superseding a previously fragmented and unequal system around fathers' and mothers' financial responsibilities after separation and divorce. While the CSA has transferred payments to mothers from the state to fathers (Lewis in this volume), its role has been complicated by a moral debate on the family and fatherhood. Much recent public, especially middle-class, concern has focused on the fathers/men who are long-term unemployed, defined as part of the "underclass," and who are seen as neglecting their fatherly duties – "a core of irresponsible and purposeless men at the center of our social malaise . . . unattached and unlovable . . . linked . . . to the erosion of the male breadwinner vocation" (Dench 1994: 10). Inspired by a "moral panic" around a relatively small group of young "irresponsible" "feckless" fathers, in practice the CSA engaged with a much larger group of fathers, who, seeing themselves as much more responsible and not at all feckless, not surprisingly, strongly contested the measures in campaigns and demonstrations against the state. The extent of ideological movement can be appreciated by the fact that the broad principles of the second Child Support Act of 1995, consolidating amendments to the first Act, were given cross-party support in the Select Committee Report of February 1995. By 1996, one-and-a-half million cases had been dealt with.

These constructions generally contrast with the Nordic equality model which has simultaneously provided relatively stronger support for family life, a route to greater public participation by women, and a much more child-centered model of welfare than the British (in Finland 21 against 2 percent of 0–3 year olds in publicly funded daycare; Millar and Warman 1996; Rubery et al. 1996). It has also been a means of protecting the father and spreading the load of caring work *amongst women*, so providing support for a relatively taken-for-granted model of fatherhood within the heterosexual family.[3] The state thus intervenes in complex ways in the construction of individual responsibility of fathers and the distribution of cash when parents separate or divorce. There is, for example, a growing state orchestration of positive models of fathering in the Netherlands and Sweden (Hobson and Knijn in this volume). Also in the Finnish case there is a more proactive promotion of the case for fatherhood and fathers' involvement. In the UK, there is less precise governmental support for fathers' caring, though even there the Labour government has initiated "Fathers Direct," which aims to offer information, advice and support to fathers, through a telephone helpline, guidance to employers on working fathers, and internet information. This modest initiative may be a counterbalance to likely increased payments by absent fathers under new child support regulations (Thomas 1999). However, the possible connections between violence, cash and care are rarely noticed in state policy.

Birth and sexuality

Historical constructions of conception, birth and sexuality lie at the very heart of the politics of fatherhood. They take us back to the base of (private) patriarchy. Debates around fatherhood usually take paternity and heterosexuality for granted. Recent years have seen growing stress in both Finland and the UK on the positive benefits of heterosexual fatherhood and positive models of heterosexual fatherhood. The question of fatherhood, and particularly young fatherhood, is a recurring, synthesizing theme throughout debates on the family and other policy arenas. Fatherhood is often assumed to be a fixed reference point within a world of rapid change. The clear message from across a broad political spectrum is that "families do need (heterosexual) fathers." Indeed the UK government is likely to increase the rights of unmarried fathers, for example, in adoption cases (Hill 1998).

Empirical research has indicated that there is no difference in developmental progress of children in lesbian, gay and heterosexual households (Rights of Women 1984; Patterson 1992). Despite this, it is now widely considered that: "children need their fathers too – as much for emotional sustenance as for paying the bills" (Coote 1995: 15). The somewhat paradoxical relationship between the critique of "feckless fathers" and the positive promotion of fatherhood, as that on "the family" more generally, rarely addresses questions of taken-for-granted (hetero)sexuality, more rarely still in any critical way.

Heterosexual hegemony in father–state relations is reaffirmed in the organization of the state, medicine, birth and conception itself. Childbirth is now a thoroughly medicalized process, but not in any simple technological way. Rather, state medical hegemony operates through responsiveness to social conditions and practices. These include the recent movements to encourage the presence and involvement of men/fathers at and around birth, whether just being there or in more active participation. "Enlightened" shades of opinion, both medical and non-medical, now agree that it is a "good thing" for fathers to be present and more involved (see Hearn 1987). Now, and particularly with new technology, such as insemination by donor and *in vitro* fertilization, the state takes an increasing interest in and control over who can have access to them, and thus who can become a father. This raises new issues around the ideologies and practices of fatherhood. The new technological possibilities may both subvert fatherhood and yet paradoxically reinforce dominant constructions of it, not least in terms of heterosexual imperatives rather than lesbian or gay parenting. The prospects of further new reproductive technologies, including cloning, and even the dispensability of the father, may bring a reassertion of "normal, heterosexual fathering," underwritten by the state, medicine and those seeking to retain the rule of the father.

Though there have been some significant legal advances in the rights of lesbians and gay men (for example, the lowering of the age of consent to 16 for male homosexuals in the UK, and the legalization of "gay marriages" in Denmark, Iceland, Norway and Sweden [see Bech 1993]), the situation of lesbian and gay parents, and thus gay fathers, remains problematic and with few civil rights in many countries. In the UK, lesbian and gay couples cannot marry, and there is extensive discrimination in relation to parenting, with "parenting rights" following from either biological status or marriage (Jackie Lewis 1998). In Finland, adoption is possible for single people and married couples; thus, although there are no reported cases of denial of parents' "parenting rights" because of their homosexuality, in practice, because of the lack of same-sex marriage, adoption is not an option for homosexual couples (Hiltunen 1998). Denmark has just (May 1999) become the first country to allow legal adoption by both parents of gay and lesbian partnerships of the biological children of one of the partners (*Helsingin Sanomat* 1999).

Men, fathers, transnational and global relations

Men and fathers cannot be understood only in terms of the nation, the welfare state or even the public patriarchies of individual societies. Increasingly, the analysis of men and fathers makes sense in the context of matters beyond the nation, within late modern relations of the state, global markets, shifting (un)employment, migration and transnational public patriarchies. In many ways, this is of course not new at all: international, imperialist and colonialist relations have long been integral to the construction of men and fathers, all the more so in the British case. Indeed, a focus on the nation-state was usually both in isolation from and in relation to other states. A national focus is usually also international in its conditions and its effects. In this section, I look beyond the immediate construction of men and fathers in the nation-state to the analysis of fatherhood within late modern relations, characterized by transnational and global relations. No longer is fatherhood simply mediated by fatherhood defined by the nation-state. The separation of biological, social and national legal definitions of fatherhood is becoming mediated by new political, economic, cultural and legal forms, often organized through organizations and managements, themselves dominated by men.

The basic building block of social analysis, the nation-state, is becoming increasingly problematic, with the growing power of transnational corporations, organizations, laws, networks and managements, including governmental, non-governmental organizations (NGOs), media, information, finance and capitalist organizations dominated by men. This is perhaps clearest with militarism, where the arms traders are men, the companies are headed by men, and the governments and their military and "defense" sections are led by men. It is also apparent in the growth of multinational corporations (the assets of many supranational corporations exceed some nation-states' Gross National Product (GNP) [Bauman 1995: 152]) and transnational alliances and unions, such as the European Union (EU) and its increasing action in legal, economic, monetary, consumer protection, social, health and safety, equal opportunities and environmental policy. Additionally, Western-dominated, yet transnational, organizations, like the International Monetary Fund (IMF) and the World Bank, impact profoundly upon nations through debt management and structural adjustment programs. Meanwhile, international resistances develop through transnational boycotts, trade unionism, fair trade movements, green campaigns, ethical consumerism and campaigns against sexual violence.

A focus on the nation as a discrete entity is increasingly unsatisfactory, at this time of crisis, change, uncertainty and polarizing inequalities (Bauman 1995: 140). Yet, while the nation-state becomes inherently uncertain, other attempts are being made to reinstate the nation either as a legal entity or an expression of communal/community identity of new imaginary centers and communities. These movements involve throwing off the grip of other previous centers (Bauman 1995: 153). The nation is simultaneously fragmenting and re-forming. It is increasingly problematic to see the nation-state as the automatic starting point of analysis. Individual identity, organization and nation, and thus fathers and fatherhood, are all problematic, in the context of global relations. The (potential) loss of identity, organization, nation and what fathers and fatherhood might mean is part of the movement toward globalization, itself assumed to be the product of fundamental change in global technology, media, communication, industry, education, governmental institutions, finance, militarism and environment.[4] The deconstruction of dominance and dominant centers occurs in the context of globalizing processes. Theorizing globalization is a fruitful avenue for deconstruction (Gibson-Graham 1996), undermining the notion of a simple center of power, whether of fathers or any other social group, and highlighting multiple, contradictory centers of power even in nation-states. However, globalization facilitates new centers of power, forms of dominance and new powerful social categories of men, for example, men with access to control of multinationals, international finance or electronic communications.

Yet, globalization debates rarely explicitly theorize the category of "men" within changing world contexts: what might be called the category of "men of the world" (Hearn 1996a). The category, "men of the world," generally remains invisible, yet needs critical attention in looking beyond the nation to various categories of men and of fathers worldwide. Changing social constructions of fathers within globalization is another missing category; a dominant needing deconstruction. Naming categories, such as "men" or "fathers" allows for a more focused critique to be developed. However, whilst naming and deconstructing categories and oppressions, it is necessary to acknowledge those that may be so obscured, for example, "black men" or "black fathers." These absences are clearest in analyses of the global, whether political, media or academic, that attempt to produce "gender-neutral" accounts. Globalization theses typically do not use gender as a central concept. More popular have been agendered conceptual frames, such as centre–periphery relations; band–tribe–chiefdom–state evolutions; stateless–state dualism (Friedman 1994); capitalism and imperialism; modernization; postmodernization; and the "world-system." Gendered interpretations are increasingly present in analyses of "international economic trends" (Fernández Kelly 1994), "third world politics" (Waylen 1996), "international relations" (Grant and Newland 1991), and the very notions of economics (Waring 1988), finance (Lehman 1996), and labor itself (O'Brien 1981; Mies 1986; Hearn 1987). Fathers and men more generally are no longer to be seen as local and national agents, but within historical and global social relations beyond the immediate nation-state.

The significance, forms, power and practices of "men as fathers" and "fathers as men" in the production and reproduction of global domination remains severely neglected in terms of not only gender, but also class and race. To look at "men of the world"/"fathers of the world" in such ways represents a major deconstruction of, indeed threat to, both dominant and most critical understandings of fatherhood and the nation-state. Most analyses of fathers and the state fail to address the power of fathers, men and nation-states in the context of international globalizing processes, including the *inability* of nation-states to fully control the financial, media, information and symbolic flows across their borders.[5]

The local global: toward late modern fatherhood?

Globalization is not just a question of moving beyond the nation. Gendered globalization is not a distant phenomenon but happens and is experienced locally. Global processes are felt through mediations by individuals locally. The movement toward transnational public patriarchal fatherhood, a form of late modern fatherhood, involves the growing impact of those globalizing processes occurring and experienced locally. The separation of biological, social and (national) legal fatherhoods is mediated by a wide range of economic, political, legal and cultural processes, both locally and globally.

The local global construction of fatherhood appears in several ways. First, global processes often entail clear *economic* effects, such as the restructuring of work, employment and unemployment through the operation of global policies of transnational corporations and transnational governmental organizations. Such organizations and managements exert all kinds of powers, controls and influences over not only individual fathers but also nation-states and their policies and practices in relation to fathers. They may move their enterprises, redirect investment, transfer labor, control information and other flows, influence governmental economic and social welfare policies, facilitate or reduce militarism, and create and diffuse images, including those of fatherhood, around the world. The individual autonomous father has been superseded not only by the (patriarchal) nation, but also partly by (patriarchal) transnational and global organizations and managements beyond the nation-state. Men in managerial positions in transnational organizations may, of course, be fathers; indeed there is some tendency for men managers to be more often married, to have children and to have more children than women managers (Alimo-Metcalfe 1993). In that sense, fatherhood may be dominantly constructed as socially compatible with management in a way that motherhood may often not be. Indeed, fathers in transnational management may be able to be fathers in ways that tend to supersede national cultural contexts.

Secondly, changing globalizing conditions are making themselves felt at the *political* levels, for example in the provision of more similar welfare, state and trans-state interventions and services, including those that affect fathers and fatherhood. International transfers of policy from the West and the North to the South, especially in the field of welfare policy, have increased, with economic and social models imported in the pressure to restructure in structural adjustment programs. Similar schemes to the CSA described above have been adopted in several countries. While in broad terms these shift the balance of cash expenditure from the state to individuals, their local meaning, and indeed the political responses to them, cannot be prejudged as they intersect with different social constructions of fatherhood. Other policy transfers have occurred across the Atlantic and within Europe and elsewhere. Under the terms of the

1996 parental leave agreement of the Social Chapter, all EU countries had parental leave arrangements except for the UK (Labour Research 1996). Parental leave of three months was introduced in December 1999 for women and men when they have a baby or adopt a child (HMSO 1998). This change should also be placed in the context of some movement toward greater UK government orientation toward children and "families" in the form of Working Families Tax Credit and the National Child care Strategy (HMSO 1998), setting out good intentions but as yet relatively little actual new child care provision (Himmelweit and Perrons 1999). Even with these limited reforms, broad contrasts between the Nordic and the British welfare models remain. In Finland where "fathers . . . are entitled to a separate allowance paid for a period of six workdays at some point during the maternity/parenthood period . . . [and] Fathers can also get an allowance for 6–12 days in connection with the birth of a child" (Families and Children 1997: 2), there is still a considerable non-take-up of their possible allowances after childbirth; similarly a limited proportion of fathers (about one-fifth) look after children when they are ill. This is generally in keeping with patterns in Nordic paternity leave schemes. For example, in Sweden most fathers do take up the six "daddy days" after the baby is born, but fewer take up the "daddy month" (Hobson in this volume). In Norway (from 1993) and Sweden (from 1995) there has been rather strong governmental policy to encourage fathers to take paternity leave, stipulating that four weeks of the joint parental leave could be taken by the father only (and is otherwise lost). This has been a "success story" as a policy intervention, in the sense that it is now taken up by about 80 percent of Norwegian fathers after childbirth (Leira 1998; Brandth and Kvande 1999).

Another transnational political question with implications for fatherhood is the current debate on time-use in families. This concerns not some abstract "crisis of masculinity" or "crisis of fatherhood," but how time is spent inside and outside families. Fathers' time-use is becoming of increasing policy interest within European debates, as expressed in the November 1993 European Directives on Working Time, calling for minimum daily rest periods, a maximum working week of 48 hours, a maximum average working day of 11 hours, minimum periods of annual leave, and some restrictions on night working and shift working. In the UK, these were also opposed by the previous Conservative governments, but have now been introduced. The growing governmental (*policy*) interest in the control and limitation on working time stands, however, in stark contradiction with the (*economic*) tendencies to "long hours culture" in some jobs (Rutherford 1999), and the growth of unlimited hours contracts and performance-related and commission-based pay systems, be they in telephone sales or health services management. These contradictions can be particularly severe for men with younger children, and may be manifested in a strange alliance between employers' pressure on extracting full value and male employees' apparent preference for the (male) world of work to that of family. The issue of fathers' time spent *within* families remains vitally important, not least because some of the longest working hours outside the home are currently being worked by fathers with children under sixteen (Fagan 1996). This is a matter of not only who does what kinds of work in families, but also the quality of contact between fathers/men and other people in families. The amount of time young people spend with their families can be a key influence on how well they do at school and work, rather than whether they grow up in a family with both biological parents (*The Relationship . . .* 1996).

A third example of the changing transnational politics of fatherhood is the growth of increased international contacts between men within what can be described as the "men's movements." These include "fathers'/men's rights" organizations (for example, the Coalition of Free Men), those that promote positive models of fathers and modes of fathering (the Fatherhood Responsibility Movement), religious reassertions of fatherhood (the Promise Keepers, the Nation of Islam), mythopoetic men's movements, and pro-feminist men's movements. With such movements, broad discourses on masculinities are transferred and translated into different societal contexts, with consequences for specific local constructions of fatherhood.

Thirdly, there are *geographical* effects. While national boundaries can be incredibly rigid for some people, globalization may involve the movement and migration of people, the availability of some degree of common social symbols, and the frequency of cross-cultural social–sexual relations, families, fathering and mothering. The development of the EU and the breakdown of the Soviet bloc have in different ways facilitated greater population movements within Europe. For example, the relative isolation and homogeneity of Finland is gradually being changed with more migrants from Estonia and Russia, and more contacts within the EU. Fathers meanwhile live in *particular* places, sometimes more than one, and probably work in a different place or places; the global is made local through the concentration of the *effects* of global forces in particular places and localities. Places have special significance as localities of family, "origin," work, migration, friendship, leisure, tourism, sexuality, affection. Other places have value or exist through electronic communication. Fathers have particular biographical relations to such multiple localities. While greater cultural contacts can have positive implications for both those concerned, transnational fatherhood can also bring major legal complications. Sometimes this involves legal disputes across and between different state, legal and cultural traditions, and, in the worst cases, violence and abduction. There is a slow development of transnational legal processes on these aspects of fatherhood.

Fourthly, globalization processes provide the social context of the *personal*, personal experience and personal relations. The (re-)formation of identities of fatherhood occur through personal relations set within this changing, globalizing context. Social and personal changes occur within this daunting globalizing context. Identity (de)construction occurs through increasingly globalized personal experience. Fatherhood may be reconstituted at the cultural and symbolic levels. Indeed one cultural and symbolic effect is the increased availability of visual and textual images of fathers throughout the world, for example, from advertising, film and the internet. Fathers as images and as texts appear to have become of increased interest in recent years. They may idealize or glamorize images of fathers, and thus may contradict dominant everyday fathering practices. Information and media technology, advertising, image-production as well as international travel and trade themselves, produce evermore contradictory global influences and global artifacts that are available for use in the process of people becoming a particular "type of father." This is not just an analytical problem but an emotional, lived and fictive one.

The implications of these changes for fatherhood, individual fathers and "fathers/men of the world" are immense. Centers of dominance, of fathers'/men's dominance, may be reinforced, relocated, fragmented and deconstructed. Men's structural power within globalization processes may increasingly be enacted by men, often fathers, who are themselves contradictory, fractured, with structures of desire mediated through global information, mass media and cyberspace. Late modern gendered globalization has made the interconnections between the real and the fictional more intense.

Searching for the dominant, deconstructing the dominant

This chapter has stressed the increasing involvement of the state, and the different, dispersing and sometimes contradictory acts of the state and its networks of power, in the definition, construction and control of fathers and fatherhood. That should not, however, necessarily be seen as a diminution of the power of fathers or an undermining of the institution of fatherhood. While there are signs of cultural change around fatherhood, much state involvement appears to be a means of reinforcing the hegemonic power of fathers and fatherhood. There has been a deep-rooted, historical and structural interdependence, even compatibility, between fatherhood and the (public patriarchal) state, even though individual fathers or particular groups of fathers may experience the opposite. We may think of this as *the fatherhood–state complex* – the complex and sometimes paradoxical ways in which the power of the father and the power of the state interconnect. With violence, the state negotiates between the historical legacy of leaving fathers alone as violence is seen as a "private matter," and the increasing signs of more serious state interventions against fathers' violence. With cash and care, there is rather different tension between the state again accepting fathers' inactivity coupled with rights, and the movement toward state sponsorship of greater cash responsibility and ideological reinforcement of fathers. With birth and sexuality, we come to some of the most taken-for-granted aspects of fatherhood, in terms of conception, paternity and heterosexuality, that have been largely reaffirmed through the recent politics of new medical technology, and only incipiently problematized through the emerging status of "gay fathers." However, complex as they are, these national relations are themselves being further problematized through global processes that appear to undermine the autonomy of the nation-state. This may usher in yet more complicated, contradictory forms of transnational public patriarchal fatherhood–state relations. Global influences may transform fatherhood, making it both part of transnational powers and deconstructing it, culturally and experientially.

Empirical studies and theoretical analyses of fatherhood rarely explicitly attend to the social construction and then deconstruction of the dominant. This applies not only to fathers/men as a general category, but also to particular groups of fathers/men, such as white, heterosexual, able-bodied men (WHAMs) (Hearn and Collinson 1993) or white, heterosexual, able-bodied fathers (WHAFs), themselves summations of race/ethnicity, sexuality, (dis)ability and gender. Deconstructing dominant forms of fatherhood involves making clearer the social construction of "men," of "whiteness," of "ablebodiedness," and so on: naming fathers as men, as socially constructed and not naturally this or that. Fathers'/men's power is neither solid nor unproblematic. While dominance persists, this is often not from any clear or solid center; rather, it is multifaceted, diffuse, dispersed, composite, shifting. Men's power as fathers and in fatherhood remains pervasive. To understand the changing relations of fatherhood, the state and beyond involves new imaginations, particularly on the changing immensity of both men's power and challenges/resistances to it. This entails attending to the cross-cutting nature of men's/fathers' gender power with other powers, oppressions, divisions and differences, along with its persistent material solidity and discursive arbitrariness. The very idea of (a center of) fatherhood may yet dissolve.

Epilogue

David Morgan

Extending the image

Representations of fathers are increasingly common and most of these show a father holding or playing with a young child or infant. The image is nearly always positive and suggesting mutual pleasure. Yet, as with all such images, what is significant is what is excluded. It edits out the range of ways of characterizing or qualifying the term "father," a range which includes terms used quite frequently in this book: "household," "biological" and "absent" for example. It focuses on fathering in relation to small children and therefore obscures the complexities of relationships between fathers and adolescents or between a father and his adult "children" who may also be fathers or mothers themselves. The depiction of pleasurable, close physical, interaction edits out not only some of the more complex and difficult aspects of looking after small children but also the possibilities of violence or abuse. Finally, the focus on a simple dyadic relationship between a father and child excludes the numerous and complex ways in which this dyad is linked to others and to wider social structures.

This book has been concerned centrally with these relationships beyond and outside this conventional picture. This has not been the exclusion of the relationships between a father and a child, the very practices of fathering, but rather we hope to have added to and to have rounded out this over-simple image. This process of elaborating or building upon this core dyadic image has been followed through in a variety of ways.

(i) In the first place, the practices of fathering are located within the domestic triangle of father, mother and child, whether or not the different individuals actually and regularly inhabit the same household. The domestic triangle serves as a reminder that the practices of, and discourses around, fathers must inevitably involve women, in this case mothers, as well as men.

This is not to argue that the identity of father is inevitably bound up with the institution of marriage as it was in the past for many

273

of the countries with which we are concerned. Even within what is usually regarded as a more traditional order, the domestic triangle did not exist on its own but was linked to other triangles through ties of extended family or kinship. Now these wider linkages are increasingly complex as a consequence of lone parenthood and divorce and remarriage or repartnering. To understand the practices of fathering we need to see it in the context of complex networks of significant others.

(ii) At a somewhat more abstract level, there are the ways in which fathers, located within households and domestic triangles, have been linked to the state and the market. This institutional triangle of family, state and market has been a central concern of this book. With this shift of level of analysis from the domestic to the institutional we also get a shift in emphasis from the practices of fathering to the rights, duties and obligations associated with fatherhood. It is at this level that the contrasts between different welfare regimes emerge sharply comparing, say, the stress on employment and market relationships in the United States, where fathers are primarily addressed as wage workers, with the more direct expression of interest in the practices of fathering as manifested in Sweden. When we use the term "state" we are not talking in theoretical abstractions but of a range of institutions and officials concerned with welfare, the policing of family practices and the maintenance of fiscal and economic policies. Further, in talking about the state, we must always be ready to consider the gaps between formal statements of law or policy and actual practice.

The inclusion of this institutional triangle in the analysis of fatherhood and fathering adds to our understanding of the gendering of fathers. To consider fathers as men entails, as Hearn argues in his chapter, that we look beyond the father–child dyad and examine fathers as they engage in all kinds of other relationships such as those within paid employment or those in relation to agencies of the state (Hearn in this volume). The notion of the father as "provider" points to the strong set of gendered linkages between fathers and the market. In relation to the state we have a wide variety of issues to do with fathers as objects of state concern or support, and men, including fathers, as employees of state agencies directly or indirectly concerned with family matters or, more generally, as gendered citizens involved, in numerous and complex ways, in the construction of public policy and debate.

(iii) If we take the two triangles, the domestic and the institutional, together, we are reminded that gender is not simply a question of differences between men and women or between fathers and mothers, but also one of inequality and power. As Hearn points out in his chapter, the conceptual shift has been one of moving from understanding patriarchy in its older sense as rule of the father to a more general understanding of the power of men over women, and that this has been paralleled by a long-term shift from private to public patriarchy (See also Walby 1990). Yet this does not mean that questions of power have departed from the private or the domestic sphere, as numerous studies of domestic violence or the divisions of household labor continue to show.

One of the merits of a concept like "patriarchy" is that it encourages the reader to think beyond the particular topic under consideration and to see wider structural connections or linkages. Just as our understanding of fathers is enhanced by looking at significant others outside the immediate father–child dyad so, too, is our understanding of fathering increased by considering practices which might seem at some distance from this relationship. One example, mentioned by Hearn (in this volume), is that of sexuality. The links between concerns about fatherhood and the constructions of the sexualities of young, often working-class, men has been discussed in several of the chapters. But it is important to note also that most of the discourses around fatherhood have been implicitly or explicitly discourses about the construction, and privileging, of heterosexual identities. Questions about gays or lesbians engaging in "fathering" practices are still highly controversial in many of the countries with which we have been concerned.

(iv) We have seen the ways in which the image of the father and child can be questioned by placing it within the wider contexts of domestic and institutional triangles and those of gendered power and patriarchies. But this does not exhaust the range of questions that we might want to ask of this core image. Thus we need to ask questions about the class and ethnic identities of the fathers being depicted. Several contributions to this book have reminded us of the importance of not considering fathers, or men, as an undifferentiated group, but rather of seeing gender and gender relationships as being shaped and modified by relations of class and ethnicity. This emerges sharply in the contributions dealing with the United States, but it is also present in some of the other essays. Is the ideal model of fatherhood frequently, if unspokenly, a white, middle-class model? And are some of the more stigmatized models of fatherhood more readily identified with ethnic minorities, with the underclass or with other ways of characterizing the socially excluded?

Extensions in space

In the remainder of this Epilogue I want to concentrate on two particular sets of extensions, one dealing with space and the other dealing with time. Beginning with space, the importance of developing a comparative perspective has been stressed throughout this volume, and the comparisons of different "welfare regimes" was one of our points of departure. Comparative analysis, as Oláh, Bernhardt and Goldscheider (in this volume) remind us, enables us to explore differences in both social attitudes and the structural dimension of state support. It serves to underline the fact that the relatively simple domestic and institutional triangles may have markedly different contents within different welfare regimes. It serves, therefore, as a valuable corrective against the ethnocentricism that has often got in the way of a more critical understanding of fatherhood and fathering.

However, there are perhaps limitations with the kind of comparative perspective being stressed here. In the first place, it should be recognized that the comparative perspective needs to be taken much further. Our analysis concentrates on a range of European nations together with the United States and there is clearly a need to go beyond these particular countries. Secondly, there are increasing limitations (recognized at several places in this collection) of treating the nation-state as the key unit of comparison.

One highly specific point we need to look at beyond the boundaries of any one particular nation-state is to consider the various agencies and practices associated with the European Union (EU) and the ways in which these impact upon specific countries. Municio-Larsson and Algans (in this volume), for example, show how important it was, in the Spanish case, to consider the EU as an engine for the reform of family policy in that country. Discussions about parental and paternal leave are increasingly being framed within a European comparative framework.

More generally, however, we have to consider the theme of globalization. This term remains controversial and its uses, where they are not actually challenged, are various (Bartelson 2000; Therborn 2000). What is clear is that the term is not simply confined to the development of international or transnational bodies of regulation. To compress and oversimplify a whole range of arguments, we may recognize that debates about fatherhood and fathering cannot be confined within any one set of national boundaries. There are connections, formal and informal, across the globe between participants in the various debates on fathers' rights or the responsibilities of men and their changing identities. In economic terms, as Hearn reminds us, the practices of fathers cannot be isolated from wider global trends in the ways in which work is organized, whether these include greater movements across national boundaries, the development of international bodies regulating the practices of employers and others, or the increasing trends in the direction of "flexibility" in working practices. The individualization which will be referred to later in this chapter should also be seen within this increasingly global context. At the same time, this perspective should be seen not as a simple substitution of a wider set of relationships for a narrower (e.g. nation-based) set but, rather, as the addition of newer and more comprehensive relationships and points of reference. The global and the local interact in numerous, complex ways and it is for this reason that Hearn refers to the "local global construction of fatherhood" (in this volume).

Extensions in time

Photographic images are necessarily static and edit out processes of change. Yet processes of social change have been at the heart of the accounts presented here; indeed, a sense of change may be said to provide much of the rationale for the book as a whole. We focus on something of a paradox. As we have argued, discussions around fathers and fatherhood have become more frequent, and often with an increasing sense of urgency, in all the countries with which we have been dealing. Yet the overall context is one in which parenthood is a "less central and stable element in men's lives" (Oláh, Bernhardt and Goldscheider in this volume). Of course, this is only a superficial paradox. It is partly because the significance of male parenthood has declined in this way, coupled with a growing perception that, economically, socially and psychologically this is an undesirable state, that there has been this varied but widespread concern.

Again, there may be some disagreement as to how the wider societal changes might be characterized. Examples include, shifts from modern to late modern or from modern to postmodern, and the development of risk society (Beck 1992) or individualization. In some cases, the changes might seem to be very specific, such as the move from dictatorship to democracy in Spain, the collapse of the Berlin Wall or the development of the European Union. However, even in the case of Spain, it is argued that there was also a "receptivity for change" already present, indicating that these wider influences were being felt even prior to the actual change in regime (Municio-Larsson and Algans in this volume).

One general way of characterizing these changes is in terms of increasing complexity, diversity and plurality. In various ways it is possible to talk about shifts from the singular to the plural. Thus, writers on the changing situations of men increasingly talk about masculinities rather than a singular "masculinity." It is possible to think of "patriarchies" rather than a single unified "patriarchy." And the addition of the word "fathering" to the terms "fathers" and "fatherhood" is also a recognition of a growing plurality of fathering practices rather than the unified normative model of fatherhood. If we continue to use this term, it is in the light of a recognition of "competing narratives of fatherhood." Knijn and Selten express this complexity and plurality well when they write:

> We might conclude that the shift to the caring fatherhood discourse is inspired by an amalgam of different, and sometimes competing, ideologies. These reflect, as well as respond to, the processes of individualization and democratization within the private triangle. Feminist movements, fatherhood movements and experts each developed their own assumptions about the responsibilities, rights, capabilities and commitment of fathers. (Knijn and Selten in this volume)

It is at this point that the more particular, if theoretically situated, discussions of fatherhood and fathering link to wider theoretical debates. As has already been mentioned, the terminologies differ as do the theoretical models which generate these terminologies. At various points in the discussion we have mentioned terms such as individualization, postmodernity, risk society, late modernity and so on, to which we might wish to add Castells' (1997) discussion of "network society." It would be misleading to impose an artificial unity on to all these terms and the theories behind them. However, very briefly and oversimply, we may identify several broad themes that emerge from this current ferment of ideas.

Declining patriarchy?

A theme which emerges from much of the current literature is the release from gender roles or, as Castells puts it, "the end of patriarchalism" (Castells 1997). We need to be clear about what is being argued here. It is not being claimed that gender, either as difference or as structured inequalities, has become irrelevant. The idea of a "release from gender roles" refers to a weakening of the determining character of gender, the idea that gender constitutes some basic role from which much else follows. Rather, individuals' life chances are now less clearly determined by their gender, and the possibilities for challenging the relevance of gender are considerably increased. In talking about "the end of patriarchalism," Castells seems to recognize that this may be overstating the case and that there is plenty of evidence from across the globe of the continuation of patriarchal practices. The continuing presence of violence against women in the home and the relatively slow change in terms of men's participations in the home may be referred to here. Further, Castells recognizes that there may be some strong reassertion of patriarchal values and practices at some stage in the future. Nevertheless, the argument is that patriarchalism is under challenge:

> However, the very vehemence of the reaction in the defense of patriarchalism, as in the religious fundamentalist movements thriving in many countries, is a sign of the intensity of the anti-patriarchal challenge. Values that were supposed to be eternal, natural, indeed divine, must now be asserted by force, this retrenching in their last defensive bastion, and losing legitimacy in people's minds. (Castells 1997: 242)

The relevance of these arguments for the discussions of fatherhood and fathering are fairly clear. This loosening, to put it no stronger, of the gender order constitutes part of the background against which current debates about fatherhood are taking place. Conversely, concerns and tensions around the practices of fathers contribute to the loosening of the gender order. On the one hand, we have assertions or reassertions of fathers' rights in the face of apparent challenges to and underminings of what might be seen as their traditional authority. The case of Spain, where women lawyers involved in family law are confronted by organized groups of separated or divorced fathers is a case in point (Municio-Larsson and Algans in this volume). In some cases, these reactions may take the form of an active assertion of the special claims of biological fatherhood. On the other hand, we have moves toward a more active or positive understanding of fathering and pressure on governments and employers to re-organize working practices in order to open up greater opportunities for such active fathering. We also have discussions about whether the gendering of fathering is strictly necessary and whether a move to more generalized parental practices might be recommended instead.

"Decline" may perhaps be too strong a word for what has been happening to patriarchal orders, but we can certainly indicate important changes. One aspect of this may be, as Hearn argues following Walby's terminology, a shift from "private" to "public" patriarchy, although this is a long-term historical trend and probably too general to take us very far in the analysis of current debates about fatherhood (Hearn in this volume). Nevertheless, the terms do underline the importance of what is happening in public life, the media and the marketplace for any current discussion of fathers. A further development might be to talk about public "patriarchies" in the plural, to draw attention to some of the variation and tensions between state and market that several of the contributors have indicated.

Another way of thinking about this is in terms of increasing complexities, a point stressed in several of the preceding chapters. Thus, Oláh,
Bernhardt and Goldscheider (in this volume) write of "the increase in
men's parental role complexity." Yet again, this is not purely a consequence of some expansion of individual choice and freedom but can be
understood in particular structural contexts. Thus, Lewis invites us to
consider such variations in the context of different gendered policy and
welfare regimes (Lewis in this volume). We may, for example, consider the
impact of the deteriorating position of the male breadwinner in the United
States (Orloff and Monson in this volume). Within this broad framework,
there may continue to be variations, as Gavanas explores in her distinctions between movements which stress fragile families and those which
are more directly pro-marriage (Gavanas in this volume). The implications for notions of patriarchalism may be quite different within these two
different tendencies, although both focus concern upon the changing and
possibly weakening position of fathers in the modern society.

Hegemonic masculinities?

Two important themes have emerged from the literature on men and
masculinities, especially in the writings of Connell: the idea of the pluralization of masculinities and the idea of hegemonic masculinity. The
importance of moving away from a single model of a unified masculinity
seemed to be particularly important in exploring the range of discourses
around fatherhood and of fathering practices. But, in the context of such
variety, what is the present status of the idea of hegemonic masculinity?

It can be argued that the concept of hegemonic masculinity was developed in order to counter the sense of complete freedom of choice that
the idea of the pluralization of masculinities might suggest if taken on its
own. There is a range of masculinities, but they are not equally persuasive
or dominant. The idea of hegemonic masculinity suggests that, despite
the apparent range of ways of "doing masculinity," there remain deeply
embedded and subtly coercive notions of what it really means to be a man.
In relation to fatherhood we can see this in the continuing stress on fathers as responsible and providing individuals. This theme continues, for
example, to be very important in the United States: "part of the very definition of masculinity, and good fatherhood, in the US has been economic
self-support" (Orloff and Monson in this volume). The good father is one
who provides economic support for his children and who does this as a
consequence of his own efforts in the marketplace, without help from
the state or charities. This value, which can be readily linked to more
general ideas of hegemonic masculinity, persists despite the continuing

uncertainties of the labor market, especially in a time of labor-force "flexibility." It remains a major aspiration.

This idea of the responsible father would be a familiar one in several of the countries explored here, although it appears to be competing with other gendered constructions of fatherhood. Lewis argues that, for the UK, the trends appear to suggest an emphasis on both the more caring and the more distant father (Lewis in this volume). Similar diverse trends are noted for the Netherlands (Knijn and Selten in this volume). While it could be argued that the more caring, especially where it is combined with responsible economic provision (i.e. both cash and care), could be seen as the model of fatherhood most in accord with hegemonic masculinity, the more distant father may also be linked to other dominant and persuasive constructions of masculinity. The more distant father may continue to be the good provider (and hence reinforce one important theme which continues to link masculinity to the world of paid employment) but, even where he is not, he may correspond to what in the UK is described as the "Jack the lad" model of masculinity. Biological fatherhood proves that he is a real man and his cheerful detachment from family responsibilities may strike a chord within certain male sub-cultures. Nationally, such behavior may be far from being in accordance with hegemonic masculinities, but, at a more local level, the picture may be more ambiguous.

This suggests the idea of competing masculinities in relation to fatherhood and fathering, even where one model may appear to be the more dominant. We may see this ambiguity, differently nuanced, in the Swedish case. Sweden has been described as one of the most men-friendly societies and one where men have been actively involved in debates about equality and emancipation (Hobson and Bergman in this volume). As Hobson and Bergman show, Sweden has been especially important in propagating new visual images of fathers and they argue that: "Being a father has become a crucial part of men's identity in Sweden." The ambiguity arises as to whether this is to be seen as the erosion of gender differences and the undermining of gendered practices or whether it constitutes the development of a new model of hegemonic masculinity. The latter would seem to be the case.

The chapters in this volume, therefore, do not suggest an abandonment of the idea of hegemonic masculinity. Rather, some would seem to suggest the need to think of a plurality of competing linkages between fatherhood and masculinities, while others would seem to suggest the emergence of a new, but equally hegemonic model. Again we are led back to stressing the importance of local and historical variations, seeing local not simply in terms of the nation-state but also in terms of certain class or ethnic identities within particular countries.

Individualization

The idea of increasing individualization, a theme most closely associated with Beck and Beck-Gernsheim (1995), although present in some other accounts as well, has been considerably influential and several of the chapters refer, directly or indirectly, to these ideas. In part this process of individualization represents a continuation of trends which were at the core of the transition from a traditional to a modern society with the weakening of traditional ties and obligations often underlined by religious and community values. In the liberal welfare regimes the links between older notions of individualism and privacy may be particularly important (Orloff and Monson in this volume). But this newer sense of individualization in part reflects and derives from new changes in the organization of paid employment and a greater sense of openness in the choice of patterns of domestic living, no longer determined by some quasi-inevitable life-course sequences from single to married and from marriage to parenthood. The use of the term "lifestyle" reflects this sense of choice and openness as does the phrase "do-it-yourself biography."

Individualization is related to parenthood partly through the idea that parenthood – or non-parenthood – may be more freely chosen and more readily fitted into an individual biography, and partly through the idea of the changing meaning of the child to its parents. Within the uncertainties of a late modern society, so the argument goes, a child represents the basis for new hopes, a projection into the future. Clearly much of the political debate and media attention has been focused upon what appear to be the more dysfunctional manifestations of these trends: the lone mother and her increasing willingness to have a child outside wedlock or a stable heterosexual relationship and the absent or "deadbeat" dad, for examples. Some might argue that it is the individualization of women that constitutes the problem (see Lewis in this volume, on some of the UK debates), while other analyses might link this to a lessening commitment in male–female relationships and the declining significance of parenthood in men's lives (Oláh, Bernhardt and Goldscheider in this volume).

Yet, clearly, these ideas of individualization and the changing significance of children also have consequences for ideas of fatherhood. The absence of some fathers may be a manifestation of this individualization process, but so, too, are the various concerns about access to children and the "rights" of fathers in relation to their biological children. Further, to use the terminology developed in this volume, the stress on fathering as opposed to or in addition to fatherhood may be seen as representing a desire to place the practices of fathers more centrally within an individually constructed biography.

Once again, it is important to provide some context for these debates about individualization. Oláh, Bernhardt and Goldscheider (in this volume) argue that notions of individualization and the practices associated with them must be related to factors such as the degree of state support. But this suggests different models of individualization. The stress on cash rather than care in the United States (Orloff and Monson in this volume) may point to one, perhaps more, traditional model of individualism, although consistent with the idea of writing one's own biography. In other contexts, a greater degree of state support for both mothers and fathers may indicate contexts where it is more possible to explore themes of individualization, or may indicate limitations or constraints on individualizing practices within welfare regimes. In some modern societies, non-parents may oppose the development of "family-friendly" employment practices on the grounds that parenthood is now a matter of individual choice and should, therefore, be an individual rather than a collective responsibility. As with the discussion of hegemonic masculinities, what our studies show is the importance of being continually sensitive to the different ways in which individualization may manifest itself, and to the limits to these ideas in what, in all other respects, would be clearly identified as modern or late modern societies. The idea of global trends along the path to individualization may not take us very far in understanding different fathering practices and discourses about fatherhood.

Reflexivity

One of the features sometimes associated with modernity is that of reflexivity. Again there are various overlapping meanings attached to this term, but the general idea is one of the increasing monitoring of the self and of a wide range of individual practices. Of particular relevance here is the monitoring of interpersonal relationships within families and households. In part, this monitoring comes from outside, from external agencies concerned, in this case, with the practices of fathering, parenting and the needs of children. Numerous professional and governmental bodies are concerned with the measurement and audit of domestic practices or the construction of a family dimension to a range of social problems such as truancy, drug or alcohol abuse or hooliganism. Several of these agencies and their concerns, insofar as they become focused upon fathers, have been identified in this book. But this monitoring also, it is argued, comes from within. Individuals are encouraged to look critically at their own practices and to see whether these measure up to some external or perhaps imagined standard. Where there is a stress on the rights and obligations of fatherhood, this monitoring, while not absent, may be less central. The allocation of the title "father" provides the basis for the rights and the duties, and it is a relatively straightforward matter to see that these rights and duties apply to individuals. Where there is a stress on fathering, on the other hand, there is a much more critical and reflexive examination of routine practices and their likely consequences for the well-being of the child. It is not, as some moralists claim, that fathers (or anybody else for that matter) are willfully disregarding their responsibilities. Rather, the evidence would seem to suggest a continuing moral reflexivity on the practices of fathering and their practical or moral adequacy (see Smart and Neale 1999).

There is another aspect of reflexivity that deserves attention. Particular discussions about, in this case, fatherhood or fathering practices, may also provide the occasion for wider reflections on the state of the society in which these practices or discourses are taking place. We have already seen how discourses around fatherhood are frequently framed by other concerns to do with morality, crime or the underclass. Or some particular aspect of fathering may cause wider discussion on fatherhood itself. Thus, Municio-Larsson and Algans (in this volume) note how, in modern Spain, conflicts over non-payment "reveal broader discursive conflicts on fatherhood in Spanish society." This constant linking of the particular issue or practice to more general concerns is very much part of what is understood by reflexivity in modern society. To some extent, of course, this particular collection of articles is part of this ongoing process of reflexivity in modern societies.

Conclusion

Individualization, the undermining of at least some aspects of the gender order, globalization and reflexivity: these are some of the key features that, it has been argued, impact upon intimacies and domestic relationships at the end of the twentieth century. Within the parameters set by these concepts, there is plenty of room for debate about their relative importance or whether a more optimistic or a more pessimistic interpretation is to be provided. There are just one or two questions that might be appropriate in conclusion. In the first place, it might be argued whether the stress on individualization (and with it, some aspects of individual reflexivity) might be overstated. The material presented in the preceding chapters has certainly shown evidence of the exercise of choice and the construction of individual biographies in the context of fathering. But it has also suggested the limitations of this process of individualization. A recognition of class and ethnic divisions entails, it would seem, a further recognition that the opportunities for individual men as fathers to shape their own life trajectories are highly variable and frequently shaped by circumstances outside their immediate control. The inclusion of the state and the market in our institutional triangle serves as a reminder that there are forces limiting, if not absolutely determining, the choices and life chances of individuals within domestic settings.

Indeed, it may be possible to identify, very loosely, a threefold division in terms of opportunities for individualization and the construction of personal autobiographies. In the first place, there are those for whom these ideas of individualization might seem to be a reality. They have reasonably high and stable incomes as well as other forms of social and cultural capital, and live in a political environment where fathering is positively valued and where there are reasonably effective attempts on the part of the state and employers to create a context favorable to the development of "good" fathering practices. These practices are "good" not only in conforming to the aspirations of the individual fathers, but also in terms of their partners and their joint children. We may also include here those who deliberately choose to opt for more conventional or established divisions of labor or more distant patterns of fathering.

Next, there are those whose life chances are somewhat less stable. They have some of the social and cultural capital of the former group, attempt to live up to the norm of "good provider" and are clearly exposed to the values and debates about the development of fathering practices. Yet for some, as a result, say, of unfavorable or uncertain working conditions, the aspirations do not necessarily match up with the reality. For others, more traditional models of fatherhood may provide the most plausible model, although here this may sometimes come up against the different expectations of mothers and partners. For yet others, upheavals in domestic circumstances following divorce or the end of a cohabitation may provide further sources of tension and ambiguity. This middle group is the one most likely to be exposed to conflictual and competing expectations as well as to some of the uncertainties of a flexible, global employment situation.

Finally, there are those who are most frequently the object of popular concern and debate. The term "underclass" would probably be inappropriate here since the circumstances, structured by age and ethnicity as well as by class, would seem to be highly various and not likely to favor the development of anything like a coherent class category. For some of these, economic or domestic circumstances may be the source of stigmatized fathering practices: absenteeism, economic under-provision and so on. For some of these, the fathering practices themselves, and the responses of the state to them, may be the source of their unfavorable position. As Castells (1997) has argued, for many men in these circumstances they see the collapse and erosion of the certainties of the old patriarchalism without having access to the opportunities provided by new models of fathering and domestic life. Yet it also has to be remembered that for others there may be heroic attempts to live up to standards of good fathering in the face of highly adverse circumstances.

We clearly need more work in delineating the different life chances and experiences of fathering in modern society. The size and durability of the three categories will vary within the different societies with which we have been concerned. There will almost certainly be considerable fluidity with men moving in and out of these loosely defined categories. Yet what is clear from our discussions is that the numerous economic and political changes affecting fatherhood do not affect all fathers equally, and there is much variation within as well as between modern societies.

The other theme running through some of these general discussions which requires careful scrutiny is the argument about the undermining of patriarchies or the release from gender roles. Clearly, there have been important shifts in the ordering of gender within all the societies with which we have been concerned. These shifts constitute a major part of the background to the debates and policies which we have been surveying and provided the point of departure for many of our discussions. Yet, there is certainly enough evidence to justify the continuing use of the word "patriarchy" (or "patriarchies") or the phrase "hegemonic masculinity," and to argue that men still directly or indirectly enjoy some benefits from their position in the gender order, however much this may be modified by considerations of class, ethnicity and the life-course.

Again we must allow for considerable variation. There are some fathers who continue to enjoy the benefits associated with their gendered positions in society and who question or resent any apparent attempts to undermine these positions. There are some fathers who might feel, on a day-to-day basis, that they enjoy relatively few benefits from being a man or a father, and may be attempting to make sense of the numerous and sometimes clashing influences to which they are opposed. And there are other fathers who, individually or collectively, are attempting not only to develop new models of fatherhood, but also to challenge many of the key features of a continuing patriarchal order. Fathers, in short, have many different standpoints and many different stories to tell about their lives and experiences. We should be prepared to listen carefully and critically to all of these accounts.

Notes

1 We use household fathers to cover those men who are living in a household with a partner's children. This term does not indicate whether these men are assuming the role of father or practicing fathering. Household father is the term employed by Oláh, Bernhardt and Goldscheider in this volume.

2 In countries without paid benefits, many corporations and public sector employers' cover paid parental leave in union contracts or sick leave provisions or special policies for parental leave benefits. In the Netherlands, for example, civil servants have paid parental leave, but only 5 percent of all union agreements include a payment for a parental leave absence (Koopmans and Stavenuiter 1999).

3 They find similarities in the current accounts of the crises in masculinities with the Christian men's movements at the turn of the century that tapped into men's anxieties over feminization, their changing position in the labor market, loss of influence in the family, and women's suffrage activism.

4 Trudie Knijn presented this innovation of the domestic/relational triangle and its interrelation to the welfare institutional triangle at the first planning meeting for our project in January 1996.

5 Authors were asked to rank their cases as strong, moderate or weak using guidelines based on both laws and administrative policies, and implementation and enforcement. For economic obligations, we considered the legal boundaries, the levels of benefits and whether the father was likely to pay them. We found the most variation among our cases in the levels of benefits assessed and the enforcement for fathers' payment. As Anne Corden (1999) shows in her study, there are some variations in the laws and penalties, but there are more administrative differences, which affect outcomes. We therefore put more emphasis on the variation that exists around the levels of payment assessed and the amounts actually paid, collected by the state or paid to the mother. For custody rights, we considered the likelihood of being awarded joint or sole-father custody, and the rights of custody fathers who were not married to the mothers' children, as well as the penalties for not allowing father access.

6 U. Hofmann v Barmer Ersalzkasse (1984), ECR 3.

1. CORESIDENTIAL PATERNAL ROLES IN INDUSTRIALIZED COUNTRIES:
SWEDEN, HUNGARY AND THE UNITED STATES

Stockholm University provided support for this research through a graduate fellowship for Livia Sz. Oláh. The Demography Unit of Stockholm University also provided hospitality and support for Frances Goldscheider between November 1997 and February 1998. The Swedish Family and Work Survey of 1992 was conducted by Statistics Sweden. Economic support for data management and processing was provided to the Stockholm University Demography Unit (SUDA) by the Swedish Council for Social Research (Grant 93-0204), which also provided research funds for Eva Bernhardt. We also wish to thank the Central Bureau of Statistics in Hungary for granting access to the Hungarian Fertility and Family Survey of 1992/93 and the Population Activities Unit at Geneva for providing data on family statuses of men and women in a set of European countries included in the descriptive multi-country analysis in this chapter. Finally, the support of Center Grant P30-HD28251 to the Population Studies and Training Center, Brown University, is gratefully acknowledged. This chapter benefited from the comments of Calvin Goldscheider, as well as those of our co-contributors at several meetings on the project, "Fathers and the State."

1 Single parents usually have fewer resources and so may appear to be taking greater advantage of means-tested programs than other groups of parents. For example, they may be more likely to receive a housing allowance and possibly a larger one, as well. Also, the fee they pay for public child care may be lower than that paid by other families with children.

2 Cohabiting couples and single youths were not eligible for the "baby bonus" housing loan unless they already had children at the time of the loan application. Other family policy benefits were not influenced by the parents' marital status, but single parents, i.e. those without a cohabiting partner, received a higher family allowance and paid less for public child care than other parents.

3 The Family and Medical Leave Act provides twelve weeks of unpaid child-care leave with a job guarantee, but only for parents who work in companies with at least fifty employees (Panayotova and Brayfield 1997).

4 The proportion of women employed part time has varied between 37 and 47% in Sweden since the late 1960s onwards (Sundström 1993), compared to about 30% in the United States in the late 1980s and c. 3% in Hungary both during socialism and in the transition period (Szalai 1991; Panayotova and Brayfield 1997).

5 There are three types of both parental and partnership statuses. The parental statuses are (1) no children, (2) only biological or adopted children and (3) some "other" children. The three partnership statuses are (1) no partner, (2) a cohabiting partner and (3) a spouse. Because many of the nine possible combinations of statuses are rare (in one or more countries), we have collapsed them into a set of six by combining three pairs of possibilities. We have six categories to analyze: married with biological children only, married with no children, married with at least some non-biological children, cohabiting with children, living with children but no partner, and unmarried without children.

The first group is the reference category for the regression. Hence, the model contains the five relations

$$\ln(P_i/P_0) = \sum_j (B_{ij} - B_{i0})X_j, \quad \text{for } i = 1, \ldots 5,$$

where P_0 is the probability of living with a spouse and biological children only, each P_i is the probability of living in one of the other family status categories, the X_j are the (binary) predictor variables, and the B_{ij} is the logistic regression coefficient for the jth variable in the ith family status. Our Table 7 contains estimates of the contrasts $B_{ij} - B_{i0}$.

6 Cohabitation has been common in the Nordic countries, and particularly in Sweden, for a considerably longer period than elsewhere (Hoem and Hoem 1988), although Western European countries as well as the US and Canada resemble the trend in Sweden, since they also experienced rapid expansion in this form of partnership beginning in the late 1960s (Bumpass, Sweet and Cherlin 1991; Toulemon 1995; Turcotte and Bélanger 1997). Hungary, like other countries in Central and Eastern Europe, on the other hand, is a late-comer regarding the frequency of cohabitation. The new living arrangement began its spread in Hungary only during the 1980s, appearing first in the divorced population and reaching the young in the late 1980s (Csernák 1996).

7 These figures may not be completely comparable, however, because of differences in legal systems and definitions.

3. COMPULSORY FATHERHOOD: THE CODING OF FATHERHOOD IN THE SWEDISH WELFARE STATE

We are very grateful to Johanna Schiratzki, a legal expert in divorce and custody in Sweden, for her insights and careful reading of our text. Livia Oláh, an author in this book, was an invaluable resource for tracking down demographic changes. We also thank Mieko Takahashi for help in sorting out the complicated statistic on how much divorced fathers actually pay back the state.

1 Helga Hernes (1987) coined this term to refer to Scandinavian welfare states that developed policies that have been enabling for women to become participant in economic and political life.

2 Registered Partnership Act, chapter 1, section 1. That parents' homosexuality does not affect custody has been a principle in Swedish law since 1955 (SOU 1984: 63, 274). Although a majority of Swedes have reported their opposition to legislation supporting the rights of gays to adopt children (60 percent), there is support for such legislation among the coalition of Social Democrats, Greens, Liberals and the Left Party.

3 Household fathers contribute to the mother's household expenses, so, in this sense, they provide indirect support for children under their roof. Still they are not required to support children fathered by another man.

4 In traditional Muslim societies, men can initiate divorce (women have to ask permission from husbands for divorces), and women often lose custody of the children after the divorce.

5 See, for example, the stories about Pippi Longstocking and Alfons Åberg.
6 The UFR (Umgängesrätts Föräldrarnas Riksförening), translated as the Association of Parents around Rights to Custody, is more representative of this kind of group. It frames its goals in terms of gender equality and accepts women members, most often partners of men claiming their rights as fathers (UFR Handbook 2000 and personal interviews May 2000).
7 The basic reduction level was increased from 24,000 (about 2,700 dollars) to 72,000 SEK (Swedish crowns; about 9,000 dollars): see Proposition 1998/99: 78, p. 18.

4. THE PROBLEM OF FATHERS: POLICY AND BEHAVIOR IN BRITAIN

1 The percentage of women working full time in Britain was higher in the 1950s than in the 1990s (Hakim 1996).
2 Nevertheless, the current forecast is for a rise in the Agency's caseload from 730,000 to 1.2 m by 2004 (Knights et al. 1999).
3 This piece of legislation was abandoned in 2001 because of difficulties in implementation, but the idea that parents should take responsibility for working out their own solutions remains.

5. A NEW ROLE FOR FATHERS? THE GERMAN CASE

I wish to thank Andreas Flegel for information on custody issues and child support.
1 See the discussion on male breadwinner regimes in the Introduction.
2 It also forbids same-sex marriage and corresponding entitlements to various marriage-related benefits.

7. MAKING SENSE OF FATHERHOOD: THE NON-PAYMENT OF CHILD SUPPORT IN SPAIN

1 Stockholm University provided support for this research through an assistant professorship for Ingegerd Municio-Larsson between July 1994 and July 1998. Economic support for traveling, transcriptions and proofreading was provided by the Swedish Council for Planning and Coordination of Research (Grant dnr. 950553:8).
2 According to data of the Council of Europe (1999), in 1997 the crude divorce rate, that is divorces per 1,000 of the average population, was 0.9 for Spain. This situates Spain at approximately the same level as Italy, 0.6, and Greece, 0.9, but lower than the Netherlands, 2.2, and Sweden, 2.4.
3 In 1981, the divorce suits filed numbered 9,483 and separation suits, 6,880 (Goode 1993: 71). The corresponding figures for 1998 were 36,072 and 56,837 (*Mujeres en Cifras* 2000).
4 There were 38.6 million persons living in these 11.8 million households. In addition to the 1.6% separated and 0.9% divorced, 8.8% were headed by a person categorized as single, 74.6% married, 14.0% widowed (Instituto Nacional de Estadística 1998: tables 1.1 to 1.2.17).

5 Amalia Gómez, then Secretary of Social Affairs, in an interview with Radio Exterior de España, January 23, 1998.

6 Another difference is that a larger proportion of women work part time, 16.7% as compared to 2.8% for men. Similarly, a large proportion of women had not worked before registering as unemployed, 26.3% as compared to 17.0% amongst men. Data from the Survey of the Able-Bodied Population second quarter of 2000. Data on wage difference refer to 1999 (*Mujeres en Cifras* 2000).

7 The central office of the federation of these associations is located in Madrid. The separated women started organizing in 1973, that is, before the men. Interview with the president, March 3, 1998.

8 The associations interviewed on the occasion of this chapter are Asociación de Padres Separados y Maltratados (Association of Separated and Mistreated Fathers), on February 24, 1998, and Asociación de Padres Separados (Association of Separated Fathers), on March 6, 1998 and March 25, 1999. Both associations are located in Madrid.

9 On the very few occasions when someone has, in fact, been sent to prison, the associations have organized protest manifestations (See Castaño 1996: 5).

10 Cousins (1995) includes Spain, as well as Portugal, Greece and Italy, in the Latin model of the welfare state. Family benefits in twelve countries of the European Union are compared in Papadopoulos 1998: 54. His conclusion is that the southern European countries and Ireland provide "the least generous packages across all family types."

11 The text of this project was never made public. The information given, as well as this last quote, is from an interview with a representative of the Instituto de la Mujer (Women's Institute), on February 27, 1998. There have been previous congressional bills on this issue.

12 The expression cited has recurrently been used in the debate about this new law. In Herrera Rivera 1992, Case A1, reference is made to an International Treaty from 1966, according to which "no-one may be imprisoned solely because of the non-compliance of a contractual obligation."

13 According to Papadopoulos (1998: 54), of the twelve countries in the European Community, Spain ranks last in regard to benefits to lone-parent families.

14 In 2000, 20.4% of the able-bodied women were unemployed, compared to 9.6% of men (*Mujeres en Cifras* 2000).

15 In 1996, there were twenty-three associations, organized into the Spanish Federation of Separated Fathers, *Crónica de Almería*, September 22, 1996.

16 For example, the TV program "Los unos y los otros," *TVE Internacional*, January 31, 1995 (see also *Crónica de Almería* September 22, 1996; *El País* March 20, 1999a).

17 In the study of separated fathers in Canada, previously referred to, demands for joint custody are similarly motivated by reference to the "goal of participatory fatherhood" (Bertoia and Drakich 1995: 240). The demands of the Canadian fathers were surprisingly similar to those expressed by Spanish fathers.

18 On case backlog in the courts, see Hernández (1996) *El País*, May 14.

8. THE FATHERHOOD RESPONSIBILITY MOVEMENT: THE CENTRALITY
OF MARRIAGE, WORK AND MALE SEXUALITY IN RECONSTRUCTIONS
OF MASCULINITY AND FATHERHOOD

1 A report on the condition of the "American Negro" entitled "The Negro family: the case for national action" published in March 1965 by Daniel Patrick Moynihan, then Assistant Secretary of Labor.

2 The term "fragile families" was coined by Ronald Mincy at the Ford Foundation's Strengthening Fragile Family Initiative, and defined as "composed by children born out of wedlock and their low-skilled biological parents who do not legitimize the birth by marrying or establishing paternity" (in Mincy 1997).

3 Federal, regional, state and local levels. It could be debated to what extent the interviewees represent their organizations. Given that they primarily represent themselves as individuals, most interviewees are key people in the field who are considered very influential.

4 The chapter also uses material from an in-depth study of one local program.

5 The term "field" is also used frequently by representatives and is their conception, not just my own.

6 I am looking at the Fatherhood Responsibility Movement in terms of four types of entities: organizations, clusters of organizations, key people and interviewees who are mainly advocates, researchers, civil or religious leaders and practitioners within the field.

7 However, this recently started to change – not the least thanks to the efforts of the Fatherhood Responsibility Movement.

8 In Gavanas (2001), I elaborate on the historical and international scope of Fathers' Rights groups and men's movements.

9 "Traditional" here means a Eurocentric, Victorian and Christian-based model of the nuclear family with its division of labor between a breadwinner husband/father and a care-working wife/mother (see Moore 1988).

10 Gavanas (2001) deals with these issues more extensively.

11 The "marriage movement" was launched by David Popenoe, Barbara Dafoe Whitehead and David Blankenhorn of the National Marriage Project, and involves organizations like The Marriage Savers, Coalition for Marriage, Family and Couples Education and Family Impact Seminar.

12 Presumptions that construct normality, maturity, sexuality and naturalness as entailing a heterosexual, monogamous, nuclear family oriented life style based on traditional notions of gender difference and complementary gender roles.

13 The exact quotation was: "That young woman's life has been transformed by her father's love, and her father's life was transformed by his love for his child. That transformation is, in my opinion, the *single* most *powerful civilizing influence* in human society. It's the glue that binds civilization together. It's not the only glue, but it's the glue that's missing right now in so many families, and in so much of our country. That's why we're here today: to encourage fathers in their irreplaceable role" (Al Gore at the National Fatherhood Initiative's second national summit on fatherhood, on June 15, 1998, original emphasis).

14 One interesting example occurred June 10–14, 1998, when, at a National Practioners Network conference in Anaheim, California, fathers' rights groups were *both represented inside* and *protested outside* the conference.

15 Phrasings extracted from interviews.

16 The family forms that are contested in the Fatherhood Responsibility Movement include single-parent families, step-parent families, cohabiting two-parent families as well as married two-parent families. Same-sex-parent families of various residential constellations are not an issue that any of the organization representatives interviewed for this study brought up or even want to discuss when asked (except for the Gay Fathers' representative, and one interviewee who talked about a particular case where a gay father came to their program). One reported explanation for not wanting to talk about gay/lesbian families is that it is too politically sensitive; another is that homosexuality is a social ill that other organizations deal with, and that the Fatherhood Responsibility Movement primarily deals with the more urgent problem of fatherlessness. However, the Fatherhood Responsibility Movement may be analyzed in terms of its heteronormative presumptions, which become particularly interesting in its constructions of masculinity, gender relations and marriage. Fragile families representatives sometimes ask: if the government is not neutral on the issue of marriage, where does that leave non-traditional families? However, non-heteronormative families could also be included in notions of non-traditional families, and the same question could be asked on behalf of gay and lesbian families. Of the interviewees who were asked or would answer, about half expressed opposition to the existence of gay and lesbian couples or families, or the idea of gay/lesbian marriage. However, it is even more interesting to analyze what is said between the lines within fatherhood discussions in this context.

17 See note 12 above.

18 Phrasing taken from a speaker at a pro-marriage fatherhood conference.

9. MEN, FATHERS AND THE STATE: NATIONAL AND GLOBAL RELATIONS

The chapter has developed from the paper, "Men and power: citizenship, welfare, nation and global relations," presented at the Third European Sociological Association Conference, University of Essex, August 1997; I am grateful to Franca Bimbi, Barbara Hobson, Arnlaug Leira, Ruth Lister, Ingaillil Montanari and Fiona Williams for their constructive comments on it, to David Collinson, Jeanette Edwards, Liisa Husu, Knut Oftung, Jennie Popay and Sue Scott for discussions on related questions, and to Sirpa Wrede and members of the Seminar that produced this book for feedback on earlier drafts.

1 The separation and boundaries of the public and private domains, or the family, state and market, need to be questioned and problematized. There also appear to be new formations of social structures and permutations of state, economy, civil society and the media, in effect new building blocks of analysis, in the process of relatively rapid development. Thus it may be more useful to consider clusters of social institutions rather than separate social arenas, for example, such clusters as "economy, (hetero)sexuality, and procreation,"

"fathers, professions and the state," "(hetero)sexuality, private violence and the state," "polity, police, military and monarchy" (Hearn 1992).

2 Cited in Rose 1996: 341.

3 For a survey of current Nordic measures on fathers see Carlsson (1998).

4 Malcolm Waters (1995: 9) sums up some of these changes as follows: "*material exchanges localize; political exchanges internationalize; and symbolic exchanges globalize*" (italics in original).

5 R. W. Connell (1993, 1998) has developed a broad historical and global political sociology of men in gender relations, through a framework of "multiple cultures and multiple masculinities." He argues that "(s)ince the agents of global domination were, and are, predominantly men, the historical analysis of masculinity must be a leading theme in our understanding of the contemporary world order" (1993: 606). This approach directs attention to the history of men in the state, militarism and warfare, industrialization, the professions, technology and management. While Connell does not here explicitly address the question of fatherhood, he provides a powerful framework for rethinking socio-historical change in fathers and fatherhood.

References

Abromovitz, Mimi 1988. *Regulating the Lives of Women: Social Welfare Policy from Colonial Times to the Present,* Boston: South End Press.

Adamik, Mária 1991. "Hungary – supporting parenting and child rearing: policy innovation in Eastern Europe," in Sheila B. Kamerman and Alfred J. Kahn (eds.), *Childcare, Parental Leave, and the Under 3s: Policy Innovation in Europe,* New York: Auburn House Press, pp. 115–144.

Adorno, Theodor W., Else Frenkel-Brunswick, Daniel J. Levinson and R. Nevitt Sanford 1969. *The Authoritarian Personality,* New York: Norton Library. [1st edn 1950].

Albrecht, James W., Per-Anders Edin, Marianne Sundström and Susan B. Vroman 1999. "Career interruptions and subsequent earnings: a re-examination using Swedish data," *Journal of Human Resources* 294: 294–321.

Alexander, Sally and Barbara Taylor 1980. "In defence of 'patriarchy,'" *New Statesman* 99(1): 161.

Alimo-Metcalfe, Beverly 1993. "Women in management: organizational socialization and assessment practices that prevent career advancement," *International Journal of Selection and Assessment* 1(2): 68–83.

Ambjörnsson, Ronny 1988. *Den skötsamme arbetaren: Idéer och ideal i ett norrländskt sågverkssamhälle* 1880–1930, Stockholm: Carlsson.

Amenta, Edwin 1998. *Bold Relief: Institutional Politics and the Making of Modern American Public Social Provision, 1929–1950,* Princeton University Press.

Anderson Elijah 1990. *Streetwise: Race, Class and Change in an Urban Community,* University of Chicago Press.

Atkinson, Paul 1979. "The problem with patriarchy," *Achilles Heel* 2: 18–22.

Backett, Katherine 1982. *Mothers and Fathers,* London: Macmillan.

Barnes, Helen, Patricia Day and Natalie Cronin 1998. *Trial and Error: a Review of UK Child Support Policy,* London: Family Policy Studies Centre, occasional paper 24.

Barrett, Michele 1980. *Women's Oppression Today: Problems in Marxist Feminist Analysis,* London: Verso.

Bartelson, Jens 2000. "Three concepts of globalization," *International Sociology* 15(2): 180–196.

Bast, Kerstin and Ilona Ostner 1992. "Ehe und Familie in der Sozialpolitik der DDR und BRD – ein Vergleich," in W. Schmäh (ed.), *Sozialpolitik im Prozess der deutschen Vereinigung,* Frankfurt: Campus, pp. 228–270.

Bauman, Zygmunt 1995. "Searching for a centre that holds," in Mike Featherstone, Scott Lash and Roland Robertson (eds.), *Global Modernities*, London: Sage, pp. 140–154.

Baxter, Janeen and Emily W. Kane 1995. "Dependence and independence: a cross-national analysis of gender inequality and gender attitudes," *Gender and Society* 9(2): 193–215.

Bech, Hennig 1993. "Report from a rotten state: 'marriage' and 'homosexuality' in 'Denmark,'" in Ken Plummer (ed.), *Modern Homosexualities*, London: Routledge, pp. 134–147.

Beck, Ulrich 1992. *Risk Society: Towards A New Modernity*, London: Sage.

Beck, Ulrich and Elizabeth Beck-Gernsheim 1995. *The Normal Chaos of Love*, Cambridge: Polity Press.

Becker, Gary 1991. *A Treatise on the Family*, Cambridge, MA: Harvard University Press. 1st edn 1981.

Beechey, Veronica 1979. "On patriarchy," *Feminist Review* 3: 66–82.

Beemyn, Brett and Michele J. Eliason (eds.) 1996. *Queer Studies: A Lesbian, Gay, Bisexual and Transgender Anthology*, New York University Press.

Bejstam, Lars and Anita Wickström 1996. *Underhållsstöd och underhållsbidrag*, Stockholm: Juristförlaget.

Bell, Linda and Richard Freeman 1995. "Why do Americans and Germans work different hours?," in Friedrich Buttler, Wolfgang Franz, Ronald Schettkat and David Soskice (eds.), *Institutional Frameworks and Labor Market Performance: Comparative Views on the U.S. and German Economies*, London and New York: Routledge, pp. 101–131.

Bennett, Neil G., David E. Bloom and Cynthia K. Miller 1995. "The influence of nonmarital childbearing on the formation of first marriages," *Demography* 32(1): 47–62.

Berger, Birgitte and Peter L. Berger 1983. *The War over the Family: Capturing the Middle Ground*, London: Hutchinson.

Berger, Horst, Wilhelm Hinrichs, Eckhard Priller and Annett Schultz 1999. *Privathaushalte im Vereinigungsprozess*, Frankfurt: Campus.

Bergman, Helena 1999. "En familj som andra: Barnavårdsmän och genuspolitik i den tidiga välfärdsstaten," *Historisk tidskrift* 119(2): 227–252.

Bergqvist, Christina 1999. "Childcare and parental leave models," in Christina Bergqvist (ed.), *Equal Democracies? Gender in the Nordic Countries*, Oslo: Scandinavian University Press.

Bernhardt, Eva M. 1992. "Working parents in Sweden: an example for Europe?" in *Human Resources at the Dawn of the 21ˢᵗ Century*, Strasburg: Eurostat, pp. 231–254.

   2000. "Repartnering among Swedish men and women: a case study of emerging patterns in the second demographic transition." Paper presented at the Family and Fertility Surveys (FFS) Flagship Conference, Brussels, Belgium, 29–31 May.

Berns, Sandra 2000. "Folktales of legality: family law in the procedural republic," *Law and Critique* 11: 1–24.

Bertoia, Carl E. and Janice Drakich 1995. "The fathers' rights movement: contradictions in rhetoric and practice," in William Marsiglio (ed.), pp. 230–254.

Billingsley, Andrew 1992. *Climbing Jacob's Ladder: The Enduring Legacy of African-American Families*, New York: Touchstone.

Björnberg, Ulla 1998. "Family orientation among men: a process of change in Sweden," in Eileen Drew, Ruth Emerek and Evelyn Mahoon (eds.), *Women, Work and the Family in Europe*, London: Routledge, pp. 200–207.

2001. "Women and family in post war Sweden," in Carl le Grand and Toshiko Tsukaguchi-le Grand (eds.), *Women in Japan and Sweden – Work and Family in Two Welfare Regimes*, Stockholm: Center for Asia–Pacific Studies.

Blanke, Karen, Manfred Ehling and Norbert Schwarz 1996. *Zeit im Blickfeld: Ergebnisse einer repräsentativen Zeitbudgeterhebung*, Stuttgart: Kohlhammer.

Blankenhorn, David 1995. *Fatherless America: Confronting Our Most Urgent Social Problem*, New York: Basic Books.

Bock, Gisela and Pat Thane (eds.) 1991. *Maternity and Gender Politics: Women and the Rise of the European Welfare States, 1880s–1950s*, New York: Routledge.

Bonnekamp, Dolly 1988. *De rechterlijke besluitvorming inzake voogdij na echtscheiding*, Utrecht: Vakgroep Rechtstheorie/Encyclopedie.

Bosanquet, Helen 1906. *The Family*, London: Macmillan.

Bradshaw, Jonathan, John Ditch, Hilary Holmes and Peter Whiteford 1993. "A comparative study of child support in fifteen countries," *Journal of European Social Policy* 3: 255–271.

Bradshaw, Jonathan and Jane Millar 1991. *Lone-Parent Families in the UK*. DHSS Social Security Research Report 6. London: HMSO.

Bradshaw, Jonathan, Carol Stimson, Carol Skinner and Julie Williams 1999. *Absent Fathers?*, London: Routledge.

Brandth, Berit and Elin Kvande 1999. "State feminism and flexible fathers," Paper presented at the Nordic–UK Collaborative Seminar on Employment Policies and Gender Relations, Stockholm, June.

Braun, Michael and Peter Ph. Mohler (eds.), 1998. *Blickpunkt Gesellschaft 4*, Opladen: Westdeutscher Verlag.

Brinig, Margret and Steven Crafton 1994. "Marriage and opportunism," *Journal of Legal Studies* 23: 869–894.

Broberg, Gunnar and Mattias Tydén 1996. "Eugenics in Sweden: efficient care," in Gunnar Broberg and Nils Roll-Hansen (eds.), *Eugenics and the Welfare State: Sterilization Policy in Denmark, Sweden, Norway and Finland*, East Lansing: Michigan State University Press, pp. 77–149.

Brown, Michael 1999. *Race, Money and the American Welfare State*, Ithaca, NY: Cornell University Press.

Bryson, Lois, Michael Bittman and Sue Donath 1994. "Men's welfare state, women's welfare state: tendencies to convergence in practice and theory?" in Diane Sainsbury (ed.), *Gendering Welfare States*, London: Sage, pp. 118–131.

Buck, Nick and John Ermisch 1995. "Cohabitation in Britain," *Changing Britain* (Newsletter for the ESRC's Population and Household Change Research Programme) 3: 3–5.

Bumpass, Larry L., James A. Sweet and Andrew Cherlin 1991. "The role of cohabitation in declining rates of marriage," *Journal of Marriage and the Family* 53(4): 913–927.

Burghes, Louie, Lynda Clarke and Natalie Cronin 1997. *Fathers and Fatherhood in Britain*, London: Family Policy Studies Centre.

Burkhauser, Richard and Karen Holden (eds.) 1982. *A Challenge to Social Security: The Changing Roles of Women and Men in American Society*, New York: Academic Press.

Burns, Ailsa and Cath Scott 1994. *Mother-Headed Families and Why They Have Increased*, New Jersey: Lawrence Erlbaum.

Busch, Gabriele, Doris Diebäcker-Hess and Marlene Stein-Hilbers 1988. *Den Männern die Hälfte der Familie den Frauen mehr Chancen im Beruf*, Weinheim: Deutscher Studien Verlag.

Bussemaker, Jet, Annemieke van Drenth, Trudie Knijn and Janneke Plantenga 1997. "Lone mothers in the Netherlands," in Jane Lewis (ed.), *Lone Mothers in European Welfare Regimes*, London: Jessica Kingsley Publishers, pp. 96–140.

Büttner, Helmut 2000. "Unterhalt für die nichteheliche Mutter," *FamRZ* 47 (13): 761–766.

Cairns, John Arthur Robert 1934. *Drab Street Glory*, London: Hutchinson.

Carlsson, Soeren (compiled by) 1998. *Men on Parental Leave – How Men Use Parental Leave in the Nordic Countries*, Copenhagen: Nordic Council of Ministers.

Carrasco, Cristina 1991. *El trabajo doméstico y la reproducción social*, Report no. 28, Madrid: Instituto de la Mujer, Ministerio de Asuntos Sociales.

Carrigan, Tim, R. W. Connell and John Lee 1985. "Toward a new sociology of masculinity," *Theory and Society* 14(5): 551–604.

Casey, Kathleen and Susan Carroll 2001. "Women in the 104th congress and welfare reform legislation," in Nancy Hirschmann and Ulrike Liebert (eds.), *Reinventing the Welfare State? Feminist Theory and Comparative Analyses of the US and Europe*, New Brunswick, NJ: Rutgers University Press.

Castaño, Santiago 1996. "La ley se alía con los padres separados. Cada vez son más los jueces que reconocen la patria potestad compartida y que las mujeres pagen la pension," *Diario 16*, May 20, pp. 2–3.

Castells, Manuel 1997. *The Power of Identity (The Information Age, Vol II)*, Oxford: Blackwell.

Castles, Francis 1994. "The wage earners' welfare state revisited: refurbishing the established model of Australian social protection, 1983–1993," *Australian Journal of Social Issues* 29(2): 120–145.

CBS 1994. *95 jaar statistiek in tijdreeksen*, The Hague: SDU.
   1995. *Statistisch Zakboek*, The Hague/Heerlen: Centraal Bureau voor de Statistiek, SDU.
   1997. *Enquete beroepsbevolking 1996*, Heerlen: Centraal Bureau voor de Statistiek.

Cherlin, Andrew 1997. "Introduction," in *Journal of Family Issues* 18(fall): 1–12.

Chiswick, Carmel U. and Evelyn L. Lehrer 1990. "On marriage-specific human capital: its role as a determinant of remarriage," *Journal of Population Economics* 3(3): 193–213.

Clarke, Sue and Jennie Popay 1998. "'I'm just a bloke who's had kids': men and women on parenthood," in Jennie Popay, Jeff Hearn and Jeanette Edwards (eds.), pp. 196–230.

Cm. 3992 1998. *Children First: A New Approach to Child Support*, London: HMSO.

Cmnd. 5629 1974. *Report* of the Committee on One-Parent Families, London: HMSO.

Cohen, Lloyd 1987. "Marriage, divorce and quasi rents; or, 'I gave him the best years of my life,'" *Journal of Legal Studies* 16: 267–303.

Collier, Richard 1995. *Masculinity, Law and the Family*, London: Routledge.

   1996. "Coming together?: post-heterosexuality, masculine crisis and the new men's movement," *Feminist Legal Studies* 4(1): 3–48.

Collinson, David L. and Jeff Hearn 1994. "Naming men as men: implications for work, organisations and management," *Gender, Work and Organization* 1(1): 2–22.

Coltrane, Scott 1996. *Family Man: Fatherhood, Housework and Gender Equity*, Oxford University Press.

Committee on Ways and Means, House of Representatives 1998. *Fatherhood and Welfare Reform*, Serial 105–78, July 30, Washington, DC: US Government Printing Office.

Connell, R. W. 1993. "The big picture: masculinities in recent world history," *Theory and Society* 22(5): 597–623.

   1995. *Masculinities*, Cambridge: Polity Press.

   1998. "Men in the world: masculinities and globalisation," *Men and Masculinities* 1(1): 3–23.

Coote, Anna 1995. "The family: a battleground in fearful times," *The Independent*, October 30, p. 15.

Corden, Anne 1999. *Making Child Maintenance Regimes Work*, London: Family Policy Studies Centre.

Cornell, Drucilla 1998. "Fatherhood and its discontents: men, patriarchy, and freedom," in Cynthia R. Daniels (ed.), pp. 183–202.

Cornwall, Andrea and Nancy Lindisfarne (eds.) 1994. *Dislocating Masculinity*, London: Routledge.

Cotarelo, Ramón 1989. "La Constitución de 1978," in José Félix Tezanos, Ramón Cotarelo and Andrés de Blas (eds.), *La Transición Democrática Española*, Madrid: Editorial Sistema (reprinted 1993), pp. 317–345.

Council of Europe 1999. *Recent Demographic Developments in Europe 1999*, European Population Committee Strasburg: Council of Europe Press, October.

Cousins, Christine 1995. "Women and social policy in Spain: the development of a gendered welfare regime," *Journal of European Social Policy* 5(3): 175–197.

Cox, Donald and George Jakubson 1995. "The connection between public transfers and private interfamily transfers," *Journal of Public Economics* 57(1): 129–167.

Crónica de Almería 1996. "Padres separados se concentran hoy ante el Congreso," September 22.

CSA 1998. *Child Support Agency Quarterly Summary of Statistics*. London: DSS.

Csernák, Magdolna 1996. "Marriage and divorce in Hungary: demographic aspects of changes," in Pál Péter Tóth and Emil Valkovics (eds.), *Demography of Contemporary Hungarian Society*, New York: Columbia University Press, pp. 37–54.

Curran, Laura and Laura S. Abrams 2000. "Making men into dads: fatherhood, the State, and welfare reform," *Gender & Society* 14(5): 662–678.

Cuyvers, Peter, Kees de Hoog and Hettie Pott-Buter 1997. "Gezinsbeleid in perspectief," in S. Grotenhuis and J. van der Zwaard (ed.), *Kiezen voor kinderen*, Gezin en beleid I, Utrecht: Elsevier/De Tijdstroom/NGR, pp. 17–36.

Dahlström Edward (ed.) 1962. *Kvinnors liv och arbete* (Women's life and work), Stockholm: SNS Förlag.

Daly, Mary 1994. "Comparing welfare states: towards a gender friendly approach," in Diane Sainsbury (ed.), *Gendering Welfare States*, London: Sage, pp. 101–117.

Daniels, Cynthia R. (ed.) 1998. *Lost Fathers: the Politics of Fatherlessness in America*, New York: St. Martin's Press.

Darvishpour, Mehrdad (forthcoming). "Immigrant women challenge the role of men," *Journal of Comparative Family Studies* 32.

Davidson Hunter, James 1991. *Culture Wars: the Struggle to Define America*, New York: Basic Books.

Davis, Gwynn, Stephen Cretney and Jean Collins 1994. *Simple Quarrels*, Oxford: Clarendon Press.

Davis, Gwynn, Nick Wikeley and Richard Young with Jackie Barron and Julie Bedward 1998. *Child Support in Action*, Oxford: Hart Publications.

de Boer, J. 1998. "Familierechtelijke vernieuwingen," *Nederlands Juristenblad* 31(1): 1–8.

Defert, Daniel 1991. "'Popular life' and insurance technology," in Graham Burchell, Collin Gordon and Peter Miller (eds.), *The Foucault Effect: Studies in Governmentality*, Hemel Hempstead: Harvester Wheatsheaf, pp. 211–234.

de Hart, Joep 1995. *Tijdopnamen, Sociale en Culturele Studies – 22*, Rijswijk: Sociaal en Cultureel Planbureau.

Delphy, Christine 1977. *The Main Enemy*, London: Women's Research and Resources Centre.

  1984. *Close to Home*, London: Hutchinson.

Dench, Geoff 1994. *The Frog, the Prince and the Problem of Men*, London: Neanderthal Books.

Dennis, Mike 1998. "Family policy and family function in the German Democratic Republic," in Eva Kolinsky (ed.), *Social Transformation and the Family in Post-Communist Germany*, Houndmills: Macmillan, pp. 37–56.

Dennis, Norman and George Erdos 1992. *Families Without Fatherhood*, London: IEA.

DeParle, Jason 1998. "Welfare overhaul initiatives focus on fathers," *New York Times* electronic edition, September 3.

de Regt, Ali 1993. *Geld en gezin. Financiele en emotionele relaties tussen gezinsleden*, Meppel: Boom.

Deven, Fred 1994. *Los hombres, los medios de comunicación y la infancia: cobertura periodística de los hombres como "cuidadores" en siete estados miembros de la*

Union Europea. Red de atención a la infancia de la Comisión Europea y otras medidas para reconciliar las obligaciones laborales y familiares.

de Vries, Annemie (ed.) 1998. *Jaarboek Emancipatie. Tijd en ruimte voor arbeid en zorg*, The Hague: VUGA.

Diario 16 1996. "Los ex cónyuges acuden a los detectives. Uno de cada cinco casos en manos de investigadores privados busca ingresos ocultos," May 20, p. 3.

Döge, Peter, 2000. "Geschlechterdemokratie als Männlichkeitskritik," *Aus Politik und Zeitgeschichte* B 31-32/2000, July 28, pp. 18–23.

Donovan, Brian 1998. "Political consequences of private authority: Promise Keepers and the transformation of hegemonic masculinity," *Theory and Society* 27: 817–843.

DS (Departmentserien) 1993. *För barnens skull* "Delrapport från regeringens pappagrupp."

1995: 2. "Pappagrupp." *Slutrapport.*

1996: 2. "Underhållstöd till barnmed särlevande föräldrar."

1999: 30. "Förslag till utfyllnadsbidrag vid växelvis boende."

1999: 57. "Gemensam vårnad för ogifta föräldrar."

DTI 2000. *Work and Parents: Competitiveness and Choice*, London: Department of Trade and Industry.

Duindam, Vincent 1997. *Zorgende vaders*, Amsterdam: Van Gennep.

Duncan, Greg J. and Saul D. Hoffman 1985. "A reconsideration of the economic consequences of marital dissolution," *Demography* 22(4): 485–497.

Duneier, Mitchell 1992. *Slim's Table; Race, Respectability And Masculinity*, University of Chicago Press.

Durán, María Angeles 1998. *De puertas adentro.* Madrid: Instituto de la Mujer, Ministerio de Cultura.

Duvander, Ann-Zofie 1999. "The transition from cohabitation to marriage: a longitudinal study of the propensity to marry in Sweden in the early 1990s," *Journal of Family Issues* 20(5): 698–717.

The Economist 1995. "leader" September 9.

Edgeworth, F. Y. 1922. "Equal pay to men and women for equal work," *Economic Journal* 32: 431–457.

Edwards, Tim 1994. *Erotics and Politics*, London: Routledge.

Eekelaar, John 1978. *Family Law and Social Policy*, London: Weidenfeld and Nicolson.

1991. "Parental responsibility: state of nature or nature of the state?" *Journal of Social Welfare and Family Law* 1: 37–51.

Eekelaar, John and Eric Clive with Karen Clarke and Susan Raikes 1977. *Custody after Divorce: the Disposition of Custody in Divorce Cases in Great Britain*, Oxford: Centre for Socio-Legal Studies, Wolfson College.

Ehrenreich, Barbara 1983. *The Hearts of Men: American Dreams and the Flight from Commitment*, London: Pluto Press.

1989. *Fear of Falling: the Inner Life of the Middle Class*, New York: Basic Books.

El Pais, 1998. "Cardenal dice que el Código Penal no es suficiente para atajar la violencia familiar," September 16, p. 18.

1999a. "Los separados reivindican en el Día del Padre la custodia compartida," March 20.

1999b. "El apellido materno será el primero si así lo acuerdan los padres. El Congreso aprueba que prevalezca que del padre si hay conflicto," May 14.

Ellwood, David 1988. *Poor Support: Poverty in the American Family*, New York: Basic Books.

1996. "Welfare reform as I knew it: when bad things happen to good policies," *The American Prospect* 26 (May–June): 22–29. (Internet edition <http://epn.org/prospect/26/26ellw.html>.)

Elshtain, Jean Bethke 1981. *Public Man, Private Woman*, Oxford: Martin Robertson.

EMNID-Institute 1978. *Sicherung des Lebensunterhalts für Kinder alleinstehender Eltern*, EMNID: Bielefeld.

Ermisch, John F. and Robert E. Wright 1991. "The duration of lone parenthood in Great Britain," *European Journal of Population* 7(2): 129–158.

Esping-Andersen, Gøsta 1990. *The Three Worlds of Welfare Capitalism*, Cambridge: Polity Press and New Jersey: Princeton University Press.

Esping-Andersen, Gøsta (ed.) 1996. "Welfare states without work: the impasse of labour shedding and familialism in continental European social policy," in *Welfare States in Transition: National Adaptations in Global Economies*, London: Sage, pp. 66–87.

Esping-Andersen, Gøsta 1999. *Social Foundations of Postindustrial Economies*, New York: Oxford University Press.

Evans, M. D. R., Jonathan Kelley, J. Dronkers, M. Borgers and L. Rollenberg 1995. "Parental divorce and children's education: Australian evidence," *Worldwide Attitudes* 17 (July).

Fagan, Colette 1996. "Gendered time schedules: paid work in Great Britain," *Social Politics: International Studies in Gender, State, and Society* 3(1): 72–106.

Faludi, Susan 1999. *Stiffed: the Betrayal of the American Man*, New York: William Morrow and Company.

Families and Children 1997. <http://www.kela.fi/english.family.htm#maternity>.

Fassinger, Polly A. 1993. "Meanings of housework for single fathers and mothers: insights into gender inequality," in Jane C. Hood (ed.), *Men, Work and Family*, London: Sage, pp. 195–216.

Ferguson, Harry 1990. "Rethinking child protection practices: a case for history," in Violence Against Children Study Group (eds.), *Taking Child Abuse Seriously*, London: Unwin Hyman/Routledge, pp. 121–142.

Fernández Kelly, Maria P. 1994. "Making sense of gender in the world economy: focus on Latin America," *Organization* 1(2): 249–275.

Ferrara, M. 1996. "The social model of welfare in Southern Europe," *Journal of European Social Policy* 6(1): 17–31.

Ferri, Elsa and Kate Smith 1996. *Parenting in the 1990s*, London: Family Policy Studies Centre and the Joseph Rowntree Foundation.

Finegold, Kenneth 1988. "Agriculture and the politics of U.S. social provision: social insurance and food stamps," in Margaret Weir, Ann Shola Orloff and Theda Skocpol (eds.), pp. 199–234.

Fineman, Martha 1995. *The Neutered Mother, The Sexual Family, and Other Twentieth Century Tragedies*, New York: Routledge.

Firestone, Shulamith 1970. *The Dialectic of Sex*, London: Jonathan Cape.

Flood, Lennart and Urban Gråsjö 1997. "Tid för barn, tid för arbete," in Göran Ahrne and Inga Persson (eds.), *Familj, makt och jämställdhet*, SOU 1997:138: 159–188.

2001. "Women and family in post war Sweden," in Carl Le Grand and Toshiko Tsukaguchi-le Grand (eds.), *Women in Japan and Sweden – Work and Family in Two Welfare Regimes*, Stockholm: Center for Asia–Pacific Studies.

Florin C. and Nilsson B. 1999. "'Something in the nature of a bloodless revolution...': Gender equality policy in Sweden in the 1960s and 70s," in Rolf Torstendahl (ed.), *Social Policy and Gender System in Two German States and Sweden, 1945–1989*, Uppsala: Uppsala Historica, Uppsaliiensa 22, pp. 11–78.

Freeman, Micheal D. A. 1987. *Dealing with Domestic Violence*, Bicester, Oxon.: CCH Editions.

Friedman, Jonathan 1994. *Cultural Identity and Global Process*, London: Sage.

Fromm, Erich, Max Horkheimer, Hans Mayer and Herbert Marcuse 1936. *Studien über Autorität und Familie*, volume 1, Paris: Librairie Félix Alcan.

Fthenakis, Wassilios E. 1988. *Väter*, Munich: DTV (two volumes).

Fukuyama, Francis 1997. *The End of Order*, London: Social Market Foundation.

Furstenberg, Frank 1988. "Good dads–bad dads: two faces of fatherhood," in Andrew J. Cherlin (ed.), *The Changing American Family and Public Policy*, Washington, DC: The Urban Institute Press.

Gampert, Christian 2000. "Der entmachtete Vater," *Kursbuch* 140: 161–169.

Gans, Herbert 1995. *The War Against the Poor: the Underclass and Antipoverty Policy*, New York: Basic Books.

Garfinkel, Irwin and Sara McLanahan 1986. *Single Mothers and Their Children: a New American Dilemma*, Washington, DC: Urban Institute.

Garfinkel, Irwin, Sara McLanahan and Daniel Meyer 1998. *Fathers Under Fire: the Revolution in Child Support Enforcement*, New York: Russell Sage.

Garnham, Allison and Emma Knights 1994. *Putting the Treasury First: the Truth about Child Support*, London: Child Poverty Action Group (CPAG).

Gastelaars, Marja 1985. *Een geregeld leven. Sociologie en sociale politiek in Nederland 1925–1968*, Amsterdam: SUA.

Gavanas, Anna 2001. *Masculinizing Fatherhood: Sexuality, Marriage and Race in the U.S. Fatherhood Responsibility Movement*, Stockholm: Department of Anthropology, Stockholm University.

Gershuny, Jonathan and John P. Robinson 1988. "Historical changes in the household division of labor," *Demography* 25(4): 537–552.

Gershuny, Jonathan, Michael Godwin and Sally Jones 1994. "The domestic labour revolution: a process of lagged adaptation?" in Michael Anderson, Frank Bechhofer and Jonathan Gershuny (eds.), *The Social and Political Economy of the Household*, Oxford University Press, pp. 151–197.

Gerson, Kathleen 1993. *No Man's Land. Men's Changing Commitments to Family and Work*, New York: Basic Books.

Gibson-Graham, J. K. 1996. *The End of Capitalism (as we knew it)*, Cambridge, MA: Blackwell.

Giddens, Anthony 1992. *The Transformation of Intimacy, Sexuality, Love and Eroticism in Modern Societies*, Cambridge: Polity Press.

Gilder, George 1981. *Wealth and Poverty*, New York: Basic Books.
1987. "The collapse of the American family," *The Public Interest* (Fall): 20–25.
Gillis, John R. 1997. *A World of Their Own Making: Myth, Ritual, and the Quest for Family Values*, Oxford and New York: Oxford University Press.
2000. "Marginalization of Fatherhood in Western Countries," *Childhood* 7(2): 225–238.
Glatzer, Wolfgang and Ilona Ostner (eds.), 1999. *Deutschland im Wandel. Sozialstrukturelle Analysen*, Opladen: Leske and Budrich.
Goldscheider, Frances K. and Linda J. Waite 1991. *New Families, No Families? The Transformation of the American Home*, Berkeley, CA: University of California Press.
Goldstein, Joseph, Anna Freud and Albert J. Solnit 1980. *Before the Best Interests of the Child*, London: André Deutsch.
Goode, William J. 1993. *World Changes in Divorce Patterns*, New Haven and London: Yale University Press.
Goodwin, Joanne L. 1997. *Gender and the Politics of Welfare Reform: Mothers' Pensions in Chicago, 1911–1929*, University of Chicago Press.
Gordon, Linda 1994. *Pitied but Not Entitled: Single Mothers and the History of Welfare*, New York: Free Press.
Gordon, Margaret S. 1988. *Social Security Policies in Industrial Countries: a Comparative Analysis*, Cambridge University Press.
Granström, Fredrik 1997. *Fertility and Family Surveys in Countries of the ECE Region. Standard Country Report: Sweden*, New York and Geneva: United Nations.
Grant, Rebecca and Kathleen Newland (eds.) 1991. *Gender and International Relations*, Milton Keynes: Open University Press.
Gregg, Paul and Jonathan Wadsworth 1995. "More work in fewer households?" in John Hills (ed.), *New Inequalities: the Changing Distribution of Income and Wealth in the UK*, Cambridge University Press, pp. 181–207.
Griffen, Clyde 1990. "Reconstruction masculinity from the evangelical revival to the waning of progressivism: a speculative synthesis," in Mark C. Carnes and Clyde Griffen (eds.), *Meanings for Manhood: Constructions of Masculinity in Victorian America*, University of Chicago Press, pp. 183–204.
Griswold, Robert 1992. *Fatherhood in America: a History*, New York: Basic Books.
Grossmann, Heidrun (ed.), 1996. *Unterhaltssituation von Kindern im Land Brandenburg. (Final Report)*. Potsdam: Ministry of Labour, Social Affairs, Health and Gender.
Grunell, Marianne 1997. *Mannen die zorgen, zijn de kerels van morgen*, Utrecht: Uitgeverij Jan van Arkel.
Guillén Ana M. and Manos Matsaganis 2000. "Testing the 'social dumping' hypothesis in Southern Europe: welfare policies in Greece and Spain during the last 20 years," *Journal of European Social Policy* 10(2): 120–145.
Gustafsson, Siv and Frank Stafford 1994. "Three regimes of childcare: the United States, the Netherlands and Sweden," in Rebecca M. Blank (ed.), *Social Protection Versus Economic Flexibility*, University of Chicago Press, pp. 333–361.

Gysi Jutta and G. Meyer 1993. "Leitbild berufstätige Frau. DDR Frauen in Familie, Partnerschaft und Ehe," in G. Helwig and H. M. Nickel (eds.), *Frauen in Deutschland 1945–1990*, Berlin: Akademie Verlag, pp. 277–292.

Haas, Linda 1992. *Equal Parenthood and Social Policy: a Study of Parental Leave in Sweden*, Albany: State University of New York Press.

Habermas, Jürgen 1969. *Protestbewegung und Hochschulreform*, Frankfurt am Main: Suhrkamp.

Hagemann-White, Carol and Maria S. Rerrich 1985. *Frauen Männer Bilder. Männer und Männlichkeit in der feministischen Diskussion*, Bielefeld: Kleine Verlag.

Hakim, Catherine 1996. *Key Issues in Women's Work*, London: Athlone.

Halsey, A. H. 1993. "Changes in the family," *Children and Society* 7(2): 125–136.

Haney, Lynne 1998. "Engendering the welfare state," *Comparative Studies in Society and History* 40: 748–767.

Hanmer, Jeff 1990. "Men, power and the exploitation of women," in Jeff Hearn and David Morgan (eds.), *Men, Masculinities and Social Theory*, London: Unwin Hyman, pp. 21–42.

Hannerz, Ulf 1969. *Soulside: Inquiries into Ghetto Culture and Community*, New York: Columbia University Press.

Harkness, Susan, Stephen Machin and Jane Waldfogel 1996. "Women's pay and family incomes in Britain, 1979–1991," in John Hills (ed.), *New Inequalities: the Changing Distribution of Income and Wealth in the UK*, Cambridge University Press, pp. 158–180.

Hatje, Ann-Katrin 1974. *Befolkningsfrågan och välfärden: Debatten om familjepolitik och nativitetsökning under 1930- och 1940-talen*, Stockholm: Allmänna förlag.

Hayden, Dolores 1984. *Redesigning the American Dream: the Future of Housing, Work and Family Life*, New York: Norton.

Hearn, Jeff 1983. *Birth and Afterbirth: a Materialist Account*, London: Achilles Heel.

  1987. *The Gender of Oppression: Men, Masculinity and the Critique of Marxism*, Brighton: Wheatsheaf.

  1992. *Men in the Public Eye: the Construction and Deconstruction of Public Men and Public Patriarchies*, London: Routledge.

  1993. "The politics of essentialism and the analysis of the 'men's movement(s),'" *Feminism and Psychology* 3(3): 405–409.

  1996a. "Deconstructing the dominant: making the one(s) the other(s)," *Organization*, 3(4): 611–626.

  1996b. "Is masculinity dead? A critique of the concept of masculinity/masculinities," in Mairtin Mac an Ghaill (ed.), *Understanding Masculinities*, Buckingham and Philadelphia: Open University Press, pp. 202–217.

  1996c. "Men's violence to known women: historical, everyday and theoretical constructions by men," in Barbara Fawcett, Brid Featherstone, Jeff Hearn and Christine Toft (eds.), *Violence and Gender Relations*, London: Sage, pp. 22–37.

  1997. "The implications of critical studies on men," *NORA: Nordic Journal of Women's Studies* 3(1): 48–60.

1998a. "Troubled masculinities in social policy discourses: young men," in Jennie Popay, Jeff Hearn and Jeanette Edwards (eds.), pp. 37–62.

1998b. *The Violences of Men*, London: Sage.

1998c. "The welfare of men?" in Jennie Popay, Jeff Hearn and Jeanette Edwards (eds.), pp. 11–36.

1999. "It's time for men to change," in Jim Wild (ed.), *Working with Men for Change*, London: Taylor and Francis, pp. 5–15.

Hearn, Jeff and David L. Collinson 1993. "Theorizing unities and differences between men and between masculinities," in Harry Brod and Michael Kaufman (eds.), *Theorizing Masculinities*, Thousand Oakes, CA: Sage, pp. 97–118.

Helsingin Sanomat 1999. "Tanskan homoille rajattu adoptio-oikeus," 21 May, p. C5.

Helwig, Gisela and Hildegard Maria Nickel (eds.), 1993. *Frauen in Deutschland 1945–1990*, Berlin: Akademie Verlag.

Hernández, José A. 1996. "13.800 causas civiles atascadas en los juzgados por la 'huelga' de magistrados" "Los asuntos no urgentes tardan 60 días desde que se registran hasta que llegan a la mesa del juez," *El País*, May 14.

Hernes, Helga 1987. *Welfare State and Woman Power: Essays in State Feminism.* Oslo: University of Oslo Press.

Herrera Rivera, Alicia 1992. *Ponencia al Consejo General de Poder Judicial*, Madrid: Memo, December 30.

1994. *Evaluación del Programa de Ejecuciones de Sentencias y Querellas por Abandono de Famila (Art. 487, bis)*, Madrid: Memo.

Higuera Guimera, Juan Felipe 1997. "El Proceso de Despenalización del Aborto en España" in *Actualidad Penal* 35, October 5, pp. 765–810.

Hill, Dave 1998. "Fathers' day," *The Guardian* G2, 11 March, pp. 14–15.

Hill, Robert B. 1993. *Research on the African-American Family: a Holistic Perspective*, Westport Connecticut: Auburn House.

1997. *The Strengths of African-American Families: Twenty-Five Years Later*, Washington, DC: R and B Publishers.

Hiltunen, Rainer 1998. "Finland" in *ILGA–Europe Equality for Lesbians and Gay Men*, Brussels: ILGA. Electronic edition <http://epn.org/prospect/26/26ellw.html>.

Himmelweit, Sue and Diane Perrons 1999. "Gender dimensions of recent labour market policies: changing patterns of work and care in the UK." Paper presented at the Nordic–UK Collaborative Seminar on Employment Policies and Gender Relations, Stockholm, June.

Hirdman, Yvonne 1989. *Att lägga livet tillrätta: Studier i svensk folkhemspolitik*, Stockholm: Carlsson.

HMSO 1998. *Fairness at Work*, London: HMSO.

Hobson, Barbara 1993. "Feminist strategies and gendered discourses in welfare states: married women's right to work in the United States and Sweden during the 1930s," in Seth Koven and Sonya Michel (eds.), pp. 396–430.

1994. "Solo mothers, social policy regimes and the logics of gender," in Diane Sainsbury (ed.), *Gendering Welfare States*, London: Sage, pp. 170–187.

Hobson, Barbara and Mieko Takahashi 1997. "The parent–worker model: lone mothers in Sweden," in Jane Lewis (ed.), pp. 121–139.

Hochschild, Arlie Russell 1989. *The Second Shift: Working Parents and the Revolution at Home*, New York: Basic Books.

1995. "The culture of politics: traditional, postmodern, cold-modern, and warm-modern ideals of care," *Social Politics: International Studies of Gender, State, and Society* 2(3): 331–346.

1996. *The Time Bind: When Work Becomes Home and Home Becomes Work*, New York: Henry Holt.

Hoem, Britta and Jan M. Hoem 1988. "The Swedish family: aspects of contemporary developments," *Journal of Family Issues* 9(3): 397–424.

1992. "Disruption of marital and non-marital unions in contemporary Sweden," in James Trussell, Richard Hankinson, Judith Tilton (eds.), *Demographic Applications of Event History Analysis*, Oxford: Clarendon Press, pp. 61–93.

Holst, Elke and Jürgen Schupp 1999. "Erwerbsbeteiligung und Arbeitszeitwünsche 1993 und 1997," in W. Glatzer and Ilona Ostner (eds.), *Deutschland im Wandel. Sozialstrukturelle Analysen*, Opladen: Leske and Budrich, pp. 289–306.

Holtrust, Nora 1988. "Het nieuwe afstammingsrecht. Van onwettige kinderen naar opgedrongen vaders," in Petra de Vries (ed.), *Aan het hoofd van de tafel*, Amsterdam: Sara, pp. 55–72.

1993. *Aan moeders knie. De juridische afstammingsrelatie tussen moeder en kind*, Nijmegen: Ars Aequi Libri.

Holtrust, Nora and Ineke de Hondt 1997. "Ontwikkelingen in het familierecht," in Niphuis-Nell (ed.), pp. 247–286.

Home Office 1998. *Supporting Families*, London: Home Office.

Hooghiemstra, Erna 1997. "Een- en tweeverdieners," in Niphuis-Nell (ed.), pp. 53–83.

Horgby, Björn 1993. *Egensinne och skötsamhet: Arbetarkultur i Norrköping 1850–1940*, Stockholm: Carlsson.

Horn, Wade F., David Blankenhorn and Mitchell B. Pearlstein (eds.) 1999. *The Fatherhood Movement: a Call to Action*, New York: Lexington Books.

Howard, Christopher 1997. *The Hidden Welfare State: Tax Expenditures and Social Policy in the United States*, Princeton University Press.

Hurstel, Françoise 1997. "De los padres 'ausentes' a los 'nuevos padres'. Contribución a la historia de una transmisión genealógica colectiva," in Tubert, Silvia (ed.), *Figuras del padre*, Madrid: Ediciones Cátedra, pp. 295–305.

Iglesias de Ussel, Julio and Lluís Flaquer 1993. "Familia y Análisis Sociológico: El Caso de España," *Reis* 61: 57–75.

Instituto Nacional de Estadística 1998. *España. Anuario Estadístico 1997*, Madrid: Instituto Nacional de Estadística.

Isberg, Hagbard 1919. "Möjlig fader," *Vårdarebladet* 1919(3): 30–33.

Jalmert, Lars 1994. *Underhållsskylydiga fäder och mödrar*, Stockholms Universitet, Pedagogiska Institutionen.

Jalmert, Lars and Eva Olsson 1997. *Bra Pappor: Om vårdnadshavande pappor och mammor*. Stockholms Universitet, Pedagogiska Institutionen.

Jarvis, Sarah J. and John Micklewright 1992. "The targeting of family allowance in Hungary," *EUI Working Paper ECO 92/96*, Florence: European University Institute.

Jensen, An-Magritt 1998a. "Fatherhood and parental Europe." Paper presented at the conference on fatherhood, Fano, Italy, May.

  1998b. "Partnership and parenthood in contemporary Europe," *European Journal of Population* 14(1): 1–12.

Jonsson, Jan O. and Michael Gähler 1997. "Family dissolution, family reconstitution, and children's educational careers: recent evidence for Sweden," *Demography* 34(2): 277–293.

Jurisprudencia Tribunal Constitucional (Jurisprudence of the Constitutional Court) No. 441. 1997. *Actualidad penal* 28, July 7–13, pp. 1125–1130.

Kälvemark, Ann-Sofie 1980. *More Children of Better Quality? Aspects on Swedish Population Policy in the 1930s*, Studia Historica Upsaliensia 115. Uppsala: Almqvist and Wicksell International.

Kamarás, Ferenc 1986. "Egyszülös családok," (One-parent families) *Demográfia* 29(2–3): 253–266.

  1999. *Fertility and Family Surveys in Countries of the ECE Region. Standard Country Report: Hungary*, New York and Geneva: United Nations.

Kavemann, Barbara and Ingrid Lohstöter 1985. *Väter als Täter: Sexuelle Gewalt gegen Mädchen*, Reinbek: Rowohlt.

Kessler-Harris, Alice 1995. "Designing women and old fools: the construction of the social security amendments of 1939," in Linda K. Kerber, Alice Kessler-Harris and Kathryn K. Slkar (eds.), *U.S. History as Women's History: New Feminist Essays*, Chapel Hill: University of North Carolina Press, pp. 87–106.

Keuzenkamp, Saskia and Erna Hooghiemstra 2000. *De Kunst van het Combineren. Taakverdeling onder Partners*, The Hague: Sociaal en Cultureel Planbureau.

Keuzenkamp, Saskia and Ko Oudhof 2000. *Emancipatiemonitor 2000*, The Hague: Sociaal en Cultureel Planbureau.

Kiernan, Kathleen 1992. "Men and women at work and home," in Roger Jowell, L. Brook and Gillian Prior (eds.), *The British Social Attitudes Survey*, 9th Report, Aldershot: Dartmouth.

Kimmel, Michael 1996. *Manhood in America: a Cultural History*, New York: Free Press.

Kitschelt, Herbert, Peter Lange, Gary Marks and John D. Stephens 1999. *Continuity and Change in Contemporary Capitalism*, Cambridge University Press.

Klatch, Rebecca 1990. "The two worlds of women of the new right," in Louise Tilly and Patricia Gurin (eds.), *Women, Politics and Change*, New York: Russell Sage, pp. 529–552.

Klinth, Roger 1999. "The man and the equal family: a study of images of masculinity in the educational and TV Programmes in Sweden, 1946–1971," in Rolf Torstendahl (ed.), *Social Policy and Gender System in Two German States and Sweden, 1945–1989*, Uppsala: Uppsala Historica, Uppsaliiensa 22, pp. 169–198.

Knights, Emma, Jon Brackwell, Simon Cox and Alison Garnham 1999. *Child Support Handbook*, London: Child Poverty Action Group (CPAG).

Knijn, Trudie 1994. "Fish without bikes: revision of the Dutch welfare state and its consequences for the (in)dependence of single mothers," *Social Politics: International Studies in Gender, State, and Society* 1(1): 83–105.

  1995. "Towards post-paternalism? Social and theoretical changes in fatherhood," in Mirjam van Dongen, Gerard Frinking and Menno Jacobs (eds.),

Changing Fatherhood: a Multidisciplinary Perspective, Amsterdam: Thesis Publishers, pp. 1–20.

1997. "Keuze voor en beleving van moederschap en vaderschap," in Niphuis-Nell (ed.), pp. 223–244.

Knijn, Trudie and Monique Kremer 1997. "Gender and the caring dimension in welfare states: towards inclusive citizenship," *Social Politics: International Studies in Gender, State, and Society* 4(3): 328–361.

Koo, Helen P., Chirayath M. Suchindran and Janet D. Griffith 1984. "The effects of children on divorce and re-marriage: a multivariate analysis of life table probabilities," *Population Studies* 38(3): 451–471.

Koopmans, I. and M. Stavenuiter 1999. *Meer werken, minder zorgen. Arbeid en zorg in wetgeving en CAO's*, Breukelen: Nyfer.

Korpi, Walter 1989. "Power politics and state autonomy in the development of social citizenship," *American Sociological Review* 54: 309–328.

Koven, Seth and Sonya Michel (eds.) 1993. *Mothers of a New World: Maternalist Politics and the Origins of the Welfare States*, New York and London: Routledge.

Krausz, Katalin 1992. "Reforming the Hungarian welfare state." Paper presented at Comparative Studies of Welfare State Development: Quantitative and Qualitative Dimensions, Bremen, Center for Social Policy Research, September 3–6.

Kungliga statistiska centralbyrån 1914. "Utom äktenskapet födda barn," *Statistiska meddelanden* A I:4 , Stockholm: Kungliga statistiska centralbyrån.

1916. "Utom äktenskapet födda barn," *Statistiska meddelanden* A I:5, Stockholm: Kungliga statistiska centralbyrån.

1917. "Utom äktenskapet födda barn," *Statistiska meddelanden* A I:10, Stockholm: Kungliga statistiska centralbyrån.

Kurz, Karin 1998. "Hausfrau oder Berufsfrau? Einstellungen zur Rolle der Frau in Ost- und Westdeutschland," in M. Braun and P. Ph. Mohler (eds.), *Blickpunkt Gesellschaft 4*, Opladen: Westdeutscher Verlag, pp. 173–220.

Kuusipalo, Jaana 1990. "Finnish women in top-level politics," in Marja Keränen (ed.), *Finnish "Undemocracy": Essays on Gender and Politics*, Jyväskylä: Finnish Political Science Association, pp. 3–36.

Labour Research 1996. "Opt-out means UK parents lose out," *Labour Research* January, pp. 15–17.

Lagberedningens förslag till revision av giftermålsbalken och vissa delar av ärvdabalken III 1915. *Förslag till lag om barn utom äktenskap m.m.*, Stockholm.

Lake, Marilyn 1992. "Mission impossible: how men gave birth to the Australian nation – nationalism, gender and other seminal acts," *Gender and History* 4: 305–322.

Laleva, María 1999. "Padres que se mojan. Todavía no pueden traer a sus hijos al mundo, pero hay padres pioneros que han decidido asumir su paternidad al 100%," in *El País Semanal* 1173, March 21, pp. 102–105.

Larner, Wendy 2000. "Post-welfare state governance: towards a code of social and family responsibility," *Social Politics: International Studies of Gender, State, and Society* 7(2): 224–265.

Lavin, Rune 1987. *Barnbidrag* (Child allowance), Lund: Acta Societatis Juridicae Lundensis.

LCD 1998. *Procedures for the Determination of Paternity and on the Law on Parental Responsibility for Unmarried Fathers*, London: Lord Chancellor's Department.

Lehman, Cheryl 1996. "Quiet whispers . . . men accounting for women, west to east," in David L. Collinson and Jeff Hearn (eds.), *Men as Managers, Managers as Men*, London: Sage, pp. 150–166.

Leira, Arnlaug 1992. *Welfare States and Working Mothers*, Cambridge University Press.

1998. "Caring as social right: cash for childcare and daddy leave," *Social Politics: International Studies in Gender, State, and Society* 5(3): 362–378.

Lewis, Charlie 1996. "Fathers and preschoolers," in Michael E. Lamb (ed.), *The Role of the Father in Child Development*, London: John Wiley, pp. 121–142.

Lewis, Charlie and Margaret O'Brien 1987. "Constraints on fathers: research, theory and clinical practice," in Charlie Lewis and Margaret O'Brien (eds.), *Reassessing Fatherhood: New Observations on Fathers*, London: Sage, pp. 1–19.

Lewis, Jackie 1998. "United Kingdom" in *ILGA–Europe Equality for Lesbians and Gay Men* <http://www.steff.suite.dk/report.htm#UNITEDKINGDOM>, electronic edition, Brussels: ILGA.

Lewis, Jane 1980. *The Politics of Motherhood: Child and Maternal Welfare in England 1900–1939*, London: Croom Helm.

1992. "Gender and the development of welfare regimes," *Journal of European Social Policy* 2(3): 159–173.

1997a "Gender and welfare regimes: further thoughts," *Social Politics: International Studies in Gender, State, and Society* 4(2): 160–177.

1997b (ed.). *Lone Mothers in European Welfare Regimes: Shifting Policy Logics*, London: Jessica Kingsley Publishers.

1998 (ed.). *Gender, Social Care and Welfare State Restructuring in Europe*, Aldershot: Ashgate.

2000. "Why don't fathers pay more for their children?" *Benefits* 27: 1–8.

2001. *The End of Marriage? Individualism in Intimate Relationships*, Aldershot: Edward Elgar Pubs.

Lewis, Jane with Jessica Datta and Sophie Sarre 1999. *Individualism and Commitment in Marriage and Cohabitation*, London: Lord Chancellor's Department.

Lichtenstein, Nelson 1989. "From corporatism to collective bargaining: organized labor and the eclipse of social democracy in the postwar era," in Steve Fraser and Gary Gerstle (eds.), *The Rise and Fall of the New Deal Order, 1930–1980*, Princeton University Press, pp. 122–152.

Lieberman, Robert C. 1998. *Shifting the Color Line: Race and the American Welfare State*, Cambridge, MA: Harvard University Press.

Liebfried, Stephan 1993. "Towards a European welfare state," in Catherine Jones (ed.), *New Perspectives on the Welfare State in Europe*, London: Routledge, pp. 13–156.

Lister, Ruth 1997. *Citizenship: Feminist Perspectives*, London: Macmillan.

2000. "Dilemmas of engendering citizenship," in Barbara Hobson (ed.), *Gender and Citizenship in Transition*, London: Macmillan, pp. 33–83.

Lye, Diane N. and Ingrid Waldron 1997. "Attitudes toward cohabitation, family, and gender roles: relationships to values and political ideology," *Sociological Perspectives* 40(2): 199–225.

MacKinnon, Catharine A. 1982. "Feminism, Marxism, method and the state: an agenda for theory," *Signs: Journal of Women in Culture and Society* 7(3): 515–544.

1983. "Feminism, Marxism, method and the state: toward feminist jurisprudence," *Signs: Journal of Women in Culture and Society* 8(4): 635–658.

Maclean, Mavis 1991. "The making of the Child Support Act 1991: policy making at the intersection of law and social policy," *Journal of Law and Society* 21: 505–519.

1994. "Delegalizing child support," in Mavis Maclean and Jacek Kurczewski (eds.), *Families, Politics and the Law*, Oxford: Clarendon Press.

Maclean, Mavis and John Eekelaar 1997. *The Parental Obligation: a Study of Parenthood across Households*, Oxford: Hart Publishing.

Maidment, Susan 1984. *Child Custody and Divorce*, London: Croom Helm.

Majors, Richard G and Jacob U. Gordon (eds.) 1994. *The American Black Male: His Present Status and His Future*, Chicago: Nelson-Hall.

Mangan, J.A. and James Walvin (eds.) 1986. *Manliness and Morality: Middle-Class Masculinity in Britain and America 1800–1940*, Manchester University Press.

Mansfield, Penny and Jean Collard 1988. *The Beginning of the Rest of your Life? A Portrait of Newly-wed Marriage*, London: Macmillan.

Marsiglio, William (ed.) 1995. *Fatherhood: Contemporary Theory, Research, and Social Policy*, London: Sage.

Martín, Concha 1998. "El fraude es la mayor injusticia del IRPF" *El País*, February 20, p. 54.

Mason, Mary Ann 1994. *From Father's Property to Children's Rights: The History of Child Custody in the United States*, New York: Columbia Press.

Matovic, Margareta R. 1984. *Stockholmsäktenskap: Familjebildning och partnerval i Stockholm 1850–1890*, Stockholm: Liber förlag.

McCaffery, Edward J. 1997. *Taxing Women*, University of Chicago Press.

McFate, Katherine, Timothy Smeeding and Lee Rainwater 1995. "Markets and states: poverty trends and transfer system effectiveness in the 1980s," in Katherine McFate, Roger Lawson, and William Julius Wilson (eds.), *Poverty, Inequality and the Future of Social Policy: Western States in the New World Order*, New York: Russell Sage, pp. 29–64.

McLanahan, Sara S. and Gary D. Sandefur 1994. *Growing Up With A Single Parent: What Hurts, What Helps*, Cambridge, MA: Harvard University Press.

McMahon, Antony 1993. "Male readings of feminist theory: the psychologization of sexual politics in the masculinity literature," *Theory and Society* 22(5): 675–696.

Menéndez Alvarez-Dardet, Susana 1994. *La implicación del padre en la crianza y la educación de sus hijos: Análisis Exploratorio con una muestra andaluza*, Sevilla: Facultad de Psicología de Sevilla.

Menéndez del Valle, Emilio 1989. "Política exterior y transición democrática en España," in José Félix Tezanos, Ramón Cotarelo and Andrés de Blas (eds.),

La Transición Democrática Española, Madrid: Editorial Sistema (reprinted 1993), pp. 715–755.

Messner, Michael A. 1997. *Politics of Masculinities: Men in Movements*, Thousand Oaks: Sage.

Metz-Göckel, Sigrid and Ursula Müller 1986. *Der Mann. Die Brigitte-Studie*, Weinheim: Beltz.

Meulders-Klein, M-T. 1990. "The position of the father in European legislation," *International Journal of Law and the Family* 4: 131–153.

Meyer, Madonna Harrington 1996. "Making claims as workers or wives: the distribution of social security benefits," *American Sociological Review* 61: 449–465.

Michel, Sonya 1993. "The limits of maternalism: policies toward American wage-earning mothers during the progressive era," in Seth Koven and Sonya Michel (eds.), pp. 277–320.

Mies, Maria 1986. *Patriarchy and Accumulation on World Scale*, London: ZedBooks.
   1998. "Globalization of the economy and woman's work in a sustainable society," *Gender, Technology and Development* 2(1): 3–37.

Millar, Jane 1996. "Family obligations and social policy: the case of child support," *Policy Studies* 17(3): 181–193.

Millar, Jane and Andrea Warman 1996. *Family Obligations in Europe*, London: Family Policy Studies Centre.

Mincy, Ronald 1997. "Delivering dads: paternalism and fragile families," in Lawrence Mead (ed.), *The New Paternalism: Supervisory approach to Poverty Reduction*, Washington, DC: The Brookings Institution.

Ministerie van Sociale Zaken en Werkgelegenheid 1997. *Kansen op Combineren. Arbeid, zorg en economische zelfstandigheid*. The Hague.

Mink, Gwendolyn 1995. *Wages of Motherhood: Inequality in the Welfare State, 1917–1942*, Ithaca, NY: Cornell University Press.
   1998. *Welfare's End*, Ithaca, NY: Cornell University Press.
   2000. "Gender in Wisconsin's child support and paternity establishment policy: An ethnographic study," Ph.D. dissertation, Department of Sociology, University of Wisconsin-Madison.

Mitchell, Juliet and Jack Goody 1997. "Feminism, fatherhood and the family in Britain," in Ann Oakley and Juliet Mitchell (eds.), *Who's Afraid of Feminism? Seeing Through the Backlash*, London: Hamish Hamilton, pp. 220–223.

Mitscherlich, Alexander 1955. "Der unsichtbare Vater," *Kölner Zeitschrift für Soziologie und Sozialpsychologie* 7: 188–201.
   1963. *Auf dem Weg zur vaterlosen Gesellschaft. Ideen zur Sozialpsychologie*, Munich: R. Piper.

Moffitt, Robert A., Robert Reville and Anne E. Winkler 1998. "Beyond single mothers: cohabitation and marriage in the AFDC program," *Demography* 35(3): 259–278.

Monahan, T. 1976. "The occupational class of couples entering into interracial marriages," *Journal of Comparative Family Studies* 7:175–192.

Monson, Renee A. 1997. "State-ing sex and gender: collecting information from mothers and fathers in paternity cases," *Gender and Society* 11: 279–95.

2001. "Gender in Wisconsin's child support and paternity establishment policy: an ethnographic study," Ph.D. dissertation, Department of Sociology, University of Wisconsin-Madison.

Moore, Henrietta 1988. *Feminism and Anthropology*, Cambridge: Polity Press.

Morgan, Patricia 1995. *Farewell to the Family: Public Policy and Family Breakdown in Britain and the USA*, London: IEA.

Moss, Peter (ed.) 1995. *Father Figures: Fathers in the Families of the 1990s*, Edinburgh: HMSO.

Moxnes, Kari 1993. "Changes in family structure: challenge for theory formation," in Arnlaug Leira (ed.), *Family Sociology: Developing the Field*, Oslo: Institute for Social Research, Report 93(5), pp. 91–109.

Muesse, Mark W. 1996. "Religious machismo: masculinity and fundamentalism," in Stephen B. Boyd, W. Merle Longwood and Mark W. Muesse (eds.), *Redeeming Men: Religion and Masculinities*, Louisville: Westminster John Knox Press, pp. 89–102.

Mujeres en Cifras 2000. Ministerio de Trabajo y Asuntos Sociales, Instituto de la Mujer. Internet edition <http://www.mtas.es/mujer/mcifras>, 27 and 28 December.

Mullins, Claud 1954. *Marriage Failures and their Children*, London: Epworth Press.

Murray, Charles 1985. *Losing Ground: American Social Policy, 1950–1980*, New York: Basic Books.

Myles, John and Paul Pierson 1997. "Friedman's revenge: the reform of 'liberal' welfare states in Canada and the United States," *Politics and Society* 25(4): 443–472.

Myrdal, Alva 1945. *Nation and Family*, London: Kegan Paul, Trench, Trubner and Co.

Näsman, Elizabeth 1995. "Time, work, and family life," in Birgit Arve-Perex (ed.), *Reconciling Work and Family Life – a Challenge for Europe?*, Commission of European Communities, Stockholm: Norstedts, pp. 93–102.

National Women's Law Center and the Center on Fathers, Families, and Public Policy 2000. *Family Ties: Improving Paternity Establishment Practices and Procedures for Low-Income Mothers, Fathers and Children*. Electronic edition <http://www.cffpp.org/commonground.pdf>.

NCHS 1995. *Monthly Vital Statistics Report* 43(9), Supplement, Hyattsville, Maryland: National Center for Health Statistics.

Neckerman, Kathryn, Robert Aponte and William Julius Wilson 1988. "Family structure, black unemployment, and American social policy," in Margaret Weir, Ann Shola Orloff and Theda Skocpol (eds.), pp. 397–346.

Nelson, Barbara 1990. "The origins of the two-channel welfare state: workmen's compensation and mothers' aid," in Linda Gordon (ed.), *Women, the State and Welfare*, Madison: University of Wisconsin Press, pp. 123–151.

Nermo, Magnus 2000. *Structured By Gender. Patterns of Sex Segregation in the Swedish Labour Market: Historical and Cross-National Comparisons*. Stockholm: Swedish Institute for Social Research 41.

Niphuis-Nell, Marry (ed.) 1997. *Sociale atlas van de Vrouw deel 4: Veranderingen in de primaire leefsfeer*. Rijswijk: Sociaal en Cultureel Planbureau.

Nordlöf, Barbro 1997. *Barnets rätt och bästa: En studie i barnavårdsmannaverk-samheten i Stockholm*, Stockholm: Stockholmia förlag.

Nutzinger, Hans G. and Martin Held (eds.) 2000. *Geteilte Arbeit und ganzer Mensch*. Frankfurt: Campus.

O'Brien, Mary 1981. *The Politics of Reproduction*, London: Routledge and Kegan Paul.

1986. *Reproducing the World*, Boulder: Westview.

O'Connor, Julia 1993. "Gender, class and citizenship in the comparative analysis of welfare state regimes: theoretical and methodological issues," *British Journal of Sociology* 44: 501–518.

1996. "From women in the welfare state to gendering welfare regimes," *Current Sociology* 44(2): 1–124.

O'Connor, Julia, Ann Shola Orloff and Sheila Shaver 1999. *States, Markets, Families: Gender, Liberalism and Social Policy in Australia, Canada, Great Britain and the United States*, New York: Cambridge University Press.

Offe, Claus and Johan De Deken 1999. "Work, time, and social participation. Policy options for dealing with labour market precariousness," Institute of Social Science. Humboldt University Berlin. Mimeo.

Olson, Mancur 1971. *The Logic of Collective Action: Public Goods and the Theory of Groups*, Cambridge, MA: Harvard University Press, 2nd edn (first published 1965).

Oppenheimer, Valerie Kincaid 1994. "Women's rising employment and the future of the family in industrial societies," *Population and Development Review* 20: 293–242.

Orloff, Ann Shola 1993a. "Gender and the social rights of citizenship: the comparative analysis of gender relations and welfare states," *American Sociological Review* 58: 303–28.

1993b. *The Politics of Pensions: a Comparative Analysis of Britain, Canada, and the United States, 1880–1940*, Madison: University of Wisconsin Press.

1996. "Gender and the welfare state," *Annual Review of Sociology* 22: 51–70.

2001. "Ending the entitlements of poor single mothers: changing social policies, women's employment and caregiving," in Nancy Hirschmann and Ulrike Liebert (eds.), *Women and Welfare: Theory and Practice in the United States and Europe*, New Brunswick: Rutgers University Press, pp. 133–159.

Orloff, Ann Shola and Renee Monson 1997. "Citizens, workers, or fathers? Men in U.S. social policy." Paper presented in the session gender and welfare" at the annual meeting of the American Sociological Association, Toronto, Ontario, Canada, August 12.

Ostner, Ilona 1997. "Lone mothers in Germany before and after unification," in Jane Lewis (ed.), pp. 21–49.

1998. "Gender, family and the welfare state – Germany before and after unification," in Eva Kolinsky (ed.), *Social Transformation and the Family in Post-Communist Germany*, Houndmills: Macmillan, pp. 82–96.

2000. "Was heißt hier normal? Normalarbeit, Teilzeit, Arbeit im Lebenszyklus," in H. G. Nutzinger and M. Held (eds.), *Geteilte Arbeit und ganzer Mensch*. Frankfurt: Campus, pp. 173–189.

Oswald, Hans 1998. "Sozialisation und Entwicklung in den neuen Bundesländern," *Zeitschrift für Soziologie der Erziehung und Sozialisation* (special issue), Weinheim: Juventa.

OTROSÍ informativa 1999. "Acuerdos entre jueces, fiscales, secretarios de familia y abogados de Madrid, Colegio de Abogados de Madrid," no. 2, III época, March 1999.

Palmer, John and Isabel Sawhill (eds.) 1984. *The Reagan Record*, Cambridge, MA: Ballinger.

Panayotova, Evelina and April Brayfield 1997. "National context and gender ideology: attitudes toward women's employment in Hungary and the United States," *Gender and Society* 11(5): 627–655.

Papadopoulos, Theodoros N. 1998. "Greek family policy from a comparative perspective," in Eileen Drew, Ruth Emerek and Evely Mahon, *Women, Work and the Family in Europe*, London and New York: Routledge, pp. 47–57.

Pateman, Carol 1988. *The Sexual Contract*, Cambridge: Polity Press.

Patterson, Charlotte J. 1992. "Children of lesbian and gay parents," *Child Development* 63: 1025–1042.

Pearce, Diana 1986. "Toil and trouble: women workers and unemployment compensation," in Barbara C. Gelpi, Nancy C. M. Hartsock, Clare C. Novak and Myra H. Strober (eds.), *Women and Poverty*, University of Chicago Press, pp. 141–162.

Pedersen, Susan 1993. *Family, Dependence and the Origins of the Welfare State: Britain and France, 1914–1945*, New York: Cambridge University Press.

Pfeiffer, Christian 2000. "Fremdenfeindliche Gewalt im Osten – Folge der autoritären DDR-Beziehung?," Hanover: Kriminologisches Forschungsinstitut.

Phillips, Melanie 1997. *The Sex Change State*, London: Social Market Foundation.

Phoenix, Ann 1991. *Young Mothers*, Cambridge: Polity Press.

Pierson, Paul 1994. *Dismantling the Welfare State? Reagan, Thatcher, and the Politics of Retrenchment*, New York: Cambridge University Press.

Piper, C. 1993. *The Responsible Parent. A Study in Divorce Mediation*, Brighton: Harvester Wheatsheaf.

Plantenga, Janneke 1996. "For women only? The rise of part-time work in the Netherlands," *Social Politics: International Studies in Gender, State, and Society* 3(1): 57–71.

1998. "Double lives: labour market participation, citizenship and gender," in Jet Bussemaker and Rian Voet (eds.), *Gender, Participation and Citizenship in the Netherlands*, Asgate: Aldershot, pp. 51–64.

Popay, Jennie, Jeff Hearn and Jeanette Edwards (eds.) 1998. *Men, Gender Divisions and Welfare*, London: Routledge.

Popenoe, David 1988. *Disturbing the Nest: Family Change and Decline in Modern Societies*, New York: Adeline de Gruyter.

1991. "Family decline in the Swedish welfare state," *The Public Interest* 102: 65–77.

1993. "American family decline, 1960–1990: review and appraisal," *Journal of Marriage and the Family* 55: 527–555.

Promberger, Markus, Jörg Rosdücher, Hartmut Seifert and Raines Trinczek 1996. "Akzeptanzprobleme beschäftigungssichernder Arbeitszeitverkuerzungen. Empirische Evidenz zweier Beschäftigtenbefragungen bei der Volkswagen AG und der Ruhrkohle Ag," *Mitteilungen aus der Arbeitsmarkt- und Berufsforschung* 29 (2): 203–218.

Promemoria 1998: 06.05. Det fortsatta med reglerna om vårdnad, boende och umgänge.

Pross, Helge 1978. *Die Männer*, Reinbek: Rowohlt.

Pujol Algans, Carmen 1992. *Código de la Mujer*, Madrid: Instituto de la Mujer, Ministerio de Asuntos Sociales.

Quadagno, Jill 1994. *The Color of Welfare: How Racism Undermined the War on Poverty*, New York: Oxford University Press.

Raad voor het Jeugdbeleid 1988. *Afstamming, adoptie en sociaal ouderschap*, Rijswijk: Ministerie van Welzijn, Volksgezondheid en Cultuur.

Rainwater, Lee and William Layton Yancey 1967. *The Moynihan Report and the Politics of Controversy*, Cambridge and London: MIT Press.

Rantalaiho, Liisa 1997. "Contextualizing gender," in Liisa Rantalaiho and Tuula Heiskanen (eds.), *Gendered Practices in Working Life*, London: Macmillan, pp. 16–30.

Reformlinjer för svensk fattigvårdslagstiftning 1907. Stockholm: Centralförbundet för socialt arbetes fattigvårdskommitté.

Relationship Between Family Life and Young People's Lifestyles, The 1996. Findings, Social Policy Research 95, York: Joseph Rowntree Foundation.

Richardson, Katarina 1997. "Are divorcing parents induced to choose joint custody? An evaluation using implementation theory," *Essays on Family and Labor Economics*, Stockholm: Swedish Institute for Social Research 28, pp. 1–28.

Rights of Women 1984. *Lesbian Mothers on Trial: a Report on Lesbian Mothers and Child Custody*, London: Rights of Women.

Riksförsäkringsverket 1993. *Vilka pappor kom hem? En rapport om uttraget av. föräldrapenningen 1989 och 1990. Statistisk rapport IS- R 1993:3*, Stockholm: Riksförsäkringsverket.

1998. *Uppgifter om bidragsförskott/underhålsstöd*, Stockholm: Riksförsåkringsverket.

2000. *Delat Barnbidrag, RKV: 2000: 3*. Stockholm: Riksförsåkringsverket.

Riley, Denise 1983. *War in the Nursery*, London: Virago.

Robertson, Roland 1995. "Glocalization: time-space and homogeneity–heterogeneity," in Mike Featherstone, Scott Lash and Roland Robertson (eds.), *Global Modernities*, London: Sage, pp. 25–44.

Rodríguez, Albor 1998. "Los padres podrán escoger de mutuo acuerdo el orden de los apellidos de los hijos," *El País*, March 25.

Rojas Marcos, Luis 1995. "Hogares sin padres," in *IS. Infancia y Sociedad, número especial dedicado a Las relaciones padres/hijos, presente y futuro*, no. 30. Ministerio de Asuntos Sociales, Dirección General del Menor y la Familia, 193–206.

Rose, Nikolas 1996. "The death of the social? Refiguring the territory of government," *Economy and Society* 25(3): 327–356.

ROW 1980. *Illegitimacy: evidence to the Law Commission*, London: Rights of Women.

Rowbotham, Sheila 1979. "The trouble with 'patriarchy,'" *New Statesman* 98: 970.

Rubery, Jill, Martin Smith and Eloise Turner 1996. *Bulletin on Women and Employment in the EU* 9 (October).

Runcis, Maija. 1998. *Steriliseringar i folkhemmet,* Stockholm: Ordfront.

Russell, Bertrand 1929. *Marriage and Morals,* London: George Allen and Unwin.

Rutherford, Sarah 1999. *Organisational Cultures, Patriarchal Closure and Women Managers,* Ph.D. thesis, University of Bristol.

Sainsbury, Diane 1994. "Women's and men's social rights: gendering dimensions of welfare states," in Diane Sainsbury (ed.), *Gendering Welfare States,* London: Sage, pp. 150–169.

1996. *Gender, Equality and Welfare States,* Cambridge University Press.

Schiewe, Kirsten 1996. "Couples, parents, children and the state: defining family obligations in Germany," Working Paper AB 1, no. 14, Mannheim: Centre for European Social Research.

Schiratzki, Johanna 1997. *Vårdnad och vårdnadstvister,* Stockholm: Norstedts Juridik.

Schmähl, Winifred (ed.) 1992. *Sozialpolitic im Prozess der deutschen Vereinigung.* Frankfurt: Campus.

Schneewind, Klaus A. and Laszlo A. Vaskovics 1996. *Optionen der Lebensgestaltung junger Ehen und Kinderwunsch,* Stuttgart: Kohlhammer.

Schoen, Robert and John Wooldredge 1989. "Marriage choices in North Carolina and Virginia, 1969–71 and 1979–81," *Journal of Marriage and the Family* 51(2): 465–481.

Schwalbe, Michael 1996. *Unlocking the Iron Cage: the Men's Movement, Gender Politics, and American Culture,* New York and Oxford: Oxford University Press.

SCP 1998. *Sociaal en cultureel rapport 1998. 25 jaar sociale verandering,* The Hague: Sociaal en Cultureel Planbureau.

Select Committee on Violence in Marriage 1975. Report, together with the Proceedings of the Committee, vol. 2: Report, Minutes of the Committee and Appendices, London: HMSO.

Seltzer, Judith A. 1998 "Father by law effects of joint legal custody on nonresident fathers' involvement with children," *Demography* 35(2): 135–146.

Sennett, Richard 1998. *Der flexible Mensch. Die Kultur des neuen Kapitalismus,* Berlin: Berlin-Verlag.

Sevenhuijsen, Selma 1986. "Fatherhood and the political theory of rights: theoretical perspectives of feminism," *International Journal of the Sociology of Law* 14: 329–340.

1987. *De orde van het vaderschap. Politieke debatten over ongehuwd moederschap afstamming en huwelijk in Nederland, 1870–1900,* Amsterdam: Stichting Beheer IISG.

SFS 1917: 376. *Lag om barn utom äktenskap.*

1927: 452. *Efterlysning av vissa underhållsskyldiga.*

1933: 229. *Lag angående blodundersökning i mål om barn utom äktenskap.*

1996: 1030. *Lag om underhållsstöd.*

2000: 1397. "Lag om ändring i lagen," *Lag om ändring i lagen* (1996: 1030) *om underhållsstöd.*

Siim, Birte 2000. *Gender and Citizenship: Politics, Agency in France, Britain and Denmark*, Cambridge University Press.

Sillitoe, Alan 1970. *Saturday Night and Sunday Morning*, London: W. H. Allen, First edition 1958.

Singly, François de 1996. *Modern Marriage and its Cost to Women. A Sociological look at Marriage in France*, London: Associated University Presses.

Sjögren, Mikael 1997. *Fattigvård och folkuppfostran:Liberal fattigvårdspolitik 1903–1918*, Stockholm: Carlsson.

Skocpol, Theda 1992. *Protecting Soldiers and Mothers*, Cambridge, MA: Harvard University Press.

1996. "Delivering for young families: the resonance of the GI bill," *The American Prospect* 7(28). Internet edition <http://www.prospect.org/archives/28/28skoc.html>.

Smart, Carol 1991. "The legal and moral ordering of child custody," *Journal of Law and Society* 18: 485–500.

1995a. "The family and social change: some problems of analysis and intervention," Research Working Paper 13, University of Leeds.

1995b. "Fatherhood and the law: the case of the UK," in Mirjam van Dongen, Gerard Frinking and Menno Jacobs (eds.), *Changing Fatherhood: an interdisciplinary perspective*, Amsterdam: Thesis Publishers, pp. 137–144.

1997. "Wishful thinking and harmful tinkering? Sociological reflections on family policy," *Journal of Social Policy* 26(3): 301–331.

Smart, Carol and Bren Neale 1999. *Family Fragments?*, Cambridge: Polity Press.

Smith, Ken R., Cathleen D. Zick and Greg J. Duncan 1991. "Remarriage patterns among recent widows and widowers," *Demography* 28(3): 361–374.

Socialstyrelsen 1996. *Socialtjänsten och omsorgnerna i Sverige*, Stockholm: Socialstyrelsen.

Solsona, Montserrat, Carles Simó and René Houle 2000. "Separation and divorce in Spain," in Teresa Jurado Maria José González and Manuela Naldini (eds.), *Gender Inequalities in Southern Europe: Women, Work and Welfare in the 1900s*, London: Frank Kass, pp. 195–222.

Soskice, David 1999. "Divergent production regimes: coordinated and uncoordinated market economies in the 1980s and 1990s," in Herbert Kitschelt et al.(eds.), pp. 101–134.

SOU (Statens Offentliga Utredning) 1935: 6. *Åtgärder mot arbetslöshet*, Stockholm.

1936: 47. *Förskottering av underhållsbidrag till barn utom äktenskap m fl*, Stockholm.

1946: 49. *Ärvdabalkssakkunnigas förslag till föräldrabalk*, Stockholm.

1957: 49. *Följdförfattningar till ny barnavårdslag m.m*, Stockholm.

1972: 41. *Familj och äktenskap*, Stockholm.

1972: 65. *Barnavårdsmannafrågan*, Stockholm.

1977: 37. *Underhåll till barn och frånskilda. Delbetänkande av familjesakkunniga*, Stockholm.

1983: 14. *Betänkande från familjeekonomiska Kommittén*, Stockholm.

1984: 63. *Homosexuella och samhället – betänkande av utredningen om homosexuellas situation i samhället*, Stockholm (Socialdepartementet).

1995: 26. *Underhållsbidrag och Bidragsförskott*, Stockholm.

1995: 79. *Vårdnad, boende och umgänge. Betankände av. Vårdnadstvisudtredningnen. Justitiedepartementet*, Stockholm.

1995: 133. *Bostadsbidragen: effektivare inkomstprövning, besparingar* (Housing allowance: more effective means-testing, cut-backs), Stockholm: Socialdepartementet (Ministry of Social Affairs).

Spain, Daphne and Suzanne Bianchi 1996. *Balancing Act: Motherhood, Marriage and Employment among American Women*, New York: Russell Sage.

Der Spiegel 1997. "The disenfranchised father," November 17.

Stacey, Judith 1996. *In the Name of the Family: Rethinking Family Values in the Postmodern Age*, Boston: Beacon.

Staples Robert and Leanor Boulin Johnson 1993. *Black Families at the Crossroads: Challenges and Prospects*, San Francisco: Jossey-Bass.

Statistics Sweden (SCB) 1993. *Vårdnad och underhåll* (Custody and support). Stockholm: Statistiska centralbyran.

1995. *Barnomsorgsundersökning 1995. Förskolebarn (3 månader–6 år)* (Survey of childcare 1995: Pre-school children (3 months – 6 years old)), Örebro: Statistiska centralbyran.

Statistisches Bundesamt 1985–1998. *Statistische Jahrbücher*, Wiesbaden: Statistisches Bundesamt.

Stein, Rolf 2000. "Familiensoziologische Skizzen über die 'Vaterlose Gesellschaft'" *Zeitschrift für Familienforschung* 12 (1): 49–71.

Steiner-Scott, Elizabeth 1997. " 'To bounce a boot off her now and then...': domestic violence in post-famine Ireland," in Maryann Gialanella Valiulis and Mary O'Dowd (eds.), *Women and Irish History*, Dublin: Wolfhound, pp. 125–143.

Stephan, Cora 2000. "Das Schweigen der Männer," *Kursbuch* 140: 105–114.

Stephens, Linda 1996. "Will Johnny see daddy this week? An empirical test of three theoretical perspectives of post-divorce contact," *Journal of Family Issues* 1: 4466–4494.

Stevens, Beth 1988. "Blurring the boundaries: how the federal government has influenced welfare benefits in the private sector," in Margaret Weir, Ann Shola Orloff and Theda Skocpol (eds.), pp. 123–148.

Stockholm Child Welfare Committee 1920–1970. *Annual Reports*, Stockholm.

Stone, Lawrence 1977. *The Family, Sex and Marriage 1500–1800*, London: Weidenfeld and Nicolson.

Sundström, Marianne 1991. "Sweden: supporting work, family, and gender equality," in Sheila B. Kamerman and Alfred J. Kahn (eds.), *Childcare, Parental Leave, and the Under 3s: Policy Innovation in Europe*, New York: Auburn House, pp. 171–199.

1993. "The growth in full-time work among Swedish women in the 1980s," *Acta Sociologica* 36(2):139–150.

1994. *Time Out for Childcare and Career Wages of Men and Women*, Stockholm University, Demography Unit.

1996. "Determinants of the use of parental benefits by women in Sweden in the 1980s," *Scandinavian Journal of Social Welfare* 5(2): 76–82.

Sundström, Marianne and Ann-Zofie Duvander 2001. "Family division of childcare and the sharing of parental leave among new parents in Sweden," in

Ann-Zofie E. Duvander, *Couples in Sweden: Studies on Family and Work*, Stockholm: Swedish Institute for Social Research Dissertation Series 46, section III, pp. 1–28.

Sundström, Marianne and Frank P. Stafford 1992. "Female labor force participation, fertility and public policy in Sweden," *European Journal of Population* 8(3): 199–215.

Sweet, James A. and Larry L. Bumpass 1989. *American Families and Households*, New York: Russell Sage Foundation.

Sweet, James A., Larry L. Bumpass and Vaughn Call 1988. "The design and content of the National Survey of Families and Households," *Working paper NSFH–1*, Center for Demography and Ecology, Madison: University of Wisconsin.

Szalai, Júlia 1991. "Some aspects of the changing situation of women in Hungary," *Signs: Journal of Women in Culture and Society* 17(1): 152–170.

Takahashi, Mieko (forthcoming). *Gender Dimensions in Family Life: a Comparative Study of Power and Constraints in Sweden and Japan*, Stockholm: Department of Sociology, Stockholm University.

Taylor-Gooby, Peter 1996. "The response of government: fragile convergence?" in Victor George and Peter Taylor-Gooby (eds.), *European Welfare Policy: Squaring the Welfare Circle*, Basingstoke: Macmillan, pp. 199–218.

Tezanos, José Félix 1989. "Modernización y cambio social en España," in José Félix Tezanos, Ramón Cotarelo and Andrés de Blas (eds.), *La Transición Democrática Española*, Madrid: Editorial Sistema (reprinted 1993), pp. 63–119.

Thane, Pat 1982. *The Foundation of the Welfare State*, London: Longman.

Therborn, Goran 2000. "Globalizations: dimensions, historical waves, regional effects, normative governance," *International Sociology* 15(2): 151–179.

Thiebaut Luis, María Paz 1992. "Las actuaciones de las instituciones europeas en relación con la familia," *IS. Infancia y Sociedad. Número especial dedicado a la Familia* 16 (July/August): 21–34.

Thomas, R. 1999. "Fathers must be more than 'walking wallets,'" *The Observer*, April 24, p. 5.

Thompson, Linda 1991. "Family work: women's sense of fairness," *Journal of Family Issues* 12(2): 181–196.

Thornton, Arland 1989. "Changing attitudes towards family issues in the United States," *Journal of Marriage and the Family* 51(4): 873–893.

Toulemon, Laurent 1995. "La cohabitation hors mariage s'installe dans la durée," *Population* 51(3): 675–715.

Trappe, Heike 1995. *Emanzipation oder Zwang? Frauen in der DDR zwischen Beruf, Familie und Sozialpolitik*, Berlin: Sigma.

Turcotte, Pierre and Alain Bélanger 1997. "Moving in together: the formation of first common-law unions," *Canadian Social Trends* 47 (Winter): 7–10.

Tweede Kamer der Staten Generaal 1998–1999. *Regels inzake het recht op aanpassing van de arbeidsduur (Wet aanpassing arbeidsduur)*. Tweede Kamer, vergaderjaar 1998–1999: 26358, no. 3.

Valentine, Charles A. 1970. *Culture and Poverty*, Chicago University Press.

Valiente, Celia 1995. "Children first: central government child care policies in post-authoritarian Spain (1975–1994)," in Julia Brannen and Margaret

O'Brien (eds.), *Childhood and Parenthood: Proceedings of ISA Committee for Family Research Conference on Children and Families 1994*. Institute of Education, University of London, pp. 249–266.

van Praag, Carlo S. and Marry Niphuis-Nell 1997. *Het gezinsrapport. Een verkennende studie naar het gezin in een veranderende samenelving*, The Hague: Sociaal en Cultureel Planbureau.

van Wel, Frits and Trudie Knijn 2000. *Alleenstaande Ouders over Zorgen en Werken*, The Hague: Elsevier Bedrijfsinformatie.

Vaskovics, Laszlo A., Harald Rost and Marina Rupp 1997. *Lebenslage nichtehelicher Kinder. Rechtstatsächliche Untersuchungen zu Lebenslagen und Entwicklungsverläufen nichtehelicher Kinder*, Köln: Kohlhammer.

Vaskovics, Laszlo and Harald Rost 1999. *Väter und Erziehungsurlaub*, Stuttgart: Kohlhammer.

Ventimiglia, Carmine 1995. "Hombres y cambio," *IS. Infancia y sociedad* 33 (September–October): 26–30.

Vestbro, Dick Urban 1992. "Från liberal rörelse till socialistisk kamp mot patriarkatet," in Annika Baude (ed.), *Visionen om jämställdhet*, Stockholm: SNS, pp. 54–73.

Visionen om jämställdhet 1992. ed. Annika Baude. Stockholm: SNS Fomag.

Walby, Sylvia 1986. *Patriarchy at Work*, Cambridge: Polity.

　1989. "Theorising patriarchy," *Sociology* 23(2): 213–234.

　1990. *Theorizing Patriarchy*, Oxford: Basil Blackwell.

Wallerstein, Judith S. and Joan Kelly 1980. *Surviving the Breakup*, London: Grant McIntyre.

Warin, Jo, Yvette Solomon, Charlie Lewis and Wendy Langford 1999. *Fathers, Work and Family Life*, London: Joseph Rowntree Foundation/Family Policy Studies Centre.

Waring, Marilyn 1988. *Counting for Nothing*, Wellington, NZ: Allen and Unwin.

Waters, Malcolm 1989. "Patriarchy and viriarchy," *Sociology* 23(2): 193–211.

　1995. *Globalisation*, London: Routledge.

Waylen, Gillian 1996. *Gender in Third World Politics*, Buckingham: Open University Press.

Weir, Margaret 1992. *The Politics of Jobs*, Princeton University Press.

Weir, Margaret, Ann Shola Orloff, and Theda Skocpol (eds.) 1988. *The Politics of Social Policy in the United States*, Princeton University Press.

Weitzman, Leonore 1981. *The Marriage Contract. Spouses, Lovers and the Law*, New York: Free Press.

　1985. *The Divorce Revolution: the Unexpected Social Economic Consequences for Women and Children in America*, New York: Free Press.

Wennemo, Irene 1994. *Sharing the Costs of Children: Studies on the Development of Family Support in the OECD Countries*, Stockholm: Swedish Institute of Social Research Dissertation Series 25.

　1997. "Family support." Paper presented at The Welfare State at the Crossroads Conference, Sigtuna, Sweden, January 9–12.

White, Lynn K. and Alan Booth 1985. "The quality and stability of remarriages: the role of stepchildren," *American Sociological Review* (50)5: 689–698.

Wilkinson, Helen 1997. *Time Out: the Costs and Benefits of Paid Parental Leave*, London: Demos.

Williams, Fiona 1998. "Troubled masculinities in social policy discourses: father-hood," in Jennie Popay, Jeff Hearn and Jeanette Edwards (eds.), pp. 63–97.

Willrich, Michael 2000. "Home slackers: men, the state and welfare in modern America," *Journal of American History* 87: 460–489.

Wilson, Elizabeth 1977. *Women and the Welfare State*, London: Tavistock.

Wilson, William Julius 1987. *The Truly Disadvantaged: the Inner City, The Under-class and Public Policy*, University of Chicago Press.

   1996. *When Work Disappears*, New York: Knopf.

Winkler, Celia 2001. *The Canary in the Coal Mine. Single Mothers and the Welfare State: the Swedish Experience*, Lanham, MD: Rowman and Littlefield.

Winkler, Gunnar (ed.) 1989. *Geschichte der Sozialpolitik der DDR 1945–1985*, Berlin (East).

Winkler, Gunnar 1990. *Frauenreport '90*. Berlin: Verlag Die Wirtschaft. "The disenfranchised father" <http://www.pappa.com/vater/entsorgt/htm>.

Winnicott, Donald Woods 1957. *The Child and the Family: first Relationships*, edited by Janet Hardenberg, London: Tavistock Press.

Working Seminar on Family and American Welfare Policy 1987. *A Community of Self-Reliance: the New Consensus on Family and Welfare*, Washington, DC: American Enterprise Institute.

Young, Leontine R. 1954. *Out of Wedlock*, New York: McGraw-Hill.

Young, Michael and Peter Willmott 1973. *The Symmetrical Family: a Study of Work and Leisure in the London Region*, London: Routledge and Kegan Paul.

Yuval-Davis, Nira 1997. *Gender and Nation*, London: Sage.

Zulehner, Paul M. and Rainer Volz 1998. *Männer in Aufbruch. Wie Deutschlands Männer sich selbst und wie Frauen sie sehen*, Ostfildern: Schwaben Verlag.

Index